U0498907

中国非洲研究评论
总第十辑

ANNUAL REVIEW OF
AFRICAN STUDIES IN CHINA

危中有机

大变局下的非洲

OPPORTUNITIES IN CRISIS

AFRICA IN TIMES OF
UNPRECEDENTED CHANGES

刘海方 王进杰＿＿＿＿主编

创于1897　商务印书馆
The Commercial Press

图书在版编目（CIP）数据

危中有机：大变局下的非洲 / 刘海方，王进杰主编 . —
北京：商务印书馆，2023
ISBN 978 - 7 - 100 - 22803 - 9

Ⅰ.①危… Ⅱ.①刘… ②王… Ⅲ.①社会发展—研
究—非洲 Ⅳ.① D740.69

中国国家版本馆 CIP 数据核字（2023）第 151188 号

权利保留，侵权必究。

危中有机

大变局下的非洲

刘海方　王进杰 主编

商 务 印 书 馆 出 版
（北京王府井大街 36 号　邮政编码 100710）
商 务 印 书 馆 发 行
北京顶佳世纪印刷有限公司印刷
ISBN 978 - 7 - 100 - 22803 - 9

2023 年 11 月第 1 版　　　开本 710 × 1000　　1/16
2023 年 11 月北京第 1 次印刷　印张 26 ½

定价：108.00 元

北京大学非洲研究中心
学术委员会

（按姓氏拼音排序）

程　莹　付志明　李安山　林丰民　林毅夫　廉超群
刘海方　潘华琼　秦大树　沙宗平　王进杰　王锁劳
王逸舟　魏丽明　吴冰冰　许　亮　查道炯　赵白生

本书的编写和出版获得福特基金会的资助

目　录

发展转型及其内生动力

中非合作：老话题、新探索

危机与豹变

——大变局下求索中的非洲

刘海方

本书的初衷，起源于本书两位主编刘海方和王进杰 2022 年 9 月的一次讨论，经历了 3 年的时空阻隔，非洲还是那个我们熟悉的非洲吗？全球大变局下，非洲正在经历的多重危机是什么样性质的危机，内生的还是外源的？非洲的表现是自我革新图存，也即积极面对并"化危为机"呢？抑或是"躺平"，顺其自然呢？当然并不存在一个叫作"非洲"的单一行为体，各国及其内部复杂的政治社会生态必然意味着千人千面、参差不齐；作为长期跟踪研究也醉心于这个大陆的美丽与丰富宽广的中国学者，我们希望透过纷繁复杂的乱象，分析内外双重力量互构中的非洲，特别是涌动着"泛非主义"精神的非洲力量如何在推动非洲的蜕变。

两位编者强烈意识到，3 年的时空阻隔，我们长久以来积累的关于这片大陆的知识很可能已经无效，因此决定广邀海内外非洲研究专家，特别是来自非洲本土的学者，借他们的眼睛和疫情期间比我们更多在非洲一线观察的经历，从不同视角和侧面，记录非洲经历的危机和其直面巨变的努力。从设计之初到作者研讨会，我们逐渐达成共识，在记录其如何应对困境的同时，力求分辨出哪些是常态的结构性局限，哪些是新的困境下带来的新挑战，从而使我们更好去研判非洲各方行为体是否在推动创新，并成为推动有利于非洲自身可持续发展的进步性动力，以便实现"化危为机"——尽管消除所有结构性限制不可能一蹴而就。

为此，需要分析的问题有以下四个方面：第一，研判非洲当下经历危机的性质与内容肌理，从一般现象归纳总结规律，研究分析传导到政治、经济和社会民生各个领域的"危机效应"；第二，从政治生态和内部各方力量构成、制度和非制度性要素等多角度，研判危机的内生或者外源属性，回答是"斯国有斯疾"、政治危机必然发生而只是时间早晚的问题，还是危机纯粹外来、内部条件只是当下困境的次要条件？第三，世界大变局背景下，非洲当下的和平与安全局势的性质如何，既有的外来的和本土的治理路径是否有效，如何革新应变？第四，政治安全困局与非洲经济不发展存在交相互构性，决定了政治－安全领域的变革与经济结构性困境的破局需要同时解决，是"发展型国家"和"转型发展"的根本要义，也应该是今天重思中国对非合作贡献和意义的最好坐标尺度，是我们在此基础上有关中非合作转型升级的新探索、新举措是否可行的衡量依据。

寡头还是改革者？——以政变塑造国家新方向

伴随 2020 年新冠疫情全球大流行，非洲国家政治大变局次第发生，以西非萨赫勒地区为例，马里（2 次军人政变）、布基纳法索（2 次军人政变）、几内亚（1 次政府被推翻），现在如多米诺骨牌一般传导到尼日尔——2023 年 7 月 26 日，总统卫队发动扣押执政总统的政变，在这个小国存在巨大军事和矿产利益的美国和法国，立即联手欧盟、英国等伙伴施加外交压力，并以切断财政援助为威胁，截至 8 月 4 日，以上国家都已经采取了撤侨行动，但宣布绝不从这个"民主联盟"和"反恐行动"的支柱国家中撤出军队。中国自古有"乱世出枭雄"的说法，疫情大流行的全球背景之下，多米诺骨牌一样接续在西非地区发生军事政变，以至于很多媒体将其称作非洲的"政变带"，是时势造英雄，还是宵小之徒在乱世中浑水摸鱼呢？

根据 BBC 统计，1960—2000 年，每年非洲大陆发生的政变数为 4 次。[1] 相比于博茨瓦纳、肯尼亚、坦桑尼亚、马拉维和赞比亚等从来没有发生过政变的国家，一些非洲国家甚至被归类为"易政变型国家"。[2] 但军事政变并非非洲独有的政治现象，政治学大家塞缪尔·亨廷顿早在

---

[1]　https://www.bbc.com/news/world-africa-46783600, 2023-08-13.

[2]　African Coups in the 21st Century | Democracy in Africa, https://democracyinafrica.org/african-coups-in-the-21st-century/, 2023-08-13.

1968 年的著作中就敏锐地提出，20 世纪 60 年代中期已经开始出现军事政变的加纳、中非、刚果、尼日利亚等国，就像 19 世纪的拉丁美洲一样，军人干政是政治现代化历程不可缺少的部分，特别是在"普力夺"性[①]的政治化社会中[②]——在两种普力夺制度中，寡头普力夺制度是"宫廷政变"式彼此取代，在激进的普力夺制度下，军人本身往往成为改革者，是从"普力夺"社会到公民秩序的制度建设者，如纳赛尔时期埃及等案例所示。[③]几乎所有寡头型社会最终会演进为激进的普力夺政府，这实际上是第三世界作为独立觉醒民族集体亮相世界舞台，并开始变求治、追寻现代化的历史进程；亨廷顿因而提出其核心主张，参照当时并存的强国，新兴第三世界国家向现代的过渡，就是要"不断克服社会动荡和防止政治衰朽"、建立"强大政府"。[④]

　　对于今天观察非洲的政治变局，或者媒体经常使用的"乱象"或"危机"，亨廷顿的提醒是，"就军队本身去解释干政现象是说明不了问题的"，因为"它是更加广泛的社会现象的特殊表现"，[⑤]必须从广阔的社会变迁视角去看待军人干政现象。60 年代，非洲从传统向现代过渡之际、变动中的社会阶级力量对比本身就意味着传统权威的合法性遭受挑战；而西方殖民主义摧毁当地原有政治制度、破坏合法性的传统源泉，使得"当地统治者的权威要看帝国主义宗主国的脸色行事"，是社会最终转向"激进普力夺"的根本原因，是作为关键力量的军官团和民族知识分子等社会各界共同参与到民族独立过程当中来的广阔背景。[⑥]

　　冷战时期，政变上台的领导人很容易通过宣布其意识形态选择而获得美国或者苏联一方支持，也就是说冷战时期的大国权力政治为政变

---

① 按照亨廷顿自己的解释，"普力夺"（Praetorianism）是指一国的职业政治领袖本身缺乏自治性、连贯性、制度性和适应性，导致各种各样的社会势力和团体都插手政治、相互赤裸裸地对抗；简言之，就是缺乏共识、各种社会势力都干政的社会，参见 Samuel P. Huntington, *Political Order in Changing Societies*, New Haven: Yale University Publisher, p. 195。

② 塞缪尔·P. 亨廷顿著，王冠华等译:《变化社会中的政治秩序》，生活·读书·新知三联书店，1989 年，第 175—177 页。

③ 同上注，第 182—240 页。

④ 同上注，第 3—4 页。

⑤ 同上注，第 177 页。

⑥ 同上注，第 183—184 页。

成功提供了条件，并有利于其传染病一样扩散。21 世纪的前 20 年，这个平均数降低了一半，被西方社会普遍解读为得益于非洲大陆更加民主化。[①] 疫情以来发生的一系列新军事政变，与 20 世纪 60 年代发生的政变不尽相同，特别是考虑到冷战后"反政变"已经成为国际通则；而 2007 年的非盟宪章中有关"民主、选举和治理"（African Charter on Democracy, Elections and Governance）的部分，明确对"非宪法性的武装夺取政权"给予严厉谴责，这都意味着之前轻易通过美苏支持获得合法性的政变领导人，今天在国际上和大陆内都没有市场。然而，外来的压力显然没能阻挡疫情以来这些国家内部陆续发生政变的动力，这些内部动因是什么呢？显然，每一个非洲国家的情况也不尽相同，需要首先从该国本身的情况入手进行具体研究，理解其当下复杂的社会矛盾是什么，那些被褫夺权力的民选领导人是否合法性不足、治理失效，社会需要经历波涛汹涌或者暗流涌动的颠覆行动挑选新的领导者。

从乍得、几内亚、马里、布基纳法索机构的情况看，被政变的对象确实有的是要修宪争取第三任期、有的是长期执政而使合法性受到质疑，而几国共同的困难都是不断升级的恐怖主义袭击、保护公众不力等困境，加之新冠疫情与俄乌冲突以来全球供应链断裂对于非洲国家经济的沉重打击和对民众生活的巨大影响，政变还是应该解释为各种严重困难施压的结果。判断政变领袖是成为"寡头"还是充当推动社会进步的"改革者"，需要听其言观其行、看其与各种社会力量之间的互动关系，包括地区内和大陆以外的各种行为体能否在不对政变表示鼓励态度的同时，用更为积极的、开放性的态度看待政变者可能扮演改革者和新的制度建设者的作用，解决国家出现的危机。本书邀请伊萨克·巴齐耶教授贡献的《在混乱中寻找契机：布基纳法索应对动荡局势和后疫情时代发展的紧迫性》一文，是作者多次往返母国布基纳法索所获一手实地观察和调研资料写成，他认为，2022 年陆续发生两次的政变，是该国正在迫切寻求解决恐袭造成的动荡不安、改善生活并还原 1987 年革命之

[①] African Coups in the 21st Century | Democracy in Africa, https://democracyinafrica.org/african-coups-in-the-21st-century/, 2023-08-01.

父桑卡拉被害真相、还社会以正义的努力，是塑造国家新发展方向的重大变革。不管是第一次举义的达米巴中将，还是第二次领导的特拉奥雷上尉，政变后都发声说要治理使 200 多万民众流离失所的恐袭，二人都得到了民众热情的拥戴；刚刚发生的尼日尔政变，国内很多观察家不断盯着政变领导者齐亚尼中将与被政变掉的民选总统巴祖姆之间的"个人恩怨"做文章，① 却往往忽略了长久以来恐怖主义活动已经令尼日尔安全形势恶化，而新冠疫情"综合征"和持续的旱灾使得 2022 年 2 月以来粮荒严重、民生无着 ② ——这也就不难理解面对各种国际媒体的镜头，尼日尔民众毫不掩饰对于政变军人的支持，并强烈质疑持续通过采掘重要矿产、货币绑定等手段实施剥削的法国，从政变开始之日到本文收稿的 8 月 10 日，大规模尼日尔民众几乎每天都在参与反对外来干预、支持军政权的和平集会，足以说明民众的诉求和期待军政权能够改变传统上对法国的依赖关系，并改善迫在眉睫的民生压力的急迫愿望。

尼日尔没有出海口，严重依赖邻国与区内和国际进行贸易物流，经贸结构也与区内国家存在互补性，作为西非经济共同体成员，任何该地区组织关闭边境、限制人员流动的经济制裁措施都会令尼日尔民众生活受到严重影响；而该次区域共同体是否出兵干预近日来如悬在尼日尔民众和侨居者头上的达摩克利斯之剑——当然，以军事介入的方式督促政变者还政于民选总统的窗口期似乎已经过去，陷在各种巨大政治经济压力之下的西非各国实际上很难有余力出兵境外，各国的传统势力和不断以和平集会形式表达对于政变军人支持的尼日尔民众，实际上都在督促西非经济共同体辩证地看待军事政变，超越简单的"反对一切非选举形式更换政府"的一刀切式思维，发展出创造性的治理思路。

---

① 国内外很多既有评论都将巴祖姆是阿拉伯人的背景作为"个人恩怨"的起点，将其下令解除总统卫队长官齐亚尼作为导火索。

② 陶短房：《尼日尔政变：从漠不关心到举世关注》，个人公众号，参见 https://mp.weixin.qq.com/s/8s-MtifIi3k6Ry5Z4Apk_A，2023-08-14。

治乱之间，国家何为？

其他非洲国家和地区虽然尚无军事政变之虞，但政府并非高枕无忧，很多国家正在经历的挑战恰恰来自政权内部，是政权的稳定性问题。2020 年 11 月，聚焦于应对新冠疫情全球大流行，埃塞俄比亚联邦政府却打响了在北部提格雷人地区的"执法行动"战役；冲突持续了整整 2 年，人们终于得以额手相庆签署和平协议——协议墨迹未干之际，总理解散各州武装的主张又激怒了阿姆哈拉州法诺，对方以叛军的形式向首都发起进攻，直到本文写作的 2023 年 8 月初，这个遭受战争创伤还在流血的国家极有可能陷入又一场战争。在东北非的另一地区大国苏丹，长期执政的巴希尔于 2019 年在民众长期静坐示威游行中倒台；2021 年 10 月，军队最高首领布尔汉又推翻并接管了文官过渡政府；而令形势再度恶化的是，另一股军事势力因不满布尔汉将军而于 2023 年 4 月与之爆发武装冲突，形势急转直下使国家陷入胶着的内战——如今 3 个月有余，曾经历史悠久、富饶美丽的苏丹已经满目疮痍，国际移民组织最新公布的数字显示，冲突已经导致 18 个州 400 多万人流离失所。

按照亨廷顿的解释，这些"社会动荡和政治腐朽"是非洲从传统社会向现代社会转型所必然经历的阶段，在拥有强大政府（既包括完善的制度，也包括扩大群众参与水平）之前都会如影随形。很多中国学人已经客观地指出，尽管对于第三世界国家的研究贡献良多，亨廷顿的襄臼仍然是以发达国家道路为第三世界国家的参照和归宿的"欧洲中心论"局限，同时也缺少了第三世界国家曾经遭受的殖民剥削以及独立后仍然受到大国干涉和控制的视角。[①] 以上面 2 个大国为例，持续的动乱、冲突、战争（和政府隐晦地称之为"执法行动"）的背后，既有殖民的遗产，也有冷战以来大国干涉的复杂影响，即便逃开了殖民占领的埃塞俄比亚也是如此；近年来美国的介入和控制持续增加（本书邀约的两位非洲

---

① 沈宗美：《中译本序》，载《变化社会中的政治秩序》，生活·读书·新知三联书店，1989 年，第 6 页。

教授的文章《国际金融机构在非洲冲突、复苏和过渡中的作用》一文，记录了美国如何通过施压这些国际组织来控制和影响这两国），在持续进入动乱期的两国发挥何种影响还需要更多研究。我们不禁要问，非洲国家为什么如此容易受到外来干涉影响，这是否导致其具有结构性脆弱性并且容易在困境下走向政变和冲突？

包括联合国教科文组织的非洲通史委员会等越来越多的非洲历长时段视角下的历史写作表明，非洲在被殖民以前有着辉煌灿烂的物质文明和制度文明、精神文明，曾经令15世纪末以来沿着大西洋沿海寻找到达"黄金和香料"之地的欧洲人倾倒，甚至有荷兰使臣17世纪来到巴刚果心悦诚服地向当时国王双膝跪倒的历史记录。[①] 然而、400多年残酷的奴隶贸易掏空了非洲青壮劳力，也停滞了一代代人创造性地建设生兹在兹家园的历史进程。[②] 1884年的柏林会议后，非洲又沦为被彻底殖民的境况，开始经受远比中国遭受的半殖民状态更为悲惨的奴役，包括在物质、制度和精神文明等多层面的剥夺和扭曲。

从非洲自身的政治传统而言，如英国历史学、人类学家John Reader（1937）所言，在欧洲人外来影响到达之前，非洲鲜明存在着不必结成国家而以小型群体和平共处的文明艺术，显然这是非洲对人类历史最明显的贡献。然而，"欧洲人到来之前的这1万多个族群、小型国家、土国、苏丹国和宗族大家庭等等多种形态的政治单元，彼此未必完全和平共处，但是都能够共存且彼此接受各自的身份认同。与其说殖民主义瓜分了他们，不如说野蛮地聚拢他们——1万多个自治的单元被强迫成为50多个国家"[③]。

作为殖民统治工具的国家机器，实际上至少是二元的折叠世界，是在殖民者居住的城市地区建立西方式的现代治理国家机器，同时因为殖民当局力所不逮而使用各种手段把广大农村地区交给当地的传统权威来治

---

① Rebecca Bayeck, "Unsung History of the Kingdom of Kongo," CLIR Postdoctoral Fellow in Data Curation for African American and African Studies, https://www.nypl.org/blog/2021/11/02/unsung-history-kingdom-kongo.

② Walter Rodney, *How Europe Underdeveloped Africa*, London: Bogle-L'Ouverture Publications, 1972.

③ Alex Thomson, *An Introduction to African Politics*, 5th Edition, London: Routledge, 2022.

理的另一重世界——英国的殖民统治貌似重视非洲"习惯法"（customary law），"尊重"不同地方族群之间的文化、习俗、语言的差异，实际上是以"传统的发明"为最小成本的治理术，来延续传统的社会。①

现代非洲国家（注：联合国认定的是 54 个，而按照非盟标准应该说是 55 个，因为承认西撒哈拉为独立国家）起步的原点，正是这巨大而沉重的殖民历史包袱。② 理解现代非洲的政治，不得不回到这个此前的政治传统被迫断裂的时间点，首先去理解其被扭曲为殖民国家时候的政治生态，特别是考虑到大多数非洲国家的独立，就是对于这个国家机器的继承，而不是通过武装斗争和革命形式建立的。整体而言，独立至今，不能代表大多数人利益基础上形成的国家机器依然是现实国家机器的沉重底座，非洲迄今尚未摆脱"柏林会议诅咒"带来的结构性、历史性的扭曲；③ 很多非洲学者痛切批判，非洲现代国家是"缺少能力、方向、灵魂、干劲儿和远见卓识的扭曲国家，不可能推动减少贫困和独立时候承诺的其他目标所需的彻底经济转型；这个扭曲的国家，其核心本质就是横征暴敛，继续剥削殖民时代已经被征服了的非洲人，只不过此刻服务于一拨又一拨本土的精英买办集团——他们正是在殖民时代被豢养起来巩固殖民统治所需"④。当然，独立以来也出现了博茨瓦纳、坦桑尼亚等国家建设完成度比较好的国家，不能简单一笔抹杀，特别是诸多国家的第一代领导人都做出了杰出的贡献。

随着 80 年代中期国际金融体制大获全胜，非洲国家被依照新自由主义方案进行改造，之前计划和发展经济、提供公共产品和社会福利的国家功能被限制到最小，而市场也作为条件被要求向全球资本彻底打开，国有公司被要求转向私有化。期待当中的"万灵的市场"并没有拯

---

① Eric Hobsbawm, Terence Ranger, eds., *Invention of Tradition*, Cambridge: Cambridge University Press, 2012.

② Basil Davison, *Blackman's Burdon: Africa and the Curse of the Nation-State*, New York: Times Books/Random House, 1992.

③ Adekeye Adebajo, *The Curse of Berlin: Africa after the Cold War*, London: Hurst & Company, 2010.

④ N. Oluwafemi Mimiko, "Contextualizing the State Structure Requisite for Africa's Development," in: Oloruntoba, S. O., Falola, T. (eds) , *The Palgrave Handbook of African Political Economy, Palgrave Handbooks in IPE*, Palgrave Macmillan, Cham., p. 147.

救非洲国家，但国门洞开引入的全球资本确实让本国和外来私有部门势力更大，很多非洲国家发生了"国家俘获（state capture）现象"（见图1），即私有部门和基于地方、族群、宗教和林林总总各种本土与外来利益集团纠缠在一起，劫持了国家。[①] 这些势力往往寓居在政府的躯体之内，因而往往主宰了公共政策的方向。执政的政治精英与经济精英往往打着地方、宗教和族群的名号，彼此间明争暗斗，力图抢夺最大份额的国家资源。劳动者在任何政治安排中则是缺失的；政府因为被各种利益集团所绑架，也丧失了独立自主性。[②]

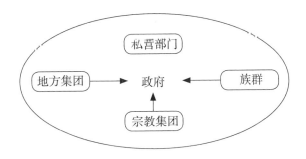

图1　"国家俘获"现象示意图

　　如果说"国家俘获"的发生，是新自由主义长驱直入、迫使国家削减功能"自断手足"以致内外资本和权贵勾结的结果，很多非洲国家的"形式民主"问题也开始成为学者们研究的热点，是对非洲广义"现代性"问题的新追索。以南非为例，种族隔离政权覆亡至今20多年了，为何依然深度割裂？ Thiven Reddy 研究发现，南非政治具有两面性，一方面是1994年以来按照西方理想设计的"自由民主制度"，规律的大选、多党制度和各种人权规范，使其看起来完美无瑕；但实际运转的是

---

①　Daniel Kaufmann, *State Capture, Corruption and Mis-Governance: Empirical Findings and Unorthodox Implications for Action from Public-Private Nexus*, a Paper Presented at the Harvard University, April 25, 2002, 转引自 D. P. Sha, "Streets and Boardrooms as Hegemonic Spaces in Shaping Political Economy in Africa," in *The Palgrave Handbook of African Political Economy*, eds. by S. O. Oloruntoba and T. Falola, Palgrave Handbooks in IPE. Palgrave Macmillan, Cham, 2020.

②　D. P. Sha, "Streets and Boardrooms as Hegemonic Spaces in Shaping Political Economy in Africa."

一个经常诉诸暴力和冲突的非正式秩序，暴露了一个碎片化、充满派系斗争的政府和结构虚弱的国家，是典型的"非常政治"[①]——这是学者 Andreas Kalyvas 提出的与"正常政治"相对立的概念，讨论的是人类现代政治永恒的困境，认为几乎所有的现代国家中都或多或少存在着某种程度政治失序的"非常"，因为无论从议程设置还是实际决策来看，随着"公共领域私人化"，政治精英、利益集团与官僚化政党操控了国家，"人民参与"的实质内涵被不断掏空，其本质是"代表性危机"，甚至有滑入阿伦特视角下极权主义的晦暗前景。[②] 从被殖民打断传统的起点上建立、经由冷战和新自由主义大国政治的控制和进一步扭曲的轨迹来看，现代非洲国家的代表性或者说包容性不足，是问题的症结所在，当前发生内战、冲突的国家中，都可以看到掌权者背后代表的少数利益集团如何挟国家之名排他性地保护狭隘小集团的利益。

简言之，400 多年非洲政治生态的轨迹，是被外来蛮横剥削、掠夺和主宰直至奋起反抗获得独立的过程，非洲国家迄今尚未摆脱沉重的负面殖民遗产，加之冷战时期代理人战争以及被国际金融体制强迫跌入"结构调整方案"深渊，可谓命途多舛。虽然整个历史中一直充斥着各种短见的利益集团和外来者沆瀣一气，但奴隶贸易以来的历史主旋律仍然是非洲人民不屈不挠保家卫国、争取实现真正的独立自主。因为了解有限，一些中文媒体对非洲政治的描述一直比较简单和负面，如"逢选必乱"。新冠疫情暴发以来，多国发生政变，似乎更无可争议地"坐实"了有关非洲政治"乱"的意象。当然，简单地将非洲的政治状况归结为乱象，并不是一些中文媒体的专利；西方媒体中一直流行着非洲人野蛮落后、天生"好战"等歪曲形象，这种深入骨髓的种族偏见难免影响到学术界的工作，1994 年卢旺达大屠杀在一些西方学术作品中被解释为部落间存在"天生的宿怨"。[③] 时至今日，撒哈拉以南非洲地区甚至不配纳

① Thiven Reddy, *South Africa, Settler Colonialism and the Failures of Liberal Democracy*, London: Zed Books, 2015.

② Andreas Kalyvas, *Democracy and the Politics of the Extraordinary*, Cambridge: Cambridge University Press, 2008, p. 6.

③ 刘海方：《十周年后再析卢旺达"种族"大屠杀》，《西亚非洲》2004 年第 3 期，第 34—38 页。

入"现代政治"研究,"阿拉伯之春"那样改变政治现状和历史轨迹的活动似乎只能发生在北部非洲,撒哈拉以南非洲民众的抗议活动被完全无视,或者被简单粗暴地赋以"骚乱""暴动"的形象。[①]长期主导着非洲政治研究的是"失败国家",特别是随着"9·11"事件刺激了西方政府、军方、智库、援助机构和国际组织,重新关注他们随时潜在伤及西方利益[②]——这些研究大体聚焦于非洲治理能力差、领导集团贪污腐败等,不乏深层次隐含的对非洲人的种族歧视与偏见,却很少关注到非洲自身积极的抗争和改善的力量。美国学者卡普兰对这种认知范式大加挞伐,认为发达国家开出的更多援助来提升政府治理能力的方剂,仍然是停留在政治的表面、治标不治本;与其个案研究的亚洲拉丁美洲案例国(阿塞拜疆、巴基斯坦、叙利亚和玻利维亚)一样,刚果(金)、索马里和西非国家案例的根本问题在于,在与外来势力相遇的过程中维系传统"社会网络"碎裂了,这种深层的脆弱性才是今日各种政治纷争的根源。[③]

公众街头抗议:面包还是政治?

疫情发生以来,"街头"(the Street)也成为非洲社会中的"热词",规模大、频率高的抗议活动直线增加——显然,城市底层民众是首先承受生活成本上升压力的,封城令和限足令导致民众陷入"饿死还是病死"的"浮士德式选择"[④],公众街头抗议的增加也正是另外一种"肚

---

① Adam Branch and Zachariah Mampilly, *Africa Uprising: Popular Protest and Political Change*, London: Zed Books, 2015, Cha.1.

② 重要的作品如 Robert I. Roterberg, *When States fail*, 2004; Robert I. Roterberg, *State failure & State Weakness in a Time of Terror*, 2003; Francis Fukuyama, *State Building*, 2004, 转引自 N. Oluwafemi Mimiko, "Contextualizing the State Structure Requisite for Africa's Development".

③ Seth D. Kaplan, *Fixing Fragile States: A New Paradigm for Development*, Westport: Praeger Security International, 2008.

④ 刘海方:《新冠肺炎全球大流行下非洲的抗疫和中非合作》,《国际政治研究》2020年第3期,第73—83页。

皮政治"的体现。^① 今日苏丹的乱局，缘起是民众大规模抗议面包涨价，浪潮之大足以颠覆长期执政的巴希尔。然而，亚当·布兰奇（Adam Branch）和撒迦利亚·曼皮利（Zachariah Mampilly）在其合著中指出，近年来被排除在政治议程之外的广大非洲公众掀起的席卷整个大陆的抗议浪潮，如同美国发生的"占领华尔街"、法国的"黄马甲"和欧洲其他国家的类似运动一样，有着非常丰富和多元的光谱，实际上继承了反帝反殖民斗争的传统——最初往往从基本生存之虞开始，目标逐渐指向一切压迫者和不平等、不公正的社会秩序；在非洲独立以后曾经分别聚焦在反对独裁政府和新自由主义政策大规模削减补贴和国家福利；21 世纪以来是非洲大陆公众的第三次抗议浪潮，仅 2005 至 2014 年间，40 多个非洲国家就发生了近百起民众抗议活动；从北非突尼斯到南非、塞内加尔，时间长的如 2017 年就开始一直持续到 2020 年的"反西非法郎运动"等，不一而足。^②

街头抗议，既有结社、联盟和群体联合的形式，也有工会、劳工运动、劳工－公众联合、行业协会（医务工作者、学生或者音乐家）、非正式部门的协会、宗教团体、泛族裔型协会、温和的反对派成员等，具体的诉求多种多样，总体上都是要求从根本上改变政治和经济不平等；而人们集结起来的动力有：一是剥削、剥夺、边缘化、压迫、镇压等外在条件形成了阶级或者其他性质的政治觉醒；二是成员组织起来用网络平台追求共同利益；三是个人或者群体形成跨协会的认同以达成共同目标。占领、罢工、学生、女性以及其他基于信仰基础的团体示威游行等形式居多，而且与反帝反殖独立运动和反对新自由主义时期往往以意识形态、族群、阶级特别是工会为线组织起来的形式不同，大众传媒时代更呈现跨阶级、族群、利益集团和各种公共社会组织联合的趋势，有时

---

① "肚皮政治"取自法国学者 Jean-Francois Bayart 的作品 *The State in Africa: The Politics of the Belly* (NY: Longman, 1993)，核心观点是非洲国家的政治与世界其他国家类似，首先是"生存政治"，其次是纠缠着各种复杂的深层文化社会制度。

② Adam Branch and Zachariah Mampilly, *Africa Uprising: Popular Protest and Political Change*, pp. 70-71；参见孟子祺：《非洲"政治社会"的能动性——〈非洲起义：民众抗议与政治变革〉评述》，载《中国国际战略评论 2021》（上），世界知识出版社，2023 年，第 176 页。

松散到辨识不出组织者，国家也往往派出军队来拦截群众示威。[①]

公众街头抗议的本质，与上一部分讨论的"国家俘获"现象是一枚硬币的两面，是非洲国家政治中的"代表性危机"的具体表现：在精英集团垄断国家利益、整体上存在代表性危机的社会中，平时相对"无声无息"的广大群众，在经济和生活压力大到不能承受而绝地求生，以"街头"为阵地发声，其目标所指是试图唤醒统治集团的注意，要求改变国家不合理的公共政策，应该视为探索和推动非洲国家由乱到治的进步力量。本书邀约长期研究埃及的专家肖坤写作的《谁来保护女性——从埃及维护女性权益的〈刑法〉修正案第 306 条谈起》一文显示，正是由于民间自发行动和女性赋能运动的推广，长期以来埃及广大女性群体饱受其苦的"性骚扰"问题，才最终以国家《刑法》修正案形式将其由轻罪改为重罪，从而迈出女性保护方面最为显著的进步。

如上所述，非洲人从反恐殖民压迫以来就形成的政治主体自觉意识，这一传统演进至今成为今天的街头抗议活动；疫情以及全球供应链中断等外来突变的条件引发经济和社会压力激增的条件下，人们更容易爆发情绪激烈的游行示威活动。以尼日利亚为例，民众 2016 年举行大规模街头行动，抗议政府突然大幅度提升电费（上涨 45%）为例，理由是政府没有依照宪法事先征询公众意见；类似地，示威活动也针对尼日利亚政府没有广泛征询意见就取消燃油补贴。[②] 被尼日利亚政府决策过程排除在外的民众，显然已经形成习惯努力通过公共空间来发声和行动，疫情期间爆发了浩浩荡荡的反对警察暴力执法的"终结 SARS"（End Special Anti-Robbery Squad，简称 End SARS）运动。类似一脉相承的精神下，2023 年发生的尼日尔政变后，尼日利亚关闭边境作为制裁行动，也停止了尼日尔主要来源的电力供应；尼日利亚民众在很多渠道发声反对本国政府，不同意用制裁的方式恶化邻国民众的生活，同时指出提布努总统是违宪的，因为没有征询议会和民众意见。

[①] D. P. Sha, "Streets and Boardrooms as Hegemonic Spaces in Shaping Political Economy in Africa."

[②] 同上。

当然，各个国家的政治生态迥异，民众"上街"的具体动因和表现形式在不同国家千差万别。2021年疫情期间，在乌干达总统竞选过程中，大量底层青年人感受着歌手 Bobi Wine 独特的热情四溢的政治音乐语言，纷纷走上街头，在他"如果议会不管贫民窟，那贫民窟就得走向议会"口号的鼓舞之下，把票投给这位敢于挑战执政35年的老总统的38岁偶像；这些人数众多的青年选民之前就在其领导号召之下，参与了反对修宪（取消总统竞选年龄限制）、反对征收社交媒体税等多次运动，笃信这位巨星会像2017年利比里亚当选总统的足球先生维阿一样，带来改变命运的可能性。选举结果是流行巨星以34.8%的选票败北，穆塞韦尼继续执政。失望的选民于是在各地上街示威游行造成骚乱，被很多国际媒体解释为"短暂狂热的"、注定失败的政治"闹剧"，但"他们的选票无疑意味着一种极其强烈的改变现状的愿望"。[①] 本书邀约的两位安哥拉学者对于安哥拉应对疫情表现的精彩分析文章《告别的时刻：安哥拉在动荡世界中寻求发展》，展现了像安哥拉这样的资源富集国差强人意的表现——巨大的资源优势迄今未转换为经济快速增长的比较优势和惠及民生的手段，大多数处于极度贫困状态且无法享受到必要公共服务的民众没有爆发大规模的"街头"行动，而是诉诸温和的、不合作性的抵抗——对公共事务报以冷漠，2022年大选中空前低落的投票率就是其对政府出现信心赤字的表现。

当然，如同美国2021年1月占领白宫的事件一样，非洲的公众街头行动和军事政变一样，都难免被别有用心的政客操控，服务于其个人的政治经济目的和权力野心，这在世界上很多国家的选举政治中都有表现——非洲最近发生的政客绑架公众抗议活动的典型案例，如肯尼亚的反对派领袖奥廷加，利用疫情和俄乌冲突以来民众反对粮食、油价上涨、政府增加税收的情绪，不断动员大规模示威游行，对国家和社会都造成了巨大破坏。

---

① 程莹：《非洲大选观察》，《北大非洲电讯》第471期，2021年2月5日。

冲突的外源性与"自由和平"的治理困境

在全球大变局下，恶性安全事件在一些非洲国家几乎达到家常便饭的发生频次，如随着气候变化影响到传统生产生活方式，尼日利亚的牧民与农民为争夺水源和土地而发生的械斗、绑架索取赎金等事件与日俱增；索马里、肯尼亚、尼日利亚、喀麦隆、乍得等国多年来一直饱受跨境恐怖组织折磨，疫情大流行以来显然活动更加猖獗。不管以上哪种形式的不安全挑战，民众首当其冲，或者被洗劫一空、流离失所，严重时更是生灵涂炭的大悲剧。如前文所述，与日增加的恐袭令马里、尼日尔和布基纳法索饱受其苦，政变的发生毋宁说是对国家社会陷入严重而复杂危机的一种反弹；与理解索马里海盗现象类似，值得深入研究的是，为什么西非萨赫勒地区成为诸多恐怖组织的温床？近年来，在恐怖主义受害国名单上新增加的莫桑比克等国，社会深层是否出现了同样的危机？

正如曾经长期担任联合国非洲经济委员会秘书长的卡洛斯教授所言，不管人们如何乐观积极地讨论和期待 21 世纪以来非洲的发展，总是迎头撞上"非洲冲突"这个词汇，因为经济发展成果总是倾向于被这个大陆上似乎更容易发生的冲突冲刷殆尽。[①] 理解冲突的原因和解决方案，同样不能离开非洲大陆的经济发展。2023 年 2 月，联合国开发署（UNDP）发布了一份题为《走向极端主义：招募通道与解脱》（在 2017 年报告基础上的更新版）的调研报告。报告长达 158 页，调查样本为 8 个非洲国家（布基纳法索、乍得、尼日利亚、尼日尔、马里、喀麦隆、苏丹、索马里）的 2000 名青年人，其中 1000 多位受访者之前是基地组织、博科圣地、伊斯兰国德国极端组织的成员，没有工作机会和基本生计来源是所有这些绝望的青年人加入这些极端组织的原因。25% 的受访者都选择没有工作机会作为最根本的极端化的原因，也是与 2017 年报告时候的统计数据相比，构成几乎全部青年走向极端化的原因（占比

---

① Carlos Lopes and George Kararach, *Structural Change in Africa: Misperceptions, New Narratives & Development in the 21st Century*, NY: Routledge, p. 16.

92%）。^① 这份调查报告受调查对象所来自的国家与上文分析的出现严重危机的国家相符，非常有说服力地显示了青年人的极端化问题与阿玛蒂亚·森定义的贫困^②（不是每天生活标准是 1.5 美元还是 2 美元，而是作为权利和能力的发展机会的贫困！）之间的根本关联——伴随着疫情流行和俄乌冲突加剧的全球供应链断裂，防疫的需要使得生产和教育都不同程度被打断，生活成本激增，而且社会流动性和上升通道更加缺乏，更多更加绝望的青年人因此选择了极端化。

也就是说，非洲国家社会经济情况的恶劣及其成因，是理解诸多形式的暴力和不安全的前提，特别是为何越来越多的青年人加入极端恐怖组织？有关"非洲为什么如此贫困"的问题，吸引了一代代学人从各个学科的角度介入研究。国际社会经历 60 年代短暂地对新独立非洲国家群体的乐观期待，70 年代石油危机爆发，20 世纪 80、90 年代非洲国家进入所谓"失去的 20 年"，非洲悲观论和对非洲的不公正批评由此而起，越来越多主导的声音是针对非洲经济和政治治理能力的批评，当然也暗含歧视和偏见的语调，与"非洲人劣等、落后"的陈词滥调并无二致。70 年代，非洲裔和非洲本土学者如罗德尼、阿克等学者加入讨论中，他们分析了沉重的殖民从政治经济社会多方面对非洲造成的剥削和重创，认为是制约非洲各国自独立以来发展的最重要结构性困境，其中包括上述当代非洲社会中的暴力和冲突问题的根源。^③ 虽然被某些学人讥讽为"还原论"，但相关结论日益得到学界共识。^④ 英国和美国的学人自 21 世纪以来陆续发表很多作品，突破欧洲人、白种人优越论视角，重新阐释了有关奴隶贸易开始的经济剥削如何让非洲的人力、物力和资源、市场源源不断转移到了欧陆和美洲，成为英国工业革命发轫、美国现代经济

---

① United Nation Development Programme, *Journey to extremism in Africa: Pathways to recruitment and disengagement*, Copyright UNDP, 2023.

② 〔印度〕阿玛蒂亚·森著，王宇、王文玉译：《贫困与饥荒》，商务印书馆，2004 年。

③ 〔圭亚那〕沃尔特·罗德尼著，李安山译：《欧洲如何使非洲欠发达》，社会科学文献出版社，2017 年。

④ Sam Moyo and Yoichi Mine (Eds), *What Colonialism Ignored: "African Potentials" for Resolving Conflicts in Southern Africa?* Cameroon: Langaa RPCIG, 2016.

繁荣和文明发展的坚实底座的相关作品。①

非洲为此付出的代价是，1200万青壮年从大西洋沿岸被运抵欧洲和美洲，而按照既有对奴隶船成功运抵人数与总人数比例的研究估算，至少是10倍于这个数字的非洲人口被奴隶贩子带出了沿岸的"不归门"，其中当然不乏那个时代最有创造性、艺术天赋和其他一身才华的优秀青年人。直到本身生产方式转变，开始通过售卖工业品、采掘矿产和经营热带经济种植业来从非洲榨取价值，欧洲才终止了从贩卖奴隶中获取暴利的肮脏生意，而强迫非洲人从农村地区进入殖民生产空间、榨取其劳动价值变成了新的暴力和剥削目标。②奴隶贸易和强迫劳动是真正意义上非洲大陆暴力和不安全的渊薮，特别是捕捉人口过程开启的"奴隶换枪支"的罪恶循环，使原本世代和平共存的非洲各个族群、酋长国之间，被挑拨着竞相抓捕别族的人去换奴隶贩子的枪支来保护族人（避免沦为别族的俘虏），非洲进入热兵器时代的同时，也滑向了群体间不信任的长久噩梦。③

第二重渊薮开始于前文所说的殖民占领时代完全罔顾历史、传统和既有社会人文基础而专横地划定的疆界。非洲统一组织1965年就以成员国共同遵守原则的形式，规定了接受既有边界不改变的原则，此后只出现过个别领土争议案例以及厄立特里亚、新独立的南苏丹等改变边界现状的案例；④然而这些人为的划出来国界线内圈住的是许许多多族际、种族、宗教分野的政治体，政权边界与原来历史形成的文化、社会和既有传统组织网络边界形成巨大张力，成为冲突和其他性质的身份认同矛盾的起点——截至20世纪末的统计显示，至少1/3独立以后的非洲国家内部经历

---

① Joseph Inikori, *Africans and the Industrial Revolution in England: A Study in International Trade and Economic Development*, Cambridge: Cambridge University Press, 2002; Howard W. French, *Born in Blackness: Africa, Africans, and the Making of the Modern World(1471 to the Second World War)*, Liveright, 2022.

② Claude Ake, A *Political Economy of Africa,* Harlow, Essex: Longman, 1981.

③ Olufemi Taiwo (2017) argues in his TED Talk, 转引自 N. Oluwafemi Mimiko, "Contextualizing the State Structure Requisite for Africa's Development"。

④〔埃及〕布特罗斯·加利著，仓友衡译：《非洲边界争端》，商务印书馆，1979年；关培凤：《非洲边界和领土争端解决模式研究》，社会科学文献出版社，2017年。

了大规模政治暴力或者战争（不包括不流血政变和偶然的暗杀行为），[①]非洲已经"为拒绝改变这个外来强加的此疆彼界付出了巨大的代价"[②]。

近些年来，更多新的殖民研究成果显示，不同殖民在今日非洲留下了不同的遗产。比如兰格认为，相较于其他国家的殖民，英国的统治更容易激发后殖民时代的族群冲突；[③]因为分而治之的统治方式，令殖民地的族群分化更加极端，也更容易进行进入冲突所需要的族群动员。美国北卡罗来纳州大学两位学者基于大量数据面板的量化研究显示，后殖民时期非洲国家的暴力冲突的方式也与英国和法国不同的殖民统治形式有直接的关联，而且遗留的遗产意味着这些后殖民国家冲突所损失的人口数目不同，造成的经济损失也不尽相同。[④]

以上有关追踪殖民统治与非洲冲突和暴力现象关联的研究，经常被当代国际问题研究者打上"还原主义"的标签，仿佛昨天的风吹不到今天的树，应该更多地从当代国际关系大棋局来研究非洲的安全问题——言外之意，非洲的暴力和不安全体现的是非洲本身的"安全治理能力赤字"，不能把责任推给西方。对此，南非约翰内斯堡大学活跃的青年学者 F. Nganje 辛辣地指出，冷战时代和后冷战时代，非洲的不安全很大程度上仍然是大国对非施加的种种经济和地缘政治影响的副产品，是这些域外行为体与某些贪婪的、短视的非洲政客勾结起来沆瀣一气的结果。因此，"非洲当下面临的安全挑战不仅是非洲的问题，也影响到域外利益相关者的福祉和安全"[⑤]。倾向于对非洲安全问题采取短期干预行为的美国，[⑥]有其

---

① Ali Mazrui, "Preface: Black Berlin & the Curse of Fragmentation," *UN Peacekeeping in Africa: From the Suez Crisis to the Sudan Conflicts* (by Adekeye Adebajo), Cape Town: Lynne Rienner Publishers, Inc., 2011.

② Elebert, Tarango, and Carter (2002), p. 1093；张春：《化边缘为中心：非洲的跨境安全研究》,《国际政治研究》2022 年第 3 期, 第 9—35 页。

③ Matthew K. Lange, "British Colonial Legacies and Political Development," *World Development* 32 (6), 2004, pp. 905-922.

④ Onah P. Thompson and Titiksha Fernandes, *Counting Lives: Colonial Institutions and Africa's Prevailing Conflicts*, https://doi.org/10.1007/978-3-030-38922-2_47.

⑤ F. Nganje and E. Ndawana, *The Political Economy of External Intervention in Africa's Security*, 2020, https://doi.org/10.1007/978-3-030-38922-2_49.

⑥ Horace G. Campbell, "The United States and Security in Africa: The Impact of the Military Management of the International System," *African Development* XLII, 2017, p. 48.

地缘政治、安全和经济利益（比如控制非洲的能源自然资源、反恐行动、打击海盗和非法贩运①），其大多数"安全援助行动"都寻求强化自身在非洲的军事影响力，包括增加武器销售和转让、军事培训、海军演习并且获取在战略性国家驻扎基地权；②继承冷战时代长期军事支持和扶植扎伊尔［今刚果（金）］、埃及独裁政权做法，2001年在全球打响反恐战争和霸权控制以来，美国也把"更换政权"（regime change）作为一种对非政策目标，瞄准那些不能够服务于美国利益的国家。③

对于前殖民地而言，打着保护人权名义来干预的前宗主国法国扮演了更糟糕的角色，带来的往往是更大的不安全和不稳定，近在咫尺的案例俄乌冲突，以及2011年法国扮演了核心角色的北约轰炸利比亚行动——12年来，溢出效应不断传导到马里和其他非洲北部与西部地区。早有学者提出，对于法语非洲国家而言，解决不断影响非洲的军事政变和其他形式的政治不稳定，"首先要重思法非关系，因为这种关系不断地将大批非洲政治精英变成法国利益的管道，特别是保障其在大陆上获取自然资源和投资机会的特权"④。如同马里和布基纳法索的案例一样，尼日尔最近的政变发生之前，国内公众已经多次游行示威反对执政者过于亲法亲美的外交政策——大众传媒时代，他们有很多途径可以了解到一些简单的事实：本国国家储备的一半在法国央行，美其名曰保证货币（非洲法郎）的稳定性，本国需要使用时要以缴利息的形式才能拿到；尼日尔的铀矿是法国大部分核电供应的来源，但95%的利润在法国人手里。面对媒体采访，政变后的尼日尔公众大声质问，"为什么前法国的殖民地都是最贫困的？"从7月26日政变开始到本文收稿的8

---

① Elisabeth Skons,"The United States," In *Security Activities of External Actors in Africa*, ed. by Olawale Ismail and Elisabeth Skons, Oxford: Oxford University Press, 2014, pp. 105-130.

② Michael Klare and Daniel Volman, "America, China and the Scramble for Africa's Oil," *Review of African Political Economy* 33, 2006, p. 299, https://doi.org/10.1080/03056240600843048.

③ Mediel Hove and Enock Ndawana, "Regime-Change Agenda: The Egyptian Experience from 2011 to 2015," *Contemporary Arab Affairs* 10, 2017, pp. 32-50, https://doi.org/10.1080/17550912.2017.1279386.

④ Rupiya Martin, "Three Reasons Why the Gabon Coup Failed," *Mail and Guardian,* January 9, 2019, https://mg.co.za/article/2019-01-09-three-reasons-whythe-gabon-coup-failed, 转引自 N. Oluwafemi Mimiko, "Contextualizing the State Structure Requisite for Africa's Development"。

月中期，公众热切地参与各种形式的公共集会，一方面表达对于政变者的支持，鼓励他们领导建设全新的国家；另一方面愤怒地呼吁抵制西方通过西非经济共同体实施武力干预，因为利比亚被干涉的教训仍然如芒在背，一旦历史在尼日尔重演，动荡就会出现在整个西非地区甚至更大范围。[①]

非洲的不安全到底如何治理？美国和其他西方大国一直打着"自由和平"的全球安全治理大旗，其思想根基可以追溯到现代欧洲早期政治哲学家如康德、亚当·斯密等人，帕里斯等学者的"民主和平论"是其当代的经典版本；问题是，后冷战时代以来，这一学说越来越成为支持美欧大国在全球进行干预的工具，[②]难掩其自私自利的实质，在非洲越来越受到质疑。例如，在此理论支撑之下的联合国维和行动，近年来也不断受到质疑，不仅效力堪忧，道德合法性也被质疑。[③]有研究发现，"随着联合国维和部队部署，西方大国与受冲突影响国家之间的贸易往往会大规模增加"；为什么与三大国（英法美）没有多少贸易往来的几内亚比绍和卢旺达，国际上在1998年和1994年分别广泛关注到其境内发生的屠杀事件，却没有得益于维和行动的支持？"西方大国似乎只干涉那些威胁到其自身利益的非洲国家的安全局势"[④]。近年来，刚果（金）等国民众多次游行反对维和行动；在马里已经被东道国叫停，本文写作之时，蓝盔部队正在加紧撤离。

很多国际观察家认为，新冠疫情全球大流行以来，随着新兴市场国家的财政吃紧，可能减少资金支持，而"新冠疫情综合征"之下的非洲国家承受了巨大的财政压力，可能会增加对于国际货币基金组织的依赖，从而开启"新自由主义"卷土重来的机会，债务重重的安哥拉、加

---

① 综合2023年7月26日以来全非网、CGTN的连续报道和采访。

② 何银：《发展和平：全球安全治理中的规范竞争与共生》，中国社会科学出版社，2020年。

③ Adekeye Adebajo, *UN Peacekeeping in Africa: From the Suez Crisis to the Sudan Conflicts*, Cape Town: Lynne Rienner Publishers, Inc., 2011; Funmi Olonisakin, *Peacekeeping in Sierra Leone: The story of UNAMSIL*, Boulder, CO and London: Lynne Rienner Publishers, 2008.

④ Szymon M. Stojek and Tir Jaroslav, "The Supply Side of United Nations Peacekeeping Operations: Trade Ties and United Nations-led Deployments to Civil War Sates," *European Journal of International Relations* 21, 2015, p. 368.

纳等国最近的走向似乎都印证了这一点，是否还要像上一轮的"结构调整方案"那样，国家功能进行大规模自废武功还有待观察。有学者认为，虽然世界银行和国际货币基金组织都声称针对脆弱国家的具体情况和需求，调整干预的方式，但两者更专注于利用战争、冲突和发展中经济体急需外汇的契机，以"新自由主义和平建设行动"来建立"新自由主义社会"，他们实际上可能更容易引发战争和经济不平等，并可能在紧缩政策下让民生更加疲敝、经济崩溃。[①] 根据本书邀约的两位长期从事安全研究的非洲名家对于苏丹和埃塞俄比亚案例的研究，近年来不断宣称调整对于脆弱国家的支持策略、更多聚焦非洲冲突的内源性社会经济发展的国际金融体制，实际上对于如何实现其宣传的"从根源解决冲突"的目标并没有清晰的思路，在两国投放的干预举措都显示出与这种"美好的叙事"相去甚远——比如在埃塞俄比亚，世界银行的项目数字自阿比总理上台以来确实有明显增加，但在 2020 年末冲突升级为内战以来，一方面要求阿比加快私有化和货币放宽管制；另一方面迟迟没有将作为"中等烈度"的冲突国家类别提升为实质性的"高烈度"冲突国家以提供更多干预；国际货币基金组织则对爆发实质性内战没有做出任何反应，只专注于压迫阿比政府与债权人的债务重组和自由兑换货币，并在重组谈判不可能情况下骤然停止所有合作。[②] 总之，以上研究显示，尽管世界银行若干重量级经济学家无数次公开自我批判过新自由主义指导下的"结构调整方案"对发展中国家产生的破坏作用，但在全球大变局背景下，国际金融体制远未发挥其宣扬的帮助冲突国家重建自由和平的目标，更不必说寻根溯源，医治殖民剥削、冷战以及当代大国影响控制给非洲带来的社会创伤，不管是针对外源性还是内生性因素。

[①]　Krishna Chaitanya Vadlamannati, Gina Maria G. Østmoe, and Indra de Soysa, "Do IMF programs disrupt ethnic peace? An empirical analysis, 1985-2006," *Journal of peace research* 51, no. 6, 2014, https://doi.org/10.1177/0022343314538478; Carol Cohn and Claire Duncanson, "Whose recovery? IFI prescriptions for postwar states," *Review of international political economy: RIPE* 27, no. 6, 2020, https://doi.org/10.1080/09692290.2019.1677743; Elliot Dolan-Evans, "Making war safe for capitalism: The World Bank and its evolving interventions in conflict," *Security dialogue* 53, no. 6, 2022, https://doi.org/10.1177/09670106221091382.

[②]　参见本书《国际金融机构在非洲冲突、复苏和过渡中的作用——以埃塞俄比亚和苏丹为例》一文。

　　非洲学者、思想家、智库和大陆以及国家层面的领导人近年来对于非洲自身的安全挑战的性质、根源以及长远的解决之道进行了深入讨论，为"非洲问题非洲方案"做出了卓越的智识贡献，也深入影响了目前非洲领导人的决策，很多向正确道路的转变正在悄悄发生。例如，关于如何认知非洲面临的安全，非洲老一代大学者、思想家马兹鲁伊教授在一本书的序言中写道，"非洲灾难的本质和核心，是西方成功地建立了全球种族等级制度，非洲被置于金字塔低端"；因而重建的关键，是"非洲人冲破种种矛盾和分裂的桎梏，达成泛非解决方案"，具体的八种方式如下：一国入境另一冲突国助力恢复秩序，如坦桑 1979 年进入乌干达案例；地区组织承认支持下，一国入境另一国，如 1976 年阿盟支持叙利亚干涉黎巴嫩案例，再如 90 年代尼日利亚在西非经共体支持下干涉利比里亚和塞拉利昂的案例；非盟和平安全委员会应该重新组织，埃及或者利比亚代表北部非洲、尼日利亚代表西部非洲、埃塞或者乌干达代表东部非洲、南非代表南部非洲地区，要都成为常任理事国，然后再选择 3—5 个非常任理事国，每隔 30 年重新审查一次；建立泛非紧急反应部队，对任何非洲国家境内的内战和冲突进行紧急灭火，以此教育非洲人达成"非洲治理下的和平"；非盟之下建立难民和流离失所人口高级专员，使用联合国难民署资源，实现非洲人领导权；临时性安排机制建立和维持的和平等。[1]

　　显然，这些建议的重点在于"泛非解决方案"，是针对非洲本土社会文化和政治网络被外来瓦解、碎片化后的形成的安全困境提出的解决方案。非洲青年学人门杜在其刚刚答辩通过的博士论文中阐述到，非洲绝大多数的不安全，本质上是国家内部的冲突，是"内向型"的，因此，难以使用"主权国家面临的外部威胁"和"单一军事维度"为定义的西方中心视角下的"国家安全观"来分析；同时，互相交织的资源短缺、环境退化、人口过剩和经济衰退等也是当前非洲安全困境的根本原因，也是其治理难度所在。21 世纪以来，非洲的安全观可以概括为"集体安全观"和在此概念基础上的集体安全机制和治理实践，其根本就是最终

---

[1]　Ali Mazrui, "Preface: Black Berlin & the Curse of Fragmentation," pp. xi-xxviii.

实现"非洲问题非洲方案"。[①]

　　值得注意的是，非洲本土的学术和智库组织方式也可以看得到这种明显的"泛非"特征，即根据美国宾夕法尼亚大学《全球智库报告2020》(2020 Global Go To Think Tank Index Report)，撒哈拉以南非洲智库总数为 679 家（仅占全球 6.07%；即使加上北非的也只占全球 8.2%）；在100 强非洲智库中，专门聚焦安全问题的仅 7 家，多聚焦整个非洲大陆的安全问题，较少仅关注特定国，加之不安全挑战日益呈现发展－安全关联（development-security nexus）叠加的复合性质，跨境安全研究的重要性远超过国家安全研究的重要性。[②] 这种安全挑战的受害者，更多体现为非洲普通民众遭受的大规模影响，即以"人的安全"的方式体现出来，其长远解决势必需要首先重思之前非洲大陆应对安全和冲突的既有方式方法——因为"之前的做法主要是跟随域外大国"的指挥棒，接受其安全援助的同时也要接受其训令和指导，目标却是"为了维护大国及其非洲帮凶们的狭隘经济和地缘政治利益"[③]。

　　非洲学人和智库开启的这一系列重思和安全重构路线中，焦点之一是西非萨赫勒地区"恐怖主义和反恐斗争的政治经济学"，Mumo Nzau、Fritz Nganje、Check Achu 等学者在承认各国政府的积极贡献和进展的同时，特别指出要深入理解恐怖主义活动激增的背后，需要同时理解受害国本身的脆弱易受攻击性和全球动荡的大背景双重互构的逻辑，西方指导的"正统的"以牙还牙的军事打击思路从来不能彻底消除恐袭，国家本身的建设是安全能力提升的根本，而外来援助者以新自由主义为路线图的"自由和平"干预方式，在不断破坏非洲国家的国家建设；非洲国家必须更多采取预防式的、真正"非洲本土创制"的反恐方式。[④]

　　新自由主义对非洲过去、现在和未来的影响，显然不限于这一部分讨论的冲突与安全领域，实际上影响是全方位的。本书特邀博茨瓦纳大

---

　　① 门杜:《当代非洲集体安全观与安全机制研究》,北京大学博士学位论文,2023 年。

　　② 张春:《化边缘为中心:非洲的跨境安全研究》,《国际政治研究》2022 年第 3 期,第9—34 页。

　　③ F. Nganje and E. Ndawana, *The Political Economy of External Intervention in Africa's Security* , p. 922.

　　④ Daron Acemoglu, Simon Johnson and James A. Robinson, "The Colonial Origins of Comparative Development: An Empirical Investigation," *American Economic Review* 91 (5), 2001, pp. 1369-1401.

学工作的陈亮博士，用细腻的笔触和敏锐的观察力，以一个大学为案例方式，记录分析了疫情下在很多国家发生的高校教职员工的罢工现象，原本相对优越的精英阶层的抗议，恰恰是新自由主义的逻辑和长期负面影响所投射的一个缩影，是高等教育本身的困境在教职员工身上的反映。尽管不是暴力形式，但高校教职员罢课的原因显然同样是出于生活压力沉重甚至前景无望而以涨工资的要求提出的，是一个微观层面的社会小冲突和小动荡，是全球问题的"地方化"。

发展型国家：绝地求生的转型发展之路

21世纪以来，非洲似乎摆脱了"黑暗大陆"的魔咒，整体经济表现越来越亮眼，"非洲狮"一时成为全世界的流行语。10余年持续的增长中，20世纪后半叶国际话语中持续忧虑的"非洲粮食安全"问题似乎也终于解决，国际粮农组织（FAO）2015年发表了《非洲粮食安全的前景前所未有过的光明》的报告，声称当年非洲的整体饥饿率相比1990—1992年的基线有31%的下降；7个国家（安哥拉、吉布提、喀麦隆、加蓬、加纳、马里和圣多美普林西比）实现了千年发展目标（MDG）1设立的"饥饿率减半"。[1] 然而，好景不长，对非洲发展的乐观期待就急转直下。卫生医疗条件极为有限的非洲大陆虽然没有迅速"沦为新冠疫情重灾区"，但是非洲经济遭遇半个世纪以来最严重的衰退，普遍的非正式就业形态使得民众在疫情期间和疫情后的生活都更为艰难——如前文所述，既没有防护设施又苦于生计无着的两难困境。[2] 俄乌冲突发生以来，非洲的发展又显露出其他亟待改进的内外部脆弱性，比如依赖俄乌两国小麦供应的国家因为供应链断裂而粮食涨价、引发"粮荒"（甚至可能引发暴动——参见峯阳一教授在本书中的论述），油气资源丰富却不能够炼油，导致政府和民众都不得不承受能源价格骤升的压

---

① FAOSTAT (Food and Agricultural Organization), *Data Extract from World Development Indicator*, 2015.

② 刘海方：《变动世界秩序中的非洲》，《世界知识》2023年第1期，第12—17页。

力。① 正如长期担任为非洲走出新自由主义魔咒做出巨大贡献的联合国非洲经济委员会② 的掌门人的 Lopes 教授所言，是时候反思持续 10 多年的关于"非洲崛起"的乐观叙事了，市场并没有自动将非洲带到持续增长的阳关大道，要做的是认真思考如何在"发展型国家"的带领下，走出依赖大宗商品价格走高的"资源泡沫"所获得的表面经济增长繁荣，实现真正的"转型发展"。③

Lopes 教授为什么会着重强调"发展型国家"和"转型发展"两个概念呢？他认为，非洲经济脆弱性的根源有几方面。首先，在 80 年代开始的"结构调整方案"要求下，非洲的市场就都被要求打开，在"自由化贸易"名义下，一方面非洲大多数经济体仍然是以资源或者原料出口为主，面对海啸般涌入的全球产品，长期陷入没有竞争力来发展本土工业化的对外不平等交换状态；另一方面，尽管近年来非洲外贸伙伴越来越多元，大陆内部的贸易、大陆与亚洲市场之间的贸易量都在增长（2016 年为 26.3%，2017 年为 27.9%）④，意味着更少受制于传统欧美市场的主宰和控制，但在毫无政府保护的情况下，非洲农业和采掘业为主的产品进入世界市场的时候，时刻受到世界市场价格波动的影响，而且农产品是与享受发达国家大量补贴的同类产品赤膊较量。另外，发达经济体彼此之间建立了越来越多的自由贸易区，彼此的产品享受免税或者低关税的待遇，这意味着来自非洲的产品通常难以进入发达国家市场。⑤

总之，疫情和大变局的教训是，非洲要种足够的粮食，而不是只种植自己几乎无缘享用的经济作物，保证"米袋子在自己手里"，要自己

---

① 刘海方：《被忽视的自强大陆——多重危机中的非洲能动性》，《文化纵横》2022 年第 4 期，第 43—53 页。

② 联合国非洲经济委员会是联合国第一个针对一个大陆的经济发展事务成立的委员会，在非洲统一组织还没有强大的社会经济和发展研究规划能力的前提下，该委员会自 20 世纪末以来主导了帮助非洲摆脱新自由主义控制的努力。

③ Carlos Lopes and George Kararach, *Structural Change in Africa: Misperceptions, New Narratives & Development in the 21st Century*, p. 3.

④ Afreximbank, *The Africa Trade Report 2018: Boosting Intra-African Trade: Implications of the African Continental Free Trade Area Agreement*, Cairo: Afreximbank.

⑤ Carlos Lopes and George Kararach, *Structural Change in Africa: Misperceptions, New Narratives & Development in the 21st Century*, p. 3.

用好自己的资源、实现自己的能源供给，要制造自己民众需要的工业品特别像防护服之类的，才能应对随时可能再次发生的更多外源危机叠加内部脆弱性的困境。简单说，以上目标所需要的最重要的变革，是农业和制造业找到可行的方式，生产本国大众消费的基本物品。非洲语境下的"转型发展"，涵义不同于一般经济学家总结的"现代化转型"（林毅夫老师强调的从低收入发展到高收入，同时完成从农业或者资源为基础向工业或者服务业为基础的经济转型[1]），也不仅仅是强调城市化过程中的人口流动增加、人口出生率和死亡率都从高向低等常用指标，而是应该首先针对其畸形外向型经济进行调矫，让依附于发达国家消费经济链条上的生产转向服务于本国民众，同时实现经济多元化、摆脱与世界经济进行单一产品交换的脆弱性。[2] 今天，非洲已经具备了一支受过良好教育的城市化劳动大军，经济向更深的工业化方向发展的时机已经具备，更何况非洲本土丰富的矿产资源和农产品，加工业能够助力一个资本产品部门的形成，而相关的科研技术和研发活动可以不必从最基础做起，而是跳跃式地通过进口技术来满足当地需要。[3]

目标清晰了，可行性具备了，关键是如何发力、谁来引领、资金支持如何解决、如何实现各方面的协同发展，特别是地缘政治的重要性卷土重来，重新成为大变局时代全球各国必须面对的新语境、新挑战的当下，亨廷顿教授当年从政治角度呼吁的非洲"强大政府"，也同样是完成今天可持续发展任务的必要前提，有同样强大的国家和国际话语权，才能够在复杂的国际环境中实现绝地重生、保护和满足本国民众当下需求，并平衡好永续发展的目标。这就是"发展型国家"再次成为非洲国家特别是领导人中高频热词的原因。

---

① 林毅夫：《中国式现代化的理论逻辑与世界意义》，北大国发院公众号，参见 https://mp.weixin.qq.com/s/dnywNsrCHwt2uxgeinM81g，2023-03-22。

② Carlos Lopes and George Kararach, *Structural Change in Africa: Misperceptions, New Narratives & Development in the 21st Century*, chp. 1.

③ ECA, *Millennium Development Goals Report 2013: Assessing Progress in Africa towards the Millennium Development Goals Food Security in Africa: Issues, Challenges & Lessons*, Addis Ababa: ECA; P. Lawrence and Y. Graham, "Structural Transformation and Economic Development in Africa," Blog, ROAPE, Http: roape.net/2015/12/18/structural-transfromation-and-economic-development-inafrica/.

　　发展型国家的观念源于非新古典经济学派，明确提出市场机制在最优化经济和发展方面的潜在不足，认为在三种情况下需要国家干预：市场缺失需要创造、市场不利需要优化提升、公共产品缺失需要引导市场加入。[①] 可以说，发展型国家既是意识形态性的，也是结构性的——国家的意识形态就是聚焦发展，实现良性增长、工业化、创造就业等结构转型的目标；同时国家必须展现出计划和实施这些目标的能力，不受破坏性社会力量的影响，能够驾驭不同的政治经济动力，最大化实现计划中的发展成果，比如投资必需的基础设施和人力资源发展。[②]

　　非洲学者最早开始关注和使用"发展型国家"概念，源于东亚国家和亚洲四小龙现象的刺激。AKE 在 1996 年的作品中，比照这些国家发展经验、质疑良治未必必须以西式民主制度为前提。[③] 享誉世界的非洲发展问题专家 Thandika Mkandawire 教授，更是批判了当时国际金融机构主导下的"妖魔化"非洲国家、要求其自动与发展"脱钩"的流行论调，提出非洲国家不缺乏"追求发展"的宗旨和目标，其人文生态环境也并不与"发展型国家"天生暌违，第一代领导人展示的正是"发展型国家"的领导力，只不过他们更多专注于政治方向的国家建设，而新一代非洲领导人转而专注于经济方向的国家建设，所以前者将资本视作"外来控制"，后者已经没有这种意识形态局限，而是拥抱资本和私有化作为政策主要选项。[④] 此后很多学者也指出，国际金融机构以非洲缺少文化土壤和机制性支持为由诊断非洲与"发展型国家"绝缘，这显然是非历史主义的，第一代领导人执行了很多国家发展计划和政府主导的项目。[⑤] 这样的诊断，特别明显的缺失之处在于对全球资本主义霸权影响非洲大

　　① Carlos Lopes and George Kararach, *Structural Change in Africa: Misperceptions, New Narratives & Development in the 21st Century*, p. 9.

　　② T. Mkandawire, "Thinking about Developmental States in Africa," *Cambridge Journal of Economics* 25, 2001, pp. 289-313.

　　③ Claude Ake, *Democracy and Development in Africa*, Washington, DC: Brookings Institution Press, 1996.

　　④ C. D'Alessandro and L. C. Zulu, "From the Millennium Development Goals (MDGs) to the Sustainable Development Goals (SDGs): Africa in the Post-2015 Development Agenda: A Geographic Perspective," *African Geographical Review* 36(1), 2017, pp. 1-18.

　　⑤ Atul Kholi, *State-Directed Development,* Cambridge: Cambridge University Press, 2004.

陆的历史和现实都避而不谈，迫使非洲国家虽然经历了抵抗但不得不重构独立之初的国家－市场关系，更多转向"市场力量"致敬效忠。[①]

21世纪以来，有关非洲国家近年来的发展问题，除了对诸如工业化、农业现代化、气候变化问题影响等专题方向的关注外，学术界的共识性议题越来越聚焦在"发展型国家"上，已有研究成果显示，相较于很多严格执行"市场万灵"的"原教旨主义式"戒律的国家，近年来录得最好发展业绩的，恰好是那些背离了新自由主义的"正统学说"、走上发展型国家之路的国家，比如埃塞俄比亚、毛里求斯和卢旺达。[②] 他们的典型特征就是允许国家参与经济活动，特别是向优先领域分配资源方面，具体案例国家因与其作为土壤的社会之间的关系模式不同而显示出不同的活力和各异其趣的结果，共同点是都开始了本土的工业化进程。[③]

与此前依据人口红利的巨大潜力、迅速推广的通信技术和快速城市化的大潮流来判断非洲未来发展优势的政治家、学者一样，Lopes 也认为，非洲国家当下具备人口、地理条件和自然禀赋、技术变革和城市化各方面交汇在一起的机遇时代，可谓天时地利人和，意味着非洲人能动性的释放和转型发展的关键时期；[④] 但他强调，非洲在21世纪前20年的增长，只看重了GDP增长和吸引国际大公司进入的资源条件，水平方向的经济扩展有限，不是有社会包容性的发展，并没有能够制造足够的生产就业机会并带来大多数人口生活水平的提高，同时非洲在全球经济中的重要性也尚未被感知到。[⑤] 当务之急就是通过转型过程来创造工作机会、增加收入和财富，而发挥农业发展的优越自然条件、以服务业和投资来带动农业转型并触发结构变革与就业机会的路径，城市和农村

---

① Mkandawire, "Thinking about Developmental States in Africa."

② S. O. Oloruntoba and T. Falola, "The Political Economy of Africa: Connecting the Past to the Present and Future of Development in Africa," *The Palgrave Handbook of African Political Economy, Palgrave Handbooks in IPE*, eds. by S. O. Oloruntoba and T. Falola, https://doi.org/10.1007/978-3-030-38922-2_1.

③ Nagar Marcel, *The Quest for Democratic Developmental States in Africa: A Study of Ethiopia, Mauritius and Rwanda*, Unpublished Doctoral Dissertation, University of Johannesburg, South Africa, 2019.

④ Carlos Lopes and George Kararach, *Structural Change in Africa: Misperceptions, New Narratives & Development in the 21st Century*, p. 17.

⑤ 同上注，第16页。

并重，同时提升人力资源，才是可持续发展的战略。提振粮食生产的最佳道路是"新绿色革命"，是以公私合作（PPP）模式将援助者、私营部门、农业生产资料供应者、农商、农产品加工者和零售商，都能够与农民连在一起，而且边远山村也有超市体系相连。[①]

这样将农业、工业和人口联动视角整体推进的战略，作为共识已经写进非盟2014年提出的"通过农业加工业触发工业化"路线图中，显然是吸取了非洲大陆本身自独立以来的多种发展经验和教训，特别是独立之初盲目效仿现代化理论的主张，片面追求工业进口替代——工业优先、牺牲农业的路线，使得人口占多数的农村凋敝，而大规模的"人口大迁徙"涌入城市周边、造就"落脚城市"，在非洲和其他许多第三世界国家形成无数城市贫民窟，教训惨痛。[②] 疫情和全球大变局，恰恰是在叫停这种"超级全球化"推动的似乎无止境的恶性城市化过程，农村如何留住人口，如何喂饱自己也喂饱本国城市人口的问题，更是人类探讨如何公平合理分配资源，允许人人可以体面、自尊并主宰自己的生活，可持续地永续发展的共同命题。

本书约请的日本著名非洲研究专家（现任日本协力团研究所所长）峯阳一教授和其津巴布韦同事共同撰写的文章，讨论的正是这个有关非洲的"三农问题"的源起、流变、现状以及解决出路。[③] 根据两位作者的研究，早在1954年，出任恩克鲁玛经济顾问的著名经济学家刘易斯就曾经鲜明提出"农村革命先于工业革命"的主张，并且认为资源有限的新独立国家如加纳，应该举全国之力首先开展"成人教育"而不是优先进行全面基础教育，因为农民亟待通过技术推广学习来提升农业发展；根据在津巴布韦等多国的一线调查，作者提出，与其等待国家自上而下解决土地不足、技术有限、市场付诸阙如等发展瓶颈，非洲小农已经自发探索组建了生产和社会一体化的农民公社，这种自发的组织很可能是

---

① C. D'Alessandro and L. C. Zulu, "From the Millennium Development Goals (MDGs) to the Sustainable Development Goals (SDGs): Africa in the Post-2015 Development Agenda: A Geographic Perspective," *African Geographical Review* 36(1), 2017, pp.1-18.

② Doug Saunders, *Arrival City*, NY: Vintage Books, 2012.

③ 参见本书《人口转型下的非洲农业发展之路：农民合作社的作用》一文。

未来非洲"三农问题"最终解决的出路。

就挑战而言，非洲大陆的经济发展同样必须解决能源需求。空气污染已经与艾滋病、疟疾并列为健康头号杀手，这意味着非洲的能源现代化面临着双重任务：既要实现超一半的人口还没有电的问题，而且在其获得足够的、可负担的能源的同时，实现能源清洁化转型的问题。除了在全球占比很高的大量传统意义上的贵金属等资源，大量的可再生能源资源意味着非洲最有机会发展绿色工业化，这是未来非洲国民经济的关键，也是地理空间、利益相关者、社会群体和社区受益的关键。解决通电非洲老大难的传统认知是"外来论"，即非洲无力自主实现，只能乞求援助国、国际组织和外来公司，资金技术甚至项目都是外来；而罗楠的研究显示，尽管可再生能源发电总量上占比还不高，非洲民众已经在探索使用相关技术解决能源需求了——前景很可能是，在国家长期未能解决的情况下，政府和外来行为体同样发挥作用前提下，非洲能源现代化很可能走一条民主化的道路，社会广泛地加入其中，甚至经常扮演引领的作用。

同样的"民主化"发展道路探索，也体现在匹配市场需求和同时均衡长远发展需求的人力资源发展方面，王进杰跟踪研究了面对疫情之下在东道国跨文化经营挑战增加的环境下，四种不同性质、不同投资方向的中资企业通过增加制度、信任、社区、文化和教育投资来探索深度扎根非洲的实践。[①]类似地，许亮对于不同华人工厂成功案例的研究显示，东道国的工业政策与中非合作，促进和塑造了华人制造业；而在非洲的经营和全球产业链中表现出经营韧性的中资企业本身的作用也非常关键，包括其雇佣女工等都是立足当地也惠及当地的探索尝试。[②]非洲"发展型国家"下一阶段的转型发展，实现经济多元化和工业化本身同样重要，是其最终摆脱"资源诅咒"、将青年人口优势转换为人口红利的关键；国家需要转变思路，自己主动参与塑造经济发展道路，也最大可能地鼓励民众和外来行为体积极探索，在国际合作中广泛吸收学习全

---

① 参见本书《多重危机下在非中国企业人力资本投资新探索》一文。
② 参见本书《非洲工业化与华人工厂》一文。

世界优秀的现代化发展经验，同时如非洲环境和可持续发展研究专家马路华教授所言，中国迄今已经成为"阻碍非洲参与经济增长的落后基础设施、交通匮乏难题"的解锁之钥，未来仍需携手共同应对环境和气候挑战，[①] 才能够充分释放和发挥非洲能动性。

结语：危机与豹变

2020年考取北大硕士项目、2022年7月毕业的加纳学生Sena，曾经多次在线上长谈中向我这个学术导师和论文指导教师憧憬疫情结束、踏入燕园的热望，但最终遗憾地成为许许多多新冠时代"在线生"中的一员，与北大只有不曾谋面的"半缘"。我以为，历史已经写就，无由弥补缺憾、找回"正常"，而Sena就像线上结识的许许多多其他学生一样，带着最真实的"新冠时代"的烙印与遗憾，继续出发向前，去拾取下一个阶段的人生了。整整一年后，这位加纳白衣青年却意外地翩然而至，来到校园与我相见——在又熟悉又陌生中，我们相对长吁，实现线下相聚，让半缘接续，才是对肆虐世间3年有余的疫情的最大胜利吧！

我问Sena，线上求学，收获是什么？他说，疫情期间一直想方设法来到校园，那些挣扎就像一次次被放在火上煎烤；但是回过头来看，没有这个过程，可能不会增加许多本领，视野不会一下从一个加纳小镇青年变成全球视野，同时对于自己的民族身份有了更清晰的认知；疫情期间克服种种艰难挑战实现在加纳和尼日利亚做有关非洲民众如何认知传统中药的实地调研，写成了获得一等奖的硕士论文的同时，自己也坚定了弘扬和复兴非洲本土传统医疗和文化的信心——这些都是在与北大的老师和同学们互动中，通过不断对比中国以及其他亚洲国家的经验获取的。

多产的美国学者布雷默反思疫情以来的世界，在其新作《危机的力量》中提出了"必要的危机"一词，认为难则难矣，关键是困难重重的时间节点下，也刚好意味着"豹变"的可能[②]——古今中外的历史，都看得

---

① 参见本书《疫情前后中国与非洲合作的环境视角》一文。

② Ian Bremmer, *The Power of Crisis*, NY: Simon & Schuster, 2022.

见这种常态的历史惰性和瞬间的历史创造性之间的辩证关系。我眼前的有志青年，3 年来的努力与蜕变，何尝不是 400 多年来历经劫难，但在我们可见的新冠疫情全球大流行时代勇敢迎接又一次源自外部"重创"的非洲大陆力量的缩影？！横行全球的新冠肺炎疫情以及 500 多天加剧全球动荡的俄乌冲突固然是突如其来的挑战，难能可贵的是，非洲一直在反思自身的局限，如联合国教科文组织助理总干事马托克所言，对非洲国家来说，重新思考发展在智力和政治上都是当务之急——新的发展模式必须从历史中吸取教训，适应非洲社会不断变化的性质。[1]

全球大变局下的非洲各行为体都在施展各种能动性，方方面面都体现出探索和打破长久以来限制其发展的结构性窘境的"破局"之努力，[2]比如本书约请的郑宇教授及其弟子们共同研究的非洲经济一体化之最新探索所示：原本对于欧盟榜样亦步亦趋，希望通过建立关税同盟来实现一体化，但发现"难比登天、遥遥无期"，但既有叠床架屋的次区域组织已经成为掣肘，必须打破这种"意大利面碗"效应，于是 2021 年 1 月"自上而下"启动大陆自由贸易区的路径，以神来之笔的方式忽然推动了非洲一体化的"关键一跃"。[3]本文基于全书作者们的精当分析，总结了大变局下非洲发生的政治、经济、社会发展领域里面方方面面的危机本质与非洲人应变的努力，既是对自身的危机求索"非洲本土创制"的解决方案，也在为全球性难题而求索奉献，比如不仅仅是在联合国大会平台上不断发声呼吁停战、2023 年 6 月南非总统更携手其他 7 国非洲领导人，器宇轩昂也不无悲壮地把"非洲方案"写进烽火硝烟的乌克兰和俄罗斯土地上——很多世界观察家当然惯常性地对此视而不见，或者蔑视和讥讽，而非洲人知其不可而为之，以此方式集体"问鼎"世界难题的勇气、胆识和智慧却值得大书特书。

---

① Firmin Edouard Matoko, Sous-directeur général, Département Afrique, UNESCO, https://oecd-development-matters.org/2020/09/17/repenser-le-developpement-en-afrique-et-pour-lafrique/.

② 刘海方：《被忽视的自强大陆——多重危机中的非洲能动性》，《文化纵横》2022 年第 4 期，第 43—53 页。

③ 参见本书《当下困境中的非洲经济一体化新进展》一文。

乱中求治：重校方向

在混乱中寻找契机：
布基纳法索应对动荡局势和后疫情时代发展的紧迫性

伊萨克·巴齐耶著　谭　威译*

摘　要：在 2019 年新冠疫情大流行期间，布基纳法索在八个月内发生了两起政变，引起了国际社会的广泛关注。西方"选举式民主"模式的捍卫者抨击这种情形是政治动荡，甚至进行非常严厉的谴责和制裁。当世界上其他国家似乎正从 2019 年新冠疫情中恢复过来的时候，国家领导人的频繁更换，体现了布基纳法索人正在迫切寻求解决疫情之前和暴发期间那些让他们焦头烂额的问题：恐怖袭击所造成的动荡不安，缺乏能够改善人民生活条件的善治，以及与犯罪有关的司法问题，其中最闻名于外的是布基纳法索革命之父在 1987 年被暗杀的事件。本文首先揭示了布基纳法索政治动荡背后的原因；然后分析了普通民众所做的努力，这有力地塑造了国家的发展方向，即加强与除前殖民者之外的其他伙伴的合作。

关键词：后疫情　布基纳法索　政治动荡　治理　发展　去殖民化

引　言

自 2022 年初以来，素有"正人君子之国"①之称的布基纳法索一直

---

　*　伊萨克·巴齐耶（Isaac Bazié），系魁北克大学蒙特利尔分校文学研究系非洲文学和文化研究方向教授；谭威，北京大学国关学院博雅博士后。

　［注］本文由刘海方、王进杰进行中文翻译校对。

　①　原文为 Burkina Faso，结合当地语言摩西语 burkina 意为正人君子，班巴拉语 faso 意为国家，译为"正人君子之国"。——译者注

备受关注，因为在其政治舞台上发生了两起非常相似的重大事件。2022年1月24日，一场政变推翻了总统罗克·马克·克里斯蒂安·卡博雷，中校保罗－亨利·桑达奥果·达米巴上台掌权。8个月后，2022年10月2日，第二次政变结束了达米巴总统短暂的统治。34岁的陆军上尉易卜拉欣·特拉奥雷执掌政权。本国所有利益攸关方都希望他能解决与恐怖分子行动有关的严峻的不安全问题，因为这关系布基纳法索40%的国土上300万人的保护和照料问题，其中三分之二的人已经逃离不安全地区，成为自己国土上漂泊的异乡人；还有与通货膨胀有关的生活成本问题，其后果让那些已经生活在动荡之中的民众惊恐不安；以及更为广泛的与善治有关的问题。

当世界的主要经济体齐聚巴厘岛（印度尼西亚），讨论后疫情时代的"共同复苏"之时，布基纳法索人所关心的问题是什么？在2020年到2022年普遍的公共卫生危机之时，他们所面临的挑战是什么？与布基纳法索在疫情之前和后疫情时期所长期面临的挑战相比，这些挑战有多重要？

为了回答这些问题，本文分为五个部分，将阐述虽然新冠疫情大流行在很大程度上是一场重大危机，但对布基纳法索的影响相对较小。为了了解布基纳法索的现状，我们有必要重回2014年，这一年应该被视为政治上的一个转折点；这个转折点开启了解决以上述问题为标志的新纪元。正是为了寻找能为这些问题提供合乎需要和紧急解决举措的领导者，该国出现了政治不稳定和社会动荡。也正是这种对卓有远见、富有革命性的领导人的追寻，人们期待新总统易卜拉欣·特拉奥雷上尉能成为托马斯·桑卡拉的化身。目前布基纳法索社会各阶层人民对总统和其他领导人的不耐烦，根源于极其窘迫的生活境况。本文的最后一部分将把布基纳法索的问题置于一个更大的脉络里，即去殖民化的背景下。肤浅的解读经常将示威中发生的事情视为反法情绪，但这些示威表明了比简单的反法情绪更为重要的东西。这种趋势不只限于布基纳法索，也波及马里和尼日尔。从内部视角看，布基纳法索目前表面上的混乱，不过是一个国家正在探寻摆脱不安全和不稳定的路径，为约2000万的人创造一个未来，这其中有77.9%的人在2019年人口普查时还不到 35 岁。[①] 在当前由中国和亚洲普遍崛起所带来的多极世界秩序里，创造了一个反抗霸权的环境，有利于布基纳法索这样的国家在世界舞台上重新定位。从这个角度来看，表面上的混乱却变成一个契机，这是一个寻求以新的方式发展的前殖民地国家可以利用的机会。

一、新冠疫情：一场对当地影响甚微的全球危机

2020 年 1 月，当我前往瓦加杜古机场搭乘飞往蒙特利尔的航班时，我听到有人说："西方人在谈论冠状病毒，但我们这里有比病毒更加严重的问题！"这场疫情已经在全球范围内夺走了众多人的生命，在接下来的两年里，这个看似逸事的笑话，变成了数百万的布基纳法索人对这场大流行病的看法。

布基纳法索在 2020 年 3 月 9 日报告了西非第一例与冠状病毒病相关的死亡病例。[②] 在一批感染和死亡报告后所采取的措施照搬了发达国家的模式：大规模地减少人口流动，在公共场所强制佩戴口罩，使用抗菌凝胶，暂停集会，关闭教育机构、宗教场所和集市。在采取这些紧急措施的同时，还每天向民众通报新增感染者、死亡病例和康复者人数。当局很快意识到，在其他国家和地方所采取的严厉措施，尤其是限制人口流动，在布基纳法索是行不通的。事实上，数百万人每天养家糊口的日常生计活动，需要流动性和开放的市集。这是该措施只施行很短时间的原因之一。布基纳法索人很快恢复到与 2020 年 3 月之前类似的生活状态的另一个原因（从公共卫生的角度来看），是感染的后果，特别与冠状病毒直接相关的死亡病例，并不像疫情开始时国内外舆论所担忧的那样触目惊心。病毒在该国出现一年多后（2021 年 6 月 17 日），下表解释了这种疾病并非布基纳法索所面临的首要问题的原因。

---

① 布基纳法索几乎有一半（45.3%）的人口低于 15 岁！National Institute of Statistics and Demography, "Depliant resultats definitifs RGPH 2019," http://www.insd.bf/contenu/documents_rgph5/Depliant%20resultats%20definitifs%20RGPH%202019.pdf, accessed November 22, 2022.

② Cf., "Burkina Faso: premiers cas de coronavirus à Ouagadougou et crise humanitaire sans précédent dans le nord," Médecins sans frontières, 24 mars 2020, https://www.msf.fr/actualites/burkina-faso-premiers-cas-de-coronavirus-a-ouagadougou-et-crise-humanitaire-sans-precedent-dans-le-nord.

表 1　布基纳法索冠状病毒（COVID-19）的统计数据[1]

2021 年 6 月 17 日的概述	
总检测数量	507
确诊病例	2
死亡病例	0
自 2020 年 3 月 9 日以来的检测总量	507
总检测数量	507

2020 年 3 月 9 日（首例冠状病毒确诊病例）至 2021 年 6 月 17 日的概述	
冠状病毒确诊人数	13464
康复者人数	13287
现有确诊病例	10
死亡病例	167

　　这些数字并不能反映病毒传播的真实状况，因为缺乏能够提供完整情况的基础设施。尽管如此，它们仍然反映了这种病毒在该国具有较低危险性，从所记录的病毒较低的传播率和相当高的康复人数就可以说明。此外，仔细阅读布基纳法索 2021 年 6 月的报告可以发现，大多数的检测是由那些需要核酸检测才能出国旅行的人所完成的。这一点很重要：事实上大多数的检测都与出国旅行有关，主要是乘坐飞机，这对普通的布基纳法索人来说是一笔很高的费用，这促使人们认为新冠是一种富人和西方人的疾病。

　　通过这些观察，我们可以理解为什么疫情大流行在全球层面是一个大问题，但在布基纳法索的影响较小。甚至在疫情开始之前，以及在后疫情时代，一个比冠状病毒更严重的问题困扰着布基纳法索人：恐怖袭击造成的不安全。这就是为什么无国界医生组织的运营总监伊莎贝尔·德富尔尼在描述 2020 年 3 月的卫生状况时，以 2019 年新冠疫情开

---

[1]　Service d'information du gouvernement du Burkina Faso, "Communiqué Infos Covid-19," June 19, 2021, https://www.sig.gov.bf/actualites/details?tx_news_pi1%5Baction%5D=detail&tx_news_pi1%5Bcontroller%5D=News&tx_news_pi1%5Bnews%5D=1265&cHash=e6452bbc8f8c6133d76062024b19639b.

始，以北部的安全问题及其对人口的影响结束。和疫情相比，这些安全问题更加突出，对布基纳法索人的生活所造成的损害也更大。当世界正试图在相对成功地控制病毒的基础之上进行重建之时，布基纳法索仍然面临在新冠疫情之前、期间和之后已经长期存在这个安全隐患。但是，为了理解在这个"正人君子之国"正在发生的事情，我们必须回到2014年10月：这是一个真正的转折点，对于布基纳法索当前的政治生活具有非常重要的影响。

二、新冠疫情前后：作为政治转折点的 2014 年

发展和司法正义问题、2015 年以来的不安全局势，以及善治的挑战，构成了 2020 年 3 月新冠疫情暴发的背景。即使在当前的后疫情时期，这些问题仍旧存在，而且比以往任何时候都更令布基纳法索人担忧。为了理解这一点，有必要简要地回顾一下 2014 年 10 月这段时期。

1. 十月起义：27 年后革命时代的终结

10 月 30 号和 31 号，现在是纪念 2014 年人民起义烈士的日子。这次大规模的人民起义终结了布莱斯·孔波雷总统长达 27 年的统治。值得一提的是，正是这个人参加了 1983 年由托马斯·桑卡拉发动的革命后，在 1987 年 10 月 15 日暗杀了桑卡拉总统，残酷地终结了这场革命。

2014 年 10 月的事件，无论是从政治上，还是从布基纳法索人的身份认同上，都不容忽视。从政治上来说，事情似乎很容易理解：起义将一个声称要"纠正"托马斯·桑卡拉发起的革命的人赶下了台。27 年来，其承诺的纠正变成了在最初几年通过暗杀来控制国家，在随后几年则通过腐败即快速致富的方式来掌控国家。所有这些都得到了西方国家的默许，它们对 1991 年以来同一个人在"选举式民主"的标签下赢得选举感到满意。此外，正是布莱斯·孔波雷试图修宪以让自己有权利再度竞选总统，激怒了民众，并导致了 2014 年 10 月 30 日至 31 日的起义。

图 1 托马斯·桑卡拉纪念碑，瓦加杜古，布基纳法索

照片来源：伊萨克·巴齐耶摄于 2022 年 6 月

图 2　革命烈士纪念碑，瓦加杜古，布基纳法索 ①
照片来源：伊萨克·巴齐耶摄于 2022 年 6 月

　　因此，从严格的政治角度来看，这场起义的前因后果非常简单。孔波雷总统在 27 年之后激怒了人民，被起义的民众赶下了台。随后是大约一年的短暂过渡时期，以 2015 年 9 月 15 日未遂的政变为标志。政治过渡总体上是成功的，因为它允许进行选举，并在 2016 年将权力移交给民选总统罗克·马克·克里斯蒂安·卡博雷。他的上台受到首都瓦加杜古市中心恐怖袭击事件（2016 年 1 月 15 日）的影响。不安全问题在不断加剧，罗克·马克·克里斯蒂安·卡博雷在第一届任期和未完成的第二届任期内未能成功地维护国家的安全，最终导致他被政变赶下台；另

---

　　① 碑文这样写道："献给在 2014 年 10 月 30 日、31 日的起义和 2015 年 9 月 16 日的政变中为祖国牺牲的儿女们，国家感谢你们。"应当指出的是，在布莱斯·孔波雷下台后的政治过渡时期，一位名叫吉尔伯特·迪安德雷的将军试图通过政变来夺取政权，但因为缺乏军队内其他成员和民众的支持而以失败告终。

一方面，从政治成熟度的角度来看，这场起义的结果并不像政治议程那样简单。事实上，在布基纳法索，任何一位政治领导人目前所面临的一个挑战，就是如何治理那些曾成功地发起过起义的民众，以及他们从托马斯·桑卡拉（1983—1987）短暂却非常重要的革命中所继承下来的政治意识。

最近的两次政变在布基纳法索受到了民众的欢迎，尽管它们遭到了国际社会的谴责。当 2022 年 1 月 24 日第一次政变发生时，民众并没有为罗克·马克·克里斯蒂安·卡博雷的下台而忧伤，而是希望新总统能够成功解决卡博雷总统无法解决的日益严重的安全问题。然而，蜜月期很短暂。2022 年 10 月，保罗－亨利·达米巴总统也被赶下台，由易卜拉欣·特拉奥雷上尉取而代之，原因与之前一样：达米巴所执行的政治议程显然并未寻求解决主要的安全问题。民间社会组织在此发挥的作用怎么强调都不为过，但更重要的是大众所发挥的监督角色，民众现在迫切地要求政府解决他们的问题，这些问题随着时间的推移只会变得更加糟糕。在最近的一次政变最初的几个小时，民众的支持起到了关键作用。也正是迫于民众的压力，被怀疑缺乏诚信的商务部长和城市规划部长，未能在 2022 年 10 月政变后组建的新政府中就职。反对派通过社交媒体敦促总理调查二人。因此，商务部长决定辞职，城市规划部长也被迫放弃职位。尽管民众为新总统的首次行动和言论喝彩，但正是这样的大众监督，不断地提醒他民众正关注着一切，并期待他为人民的福祉而采取实质性的、辛勤的和行之有效的行动。

2. 一个革命的民族在呼唤一个革命的领袖

布基纳法索发生 2014 年革命后的几年里，"街头"的作用一直没有正确分析：民众的呼声动员了各方人士，成功罢黜总统，并阻止了涉嫌不端的部长就职。确实，该国爆发的几次街头示威，造成了悲剧性的后果：最近，他们以瓦加杜古的法国大使馆和法国文化中心为目标，造成了严重的破坏。当然，这种破坏和阻扰国家机构的偶发行为应该受到谴责。然而，这种社会压力的氛围与将国家从布莱斯·孔波雷的统治中解放出来的伟大抗争有关。苏加诺总统在向联合国大会发表的著名演讲中谈到这种骚动和民众游行时说道："从我们自身的经验来看，我们也知道发展本身会造成动荡。一个动荡不安的国家需要领导和指引，它最终会产生自己的领导和指引。"① 布基纳法索除了所面临的安全和发展的挑战之外，动荡之中的治理也是一个挑战：要了解后革命时代的布基纳法索，它继承了托马斯·桑卡拉的理想和模式，这是一个动荡不安的地方，也是一个久经考验的地方。这要求领导人具备能力且正直，并拥有投身于国家福祉的理想与价值观，以此来动员人民。一些领导人未能完成这项任务，他们宁愿去指责这些通过街头抗议和社交媒体表现出来的革命力量。这些都是年轻一代的声音，政治领导人需要关注，并应当设法让他们参与到国家的重建之中。

三、易卜拉欣·特拉奥雷上尉：托马斯·桑卡拉的化身？

易卜拉欣·特拉奥雷上尉上台后不到 2 个月，布基纳法索的民众和一些外国媒体就开始寻找他与托马斯·桑卡拉的相似之处。尽管易卜拉欣·特拉奥雷没有公开声称自己是这位神话般总统的化身，但是他的行动和演讲都强烈地支持这样一种观点，即他正在追随这位在 4 年内使布基纳法索实现粮食自给自足，并给布基纳法索人民带来极大尊严和自豪感的人的脚步。

将易卜拉欣·特拉奥雷和托马斯·桑卡拉相提并论的声音与日俱增，这些事实代表了公众的舆论，并赢得了一定的尊重：

——他像托马斯·桑卡拉一样，都是通过政变上台，在 34 岁跻身上尉。

——在托马斯·桑卡拉被暗杀的周年纪念日，象征性地参观他的纪念碑。

---

① President Soekarno, "Create the World Anew," September 30, 1960, https://bandungspirit.org/IMG/pdf/soekarno-to_build_the_world_anew-un-General-assembly-1960.pdf.

图3　身着军装的易卜拉欣·特拉奥雷总统在托马斯·桑卡拉纪念碑前举着"革命的火炬"
照片来源：https://faso7.com/2022/10/15/burkina-faso-memorial-thomas-sankara-le-flambeau-de-la-revolution-remis-au-capitaine-ibrahim-traore, accessed 19 November 2022

　　——直接着手解决实际问题，同时明确地指出政治领导人对国家当前所面临的危机的责任。

　　——决定保留自己的上尉工资，而不是领取总统的工资；这一决定将他置于与托马斯·桑卡拉相同的地位，桑卡拉在公众形象中是谦逊的，他明确地希望其生活条件不超过普通人的生活水平。应当补充的是，这一决定带来了影响：新任命的部长们也决定放弃他们11月的一半工资，用来帮助逃离不安全地区的人们。

　　至少从其短短2个月执政情况上可以判断，布基纳法索的新领导人已经踏上由托马斯·桑卡拉所开创的道路。这种决心和由鼓舞人心的桑卡拉所传递的革命薪火，可以从现任总理最近发表的《总方针宣言》看到。①简而言之，这篇演讲的题目是"敢于创造未来"，这句话引自托马

---

　　①　Prime Minister Apollinaire Kyelem, "Déclaration de Politique Générale," November 19, 2022, https://www.sig.gov.bf/actualites/details1?tx_news_pi1%5Baction%5D=detail&tx_news_pi1%5Bcontroller%5D=News&tx_news_pi1%5Bnews%5D=1365&cHash=bc846f2a531c6c3454764bc9acc69e1f.

斯·桑卡拉，在宣言中多次出现。总理的讲话在绝大多数的布基纳法索人中产生了共鸣，并加强了他们对布基纳法索正在回到由桑卡拉所设定的积极变革之路的看法，总理的讲话受到了热烈欢迎。

四、继续未完成的去殖民化事业

1. 理解国内外的民众抗议

要理解布基纳法索正在发生的事情，就必须关注当前问题所超越国家的层面：它不仅是蔓延到布基纳法索之外的恐怖主义，而且也是一股席卷于马里的变革之风。这两个国家的情况在许多方面都很相似，只是马里现在与前殖民国法国的关系几乎完全破裂。作为对法国停止对其发展援助的回击，马里刚刚暂停了由法国资助的非政府组织的活动。雪上加霜的是，马里刚刚宣布与俄罗斯签署了合作协议。

在布基纳法索，第二次政变之后有许多警告和惩戒措施：欧盟发表声明："警告布基纳法索不要与瓦格纳集团合作"；美国将该国从《非洲增长和机会法案》中排除，并指责布基纳法索没有采取必要举措来确保"选举式民主"。[①] 但这似乎并没有削弱人们对新总统的支持，也未削弱那些经常要求法国离开布基纳法索的示威者的决心。在法国大使馆前的示威游行，在首都焚烧法兰西的象征符号，在城市的街道上挥舞着俄罗斯的国旗并要求"法国撤离"，这意味着什么？我们必须超越反法的情绪，才能理解正在布基纳法索和更为广阔的萨赫勒地区孕育的更深层次和更持久性的动力。

在布基纳法索，特别是在瓦加杜古，经常发生的示威活动，在表达对新政府的支持和挥舞俄罗斯国旗的同时，也将矛头指向了法兰西的象

[①] 布基纳法索总理阿波里耐·基耶朗·德坦贝拉在回答美国智库国家民主研究所（NDI: https://www.ndi.org/staff）的中非和西非项目区域主管时主张对治理要有新的理解："这种输出与我们社会格格不入的文化、传统和习俗的时代已经结束。你们在我们国家所推行的西方的民主观念不符合我国人民的愿望，因此我们国家反复出现不稳定的局势。" https://www.gouvernement.gov.bf/informations/actualites/details?tx_news_pi1%5Baction%5D=detail&tx_news_pi1%5Bcontroller%5D=News&tx_news_pi1%5Bnews%5D=790&cHash=601d6ccfff08841a9eb5cc15255ab678, accessed 30 November 2022.

征符号，这引发了重大担忧，有时这种担忧不是没有道理的。然而，从西方主流媒体的角度来看，这些都是反法情绪。毫无疑问，法国是象征性的和直接性的被击目标，但是将这些年轻人的愤怒视为由莫斯科操纵的肤浅解释并不合理。主流媒体和法国政客只是通过反法情绪的棱镜来解读这些示威活动。但真正的原因是萨赫勒地区的民众，尤其是年轻人已经深刻地认识到，霸权主义和帝国主义结构的存在阻碍了这个国家的自治和繁荣。因此，深层的愤怒是诚挚地要求更好的生活条件，并摆脱对这个目标可能构成障碍的一切事物。因此，对内攻击法国象征符号的青年和公民社会组织毫不犹豫地抨击本国的领导人，认为这些领导人缺乏引领他们走向繁荣和正义的能力；对外，基于历史和现实的原因，都是法国饱受这些运动的批判，而现实原因则是其在萨赫勒地区打击恐怖主义的斗争中所扮演的争议角色；法国被认为并非为当地人民的福祉而服务，而是试图剥削他们。

包括布基纳法索在内的萨赫勒地区的民众运动，一直被指责为莫斯科的阴谋或明显的操纵。具有讽刺意味的是，当 2022 年 2 月卡车司机围堵在加拿大的首都抗议卫生措施时，西方的媒体或政客大多将其视为加拿大的国内问题，尽管他们明显得到了美国的支持。[1] 萨赫勒地区尤其是在布基纳法索所发生的这些事件，却并没有被解释为国内事件；它们很快被报道为受境外势力的影响，好像民众没有能动性、缺乏政治意识，不能批判性地理解他们所处的国内和国际环境。为什么所发生的这一切都像一场革命一样——参与者强烈地希望改变非洲的社会和政治结构——却被西方政客傲慢地看作是受境外势力影响的结果？与此同时，法国总统马克龙不假思索地将伊朗的抗议示威视为一场革命。[2]

2.西方霸权的终结被视为非洲国家的一个契机

早在 2022 年 1 月第一次政变后，新的领导层就明白有必要明确地表

---

① Laurence Niosi, "Camionneurs : un financement aux couleurs de l'extrême droite," Radio-Canada, 09 February 2022, https://ici.radio-canada.ca/nouvelle/1860971/camionneurs-financement-extreme-droite-americaine.

② *See* Yves Bourdillon and Virginie Robert, "Pour Macron, une révolution est en cours en Iran," Les Échos, 14 November 2022, https://www.lesechos.fr/monde/enjeux-internationaux/pour-macron-une-revolution-est-en-cours-en-iran-1878586.

达布基纳法索要在国际舞台上发展"多元化的伙伴关系"的意愿。新总理刚刚（2022 年 11 月）在其宣言中又着重地重申了这一意向：

> 到目前为止，我们对我们伙伴的关系是不是太过天真呢？毋庸置疑，我们必须进行自我反省。我们将尽可能地使我们的伙伴关系多元化，直到找到符合布基纳法索利益的正确方案。但是我们绝不允许被任何一个合作伙伴牵着鼻子走。[①]

政治领袖和民间社会组织都已经认识到，我们正在经历一个多极化的世界，从亚洲的崛起，中国在非洲的关键角色以及乌克兰战争等迹象上就可以看到。新总理所讲的不止是一个简单的意图声明。他只是在表明在布基纳法索和其他非洲国家，特别是法语国家日益彰显的一种心态，即不再满足与主要的"历史伙伴"法国维持一如既往的合作态势。迄今为止，这一立场转变广受好评，并在英联邦秘书长的专栏文章中得到了呼应，其在评价曾为法属殖民地的多哥和加蓬时表示：

> 他们加入的动机不仅是希望在法语国家的网络之外扩大其政治、贸易、社会和外交关系，更为重要的是，他们被我们英联邦宪章中的价值观和愿景所吸引。这个重要的、富有活力的和不断发展的网络具有无法抗拒的吸引力，它提供了与国际伙伴多元化的互动，并加强与英联邦国家的大家庭合作的机会。[②]

在不久的将来，密切关注非洲，尤其是法语国家的去殖民化运动的快速进展将是有意义的。这将具体地实现与法国这个控制它们的单一大国脱钩的愿望，同时也使它们的国际合作伙伴变得多元化。我们应当从

---

① Prime Minister Apollinaire Kyelem, "Déclaration de Politique Générale," 19 November 2022, https://www.sig.gov.bf/actualites/details1?tx_news_pi1%5Baction%5D=detail&tx_news_pi1%5Bcontroller%5D=News&tx_news_pi1%5Bnews%5D=1365&cHash=bc846f2a531c6c3454764bc9acc69e1f.

② "Op-Ed: Gabon and Togo join the Commonwealth family," 30 August 2022, https://thecommonwealth.org/news/op-ed-gabon-and-togo-join-commonwealth-family.

这个意义上理解他们与中国和俄罗斯当前和未来的合作关系。在外部看来的混乱不堪和暂时显现的反法情绪，实际上可以转化为一个契机，即这是一个关注其他国际合作伙伴的良机。这或许是一个向前殖民者挥手告别、欢迎多元平等的合作者共同协力解决布基纳法索和其他西非国家问题的契机。

结论：西瓜、怀孕和期盼

有一天，我在瓦加杜古向一位老妇人买西瓜时问道："西瓜瓤红不红，熟不熟？"她回答道："我的孩子，我怎么知道呢？你必须等到打开它时才能看到。这个西瓜就像怀孕一样：你必须等看到孩子，再做评判！"这则逸事的含义是，有些事情只有等它们实际显现的时候才能做出判断。

在布基纳法索，人们正在经历一个充满希望和期盼的时刻。这些期盼是深切的，因为这个"正人君子之国"多年来一直遭受着各种灾难。在2个月不到的时间里，第二次政变后成立的新政府，似乎给那些期待着社会重建、守护国土安全和创造实现更加繁荣和公正的有利条件的人们带来了希望。正在进行的政治过渡将持续20个月左右：这对那些不能再忍受岌岌可危生活境况的人来说太过漫长了，但对于满足所有的期盼又太短了。为了实现这一目标，在当前进行全国动员是一项关键举措，[①]但这不应该只此一项；另一项关键举措应该是争取新伙伴的实际支持，它们与布基纳法索的团结将使该国从替代合作的梦想转变为真正的联盟。虽然布基纳法索国内最近的事态动荡不安，但所有的利益攸关者应该将其视为历史的机遇，并在相互尊重、团结与共和互利互惠的基础上，书写布基纳法索乃至整个非洲大陆与中国和许多其他亚洲伙伴之间关系新的篇章。

---

① 易卜拉欣·特拉奥雷总统下令招募五万人来充实正规军的力量。超过9万人响应他的号召进行了登记，民间也发起为支援反恐斗争提供捐赠的行动。

附：本篇英文

To Make a *Kairos* out of Chaos: Burkina Faso tackling with Insecurity and Post-Covid Developmental Urgency

Isaac Bazié[*]

Abstract: Burkina Faso has attracted plenty of international attention because of the two coups took place in eight months amid the pandemic of Covid-19. The defenders of "elective democracy" in term of the Western model denounced this situation as political instability, even with very harsh condemnations and sanctions. While the rest of the world is seemingly recovering from Covid-19 at the moment, the frequency of changing leaders of the country reflects an urgent search for solutions to problems that tormented the Burkinabe before and during the pandemic: the problem of insecurity caused by terrorist attacks, lack of good governance capable of improving the living conditions of the population, and the problem of justice concerning crimes, the most famous of which was the assassination of the father of the Burkinabe revolution in 1987. The paper first exposes the reasons for the apparent political chaos in Burkina Faso; it finally analyses the efforts of average people which greatly help to shape the way forward of the country, i.e. to strengthen collaborations with other partners but its former colonizer.

Keywords: Post-Covid; Burkina Faso; Political instability; Governance; Development; Decolonization

---

* Isaac Bazié, Professor of African Literary and Cultural Studies, Department of Literary Studies, Université du Québec à Montréal.

1. Introduction

Burkina Faso, Land of the Upright People, retains attention since the beginning of 2022 because of two major and very similar events that occurred on the political scene: a coup d'état that overthrew President Roch Marc Christian Kaboré and allowed Lieutenant Colonel Paul-Henri Sandaogo Damiba to take power on 24 January 2022; eight months later, on 2 October 2022, a second coup d'état ended the short-lived reign of President Damiba. The governance of the country was in the hands of a thirty-four-year-old captain, Ibrahim Traoré. All stakeholders in the country are looking to him to solve the serious problems of insecurity linked to terrorist acts that have deprived Burkina Faso of forty percent of its territory; the care of three million people, two-thirds of whom have fled insecure areas and are now migrants in their own country; the problems of the cost of living linked to inflation, the consequences of which are alarming for populations already living in precarious conditions; and, more generally, the problems linked to good governance.

As the world's major economies meet in Bali (Indonesia) to "recover together" in a post-pandemic world, what issues are of concern to Burkinabè? What were the challenges they faced during the generalised health crisis between 2020 and 2022, and how important were these challenges compared to others that Burkina Faso faced long before and after the pandemic?

To answer these questions, this article is divided into five parts: We will look at the extent to which the Covid-19 pandemic was a major crisis, but with a minor impact in Burkina Faso. To understand the current situation in Burkina Faso, it will be necessary to go back to the year 2014, which should be considered a turning point in political terms; this turning point initiated a new era marked by the problems listed above. It is the search for a leadership capable of providing adequate and urgent solutions to these problems that justifies the political instability and social unrest observable in the country. It is also this search for visionary and revolutionary leadership that has led the population to expect a kind of reincarnation of Thomas Sankara in the person of the new president, Captain Ibrahim Traoré. The current impatience of the people with their presidents and other leaders at all levels of Burkina's society reflects their precarious living conditions. The last part of this article will situate the Burkinabe question in a larger context, which is that of decolonisation: a superficial reading of what is happening in the demonstrations presents them as an anti-French ressentiment. But these demonstrations are the signal of something more important than a simple anti-French feeling. It is a trend that is not limited to Burkina Faso but has waves in Mali and Niger as well. The current apparent chaos in Burkina Faso, seen from inside, is nothing more than the march of a country searching its way out of insecurity and precariousness, to give a future to a population of some twenty million people, 77.9% of whom were under thirty-five years old at the time of the 2019 census.[1] In the current multipolar world order carried by the rise of China and Asia in general, creates an anti-hegemonic context that is favourable to the repositioning of countries like Burkina Faso on the world stage. Seen in this light, the apparent chaos becomes a *kairos*, an opportunity to be exploited by formerly colonized countries seeking to develop in new ways.

2. Covid-19: a global crisis with small local impacts

In January 2020, I was on my way to the airport in Ouagadougou to catch a flight to Montreal when I heard someone say: "Westerners talk about the Coronavirus, but we here have worse problems than the virus!" What seemed to be an anecdotal joke became, in the following two years, the point of view of millions of Burkinabè on the pandemic that had claimed so many victims at a global level.

Burkina Faso reported the first Covid-19-related death in West Africa on 9 March 2020.[2] The measures that followed the first reports of infection and

---

[1] Almost the half of the whole population (45.3%) is under fifteen years old! *See*: National Institute of Statistics and Demography. Accessed 22 November 2022. http://www.insd.bf/contenu/documents_rgph5/Depliant%20resultats%20definitifs%20RGPH%202019.pdf.

[2] Cf., "Burkina Faso: premiers cas de coronavirus à Ouagadougou et crise humanitaire sans précédent dans le nord". Médecins sans frontières, 24 mars 2020, https://www.msf.fr/actualites/burkina-faso-premiers-cas-de-coronavirus-a-ouagadougou-et-crise-humanitaire-sans-precedent-dans-le-nord.

death were copied from the model of developed countries: massive reduction of population mobility, mandatory wearing of masks in public places, use of antimicrobial gel, suspension of gatherings, closure of educational institutions, places of worship as well as markets. All these emergency measures were accompanied by a daily report that informed the Burkinabe population of the number of new infections, deaths and recoveries. Very quickly, authorities realised that the drastic measures applied elsewhere, particularly the confinement of the population, would not work in Burkina Faso. Indeed, millions of people live from day to day and feed their families through daily activities that require mobility and open markets. This is one of the reasons why this measure has been retained only for a very short period. The other reason that justifies that the Burkinabè populations returned rather quickly to a life similar (from a sanitary point of view) to that of before March 2020 is the following: the results of the contagions, and especially that of the deaths directly related to the Coronavirus were not as alarming as the national and international public opinion feared at the beginning of the pandemic. A little more than a year after the appearance of the virus in the country (17 June 2021), the balance sheet - below - gave reason to those who think that the disease is not the first problem of the Burkinabè:

Statistics on Coronavirus (COVID-19) in Burkina Faso[①]

Overview for 17 June 2021	
Total number of tests	507
Confirmed Covid-cases	2
Deaths	0
Total number of tests since 9 March 2020	507
Total number of tests	507

---

① "Communiqué Infos Covid-19". Service d'information du gouvernement du Burkina Faso, 19 juin 2021, https://www.sig.gov.bf/actualites/details?tx_news_pi1%5Baction%5D=detail&tx_news_pi1%5Bcontroller%5D= News&tx_news_pi1%5Bnews%5D=1265&cHash=e6452bbc8f8c6133d76062024b19639b.

General Overview from 09 March 2020 (first Covid-19 confirmed case) to 17 June 2021	
Number confirmed Covid-cases	13464
Number of recoveries	13287
Number active cases	10
Number of deaths	167

These numbers do not reflect the real state of the virus' spread, given the lack of an infrastructure capable of giving a complete picture of the situation. That said, they are still good indicators of the much less alarming danger of the virus in the country, documented by a low rate of spread and a very high number of recoveries. Furthermore, a careful reading of this June 2021 report in Burkina Faso shows that most tests were done by people who needed a Covid test to travel abroad. This is important: the fact that most of the tests are related to travel, mainly by air, and their high cost to the average Burkinabè, have contributed to the idea that Covid-19 is a disease of rich people, and Westerners.

From these observations, we understand why the Covid-19 pandemic has been a major problem at the global level, but with a minor impact in Burkina Faso. Even before the pandemic began, and in the post-Covid period, a more serious issue than the Coronavirus preoccupied Burkinabè: that of insecurity due to terrorist attacks. This explains why the Director of Operations of Médecins Sans Frontières, Isabelle Defourny, while describing the health situation in March 2020, begins with Covid-19 and ends with security issues in the North, and its consequences on the population. These security issues are more prominent and more damaging to the lives of Burkinabè than the Coronavirus. At a time when the world is trying to rebuild itself based on a relatively successful control of the virus, Burkina Faso continues to face this security priority that was present long before, during and after the Coronavirus. But to understand what is happening in the Country of Upright People, we must go back to October 2014: a real turning point whose consequences are very significant in the current political life of Burkina Faso.

3. Before and beyond Covid-19: 2014 as a political turning point

The issues of development, justice, and since 2015, insecurity, in addition to the challenges of good governance, are the context in which the Covid-19 pandemic began in March 2020. These problems remain present and more than ever worrying for Burkinabè, even in the current post-Covid period. To understand this, a brief look back at the days of October 2014 is necessary.

3.1 October Insurrection: The End of 27 years of post-revolution era

30 and 31 October are now commemorative dates for the martyrs of a popular uprising that took place in 2014. This massive popular uprising ended the twenty-seven-year reign of President Blaise Compaoré. As a reminder, it was the same one who, after having participated in the revolution started in 1983 by Thomas Sankara, put a brutal end to it by the assassination of President Sankara on 15 October 1987.

The events of October 2014 are not to be taken lightly, either politically or in terms of the identity of the Burkinabe people. Politically, things seem simple enough to understand: the insurgency removed from power a man who took it claiming to "rectify" the Revolution initiated by Thomas Sankara. Twenty-seven years later, the promised rectification turned out to be a control of the country through assassinations in the first years; and corruption, get-rich-quick schemes in the following years. All this happened with the assent of Western countries satisfied with the organisation of elections that the same man won since 1991, under the label of "elective democracy". It was, moreover, Blaise Compaoré's attempt to amend the country's constitution to give himself the right to run for president again that outraged the population and led to the uprising of 30-31 October 2014.

From the strict point of view of the political agenda, the balance sheet of this insurrection is therefore quite simple: President Compaoré, having exasperated the population after twenty-seven years, was driven from power by the revolting people. This was followed by a short transition period of about a year, marked by a failed coup attempt on 15 September 2015. The political transition was generally successful, as it allowed elections to be held and power to be returned to a democratically elected president in early 2016: President Roch Marc Christian Kaboré. His arrival in power was affected by the terrorist attack in the heart of the capital Ouagadougou (15 January 2016). This problem of insecurity, while growing, will lead to the departure by coup d'état of Roch Marc Christian Kaboré: he has not succeeded after a first term, and an unfinished second, to secure the country.

On the other hand, the outcome of the insurgency, from the point of view of political maturity, is not as simple as that of the political agenda. Indeed, one of the current challenges for any political leader in Burkina Faso is that of governing people who have to their credit a genuine and successful popular uprising, and a political consciousness inherited from the short but very significant revolution of Thomas Sankara (1983-1987).

The two recent coups d'état were welcomed by the population in Burkina Faso, even though they were denounced by international community. When the first one took place on 24 January 2022, the population did not mourn the departure of Roch Marc Christian Kaboré, but rather hoped that the new president would succeed in solving the growing problem of insecurity that President Kaboré could not solve. The honeymoon was short-lived, however. In October 2022, President Paul-Henri Damiba was also ousted from power and replaced by Captain Ibrahim Traoré, for the same reasons as before: the fulfilment of a political agenda that apparently did not pursue the resolution of the main problem of insecurity. The role of civil society organisations cannot be overemphasised, but even more importantly, the role of populations who are on the lookout and who now demand urgent answers to their problems, which are only getting worse with time. The support of the population played a key role in the first hours of the recent coup. It was also popular pressure that prevented the minister of commerce and the minister of urbanism suspected of lacking integrity from taking office in the new government formed after the October 2022 coup. The opposition went via social media and motivated the Prime minister to investigate. Consequently, the minister of commerce decided to step down, while the minister of urbanism was obliged to give up his position. While applauding the first acts and words of the new president, it is also this popular watch that constantly reminds him that it is watching everything and expects concrete, diligent and effective actions for the benefit of the people.

3.2 A Revolutionary People on the Quest for a Revolutionary Leader

In the years following the insurrection, there has been a significant failure in Burkina Faso to properly analyse what is now called "the street": the popular voices that mobilise a wide range of actors, which succeed in ousting a president and preventing suspected minister to be confirmed in their positions. There have been several street demonstrations which tragic consequences in the country: Recently, they targeted the French Embassy and the French Institute in Ouagadougou with severe damages. Of course, such punctual actions of destruction and obstruction of state institutions should be decried. However, this atmosphere of popular pressure has to do with the great protest that liberated the country from Blaise Compaoré's rule. President Sukarno said in his famous speech to the Assembly of the United Nations about that kind of agitation and popular march: "We know, too, from our own experience, that development itself creates turbulence. A turbulent nation needs leadership and guidance, and it will eventually produce its own leadership and guidance".[①] In addition to the challenges of insecurity and development in Burkina Faso, governance in turbulence is thus another challenge: understanding that post-insurgency Burkina Faso, heir to the ideals and model of Thomas Sankara, is a place of turbulence and of proven forces; these forces require political leaders with the capacity to mobilize people around ideals and values such as integrity and commitment to the well-being of the nation. Some leaders have failed in this task and have preferred to blame these insurrectional forces manifested through street protests and social media. These are the voices of a generation of young people that requests attention from political leaders, who should manage to get them involved in the country's reconstruction.

---

① President Soekarno, "Create the World Anew", 30 September 1960, https://bandungspirit.org/IMG/pdf/soekarno-to_build_the_world_anew-un-general-assembly-1960.pdf.

4. Captain Ibrahim Traoré: Reincarnation of Thomas Sankara?

Less than two months after Captain Ibrahim Traoré came to power, people in Burkina Faso and some foreign media looked for similarities between him and Thomas Sankara. Even if he does not publicly claim to be the reincarnation of the mythical president, Ibrahim Traoré's actions and speeches strongly support the idea that he is following in the footsteps of the man who, in four years, succeeded in making Burkina Faso self-sufficient in food, while instilling great dignity and pride in the Burkinabè people.

The points of comparison between Ibrahim Traoré and Thomas Sankara are cumulating by the day,[①] with facts that mark public opinion and command a certain respect:

-Coming to power by a putsch, like Thomas Sankara, at the age of thirty-four, with the rank of captain.

-Symbolic visit to the Thomas Sankara Memorial on the anniversary of his assassination.

-Directly addressing the real issues while clearly pointing out the responsibility of political leaders for the current crisis in the land.

-The decision to keep his salary as a captain instead of receiving a presidential one; this decision places him in the same position as Thomas Sankara, whose image is associated with modesty and a clear desire not to live in conditions superior to those of ordinary people. It should be added that this decision had consequences: the newly appointed ministers have also decided to forgo half their November salaries and use them to help people who have fled insecure areas.

There are signs, at least as far as can be judged in just two months of rule, that Burkina Faso's new leaders have embarked on a path initiated by Thomas Sankara. The determination and the torch relayed from the inspiring Sankara could be seen from the incumbent Prime Minister's recent Declaration of General

---

① *See* Damien Glez, "Ibrahim Traoré: sobriété affichée et mythe en construction". *Jeune Afrique*, 18 novembre 2022, https://www.jeuneafrique.com/1394073/politique/ibrahim-traore-sobriete-affichee-et-mythe-en-construction/.

Policy.[①] To put it briefly, this speech could be entitled "Dare to invent the future", a sentence quoted from Thomas Sankara, which appears several times in the Declaration. Appealing to the vast majority of Burkinabè and reinforced the perception that Burkina Faso is returning to the path of positive change, the milestones of which were set by Sankara, the speech of the Prime minister was very well received.

5. Continuing the unfinished Decolonisation Project

5.1 Understanding the Popular Protests within and outside

To understand what is happening in Burkina Faso, one must look at the supranational aspect of the issues at hand: it is not only terrorism that goes beyond the borders of Burkina Faso, but also a wind of change that also blows furiously in Mali. The situations between the two countries are in many ways similar, only Mali is now in a quasi-total rupture of its relations with the former colonizing power, France. In response to France's cessation of development aid, Mali has just suspended the activities of non-governmental organizations working with French funding. To add insult to injury, it has just made public the signing of a cooperation agreement with Russia.

In Burkina Faso, there are many warnings and punitive measures in the wake of the second coup: the European Union has issued a statement "warning Burkina Faso against cooperating with the Wagner Group"; the United States has excluded the country from the African Growth and Opportunity Act, blaming Burkina Faso for not taking the necessary steps to ensure an "elective democracy".[②] But this does not seem to dampen the support for the new

---

① Prime Minister Apollinaire Kyelem, "Déclaration de Politique Générale", 19 novembre 2022, https://www.sig.gov.bf/actualites/details-1?tx_news_pi1%5Baction%5D=detail&tx_news_pi1%5Bcontroller%5D=News&tx_news_pi1%5Bnews%5D=1365&cHash=bc846f2a531c6c3454764bc9acc69e1f.

② Prime Minister of Burkina Faso, Apollinaire Joachim Kyelem de Tambela advocated for a new understanding of governance in his response to the Regional Director for Central and West Africa Programs of the American Think Tank NDI (National Democratic Institute: https://www.ndi.org/staff): "We are no longer in phase with this kind of transfer of culture, tradition and practices alien to our society. This Western vision of democracy that you are implementing in our country is not in line with the aspirations of our people, hence the recurrent instability of our states." https://www.gouvernement.gov.bf/informations/actualites/details?tx_news_pi1%5Baction%5D=detail&tx_news_pi1%5Bcontroller%5D=News&tx_news_pi1%5Bnews%5D=790&cHash=601d6ccfff08841a9eb5cc15255ab678 (accessed 30 November 2022).

president, nor the determination of the demonstrators who regularly demand France's departure from Burkina. What is the meaning of the demonstrations in the country in front of the French embassy, the burning of French symbols in the capital, the waving of the Russian flag in the streets of the city while demanding "the departure of France"? One must go beyond anti-French sentiment to understand that a deeper and more lasting dynamic is underway in Burkina Faso and in the Sahel more generally.

The regular demonstrations in Burkina Faso, and particularly in Ouagadougou, which have targeted French symbols while showing support for the new authorities and waving the Russian flag, have fuelled - and sometimes rightly so - major concerns. However, from the point of view of Western mainstream media, this is all anti-French sentiment. For sure, France that is targeted, symbolically and directly. But the superficial explanation of this popular anger of the young people are manipulated by Moscow is not reasonable. Mainstream media and French politicians have interpreted these demonstrations only through the prism of anti-French sentiment; But the real reasons are the deep awareness of the population in the Sahel and especially at the level of young people of the existence of hegemonic, imperialistic structures that prevents the country from enjoying its autonomy and flourishing. So, the deep anger is about a sincere request for better living conditions and getting rid of everything suspected to be a blockade for the goal. Thus, at the national level, the youth and the organisations of civil society that attack the French symbols do not hesitate to criticise local leaders whom they judge lack of capacity to lead them to prosperity and justice; regarding external hinderances, France has been very much affected by these movement for both historical and present reasons: its controversial role in the fight against terrorism in the Sahel region. France is seen as not serving the interests of local people but rather coming to seeking to exploit them.

The movements in the Sahel region, including Burkina Faso, has constantly been denounced as conspiracy or overt manipulation by Moscow. Ironically, when truckers blocked the Canadian capital in February 2022 protesting health measures, the Western media or politicians treated it mostly as a Canadian domestic problem, even though evident support from the US was identified.[1] The events in the Sahel and particularly in Burkina Faso do not benefit of such intern explanation; they are quickly reported to be of foreign influence, as if the populations have no agency, no political sense and no critical understanding of the national and international context that they live in. Why everything happened like a revolution – with a deep desire from the participants to change social and political structures in Africa – is condescendingly perceived by the Western politicians as the result of foreign influences? At the same time, President Emmanuel Macron did not hesitate to comment on the protests in Iran as a revolution.[2]

5.2 The End of Western Hegemony seen as a Kairos for African Countries

Already in the aftermath of the first coup d'état in January 2022, the new leadership understood that it was necessary to clearly state the willing to "diversify the partnerships" of Burkina Faso on the international scene. The new Prime Minister has just vigorously reaffirmed this intention in his Declaration:

Have we not been too naive in our relations with our partners up to now? No doubt. An introspection is necessary. We will try, as much as possible, to diversify our partnership relations until we find the right formula for the interests of Burkina Faso. But there will be no question of allowing ourselves to be dominated by any one partner.[3]

Political leaders and civil society organizations have understood that we are experiencing a multipolar world whose signs are visible in the rise of

---

① Laurence Niosi, "Camionneurs: un financement aux couleurs de l'extrême droite". *Radio-Canada,* 09 February 2022, https://ici.radio-canada.ca/nouvelle/1860971/camionneurs-financement-extreme-droite-americaine.

② *See* Yves Bourdillon and Virginie Robert, "Pour Macron, une révolution est en cours en Iran". *Les Échos,* 14 novembre 2022, https://www.lesechos.fr/monde/enjeux-internationaux/pour-macron-une-revolution-est-en-cours-en-iran-1878586.

③ Prime Minister Apollinaire Kyelem, "Déclaration de Politique Générale", 19 novembre 2022, https://www.sig.gov.bf/actualites/details-1?tx_news_pi1%5Baction%5D=detail&tx_news_pi1%5Bcontroller%5D=News&tx_news_pi1%5Bnews%5D=1365&cHash=bc846f2a531c6c3454764bc9acc69e1f.

Asia, the determining role of China in Africa, and the war in Ukraine, among others. What the new Prime Minister said is more than a simple declaration of intent. He simply has shown increasingly visible mindset in Burkina and other African countries, particularly francophone ones, to no longer be satisfied with continuing the same dynamics of collaboration with the main "historical partner", namely France. This has so far been well received and echoed from what the Op-Ed of the Secretary General of the Commonwealth said while welcoming Togo and Gabon, both historically francophone:

> They were motivated to join not only by the desire to expand their political, trade, social and diplomatic relations beyond the Francophonie network, but, most importantly, were attracted to the Commonwealth's values and aspirations as enshrined in our Charter. The attraction of this important, dynamic, and evolving network, which provides the opportunity to diversify and engage with international partners and strengthen cooperation with the Commonwealth family of nations was irresistible.[1]

It will be interesting to keep a close eye on the rapid progress of the decolonising movement in the African and specifically Francophone states in the immediate future. It would be the concrete realization of the desire for delinking from France as a single power to control them and simultaneously diversification of their international partners. Ongoing and future cooperation with China or Russia should be understood in that sense. What appears from outside to be a chaos and an ephemeral manifestation of anti-French sentiments could be translated into a de facto *kairos*, (in which language) a favourable moment to look at elsewhere. That might be a moment to be enjoyed by waving hands to the former coloniser and heralding in diversified equal collaborators to jointly help with problems solving in Burkina Faso and other West African countries.

---

[1] "Op-Ed: Gabon and Togo join the Commonwealth family", 30 August 2022, https://thecommonwealth.org/news/op-ed-gabon-and-togo-join-commonwealth-family.

Conclusion: On watermelon, pregnancy, and positive expectations

One day, while buying a watermelon from an old woman in Ouagadougou, I asked her: "Is the watermelon red and ripe inside?" She answered: "My son, how can I tell? You must wait until you open it, and you will see. This watermelon is like a pregnancy: you must wait to see the child, and then judge!" The meaning of this anecdote is that there are things that can only be judged with time when they are concretely manifested.

In Burkina Faso, people are experiencing a moment with great hopes and expectations. These expectations are huge because the Land of Upright People has been suffering from all kinds of plagues for years. In less than two months, the new established authority out of the second coup seems to have given reason to the people who hope high for rebuilding a society by securing national territory and providing them with favourable conditions for more justice and prosperity.

The political transition that is underway would last about twenty months: a short time to meet all expectations, but too long for those who can no longer live in precariousness. To achieve this, the current national mobilisation serves as one main key,[①] but there should not be the only one; another key should be the concrete support of new partners whose solidarity with Burkina Faso will allow the country to move from dreams of alternative collaborations to real alliances. The latest development within the country, turbulent though, should be seen by all stakeholders as historical opportunities to write a new story of relations between Burkina Faso, indeed the whole Africa continent in general, and China and lots of other Asian partners, based on shared values of mutual respect, solidarity, and mutual benefit.

---

① President Ibrahim Traoré ordered the recruitment of 50,000 people to support the regular army. In response to his appeal, more than 90,000 people registered. Private initiatives also make financial contributions to support the fight against terrorism.

谁来保护女性?

——从埃及维护女性权益的《刑法》修正案第306条谈起

肖　坤[*]

摘　要: 2021年8月，埃及《刑法》修正案获得总统的批准而正式施行，该修正案中第306条将"性骚扰"由轻罪改为重罪，加重了其量刑惩罚。这项修正案也成为埃及继2014年正式将"性骚扰"行为入罪以来，在女性保护方面取得的最为显著的进步。这一法案是塞西政府着手提升埃及女性权益的重要举措之一，也被视作埃及人权状况的重大改善。埃及政府直面社会性骚扰问题并以强有力的手段加大惩处力度，极大地提高了埃及女性的社会安全保障，可以看作埃及女性赋能运动中的重大成果。在针对性骚扰入罪的议题上，主要有三个影响性因素:首先，政府作为决策机构应起到决定作用，由政府充当制度供给者的角色可以最大程度上降低社会交易成本，保障立法的有效施行;其次，在政府作为制度供给者缺位或立法空白的情况下，性骚扰甚至性侵害犯罪问题久置不决，民间社会组织活动在这个时期内的兴起和推广，能够在一定程度上起到补位的作用，但远不能满足社会的需要，民间自发的行动需在政府主导下相互配合才能更好地发挥效用;最后，埃及政府近年所倡导的女性赋能运动使女性的声音能够被关注，也使更多的女性参与到国家政治生活，从而要求政府回应女性安全诉求，有利于更多的性别敏感政策和立法的出台以及女性友好的社会环境的塑造，也在更大范围内维护了女性权益。因此，在埃及政府与民间组织或民间行动之间形成有效互动，加上埃及女性赋能运动的不断普及发展，共同促成了由政府主导的公共政

---

　* 肖坤，北京大学外国语学院阿拉伯语系讲师。

策和法规的施行，对性骚扰犯罪起到了相当的遏制和威慑作用。

关键词：性骚扰　埃及女性赋能　埃及《刑法》修正案

引　言

2021年8月，埃及《刑法》修正案最终获得总统的批准而准予施行。根据《刑法》第306条第1款规定："任何人在公共场所或私人场所通过手势、言语、行为或任何方式，包括有线、无线或电子通信手段，使他人遭受含有性意图或猥亵的行为、倾向或暗示，都将被判处不少于6个月的监禁或处以3000—5000埃镑的罚款，或是监禁并处罚款。若是被发现再次跟踪尾随他人则会被判处不少于1年的监禁，或处以5000—10000埃镑的罚款，或监禁并处罚款；重犯和累犯在监禁量刑和罚金数额上都会加倍。"《刑法》第306条第2款对性骚扰犯罪作了进一步的明确："若实施本法第306条第1款所述罪行的意图是为了从被骚扰者处获得具性本质（sexual nature）的利益，也将被视为性骚扰，行为人将被处以不少于1年的监禁或10000—20000埃镑的罚金，或者监禁并处罚金。如果行为人是本法第267条第2款所述人员之一，或者对被害人拥有职业的、家庭的或者教育的权威，通过向被害人施压而实施犯罪，或者有2名或2名以上的行为人实施犯罪，或者至少有1名犯罪行为人携带武器，则将面临2—5年监禁并处以20000—50000埃镑的罚金。"①

该修正案被认为是针对"性骚扰犯罪"的史上最严厉法律，旨在以法治强力根治长期困扰埃及女性的性骚扰问题，但它的出台并非一蹴而就，在经历了各方的尝试、努力甚至挫败之后，这部修正案才能够最终呈现于世人眼前。

一、埃及社会性骚扰问题

早在2009年，埃及全国妇女委员会所做的调查显示：大多数妇女都

---

① 资料来源：*Egyptian Penal Code*, Article 306(a), 306(b), https://harassmap.org/laws/law-text。

曾在公共场所或者交通工具上受到过持续性骚扰，74%的已婚女性和92%单身女性都表示曾在街头遭受过言语性骚扰。17%的已婚女性和22%的未婚女性表示身体曾被男性不当触摸，13%的已婚女性和12%的未婚女性表示，她们认识曾遭遇侵犯或者性暴力的女性。尽管埃及很早就开始想办法应对、解决此类问题，诸如在火车或地铁上设立女性专属车厢，也有专门的车辆工作人员提供帮助，但性骚扰问题还是未能得到根本性解决。

2011年之后，埃及性骚扰和针对女性的性暴力犯罪问题呈现激增。根据2013年联合国妇女署一项题为《减少埃及性骚扰的途径和方法研究》的报告指出，在3000名10—35岁的受调人群中，约有99.3%的埃及女性曾遭受过不同程度的性骚扰，但苦于没有连贯性的有效法规保护，而往往无法申诉。当被问及哪些年龄段更容易受到骚扰时，57.9%的人回答是"所有年龄段都会受到骚扰"；对于何种着装会让女孩更容易受到骚扰，72.4%的人回答是"所有女孩，无论穿着如何，都会受到骚扰"；对于哪个婚姻状况导致女性受到骚扰的问题，81.2%的人回答是"她们都有可能受到骚扰"。当被问及哪个社会阶层更容易受到骚扰时，87.7%的女性受访者回答"所有社会阶层都容易受到骚扰"；而在被问及"性骚扰事件一般会发生在何时"，68.9%的受访女性回答是"随时"。对受害者所受侵害的频率的问题上，竟有49.2%的受害者选择了"每天"。以上结果显示，性骚扰已经成为埃及所有女性共同面临的严重社会问题。受访女性遭受不同性骚扰形式的百分比分布如图1。[①]

2017年，汤姆森路透基金会的调查显示，开罗被认为是世界上对女性最危险的特大城市；2019年，路透社开展了一项对女性安全环境评价的调查，结果在全球19个人口超百万的城市中埃及仅排在第16位，紧随其后的是新德里、卡拉奇和金沙萨。埃及女性往往在公众场合或私人场合会遭受诸如故意触摸、言语挑衅、恶意侵犯等各种形式的性骚扰，并且受害人不仅限于埃及女性，诸多旅埃的女性也不堪

---

① United Nations Entity for Gender Equality and the Empowerment of Women, UN Women, *Study on the Ways and Methods to Eliminate Sexual Harassment in Egypt*, https://www.peacewomen.org/node/90812.

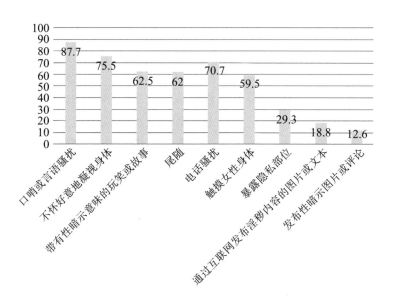

图1　埃及女性遭受不同程度性骚扰的形式与百分比

资料来源：联合国妇女署，https://www.peacewomen.org/node/90812

其扰。

　　性骚扰已经越来越成为公众领域中严重干扰社会治安环境的行为，单靠非政府的、非正式的社会制度如思想道德、习俗观念或是民间社会组织的救助行动无法完全保障女性的安全，此时必须由政府出面，提供相关的具有强制性的制度供给来加以保证，而该制度的有效执行会直接影响到女性的生存状况，是其维持正常社会生活甚至生命的保障性因素。这也使得埃及女性乃至社会要求埃及政府作为制度供给主体，加强针对"性骚扰"的立法和惩戒。

二、作为制度供给者的埃及政府

　　立法通常被看作是一种"公共品"，由国家或政府来扮演"供给者"的角色能够在最大程度上保障其实施的有效性并降低成本。埃及在2011年之后经历了社会动荡，接踵而至的是经济发展停滞，民生困顿，经济条件恶化，进而催生了各种社会问题，也是埃及性骚扰事件呈爆发式增长的主要原因。人们需要国家立法和强力执法保障女性权利和安全不受侵犯，但由于执政的穆尔西政府在制度供给者角色上的缺位，导致埃及针对"性骚扰"犯罪的立法实施迟迟得不到贯彻落实，性骚扰事件持续频发并升级，埃及女性的生活质量和权益都受到了严重的影响。

　　回顾埃及社会近几十年的发展情况我们不难发现，2011 年中东变局之后，埃及经济严重停滞，2010 年，也就是阿拉伯之春爆发的前一年，埃及的国内生产总值（GDP）增长为 5.1%，2011 年迅速下滑至 1.8%，2012、2013 年持续低位运行，直到 2014 年才勉强回到 2.9%（见图 2）。[①]低迷的经济发展导致了各种社会问题，首当其冲的是居高不下的失业率，自 2010 年起，埃及失业率猛增至 11.9%，2012 年继续上行至 12.6%，接下来 2013、2014、2015 的三年中持续 13.1% 的高失业率（见图 3），[②]而失业问题冲击最大的群体就是该国占到一多半的青年人口，这给社会带来了安全隐患，加之立法迟迟不能出台，执法机构的消极应对，对性骚扰犯罪无法形成有效的约束和惩戒，该问题屡禁不绝也就不足为奇了。

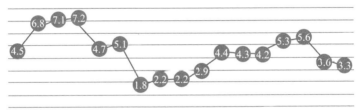

2005 2006 2007 2008 2009 2010 2011 2012 2013 2014 2015 2016 2017 2018 2019 2020 2021

—●— GDP 年增长（%）

图 2　埃及 GDP 年增长（%）（2005—2021 年）

资料来源：世界银行，https://data.worldbank.org/indicator/NY.GDP.MKTP.KD.ZG?end=2021&locations=EG&start=2005

---

　　① *GDP growth (annual %) - Egypt, Arab Rep.*, World Bank national accounts data, and OECD National Accounts data files, https://data.worldbank.org/indicator/NY.GDP.MKTP.KD.ZG?end=2021&locations=EG&start=2005.

　　② *Unemployment, total (% of total labor force) (modeled ILO estimate) - Egypt, Arab Rep.*, International Labour Organization, ILOSTAT database. Data as of June 2022, https://data.worldbank.org/indicator/SL.UEM.TOTL.ZS?end=2021&locations=EG&start=2005&view=chart.

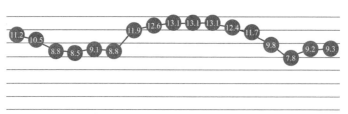

2005 2006 2007 2008 2009 2010 2011 2012 2013 2014 2015 2016 2017 2018 2019 2020 2021

→ 埃及当年失业率（%）

图3　埃及 2005—2021 年失业率（总劳动力人口占比 %）

资料来源：世界银行，https://data.worldbank.org/indicator/SL.UEM.TOTL.ZS?end=2021&locations=EG&start=2005&view=chart

2011 年之后，有许多埃及女性走上街头参与大规模游行示威活动，但是这也使她们成为性暴力犯罪的目标，在 2011 年，埃及街头爆发反对穆巴拉克的大规模政治集会的数周后，便有媒体开始爆出在活动中出现的针对女性的性侵犯和性骚扰行为，之后的街头性骚扰和性暴力事件愈演愈烈，甚至导致了某些受害人的死亡。随即有媒体描述了其中出现"非个体的、有组织有目的的对妇女的侵犯"，于是关于性骚扰是"国家共谋的对女性的暴力"的言论开始见之于各种关于此期间活动的报道中，发生在埃及的"大规模性侵事件"（mass sexual assault）一时成为媒体焦点，更有埃及安全部队被指控参与针对女性示威者的性暴力，这些行为被认为是有组织有策划地实施，目的是阻止妇女参与解放广场的抗议行动，并迫使女性受害人相信自己不应参与到游行示威中来。性暴力逐渐被看作是凌辱女性的性权利，成为让女性害怕政治表达的方式，从而迫使她们放弃发声。2011 年，有媒体爆出 17 名女性被埃及军事部门扣押并被迫接受"贞洁测试"（virginity testing），军方解释其原因是：要证明这些女性的清白以洗刷所谓的"军事人员对她们进行性侵"的虚假指控。自此，埃及社会中的性骚扰问题愈发严重，恶劣事件频出，引发国内民众的强烈不满，导致了国内及国际上对埃及政府消极应对的批评。人们不满于政府的处置态度，对国家立法解决性骚扰和性暴力的呼声日益高涨。尽管埃及政府曾多次做出承诺会解决这样的行为，保障妇女生存的安全环境，但性骚扰行为仍旧屡禁不止。"反性骚扰行动"组织(OpAntiSH)就曾批评穆尔西政府对性骚扰事件的处置力度不够。在 2013 年联合国对埃及女性调查结果显示,至少 48.9% 的受访女性表示性骚扰案件较 2011 年之前有所增长,44% 的女性认为与之前持平。[①] 九成以上的受访女性认为"制定严厉的处罚措施、切实贯彻执行现有法律"对减少性骚扰案件的发生至关重要。[②] 这说明,从立法角度入手并加大对犯罪行为的惩处是解决埃及性骚扰问题的关键手段。

同样,即使是女性选择了报案,希望以司法程序来保护自己的安全,但执法系统对性骚扰犯罪事件的处置往往并不积极。在实际操作上,极少有性骚扰案件被立案调查或是交法庭判处,而性骚扰罪的认定也非常困难,一方面是由于受害人面临举证困难的情况,也可能是无法提供足够立案所需要的证人,加上执法机关受理此类案件的消极作为,被举报的性骚扰案件立案起诉的困难较大;另一方面则是受害人担心报案可能会遭到家人的反对,甚至受到来自外界的鄙视或指责,诸如"女性遭受性骚扰多数与其不得体的着装或行为有关"等此类"被害人有罪"论调,而法律规定的对罪犯的后续惩戒力度较低或者执行力较差,由此导致了许多女性被害人选择缄默不予追究或者回避。在 2013 年联合国的调查报告中,93.4% 的受害人表示不会在遭到性骚扰时向警方求助,即使警方的介入能够及时制止侵害行为,但多数女性会出于对后续的司法程序的担忧而放弃报警。因此,长久以来埃及愈演愈烈的性骚扰问题和性骚扰犯罪都未能得到解决。

对"性骚扰"犯罪的立法作为一项公共制度,需要由政府承担起制度供给者的角色,并对其施行提供强力保障,穆尔西政府在性骚扰的问题上始终秉持着一种模棱两可的处置态度,2012 年,埃及全国妇女委员会(NCW)指责掌权的穆兄会自由与正义党(FJP)试图剥夺女性已获

---

① *Study on Ways and Methods to Eliminate Sexual Harassmen in Egypt*, UN Women, May 23, 2013, https://www.peacewomen.org/node/90812.

② UN Women Sexual Harassment Study Egypt, https://web.law.columbia.edu/sites/default/files/microsites/gender-sexuality/un_womensexual-harassment-study-egypt-final-en.pdf, accessed May 28, 2023.

得的符合伊斯兰教法规定的权利，并拒绝承认埃及已经批准的妇女权利相关的各项条约；穆兄会则称："全国妇女委员会是前政权分裂和摧毁家庭的武器。"[1]埃及政府作为制度供给者的缺位放任了性骚扰问题的恶化，滞后的反应速度和消极的处理态度无疑将会拉低民众尤其是女性对政府的信心。对明确性骚扰行为的立法空白和消极执法导致了外部制度供给缺失或者失效，直接影响到埃及女性的生存环境和人身安全。

对此，2014年之后塞西政府的处置方式就相对更加主动，面对民众尤其是女性公民对惩治性骚扰犯罪的强烈要求，塞西政府在2014年上台之后，即做出了一系列的举措以遏制该犯罪在社会上的不良影响。首先第一步就是重塑政府权威，严格立法，使公众重拾对法治的信心。2014年《刑法》修正案首次将性骚扰行为认定为刑事犯罪。《刑法》将暴力侵害女性的犯罪区分为"轻罪"和"重罪"两种，其中"性骚扰"属于轻罪，而重罪则包括强奸、绑架女性、性侵犯以及切割女性生殖器。性骚扰被划分为"身体性骚扰"和"言语性骚扰"，其中身体性骚扰属于"猥亵罪"（《刑法》第278条），由犯罪者对受害者身体或者自己的身体实施，刑事法院对其最高可判处3年有期徒刑；而"言语性骚扰"属于"侮辱罪"（《刑法》第306条），可以被判处100埃镑的罚金和1个月的监禁。同时对立案调查程序等进行修改，保护女性被害人的隐私和安全，也鼓励更多女性勇敢曝光并起诉性骚扰犯罪。

2015年4月，埃及通过了《打击暴力侵害妇女行为国家战略2015—2020》(*The National Strategy for Combating Violence against Women, 2015-2020*)，该战略通过重新整合财力和人力资源，协调有关各方的配合和沟通机制，针对2011年以来极速增长的以女性为目标的街头暴力犯罪提出应对解决策略，包括详细的活动计划、执行时间表、预期效果、预算、绩效指标、执行机制以及可能出现的执行障碍等等。[2]此战略由一个经总

---

[1] Shaymaa Fayed, *Egypt Female Rights Official Battles Islamists*, June 8, 2012, https://www.reuters.com/article/idUSBRE85612X20120607.

[2] National Council for Women (NCW), *The National Strategy for Combating Violence against Women, 2015-2020*, https://learningpartnership.org/sites/default/files/resources/pdfs/Egypt-National-Strategy-for-Combating-VAW-2015-English.pdf.

统批准的委员会负责监督执行，由总理领导，同时，政府各个部门内开设"机会均等"部门，专门处理工作场所对女性的暴力、骚扰或歧视行为；在内政部下属省级单位和司法部内都设立专门部门，负责处理暴力侵害女性事件。最为显著的是该战略提出了完善法律程序的重要性，提议设立特别法庭以便快速审理和裁决暴力侵害妇女的犯罪，敦促司法部建立支持和启动法律框架的制度，"分析研究女性暴力侵害有关法律，并对其进行相应的修订"。①整个战略行动纲领覆盖了内政部、司法部、教育部、高教部、文化部、瓦克夫宗教基金部（Waqf）等多部门，各个部门协同合作，战略中还呼吁宗教参与到制止暴力侵害女性的行动中来。同时，政府还与联合国人口基金会合作，相继在全国公立大学中设立了29家反性骚扰的处置机构，为校园中女性受侵害案件提供援助支持。

由此可见，由政府主导的针对性骚扰犯罪的行动能够极大地调动社会资源和国家力量，致力于该问题的根治，以中央政府为驱动核心是保障该制度稳定有效的基本要素。当然，对性骚扰犯罪的后续处置方面仍存在很多的缺陷或不足，例如，由于历来案件受理比例低下、性骚扰的判罪太轻、对被害人/报案人缺乏有效的保护等，往往使得女性投诉无门或惴惴不安，结果不得已保持缄默或自我消解。2017年10月就曾爆出有性骚扰罪犯在被判处监禁2周后携凶器向被害人实施报复，被害人在逃避过程中被其刺伤脸部，而在这整个案件中，这名受害女子不仅要承受身体上的伤痛，还有心理上的恐惧和被外界指责的痛苦。但值得肯定的是，塞西政府对性骚扰犯罪的立法是在打击该项犯罪中历史性的进步，弥补了新制度产生和推行上关键一环的缺失。现实依然严峻，沉疴痼疾显然不可能在一夕间轻易消除。在2019年国际民调机构"阿拉伯晴雨表"（Arab Barometer）的研究报告显示，在过去的12个月中，受访的埃及女性中曾在公共场所遭受性骚扰的比例仍高达63%，其中年轻女

① National Council for Women (NCW), *The National Strategy for Combating Voilence against Women, 2015-2020*, https://learningpartnership.org/sites/default/files/resources/pdfs/Egypt-National-Strategy-for-Combating-VAW-2015-English.pdf.

性（17—28 岁）遭受过性骚扰的比例更甚，达到了90%。[①] 政府必须发挥其主导作用，以强力手段制止性骚扰甚至性暴力非法行为继续发展下去。面对持续高涨的民意和女性更强烈的安全诉求，埃及政府在坚持作为打击性骚扰犯罪的主导力量的前提下，允许甚至鼓励民间社会组织的行动和更多的民众参与。

三、民间行动从"补位"到"协同"

2011 年后，埃及民间内部便开始内生出一种主张和行动：人们自发组织起来，走进街道走进广场，走近被侵害的女性，为她们提供救援和人身安全保护，以民间组织或是一种私人领域自发行动填补公共领域外部制度的缺失。非政府组织的救援开始成为埃及女性在街头、在广场等地的安全屏障，有不少志愿者身着统一服装，以小组行动的方式深入聚集人群，搜索并援助受困的被骚扰女性。这其中，不断发展更新的互联网技术发挥了巨大作用，许多在线服务和追踪系统相继出现，为女性保护提供了一种新的手段和方式，有效填补了在国家公共政策缺失、不足或制度失效的情况下妇女保护的空白。"骚扰地图"（HARASSmap）便是其中之一。

HARASSmap 是一个在线的非营利性组织，通过提供交互式地图来降低性骚扰犯罪的发生。当人们遭受或目睹性骚扰时，可以通过短信、邮件、推特（Twitter）、脸书（Facebook）等社交媒体发送在线报告，报告可包含犯罪现场的地区、街道等详细信息，并借助谷歌埃及地图在事发地点进行标注，提示风险点位，随后由 HARASSmap 志愿者前往当地，通过与社群、执法人员的合作，降低乃至消除当地的性骚扰犯罪。同时，HARASSmap 还致力于促进国家针对性骚扰行为的立法、为女性和男性提供自我保护课程和教育培训，以图实现全社会对以性骚扰为代表的性别暴力犯罪零容忍，为全埃及女性打造一个安全的生存生活环境，

---

① Donia Smaali Bouhlila, *Sexual Harassment and Domestic Violence in the Middle East and North Africa*, Arab Barometer, December 2019, p. 6, https://www.arabbarometer.org/wp-content/uploads/Sexual-Harassment-Domestic-Violence-Arab-Citizens-Public-Opinion-2019.pdf.

HARASSmap 得到了埃及女权中心的认可与助力。同时 HARASSmap 还帮助"反性骚扰行动"（OpAntiSH）等组织，保护女性在参加宗教节日或大规模集会时的安全。OpAntiSH 成立于 2012 年，目标主要是防范宗教节日期间发生的大规模性侵犯，并为女性提供法律、医疗和心理支持。它虽属于民间组织，但在抵抗开罗广场暴徒对女性袭击、侵害上发挥了重要的作用。OpAntiSH 组织的志愿者救援小组会通过网络、电话等方式获得女性侵害行为发生的信息，随即赶往事发地点、驱散暴徒、将受害人保护起来并带往安全地带。

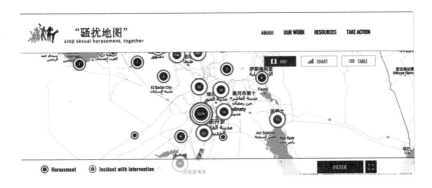

图 4　HARASSMap 网页地图
资料来源：Harassmap, https://harassmap.org/en/

　　自发的民间行动对保护女性起到了一定的积极效果，也受到了广大女性的支持和信赖，但它在实际操作上仍有很大的不足，如救援人员在现场施救过程中可能会遭到阻碍或攻击，而其中的女性救援者则也有被性骚扰或者被侵害的风险。

　　此后，埃及先后涌现了"埃及女孩是条红线""我看到了性骚扰""Me Too"等民间自发的活动，其不断发展升温，从而形成了一个全社会反对性骚扰犯罪的浪潮。2020 年 7 月，一个名叫"扎基"的青年男子（Ahmad Bassam Zaki）被指对多名女性实施性骚扰和性侵害行为；社交网站爆出的 2014 年埃及菲尔蒙德酒店强奸案，再次挑动了埃及公众对政府政治腐败的不满神经，同年 8 月，埃及公诉机关收到全国妇女委员会针对该案件的投诉。2020 年 7 月，埃及权威宗教机构判例局（Dar alifta）与爱资哈尔先后发布声明，宣布"性骚扰是一种犯罪、一种重大的罪行和虚伪行径"，并呼吁"国家专门机关应肩负起严厉打击一切形式的道德败坏和可耻的性骚扰犯罪"。[①] 爱资哈尔的声明中强调"性骚扰是非法的，无论它的形式为何——眼神、手势或是行为，都不能为其开脱或者认为它可接受"，应以法律对其进行严厉的打击。为了重塑统治权威，也迫于公众舆论带来的压力，塞西政府一方面开始加大对政治腐败的惩处力度，另一方面也着力推动对针对女性犯罪的严格立法，力图缓解民众尤其是女性对埃及社会性暴力事件的不满，"Me Too"运动带来的这次曝光也成为推动2021年《刑法》修正案获得通过的主要契机。

2020年8月16日，埃及议会全体会议上，三分之二的议员投票赞成通过了一项新的法律，以保护前来举报性骚扰或性侵犯被害人的个人隐私，并给予被害人在举报中匿名的权利，以鼓励女性举报此类案件。埃及全国妇女委员会也对此表示支持，并专门设立"投诉办公室"接待女性在受到骚扰或侵害后的投诉，强调会保证受害人个人信息和隐私安全。这在无形中鼓励着众多的女性勇于反抗性侵害和性骚扰，改善人们对此类事件的认知，降低受害人所承受的心理压力和来自外部社会的舆论压力，无疑有助于一个更安全环境的塑造。2020年开始，有大量的性骚扰受害者站出来揭露犯罪，法律支持了这些诉讼并制裁了犯罪嫌疑人。

总的来看，新的立法需要动力，2011年的埃及社会运动提供了变革的机会，但是我们观察到的是，作为社会主体之一的男性并不具备推动该项立法的天然动力，或者说天然的差异造成了男女双方对制度变迁的偏好和收益预期不同，而社会的另一半——女性，则缺乏有效的有力发声机会和机制，加上女性受高等教育、工作的比例较低，边远地区的女性政治参与率低，导致了通过社会变革来推动立法的动力不足，或者说不足以引起人们对女性问题的关注。因此私人领域、个体行为或个别非政府组织行为无法从根本上解决这个问题，在中央政府作为立法者缺位

---

① *Egypt's Dar al-Ifta in an official statement: Sexual harassment is a crime and an abominable sin*, https://www.dar-alifta.org/Foreign/ViewArticle.aspx?ID=7169&text=harassment.

的情况下，民间组织的补位虽然部分填补了这项需求，但其力量和能力所限，是无法从根本上解决这项社会顽疾的；政府和社会力量二者之间必须形成有效互动和支撑。所幸的是，由埃及政府倡议并主导的埃及女性赋能运动日益高涨，为这项立法的最终出台实施带来了新的希望。

四、埃及女性赋能运动与性骚扰犯罪入刑

埃及女性赋能运动的兴起与活跃，也为该立法的诞生提供了充足的驱动力。女性赋能是《埃及可持续发展 2030 愿景》提出的目标之一，义中明确"要消除公共领域和私人领域中一切形式的对妇女和女孩的暴力，包括贩卖、性剥削以及其他一切形式的剥削"，"通过并加强健全的政策和可执行的立法，以促进两性平等和在各个层级的女性赋能"。[①]根据 1956 年《宪法》规定，埃及女性享有包括选举权在内的充分政治权利，《宪法》明确保证两性享有平等的公民权利。埃及 2014 年《宪法》再次明确了"埃及女性与男性享有平等的公民、政治、经济和社会权利"。2018 年《宪法》修订案中第 180 条规定：通过选举产生的地方议会中，确保 1/4 的席位配额属于妇女。而在埃及新一任期（2016—2021）的议会中，女性拥有 162 个席位，占议会的 27%，这是这一比例首次超过 15%。[②]

根据 2021 年统计数据，埃及人口总数约为 1.04 亿，其中半数为女性，她们的政治参与具有相当大的影响，作为主要女性权益保障机构的埃及全国妇女委员会一直在鼓励女性参与选举，并向女性发放身份证，倡导"你的身份、你的权利"（Your ID, Your Right），鼓励女性参与市级选举投票，甚至是竞选候选人，以促进女性发声、表达政治诉求和主张。2015 年起，一项由联合国妇女署、联合国性别平等基金支持，埃及女权中心（ECWR）负责的项目"女性之声浪潮"（A Wave of Women's Voices）正式启动，总预算为 54.5 万美元，成为引导女性参政议政的行

---

① *Sustainable Development Goal-5-Gender Equality*, https://egypt.un.org/en/sdgs/5.

② *Women's Political Participation in Egypt*, https://borgenproject.org/womens-political-participation-in-egypt/.

动纲领之一，该计划旨在深入广大女性群体，从教育入手，以一及十，以十及百，以百而及千万，逐步引导女性在政治领域中自主发声、表达诉求并主动参政，推动女性参与公共事务决策、提高参政比例，参加包括地方议会在内的选举，有效利用国家法律规定的配额，从而推动性别问题敏感的法律法规的提案、讨论乃至最终通过并实施，使全社会不得不关注女性的诉求与话语权，进而谋求整个埃及社会女性自我意识的觉醒与提升。

与之相辅相成的是埃及新闻媒体和大众传媒的助力，2015 年，埃及妇女传媒联盟（Egyptian Women's Media Union）成立，女性开始学习利用网络媒体向政府或公共部门施压，迫使他们回应女性关切，从而促成更多符合女性发展利益及两性平等关系的政策出台，有女性媒体人开始报道全国各地的女性生活和生存状态，同时加强对性别敏感问题的关注和追踪报道，例如 Masr el-Nas 网站就着重培养女性新闻从业者，报道边远地区女性生活的故事。

由此，在政府主导的前提下，社会层面出现了三个相辅相成的因素在推动国家针对性骚扰犯罪的立法，其一是民间组织或者说民众自发地在保护女性、回应女性对性骚扰入罪的要求，发挥了社会动员的作用；其二是一个国家性的女性赋能运动，尤其是政治赋能，使女性的要求在社会范围内得到了表达、受到了关切，女性在议会中占有更多席位，更有利于符合女性需求的立法出台；其三是大众媒体和网络科技的发展，使这样的需求和表达能够为更多人知晓，能够唤起更多的女性乃至男性的互动，最终解决"性骚扰入罪"立法这一制度供给问题。就在该修正案通过后不久，2021 年 10 月 17 日，一名被指控在开罗地铁站骚扰女性的男子被判处 3 年零 6 个月的监禁；11 月 9 日，医生迈克尔·法赫米（Michael Fahmy）被北开罗刑事法院判处终身监禁，罪名是他利用职务之便在诊所内强制猥亵 6 名女孩。① 越来越多诸如此类的案件被公布于众，罪犯受到了应有的刑事处罚。这极大程度上维护了埃及女性的生存

---

① United States Department of State, Bureau of Democracy, Human Rights and Labor, *Egypt 2021 Human Rights Report*.

安全，成为提高女性生活质量的重要举措。

与此同时，法律也力求在最大程度上保障被害人权利和隐私不受侵犯，一名在 2020 年米特加穆尔（Mit Ghamr）大规模性骚扰事件中的受害者，在报案后受到了来自辩方律师的恐吓，称其视频和照片将被发布于网络之上；2021 年埃及检方对该案件判决提起抗诉，最终法院判决支持了被害人并将两名进行恐吓的律师判处监禁与罚款。2022 年一名餐厅员工在餐厅卫生间放置手机进行拍摄，被指控性骚扰并移交马特鲁哈刑事法院进行审理；也是在 2022 年，一名男子因在开罗街头言语骚扰一名带着孩子的母亲并试图触摸她而遭到逮捕和起诉。所有这些事实证明，该项修正案切实加大了对受害人的保护力度，在遏制性骚扰犯罪方面起到了有效的威慑作用，同时加强了公众对政府的信赖。

这项修正案的到来，为埃及政府和埃及女性开创了一个双赢的局面，在女性身心安全获得了真实有效的保障的同时，塞西政府也能够借此获得更多的国内支持，加强其统治权威和民意合法性，同时该修正案也提升了国际社会对埃及两性平等关系方面的认可度和评估值。2022 年 6 月 29 日，世界银行执行董事会在华盛顿批准了一笔给埃及的高达 5 亿美元的贷款，以支持埃及政府长久以来的工作，并使之有能力应对粮食危机；同年 10 月 3 日，世界银行执行董事会再批准一笔 4 亿美元的发展融资协议，旨在提升埃及物流和交通运输部门的绩效，促进大开罗—十月六日城—亚历山大之间铁路向低碳运输的转变，尤其是"为女性雇员提供职业发展和幼儿看护等便利，鼓励女性就业"[①]。

结　语

总的来看，在处置 2011 年以后埃及性骚扰事件频发升级的问题上，中央政府、民间组织以及日益活跃的女性赋能运动相互作用，共同促进了埃及关于性骚扰犯罪的立法出台。在初始阶段，也就是 2011 年之后几

---

① *Egypt: US$ 400 Million Project will Help to Improve and Decarbonize Logistics and Transportation Sectors*, https://www.worldbank.org/en/news/press-release/2022/10/03/egypt-us-400-million-project-will-help-to-improve-and-decarbonize-logistics-and-transportation-sectors.

年中，埃及政府在处置性骚扰犯罪问题上的迟滞导致了针对该犯罪的立法缺失，其实质是政府作为制度供给者的缺位，而民间的或私人领域的补位虽然有一些效果，但其动员能力有限，无力阻挡性骚扰犯罪的激增恶化，国家亟待推动新制度的出台和有效施行。及至 2014 年塞西政府执政后，政府成为新制度推行的主导者，并以司法机关强制手段保障其施行，同时允许和鼓励民间组织的有效补充，形成了政府与民间的共同推力，2020 年前后以"Me Too"为代表的反性骚扰运动在埃及的广泛兴起，真实地反映了女性诉求，进一步推动了政府对性骚扰犯罪的处置行动；同时，在政府主导的女性赋能运动获得女性公民乃至全社会所产生的积极效应加持下，埃及最终实现了应对性骚扰犯罪的历史性进步。这一进步反过来也有助于埃及政府公信力和执政满意度的提升，坚实其政治统治合法性根基，获得更广泛的民意支持。尽管该《刑法》修正案的效果和后续影响还需经过时间检验，有可能会经常面对现实操作上的困难，但迄今为止其为女性权益的提升和女性生存环境的改善还是带来了积极的效果。

告别的时刻：安哥拉在动荡世界中寻求发展

蒂亚戈·卡翁戈·穆通博　佩德罗·特赛·莱尔·布兰奇著

王瑞凡译*

摘　要：安哥拉内战结束至今已20年，但仍未能实现包容性发展。本文分析了制约安哥拉经济腾飞的障碍，指出现任政府面临的挑战，并对如何克服挑战提出建议。本文假设，影响安哥拉发展的关键阻碍在于其政治制度结构。通过研究安哥拉国家建设的历程，我们认为殖民主义和内战遗留下一个不负责任却对体制变革充满弹性的中央集权国家机构。尽管发展成果和公共产品无法有效惠及内陆地区，但通过在庇护关系中分配石油收入、笼络农村社区的传统权威，形成了一种去集权化的社会治理机制，这一安排得以维持体制稳定。这种组织形式使社会经济的二元结构长期存在，其中，精英阶层与资本密集型的采掘业绑定，而大多数人口则依靠自给农业和非正规工作维持生计。尽管当前针对稳定宏观经济、吸引外国投资和加强国家私营部门采取了必要的措施，但都不足以克服这种历史性根深蒂固的二元结构。安哥拉迫切需要增强国家能力建设，构建一个以快速实现工业化、振兴农业、缓解贫困和普及公共产品为目的发展规划。鉴此，我们提出以下研究课题：安哥拉如何利用潜在的比较优势实现经济快速增长、提高劳动生产率和产业多元化？

关键词：安哥拉　发展　制度　国家能力　二元结构

---

* 蒂亚戈·卡翁戈·穆通博（Tiago Caungo Mutombo），安哥拉卫理公会大学副教授、副校长，分管科研领域、研究生工作、推广教育、博士后工作，电子邮箱：mtiagocaungo@gmail.com；佩德罗·特赛·莱尔·布兰奇（Pedro Txai Leal Brancher），巴西南大河州联邦大学（UFRGS）国家公共政策、战略和发展科学与技术研究所博士后研究员，安哥拉卫理公会大学国际事务部主任，电子邮箱：brancherpedro022@gmail.com；王瑞凡，现就职于中国进出口银行，北京大学国际关系学院硕士在读研究生。

［注］本文由刘海方、王进杰进行中文翻译校对。

引　言

安哥拉的国家英雄安东尼奥·阿戈什蒂纽·内图生于 1922 年，他的出生地位于首都罗安达 60 公里外伊科洛本戈县一个名为卡西卡内（Kaxikane）的村庄。他的父亲阿戈什蒂纽·佩德罗·内图是卫理公会的牧师，母亲玛莉亚·达席尔瓦·内图是一名老师。萨拉查的军事独裁政权在葡萄牙掌权并对殖民地加强镇压统治时，阿戈什蒂纽·内图仅有 4 岁。作为被殖民当局归类为开化黑人群体的一员，阿戈什蒂纽得以就读于一所体面的学校。26 岁时，他前往葡萄牙就读医学。在那里，他不仅开始使用文学和诗歌来描绘安哥拉社会，还开始为安哥拉独立开展激进的政治活动。1951 年，他和阿米尔卡·洛佩斯·加布拉尔和马里奥·科埃略·平托·德安德拉德等一些非洲同学创办了非洲研究中心。在接下来几年里，他被葡萄牙"国际和国家防卫警察"（PIDE）以分裂主义罪名多次逮捕。1959 年，内图回到罗安达并成为安哥拉人民解放运动（葡语缩写为 MPLA，以下简称安人运）的主席。自 1962 年起，他在安哥拉独立战争中指挥安哥拉人民解放武装力量对抗葡萄牙军队。1975 年，安哥拉最终实现独立，阿戈什蒂纽成为这个年轻国家的首任总统，直至1979 年去世。

2022 年，安哥拉和国际社会热烈庆祝阿戈什蒂纽·内图诞辰 100 周年，但安哥拉在许多方面已和 20 世纪 70 年代末他离世时存在着本质区别。作为非洲出生率最高的国家，安哥拉的人口自 1979 年至 2021 年已由 800 万增长到了 3400 万，城市人口比例由 23% 增长到 67%；[①] 坐拥国土面积 1246700 平方公里和海岸线 1650 公里，其上分布着丰富的自然资源；GDP 自 1980 年的 221 亿美元提高至 2020 年的 780 亿美元，成为非

[①]　World Bank, *Angola-Agriculture Support Policy Review: Realigning Agriculture Support Policies and Programs* (*English*), Washington, D. C.: World Bank Group, 2021, http://documents.worldbank.org/curated/en/719131625036855154/Angola-Agriculture-Support-Policy-Review-Realigning-Agriculture-Support-Policies-and-Programs.

洲第六大经济体。[①] 在制度上，安哥拉抛弃了马克思列宁主义的意识形态，并承诺建立多党制政治体制和以私营经济为主导的市场经济体制。选择这条道路后，从前军事上的敌人变成了政治上的对手，在每五年一次的大选中和平地争夺安哥拉民众的选票。

尽管如此，内图生前一直批评的经济落后和对外依赖问题不仅没有消失，反而在过去的 40 年里不断恶化。殖民时代后期兴起的多元化农业产业和新生轻工业已经让位于利润丰厚的石油经济，后者构成了当下绝大部分的政府收入。资本密集型的石油产业与国际市场联系紧密，但仍脱离于安哥拉经济的其他组成部分，即大多数人口所依赖的主要是农业和非正规经济。这种二元社会经济结构造成了明显的分化和普遍贫困问题，一旦原油价格下跌，这些问题就会激化，导致安哥拉货币宽扎贬值、食物进口成本急剧上升。因此，发展并未伴随安哥拉的城市化、人口增长和经济增长一同而来。

安哥拉的结构性矛盾加剧了新冠肺炎疫情和俄乌冲突等外部冲击所带来的经济和社会影响。虽然新冠病毒的致死率并不高，但疫情减少了国际原油需求，导致该国唯一能赚取外汇的商品价格进一步下降。此外，由于安哥拉的大部分劳动者依赖于非正规经济，政府实施的封控措施致使这些最弱势群体的人均收入大幅减少。因此，出口产品单一和非正规经济成分过高，使得安哥拉人民面对新冠疫情的暴发显得格外脆弱。尽管原油价格在俄乌冲突爆发后得以复苏，但安哥拉是小麦、大米、棕榈油和化肥的净进口国，且农业生产率低下，[②] 全球产业链的断裂暴露了这个国家岌岌可危的处境。俄乌冲突引发的食品和农产品进口通胀加剧了 160 万安哥拉人正在面临的粮食危机，他们在 2021 年遭受了近

---

① Tatiana Costa, "Angola could become Africa's fourth-largest economy by 2050," *Ver Angola*, 20 July 2020, https://www.verangola.net/va/en/072020/Economy/21023/Angola-could-become-Africa's-fourth-largest-economy-by-2050.htm, accessed 10 November 2022.

② Cedric Okou, John Spray, and Filiz Unsal, *Stable Food Prices in Sub-Saharan Africa. An Empirical Assessment*, IMF Working Paper. New York: International Monetary Fund, 2022.

40 年最严重的旱灾，粮食问题进一步恶化。[1]

本文将探究为何安哥拉在内战结束 20 年后仍然无法克服二元经济社会结构，以致在外部冲击面前显得格外脆弱。换言之，为什么安哥拉在战后未能实现包容性发展和经济多元化？本文假设安哥拉的经济进步的关键阻碍在于政治制度结构。通过研究安哥拉国家建设历程，我们提出，殖民主义和内战遗留下一个不负责任的中央集权国家机构却能适应体制变革；[2] 尽管发展成果和公共产品无法有效惠及内陆地区，但运用政治手段在庇护网络中分配石油收入、笼络农村社区的传统权威，形成了一种去集权化的社会治理机制，这一安排得以维持体制稳定。因此，安哥拉的精英阶层没有动力去培养促进结构转型的发展能力，也无法切实投入到活力型市场经济体制建设中。

安哥拉的制度安排能适应变化，并非意味着本身一成不变。与其他资源型国家相似，安哥拉的制度变革模式与原油在国际市场上的价格波动相关。20 世纪 80 年代末期的油价下跌引发了渐进式的政治和经济自由化，由此形成了一种路径依赖的轨迹，增加了执政党的改革压力。2014 年以来，在油价再次下跌、腐败丑闻百出、新冠肺炎疫情的交织叠加作用下，安哥拉的社会经济矛盾激化到令其人民难以承受。面对内战结束后最严重的危机和过去两届大选中的疲软表现，安人运承诺将下放国家权力并按照国际货币基金组织（IMF）的指导进行结构性调整计划。虽然这一议程在短期发展成果方面存在相当大的局限性，但这将是首次为安哥拉探索更高效的治理形式的系统性尝试。

本文将分为三部分，外加结论部分。首先，我们将围绕落实基层自治的挑战展开探讨，考虑到安哥拉国家建设历程和原油出口导向经济对政治活力的影响，这将是安哥拉权力下放议程中的核心因素。其次，我们将分析安哥拉二元经济对生产力的负面影响，强调普遍贫困、基建落

[1] Observador, "Quase 1,6 milhões sofrem de insegurança alimentar grave no sul de Angola, indica ONU," *Observador*, 4 May 2022, https://observador.pt/2022/05/04/quase-16-milhoes-sofrem-de-inseguranca-alimentar-grave-no-sul-de-angola-indica-onu/, accessed 5 November 2022.

[2] *See* Given Yurtseven, "State Failure or State Formation? Neo-patrimonialism and Its Limitations in Africa," *E-International Relations*, 29 June 2021, https://www.e-ir.info/2021/06/29/state-failure-or-state-formation-neo-patrimonialism-and-its-limitations-in-africa/, accessed 10 November 2022.

后和严重分化等因素对经济发展具有较强的制约作用。再次，根据安哥拉的二元结构和面对新冠肺炎疫情展现出的脆弱性，我们将分析现行公共政策的可行性。最后，我们将总结主要论点，并梳理出进一步的研究课题。

一、安哥拉国家制度因素：中央集权、传统权威、基层自治

20世纪60年代末安哥拉与殖民统治抗争时期，阿戈什蒂纽·内图出版了一本诗集，名为《神圣的希望》。在一众诗歌中，这首《告别的时刻》因抒发了为自由而战的民族忧虑而广为人知。通过与"所有与儿子分离的黑人母亲"对话，他试图表达未来由自己筑造，以唤起人们的希望：

> 我已经不再等待
> 我就是那个被等待的人
>
> 我就是希望，妈妈
> 我们就是希望
> 你的儿子们
> 出发去寻找可以滋养生活的
> 信仰 [①]

2022年9月15日，安哥拉宪法法院院长劳琳达·卡多佐在总统任命仪式的开场讲话中引用了内图的诗句。卡多佐直截了当地向当选总统强调："安哥拉不能再拖延下去了。繁荣的安哥拉再也不能只停留于空想之中，而应成为愉悦的现实，即使最底层的公民也能被惠及。"她指出，大选结果表明安哥拉百姓对未来缺乏希望。因此，新一届政府必须"处

[①] Agostinho Neto, *Sagrada Esperança*, Lisbon: Sá da Costa, 1978, p. 10. 译文出自《神圣的希望》，张晓非译，江苏凤凰文艺出版社，2018年。

理好选举中出现的大量弃票现象，令人们重新相信国家有能力处理好各项事务并引领国家命运走向"①。

卡多佐的精彩讲话展现了安哥拉司法机关面对行政机构的独立性，这是向多党政治体制过渡的重要制度特征。另一方面，卡多佐之所以强调亟需重获人民对国家引领公共事务的信心，是由于大部分安哥拉人处于极度贫困状态且无法享受到必要的公共服务。根据 2021 年人类发展指数（HDI）排名，安哥拉在 190 个国家中排第 148 位，人均预期寿命为 61 岁，平均受教育年限为 5.4 年，② 48% 的人口缺乏基本的卫生设施。③

鉴于安哥拉落后的国情，政界和学界认为权力下放改革是改善公共服务和提高政治问责制的核心机制。例如，社会复兴党全国青年常务秘书加斯帕尔·多斯桑托斯·费尔南德斯认为，安哥拉市政选举的制度化是解决主要社会问题的重要抓手。④ 克拉丽丝·贝乌指出，权力下放将改善公共服务并提高民众对政治和经济事务的参与度。⑤ 纳尔逊·佩斯塔纳和阿斯拉克·奥雷提出，权力下放是一个可以确保"民主参与、促进发展、维护公民安全和政治安全"的工具。⑥

---

① Adéritco Casimiro, "'Angola não deve continuar a ser um mero sonho' – Laurinda Cardoso," *Correio da Kianda*, 15 September 2022, https://correiokianda.info/angola-nao-deve-continuar-a-ser-um-mero-sonho-laurinda-cardoso/, accessed 5 November 2022.

② UNDP, *Human Development Report 2021/2022 Overview. Uncertain Times, Unsettled Lives*: *shaping our future in a transforming world*, New York: United Nations Development Program, 2022, https://hdr.undp.org/system/files/documents/global-report-document/hdr2021-22overviewenpdf.pdf, accessed 10 November 2022.

③ World Bank, *People using at least basic sanitation services (per cent of population) - Angola.* The World Bank Group, 2022, https://data.worldbank.org/indicator/SH.STA.BASS.ZS?locations=AO, accessed 3 November 2022.

④ Angola Telegraph, "Autarchy is the main lever for solving Luanda's social problems, says PRS youth leader," *Angola Telegraph*, 5 November 2022, https://angolatelegraph.com/politics/autarchy-is-the-main-lever-for-solving-luandas-social-problems-says-prs-youth-leader/, accessed 7 November 2022.

⑤ Clarice Beu, "The Implementation of Autarchies in Angola as Leverage for Local Problems," *Constituição, Economia e Desenvolvimento: Revista da Academia Brasileira de Direito Constitucional. Curitíba*, vol.9, no. 17, 2017, pp. 346-360.

⑥ Nelson Pestana and Aslak Orre, "Para quando as autarquias em Angola," *Angola Brief*, v.4, no.8, 2014, p. 2.

　　安哥拉宪法和安人运领导人都同意将战争时期遗留下的单一国家结构进行去集中化改革。1992 年《宪法》引入了基层自治的概念，即基层选举出的对地方事务拥有自治能力和自主决策的管辖机构。在安哥拉的社会情况下，基层选举出的自治机构会在领地和民主问题上与传统权威和中央派出机构意见相左。2010 年，新版《宪法》不仅将地方自治机关的职权划定为教育、卫生、能源、水务、农村和城镇设备、文化科学、交通通信、休闲体育、住房、社会行动、民事保护、环境卫生、消费者保护、社会经济发展、土地规划、市政警察和分权合作等领域，还强调他们应从国家总预算和地方税收中获得与以上职能相匹配的财政资源。① 2014 年，若泽·爱德华多·桑托斯在安人运中央委员会的一次讲话中表示："基层政权是国家发展之本。"②

　　尽管有宪法规定且有执政党和反对党的支持，截至 2022 年，安哥拉 18 个省、164 个市和 532 个乡镇的领导人仍然由行政任命指派。③ 为何如此？为何在安哥拉下放政治权力和行政权力如此具有挑战性？与其推测是否因为安人运迷恋权力，我们认为更应在安哥拉长期国家建设进程中来理解为何地方政权的组建如此缓慢。④

　　葡萄牙于 15 世纪末建立了远洋黑奴贸易体系，现代安哥拉国家是这一体系所孕育的副产品。由于经济活动中心转移至大西洋沿岸，葡萄牙当局并不重视发展内陆地区行政基础设施，也不关心如何建立合法税收形式。3 个多世纪以来，殖民者占领区仅限于沿海地带和主要河流沿

---

① Lázaro Jaime, *O Conceito de Autarquias Locais na Constituição da República de Angola - o caso do Município*, Dissertation, Minho: Universidade do Minho, 2015.

② David Filipe, "Autarquias são fundamentais para o desenvolvimento do país, Eduardo dos Santos," *Novo Jornal*. 30 May 2014, https://novojornal.co.ao/politica/interior/autarquias-sao-fundamentais-para-o-desenvolvimento-do-pais-eduardo-dos-santos-3477.htm>l, accessed 1 November 2022.

③ Angola Telegraph, "Luanda governor appoints municipal administrators," *Angola Telegraph*, 8 November 2022, https://angolatelegraph.com/politics/luanda-governor-appoints-municipal-administrators/, accessed 10 November 2022.

④ 安人运的权力依附假说通常被反对派成员所提倡。它将权力下放改革的迟缓归因于执政党不愿意构想多元化的治理安排。尽管政治行为体的作用是理解制度结果的一个相关变量，但我们认为历史和结构因素具有更强的解释力，可以说明中央集权制度安排的长期弹性，即使在反复发生的经济危机面前也是如此。

岸的补给点，同时，他们与当地王国和酋长族群沆瀣一气，确保内陆地区能够源源不断地输送黑奴出来。一个经济发达的海洋地区同一个传统习惯法统治之下的内陆地区被捆绑在一起，难舍难分，形成了二元结构的雏形，至今仍在影响着安哥拉经济。

19 世纪末期，安哥拉的领土仍被划分为多个地理区块，每片领地上的人都拥有不同的政治、语言和文化特征。在 1885 年柏林会议之前，不同族群之间缺乏社会融合，成为独立后冲突的根源之一。在德国、法国和英国等其他欧洲大国的领土入侵压力下，葡萄牙开始占领内陆地区。当时，一名非裔葡萄牙籍大奴隶贩子已在罗安达和本格拉周边地区建立起初步的管理组织形式。这名非裔葡人与葡萄牙军队合力打败了中部高地的传统统治势力，从而在 20 世纪初逐步开展税收。[1]

至 1924 年末，宽扎河道已建立起蒸汽轮船航线，通往钻石开采区的铁路也已初步建成。1926 年，安东尼奥·萨拉查在葡萄牙掌权执政后，重新加强了殖民地的行政化管理，主要由派驻罗安达的葡萄牙人担任官职，而非裔葡人精英则被边缘化。1950—1960 年，在安哥拉生活的白人由 78825 人增至 172529 人。[2] 虽然萨拉查的经济政策带来了些许工业化浪潮和农业多元化，但大多数本地人仍在遭受强迫劳动，这种治理模式的目的在于将安哥拉打造成一个专为葡萄牙提供补给的出口平台。[3]

因此，在近 5 个世纪的殖民统治下，大部分安哥拉人在地理上被隔绝开来，无法接受正规教育或参与公共治理。尽管如此，有两种本土精英仍在殖民社会结构的夹缝中成长起来。第一种是传统权威，即所谓的"酋长"（Sobas），作为族群首领，其统治权来自世袭和宗教规定。[4] 凭借对领地的熟悉和族群民众的支持，酋长们成为殖民地行政机构的重要盟友，他们负责在领地内开展税收、募工和维持政治秩序工作。葡萄牙当

---

① Malyn Newitt, "Angola in Historical Context," in Patrick Chabal and Nuno Vidal (eds.), *Angola The Weight of History*, New York: Columbia University Press, 2008, pp. 19-92.

② Washington Nascimento, "Políticas coloniais e sociedade angolana nas memórias e discursos do escritor Raul David," *Anos* 90, v. 23, no. 44, 2016, pp. 265-289.

③ Malyn Newitt, "Angola in Historical Context," pp. 19-92.

④ *Soba* 是葡萄牙语对班图人土著语言金邦杜语（*Kimbundo*）中 *Sowa* 一词的翻译，原意为某地区的首领。

局通过操纵利用酋长具备的自下而上社会认同，可以在不使用大量士兵和官员的情况下广泛地投射权力。

在安哥拉内战期间（1976—2002），安人运首次尝试削减传统权威的权力。但内战结束后，考虑到新生政权的行政水平低下、基础设施薄弱，总统若泽·爱德华多·多斯桑托斯毫不犹豫地将酋长们纳入国家体系中。2010年版《宪法》充分认可了传统权威的习惯法，使安哥拉形成法律多元的特殊格局。截至2010年，在安哥拉全境，统治200至300人社区的传统权威注册数量为31845个。除了享受公共财政派发的薪水外，酋长们也是官员们寻求社区合法性的咨询对象，以帮助他们解决地方纠纷。酋长的身份属性与官方机构存在重合，成为建立竞争性基层机构选举制度的重要阻碍。

与酋长相同，同化者（assimilados）是殖民时期出现的另一类本土精英。与酋长不同的是，同化者是接受过葡萄牙教育的安哥拉男性，并且必须"举止有度"，以显示他们已经达到"文明"阶段，这使他们不用参加强迫劳动，可以担任公职、投票、在全国各地旅行以及考取驾照。要获得文明地位，必须精通葡萄牙语、穿着西服、实行一夫一妻制、放弃非洲传统、信仰基督教、证明收入水平可以维持家用，并在餐桌上遵从欧洲习俗。[1]

截至1960年，安哥拉登记人口中有2.5%是同化者。安哥拉第一代作家和民族运动的先驱大部分都是同化者，譬如阿戈什蒂纽·内图、若纳斯·萨文比、曼努埃尔·佩德罗·帕卡维拉、乌安亨加·西图、杰克·阿尔林多·多桑托斯、阿德里亚诺·塞巴斯蒂安、劳武·马特乌斯·戴维等人，他们大部分时间都在罗安达周边地区度过，并接受过新教传教士和欧洲大学的教育。[2]

内战结束后，国家建设依靠在安哥拉社会中占有主导地位的酋长和同化者们开展。中央政府将酋长纳入国家体系，利用这些首领在农村人

---

[1] Iracema Dulley and Luísa Sampaio, "Accusation and Legitimacy in the Civil War in Angola," *Virtual Brazilian Anthropology*, no.17, 2020, pp. 1-20.

[2] Washington Nascimento, "Políticas coloniais e sociedade angolana nas memórias e discursos do escritor Raul David," pp. 265-289.

群中拥有的神圣地位来实现对偏远地区的低成本的精细管理。在里卡多·苏亚雷斯·德·奥利维拉和苏珊·塔波尼尔看来，酋长与国家的关系应被视为安哥拉国家建设进程的分水岭，因为"与现代化话语相反，执政党和国家实际上正在制造变成一个陈旧腐朽的农村隔离区"①。非洲晴雨表显示，2020年，传统权威是安哥拉第三大最值得信任的机构，仅次于宗教领袖和军队，排在司法机构、警察机构和总统之前。②换句话说，虽然没有基层民选组织，但安哥拉拥有帮助其维持政治秩序的基层治理机制，并且无须对公众负责。

尽管1975年颁布的《国籍法》在制度层面不再区分土著群体和同化者群体，但在后殖民时代的安哥拉，城市中受过教育的精英阶层和内陆社区之间的经济、政治和文化距离依然存在。例如，"在安人运中，社会声望与葡语变位的熟练度、语言模式和生活方式相关；达不到这些标准则意味着粗鄙或非安哥拉式的狭隘"③。在安哥拉内战期间，关乎国民经济的基础设施遭到破坏，安人运依靠罗安达省周围飞地产出的原油作为战争资本补给，该政权的社会基础进一步脱离农村，从而强化了上述趋势。例如，在1985年参加第二次安人运党代会的628人中只有12人是农民。④伴随国内冲突的结束，酋长与国家的合作模式保障了内部治理，大多数社会优势资源依然被控制在安人运党内关系网络和国家资本手中，殖民时代遗留下来的城乡分化问题被自我复制。

综上所述，当和平来临时，这种传统权威和罗安达的同化精英们的组合抑制了基层代表机构的建设动力。然而，若不是安哥拉能够长期从石油出口收入中赚取大量外汇储备现金流，这个集权的非负责制国家对

① Ricardo Soares de Oliveira and Susan Taponier, "'O Governo Está Aqui': post-war state making in the Angolan Peiphery," *Politique africaine*, n° 130, Jun, 2013, p. 179.

② Carlos Pacatolo and David Boio, "Religious leaders enjoy greater popular trust than other institutions in Angola, Afrobarometer survey shows," *Afrobarometer*, 25 June 2020, https://www.afrobarometer.org/articles/religious-leaders-enjoy-greater-popular-trust-other-institutions-angola/, accessed 15 October 2022.

③ Ricardo Soares de Oliveira and Susan Taponier, "'O Governo Está Aqui': post-war state making in the Angolan Peiphery," p. 171.

④ Nuno Vidal, "The Angolan Regime and the Move to Multiparty Politics," in Patrick Chabal and Nuno Vidal (eds.), *Angola The Weight of History*, New York: Columbia University Press, 2008, pp. 1-14.

体制变革的抵制也不会这么强。

二、危机接踵而来：石油依赖与制度变革的关系

1957 年，标准石油公司和海湾石油公司从葡萄牙殖民者那里取得了独家开采权，拉开了安哥拉石油工业的序幕。[1] 20 世纪 60 年代末，原油超过咖啡成为最有价值的出口产品，并在内战期间一直领先。由于安哥拉的原油储备位于罗安达、卡宾达和扎伊尔等西北部省份易于保护的近海飞地，在内战期间成为安人运的主要收入来源。[2] 1976 年，通过将葡萄牙石油公司（ANGOL）国有化，安哥拉组建了国有石油公司安哥拉国家石油公司（Sonangol），远离了国内的政治斗争，Sonangol 变成了国家体系中飞地一般出色的官僚机构。通过与前任葡萄牙管理层签订的谅解备忘录，公司保留了大部分欧洲雇员。一名在国有化之后留任的员工如此说道："你看，从殖民统治到外国入侵，再到马列主义，又到资本主义，我一直都在这栋楼里工作。"[3]

21 世纪的头十年里，油价从 32 美元 / 桶飙升至 187 美元 / 桶，安哥拉原油产量也如火箭般飞升。2008 年，安哥拉超越尼日利亚成为撒哈拉以南非洲最大的石油出口国。2007 年，安哥拉成为石油输出国组织（OPEC）成员。高利润率吸引了 87% 的外国投资直接涌入安哥拉的石油天然气产业，[4] 无论是公共的还是私有的基础设施投资都向沿海地区倾斜，而忽视了内陆地区。最终的结果是，采掘业与国际市场接轨，但与大多数人口从事的其他维生经济活动脱节，殖民统治最后几十年崭露头角的多元化农业和新兴制造业让位于这种典型的二元制经济。

石油主导型经济与安哥拉体制变革动力的关系在于，石油收入全部处于总统的控制之下。通过把持 Sonangol 的财务，总统内阁成员可以绕

---

[1]　Jorge Cacuto, "Angola Pós-Independente: Implicações Econômicas da Herança Colonial," *Economia e Pesquisa*, v.3, no.3, 2001, pp. 22-39.

[2]　Eduardo Haddad et al., "Uneven Integration: the case of Angola. Research Paper," RP-20/02, Riad: Policy Center for the New South, 2020.

[3]　Ricardo de Oliveira, *Magnificent and Beggar Land*, London: Oxford University Press, 2015, p. 46.

[4]　Eduardo Haddad et al., "Uneven Integration: the case of Angola," 2020.

开国际审计，在国家预算外开展活动。这意味着最高行政机构拥有一个充裕且可自由支配的资金来源作为国内外政治博弈的筹码。一方面，由于石油租金是令个人致富的主要手段，通过这种利益分配可以拉拢盟友或惩罚异己。以总统为中心的庇护网络使权力寻租行为变得正常化，成为重塑精英阶层和排斥普通民众的主要形式。[1]另一方面，石油收入为国家提供的财政资源，使安哥拉能够与前来开采石油的跨国公司讨价还价，并有底气拒绝国际组织的改革要求。换句话说，与其他发展中国家相比，安哥拉的石油储备使其在全球经济中拥有更大的政策空间。

在安哥拉的制度安排中，石油收入的集中为集权政治模式的韧性创造了坚实的物质基础。2019 年，Sonangol 的营业收入相当于安哥拉 GDP 的 25%，总资产相当于 GDP 的 40%。[2]社会大部分群体仍生活在多维贫困之下，并饱受数十年战争的折磨，国家精英们则沉溺于炫耀性的奢侈品消费，而无意进行负责或切实的体制改革。此外，由于石油产业的控制权是确保国内和国际层面政治权力的关键，失去行政管理等同于丧失对庇护网络的控制权。因此，石油的经济中心地位"将政治博弈的赌注下得相当之高——赢家通吃全盘"[3]。

因此，类似于大宗商品价格对拉丁美洲政治周期的作用，安哥拉的体制变革模式也和国际油价浮动相关。流入 Sonangol 账户的石油收入与执政党需要接受的去集权化国家体系和多党竞争体制的完善程度形成反比关系。

例如，安哥拉的石油经济得益于 1979 年的第二次石油危机。国际油价的上涨使西方跨国石油公司投身到新区块的勘探中来，其中包括美国雪佛龙公司（American Chevron）——尽管美国政府正在试图推翻安人运的政权。与此同时，虽然多数人口的生存还需依靠国际援助，但外国人和高级公务员可以出入专营进口奢侈商品的商店。有利的外部环境使安

---

① Nuno Vidal, "The Angolan Regime and the Move to Multiparty Politics," 2008.

② World Bank, *Creating Markets in Angola. Opportunities for Development Through the Private Sector*, Washington: International Finance Corporation, 2019.

③ Patrick Chabal, "*E Pluribus Unum*: Transition in Angola," in Patrick Chabal and Nuno Vidal (eds.), *Angola The Weight of History*, New York: Columbia University Press, 2008, pp. 1-14.

人运得以招募扩张并在城市范围内扩大支持基础。南非在 1981 年发动对安哥拉南部省份的入侵，反过来诱发了新一轮围绕多斯桑托斯总统个人的集权化。[①]

1982 年，油价上升趋势逆转导致政府收入下降、外债增加，安人运中央委员会批准通过了《全面紧急计划》（Plano Global de Emergência），将预算集中投入到国防部门。然而，1986 年油价的再次下探令安哥拉外债大幅飙升，国际市场停止向安哥拉提供融资。此时，政府开始与 IMF 建立联系，试图通过《经济和金融复苏计划》（Programa de Saneamento Econômico e Financeiro）施行政府管控的私有化和谨慎的市场化改革。但 IMF 要求的核心措施——宽扎贬值，一直到 1992 年才得以实施，当时苏联解体使安哥拉面临的外部环境进一步恶化。1991 年，在华盛顿和国际金融机构的压力下，安人运同意签署《比塞斯协定》，该协定要求 1992 年 9 月前实现大选。

1992 年，由于争取安哥拉彻底独立全国同盟（UNITA，以下简称安盟）不认可大选结果，政治和经济自由化的政策被迫转向。内战自此进入白热化阶段，直至 2022 年安盟领袖若纳斯·萨文比被击毙后内战才得以结束。此后，油价再次进入上升通道，伴以军事上的胜利，安人运自信无须重新执行 1994 年签订的《卢萨卡议定书》。2004 年的立法选举被推迟至 2008 年。接下来，因 2010 年《宪法》规定总统由赢得议会多数席位的政党领袖担任，总统大选由 2009 年推迟至 2012 年。

随着石油收入的再次增加，安人运在全国范围重新制定了成员招募政策，将触手伸及安盟的票仓，如比耶、万博和威拉等省份，并将传统权威纳入到自身的势力范围中来。[②]因此，2012 年，安人运面对大选准备充分，已将败选风险降到最低，最终获得了 71% 的选票，确保了国民议会中 175 名代表的绝对多数席位和多斯桑托斯连任总统的地位。

---

① Nuno Vidal, "The Angolan Regime and the Move to Multiparty Politics," 2008.
② 同上。

三、危机驱动：基层自治制度化的新动力

战后的繁荣期结束于油价上升趋势的急转直下。2014—2020 年，布伦特原油报价从 100 美元 / 桶跌到 21 美元 / 桶，安哥拉政府的财政收入相较同期降低了 40% 以上。[①] 安人运被迫再次采取紧缩的措施，以维持金融市场的信心。在 IMF 的指导下，安政府开启了宏观经济稳定计划（MPS）和私有化改革计划（PROPRIV）。政府将举借贷款作为短期调控财政赤字的举措，这导致 2015—2020 年宽扎贬值了 38.9%，政府负债率从 83% 上升至 131%。汇率贬值降低了进口能力，造成粮食短缺和生活成本增加。[②] 2019 年，全国总体失业率达到了 32%，青年失业率高达 56.5%，70% 的公司关门停业，约有 1.1 万家公司彻底倒闭。[③]

因此，当若昂·洛伦索将军在 2017 年竞选总统时，国际环境已经使安哥拉的结构性矛盾越来越难以为继。除了经济危机外，国内外媒体大范围揭露了多斯桑托斯时期的高层人士腐败丑闻，使庇护系统被公之于众。安人运出现了严重的声誉危机，大城市中民众开始发起抗议。[④] 人们普遍认为，安哥拉黄金时代的财富都被揽到了私人腰包里，导致国家没有用于公共服务和经济发展。

与 20 世纪 80 年代末期的危机不同，此前十年政治自由化的影响增加了安人运的败选风险。随着反对的声音越来越强，洛伦索在竞选中承诺将打击腐败，并将基层自治的制度化作为主要议程。在投票前夕的动员会上，洛伦索要求安人运鼓起勇气落实权力下放改革。据他所说，政府将与基层自治组织共同帮助"居民们足不出县即可享受市政服务、解

---

① República de Angola, *Plano de Desenvolvimento Nacional 2018-2022 v.*1, Luanda: Governo de Angola, 2018.

② Zahabia Gupta, *Angola: Deep Dive into Dept*, Sydney: Standard & Poor's Financial Services, 2022.

③ INE, *Indicadores de Emprego e Desemprego. Inquérito ao Emprego em Angola*, Luanda: Instituto Nacional de Estatística, 2019.

④ Zefanias Matsimbe and Nelson Domingos, "Angola's 2017 Elections and the Start of a Post-Dos Santos Era," *Journal of African Elections*, v.17, no.1, 2018, pp. 1-24.

决日常难题"①。即便如此，与 2012 年的选举相比，安人运的支持率还是下降了 10%，尽管仍在国民议会中获得多数席位，但这是安人运失去社会支持的明显信号。②

迫于公众舆论压力，且出于瓦解支持多斯桑托斯总统的庇护关系的需要，洛伦索迅速采取行动，安插效忠于他的干部取代多斯桑托斯派系官员，③同时大力推进反腐工作，从而巩固了自身权力。2018 年，洛伦索颁布了《2018—2022 年预防和打击腐败战略计划》，根据该计划精神，安哥拉通过了多项反腐法案和反洗钱法案。④ 2017—2021 年期间，新的立法指导了 1500 多起腐败案件的开庭，追回赃款超过 53 亿美元。其中包括最著名的两个案件：一是针对多斯桑托斯的儿子若泽·菲洛梅诺·多斯桑托斯的诉讼，他因从安哥拉主权基金挪用 5 亿美元而被判处 5 年监禁；二是针对多斯桑托斯的女儿、Sonangol 前董事长伊莎贝尔·多斯桑托斯的诉讼，她有超过 10 亿美元的资产被冻结。

洛伦索的反腐运动难以立即解决安哥拉治理模式的顽疾。事实上，2020 年民调显示 54% 的安哥拉人认为政府在反腐方面的表现不佳，39% 的人认为反腐是对付安人运内部反对派的政治工具。⑤但从中长期来看，通过为检察官赋权并承认庇护系统的普遍存在，洛伦索政府为推进建设透明且负责的政府贡献了一份力量。

另一方面，基层自治改革较预期进展缓慢。2018 年，国土管理与国家改革部部长亚当·德阿尔梅达宣布将在 2020 年前举行基层选举，但

① Confina Media, "Angola/Eleições: João Lourenço pede 'coragem' ao MPLA para implementar autarquias," *Cofina Media*, 19 August 2017, https://www.cmjornal.pt/cm-ao-minuto/detalhe/angolaeleicoes-joao-lourenco-pede-coragem-ao-mpla-para implementar-autarquias?v=cb, accessed 29 October 2022.

② CNE, "Eleições – 2017," *Comissão Nacional Eleitoral de Angola*, 6 September 2017, https://www.cne.ao/elei%C3%A7%C3%B5es/2017, accessed 30 October 2022.

③ Benjamin Augé, *Angola under Joao Lourenço: Who Are the New Players of MPLA State?* Paris: Policy Center for the New South, 2019.

④ Republica de Angola, "Plano Estratégico de Prevenção e Combate à Corrupção 2018-2022," *Procuradoria Geral da República*. 2017, https://dnpcc.pgr.ao/wp-content/uploads/2022/05/Plano-Estrategico.pdf, accessed 28 October 2022.

⑤ Carlos Pacatolo and David Boio, "Apesar dos ganhos, os angolanos mostram-se insatisfeitos com os esforços do governo no combate à corrupção," A*frobarometer*. no.396, 9 October 2020.

被执政党与反对党在《基层自治制度化法案》上的僵持对峙拖延了进度。安人运主张采用地理渐进式改革，而安盟和其他反对党则支持进行功能渐进式改革。前者意味着该进程将先在个别地区开启作为试点，为以后的全国实行提供指导。后者则是将权限分阶段从省政府转移到基层机构。就在国民议会为此辩论不休时，新冠肺炎疫情蔓延开来。突发公共卫生事件促使政府毫不犹豫地推迟该议程，断绝了 2022 年实现基层治理机构选举的希望，并引起了反对党和民间社会活动家的抗议。

2022 年，洛伦索参选第二任期时，重申了建立基层自治的意愿。在北隆达省会邓多市的一次集会中，总统强调："我们必须建立市级基层自治制度……我们比所有人都清楚权力需要下放给公民。"但洛伦索仅以 51.17% 比 43.95% 的得票率击败了安盟领袖阿达尔贝托·科斯塔·儒尼奥尔比，这是有史以来最微弱的优势。该结果导致安人运在议会中的核心成员减少 26 人，安盟的核心成员增加 39 人。此外，安盟在最大选区罗安达省的大获全胜，以及安哥拉有史以来最低的投票率（仅 44% 的选民参与投票），都清楚地表明安人运的统治正遭到前所未有的挑战。[①]

激烈的竞选结束后，安政府宣布成立一个部际委员会，以推进基层自治制度化改革，并建立 35 个市政议会设施。在议会中，安人运将基层自治委员会主席职位授予安盟，这一姿态被解读为未来可能达成协议的表现。即便如此，仍有反对党指责安人运是在故意拖延审议。这种看法在 11 月被佐证，安人运议员鲁伊·法尔考确认表示基层政权的选举不会在 2023 年举行，而将在"2024 年解决立法层面的问题后"[②]。

总体而言，安哥拉独立后的体制变革动力主要来自执政党在油价下跌时面临的威胁增加，而不是以克服殖民时期遗留的二元社会经济结构

---

① CNE, "Edital referente às Eleições Gerais do dia 24 de Agosto de 2022," *Comissão Nacional Eleitoral*, 22 August 2022, https://www.cne.ao/storage/arquivos/EDITAL%20dos%20 resultados%20definitvos%20do%20Apuramento%20Nacional,%20referente%20%C3%A0s%20 Elei%C3%A7%C3%B5es%20Gerais%20do%20dia%2024%20de%20Agosto%20de%202022.pdf, accessed 3 November 2022.

② DW, "Angola: 'Não queremos acreditar que o PR tenha medo do poder local'," *DW*, 18 October 2022, https://www.dw.com/pt-002/angola-n%C3%A3o-queremos-acreditar-que-o-pr-tenha-medo-do-poder-local/a-63469269, accessed 5 November 2022.

这一战略目标所推动。在繁荣时期，沿海城市地区的石油收入富足，通过与内陆的传统权威合作，即使大多数人口的生活条件无法得到实质性改善，也能维持政权的合法性。然而，当受到新冠肺炎疫情等外部冲击时，安哥拉增长模式的矛盾开始显现，安哥拉人民被迫面对极度严重的经济和社会危机。在这种情况下，体制改革往往会由谨小慎微转为阔步前进，只有油价回升后改革才会被再次推迟。

尽管基层自治制度化不应被当作万能良药，但越来越多的文献表明，在非洲的社会情况下，精心设计的权力下放改革对提供公共服务、提高农业生产力和经济多元化具有积极作用。这些制度化改革正成为维持政权的当务之急，正如 2022 年大选结果所示，安人运由于没能降低安哥拉面对外部冲击的脆弱性，而扩大了安盟的投票基础。2023 年，俄乌冲突将使油价保持高位，但安人运在大选中的不力表现是否还足以让若昂·洛伦索政府继续推进竞选时受到民众盛赞的权力下放改革将成为疑问。

四、安哥拉社会经济结构的二元性

1975 年 11 月 11 日，阿戈什蒂纽·内图发表了一番精彩演讲宣告安哥拉的独立。除了称赞安哥拉人民在反殖民斗争中的勇气，内图还强调了这个新生国家面临的两大挑战。其一，从"安哥拉人民生活在水深火热中的景象"可以看出他深知安哥拉仍是一个落后国家；其二，内图认为安哥拉是一个依附于帝国主义的卫星国家。据他表示，这两个特质间的相互作用产生了安哥拉社会经济结构的二元性。也就是说，国民经济如此"严重地扭曲"，原因在于"发达地区和落后地区的发展水平两极分化"，以及被"不公平的社会关系"所推动。[①]

内图的演讲发表近 40 年后，社会经济二元性问题依然严重困扰着安哥拉。一方面，资本密集型的石油产业成为国民经济运行中的一块

---

① Agostinho Neto, "Discurso de Proclamação da Independência de Angola," *Nova Cultura*, 11 November 2021, https://www.novacultura.info/post/2021/11/11/discurso-de-agostinho-neto-na-proclamacao-da-independencia-de-angola, accessed 25 October 2022.

独立领地。2020 年，虽然石油产业占 GDP 的 33%，但只能解决 1.94% 的劳动就业，非石油经济则仅占 GDP 的 4%。[①]另一方面，石油产业几乎不与其他经济存在任何前向关联（forward linkages）或后向关联（backward linkages）。即使在石油超级周期里，安哥拉因自身缺乏炼化能力，80% 的石油衍生品仍需进口。例如，2019 年国家外汇锐减时，这种进口依赖造成了 2 个星期的燃料短缺。

作为非洲第二大原油出口国的同时，安哥拉还是全球第四大钻石生产国，2021 年钻石产量为 930 万克拉。石油产业和钻石产业相结合，构成了维持安哥拉资产阶级进行进口奢侈品炫耀性消费的物质基础。通过国内庇护网络与跨国财富管理公司、避税天堂、企业服务供应商、咨询和会计事务所的相互作用，安哥拉的精英们可以将利润轻松转移到国外，而不会在国内用于投资再生产活动。通过参与国际资本的循环，当前安哥拉的上流社会在文化和意识形态上与其他人民的关系变得更加疏远，就像殖民时代的同化者一样。[②]

与之形成鲜明对比的是，大部分人口从事劳动密集型的自给农业产业和非正规活动。自给农业吸纳了 45% 的劳动力，占 GDP 的 9.4%。主要作物是木薯、玉米、豆类、土豆、红薯、大豆、香蕉、咖啡和水稻，原始落后的小型家庭农场占据了农耕用地的 92%。同时，农村地区电网覆盖有限，无法支撑起农业加工和灌溉农业。因此，农业产出无法满足国家需求，安哥拉 50% 以上的粮食和农业产品不得不依靠进口。

2016 年，农村地区多维贫困指数高达 87.8%，大部分人口无法获取充分的烹饪燃料、电力、净水和公共卫生设施。[③]乌克兰战争爆发后，对外部市场的依赖导致肥料短缺，食品通胀率飙升至两位数，粮食危机加剧。[④]更糟糕的是，气候变化已对安哥拉的农业产生影响。该国正面临 40 年来最严重的干旱，这可能导致畜牧业和渔业部门损失约 7.49 亿

---

① CEDESA, "Um projeto de industrialização para Angola," 23 December 2020, *CEDESA*, https://www.cedesa.pt/2020/12/23/um-projeto-de-industrializacao-para-angola/, accessed 6 November 2022.

② World Bank, *Angola-Agriculture Support Policy Review*.

③ INE, *Pobreza Multidimensional em Angola*, Luanda: Instituto Nacional de Estatística, 2020.

④ WFP, *Implications of the Ukraine Crisis: food, fuel, fertilisers prices in the southern Africa region*, Johannesburg: World Food Programme, 2022.

美元。[1]

今天安哥拉的农村地区已不可同往日而语。殖民经济时代末期，安哥拉肥沃的土壤、丰富的淡水资源（安哥拉有 77 个河流流域和 43 个水文盆地）和有利的气候条件造就了高产的农村经济，该国实现了对咖啡、木薯、水果和玉米等作物的自给自足。然而，27 年的内战摧毁了连接生产区和市场的大部分基础设施，乡间遍布地雷和遗留炮弹，大量农村人口外流。自从实现和平以来，由于政府的投资政策和公共政策，谷物、豆类和禽类等农产品的产量有了大幅提升。但安哥拉的农业潜力在很大程度上尚未得到开发，45.7% 的可耕地面积中（几乎相当于法国的面积），目前只有 7% 的土地被耕种。[2]

同时，安哥拉的非正规经济约占国内生产总值的 39%，对 75% 的安哥拉人来说是必不可少的。从擦鞋匠、商贩、家庭服务到运输和黑市换汇，包括各种活动。顶篮女贩（Zungueiras）是安哥拉非正规经济的特色之一，这些妇女们把巨大的篮子顶在头上的，整日走街串巷出售各种货物。[3] 面对失业率上升问题，劳动者们尝试通过非正规经济补充收入来源，但无法受到社会保护，不仅缺乏启动资金，还常常需要经历长途跋涉。

相对而言，在 2018 年，安哥拉的非正规就业者占总就业人数的 94.1%，高于南部非洲共同体（77%）和撒哈拉以南非洲（89.2%）的平均水平，高于喀麦隆（90.9%）、乍得（94%）和刚果（85.3%）等国家。农业的非正规就业率（99.4%）高于服务业（90.2%）和工业（85.1%）。[4]

罗安达作为安哥拉最大的都市圈，同时汇集了高收益的石油工业服

---

[1]　Izabela Leao, "Angola's agricultural sector could become Africa's powerhouse. Here's why," *World Bank*, 13 September 2022, https://www.weforum.org/agenda/2022/09/angola-agricultural-sector-powerhouse-of-africa/#:~:text=However%2C%20Angola%20may%20soon%20be,a%20variety%20of%20agricultural%20products, accessed 10 November 2022.

[2]　World Bank, *Angola. Agriculture Support Policy Review*.

[3]　The Portuguese word *Zungueira* derives from the Kimbundo word *zunga*, which means surround, walk around, or circulate.

[4]　ILO, *Angola: Study on the migration from the informal economy for formal economy*, Geneva: International Labour Organisation, 2021.

务产业和最多的非正规劳动者，56% 的人口（约 400 万）[1] 从事非正规经济活动。路易卡基奥·阿方索指出，罗安达的二元结构被转化为不同生活水平的城市核心区（Baixa da Cidade）、半边缘区（过渡区）和边缘区在社会空间结构上的不平等。城市核心区聚集了 31% 的人口，包括英贡博塔、马扬加和桑比赞加等街区，不仅是中央政府、国家和跨国公司办公驻所的所在地，也是大多数学校和医院的所在地。[2]

边缘区包括在卡森加、卡库阿科和维亚纳等周边城市，50% 的人口居住于此，主要居住在基础设施薄弱、治安混乱的贫民窟（musseques）和大型露天违建市场中。[3] 过渡区包括塔拉托纳、贝拉斯和基兰巴基亚西等城市，拥有 15.5% 的人口，现代经济区和豪华住宅与穷困遍布的贫民窟并存。由于连接这三个地区的基础设施和交通服务稀少且分散，边缘区居民不得不长时间乘坐危险的无证交通工具（candongueiros），在交通堵塞中往返于核心区工作。

同时，省际空间上的不对称性也很突出。人口仅占 32% 的罗安达、卡宾达和扎伊尔等产油省贡献了 GDP 的 66.7%，而拥有 68% 人口的其他 15 个省份只贡献了约 33% 的 GDP。沿海地区和内陆地区之间缺乏基础设施相连制约了经济一体化发展，并进一步加剧了区域分化。截至 2020 年，安哥拉是南部非洲公路网总里程最低的国家之一，大部分公路缺乏修缮。墨西哥、埃及和哥伦比亚等许多发展中国家区域间贸易额高于国际贸易额，而安哥拉的国际贸易额与 GDP 的比例高达 94%，区域间贸易额仅 29%。[4]

基础设施不足和基本服务匮乏解释了为何普及小学教育仍然是一个遥远的梦想，为何中学和大学教育是少数人的特权。根据最新人口福利综合调查结果，2009 年，29% 的安哥拉儿童必须步行 2 公里以上才能

---

[1] Luís Morais, *O Mercado Informal em Luanda*, Dissertação, Lisboa: Universidade de Lisboa 2019.

[2] Luiekakio Afons, "Uma leitura da urbanização recente da cidade de Luanda partir da teoria dos dois circuitos da economia urbana," *PerCursos*, v. 23, no.51, 2022, pp. 167-210.

[3] The Portuguese word *musseque* also derives from the Kimbundo word – *mu seke* -, which means red sand, as were the color of the materials used in the first occupations in Luanda's suburbs.

[4] Eduardo Haddad et al., "Uneven Integration: the case of Angola."

上学，26% 的 6—9 岁儿童从未上过学，中高等教育分别仅惠及 27% 和 9% 的人口，文盲比例达到 34%。[①] 尽管到 2020 年情况有所改善，但仍有 130 万儿童无法入学，18 岁及以上的群体中有 48% 的人没有完成过任何阶段的教育。[②]

关于高等教育，虽然 2002—2018 年期间学生总数增长了 250 万，达到 1000 万，全国 72% 和 6.9% 的大学新生来自罗安达和本格拉。此外，大多数大学饱受设施不足、资金有限和缺乏结构化教师岗位等问题的困扰。在新冠肺炎疫情期间，鸿沟愈加凸显，比如只有不到 36% 的安哥拉人能用上互联网，只有 4% 的人用得起每月 1GB 的流量包。[③]

安哥拉教育系统的状况反映出该部门在国家预算中的低优先级，2021 年国家预算仅将 GDP 的 2.4% 用于教育，而纳米比亚为 9.6%，南非为 6.2%，乍得为 2.9%。社会救济和卫生系统也同样是这种情况。2020 年，政府分配给社会救济的资金不到 GDP 的 0.1%，[④] 而卫生支出（占 GDP 的 2.53%）仍然远远低于乍得（4.35%）、纳米比亚（8.5%）和南非（9.11%）在 2019 年的水平。因此，安哥拉百姓易受到疟疾、霍乱、黄热病和寨卡等疾病暴发的影响，儿童和产妇死亡率较高。

上述指标说明，安哥拉当下的二元社会经济结构，是殖民时期开始的不对民众负责的国家的历史再现。分化问题极为突出，最富有的 1% 集中了国民收入的 58%，而最底层的 50% 人口只拥有 9% 的财富。[⑤] 长期以来的贫富差距问题使该国在大多数全球排名中处于末位。例如，2020

① INE, *Inquérito Integrado sobre o Bem-Estar da População*, Luanda: Instituto Nacional de Estatística, 2011.

② Onélio Santiago, "Mais de 30 por cento das crianças fora do sistema formal de ensino," *Novo Jornal*, 2021, https://novojornal.co.ao/sociedade/interior/mais-de-30-das-criancas-em-idade-escolar-fora-do-sistema-formal-de-ensino---estatisticas-de-julho-falam-em-quase-2-milhoes-105413.html, accessed 10 November 2022.

③ AUC/OECD, *Dinâmicas do Desenvolvimento em África* 2021. *Transformação Digital e Empregos de Qualidade*, Addis Ababa: AUC/OECD Publishing, 2021.

④ World Bank, *Angola Poverty Assessment*.

⑤ WID, *Angola*, World Inequality Database, November 2022, https://wid.world/country/angola/, accessed 10 November 2022.

年全球优质基础设施指数中，安哥拉在 182 个国家中排名第 128 位；[①]
2022 年世界知识产权组织的全球创新指数中，安哥拉在 132 个国家中排
名第 132 位；[②] 2022 年《经济学人》的全球粮食不安全指数中，安哥拉在
113 个国家中排名第 101 位。[③]

　　安哥拉的落后状况和其自然资源禀赋形成的强烈反差，说明阿戈什
蒂纽·内图在 1975 年所强调的问题切实存在。最大的体制困境是如何
引导石油和钻石收入投入到发展目标。在这方面，通过提高国家"区分
各地具有经济潜在比较优势的宏观战略"的能力，基层自治制度化可能
发挥积极作用，同时为改善基础设施和人力资本提供条件。[④]

　　随着安哥拉正式加入南部非洲发展共同体自由贸易区（SADC）和
非洲大陆自由贸易区（ACFTA），市场扩张和进口成本降低的机会或可
有益于提高工业和农业生产力。最后一提，安哥拉完全可以从能源绿色
转型中获利。该国拥有非洲第二大的水力发电装机容量（目前仅 5% 的
潜力得到了开发）；同时拥有高强度且稳定的太阳能资源、西南地区的
风力走廊以及丰富的绿色氢气开发前景。[⑤]

五、若昂·洛伦索时期安哥拉的发展探索

　　在持续经济危机的压力下，若昂·洛伦索政府于 2018 年 1 月 1 日
颁布了《国家发展计划（2018—2022）》。作为中期规划工具，该规划本
应与 2007 年颁布的《安哥拉 2025 年长期战略发展规划》（以下简称《安

---

① Juan Oteiza, "Global Quality Infrastructure Index 2020," *Tableau Software*, 2021, https://public.
tableau.com/app/profile/juan.jos.oteiza/viz/GQII2020_public/MAP, accessed 13 November 2022.

② WIPO, *Global Innovation Index* 2021 *Tracking Innovation through the COVID-19 Crisis*,
Geneva: World International Property Organization, 2021.

③ The Economist Newspaper, "The Global Food Security Index 2022," *Economist Impact*, 2022,
https://impact.economist.com/sustainability/project/food-security-index/, accessed 9 November 2021.

④ Justin Lin and Célestin Monga, *Beating the Odds. Jump-Starting Developing Countries*,
London: Princeton University Press, 2017, p. 4.

⑤ Energy Capital & Power, "Identifying Opportunities in Angola's Renewable Energy Sector,"
Energy Capital & Power, 21 July 2022, https://energycapitalpower.com/angola-opportunities-renewable-
energy/, accessed 1 November 2022.

哥拉2025》）相一致，但考虑到《安哥拉2025》的愿景是在乐观的石油繁荣周期制定的，《国家发展计划（2018—2022）》不得不针对该预期做出调整。例如，虽然《安哥拉2025》设想在2025年实现10%的相对贫困率，但《国家发展计划（2018—2022）》在2022年将该目标修订为25%。2007年制订的规划预期在2025年前的生产力年均增长率为4.1%，而《国家发展计划（2018—2022）》则预期在2022年降至2.8%。《安哥拉2025》预计2022年全国水资源的覆盖率为95%，但《国家发展计划（2018—2022）》则预期水资源的覆盖率从2017年的60%，至2022年仅上升到85%。

《国家发展计划（2018—2022）》作为宏观框架，包括五个中心、二十五项战略政策和八十三项行动计划。更具体地来说，正如20世纪80年代的《经济和金融复苏计划》（Programa de Saneamento Econômico e Financeiro）是向IMF发出一封意向信，《国家发展计划（2018—2022）》采取了整体紧缩的目标以迎合国际金融机构。例如，规划安哥拉政府将"逐步成为经济的监管者、促进者和协调者，逐步减少自身对经济的参与"。此外，还规划通过大规模的私有化计划重整企业体系，该计划侧重于促进国家私营部门发展和提高外国投资吸引力。换言之，面对石油收入下降和外债上升的压力，该计划采用新自由主义范式指导改善商业环境和竞争力。

《国家发展计划（2018—2022）》的战略方针分为两个核心计划：宏观经济稳定计划（MSP）和支持国家生产、出口多样化和进口替代计划（PRODESI）。在安哥拉财政部于2018年提出申请后，IMF提供了政策合作工具（PCI）支持MSP，该工具旨在减少国家主导的经济破坏，以维持宏观经济稳定，以及排挤私人投资。

汇率高估是安哥拉经济的主要畸形现象之一，这虽有利于刺激进口，但削弱了出口竞争力，并导致货币黑市的出现。因此，安哥拉中央银行（Banco Nacional de Angola, BNA）于2018年1月取消固定汇率制度，并通过外汇拍卖的方式逐步向浮动汇率制过渡。财政整顿是MSP提出的另一项政策，通过压缩初级财政支出、出让国有资产、取消补贴、加收增值税（VAT）扩大非石油收入以及批准《财政问责法案》等落实。

最后，MPS 将债务与 GDP 的比率从 2018 年的 90% 降至 2023 年的 65% 作为财政整顿工作的目标。[①]

这项财政紧缩的议程在议会中得到了支持。在接下来的几个月里，国民议会通过了一批支持市场化的立法。《安哥拉竞争法案》首先于 2018 年 4 月通过，该法案由新成立的竞争监管局（CRA）负责执行。受欧盟和葡萄牙竞争法案的启发，安哥拉的法律框架对反竞争行为、控股合并程序和国家兜底制度都予以明令禁止。

而后，国民议会于 2018 年 6 月批准了《私人投资法案》。新法案对外国投资取消了最低投资额限制，不再要求必须有安哥拉公民或公司参加，同时新建 2 个开发区、列出 9 个具有特定利益的优先部门，并建立投资和出口促进局（AIPEX）。3 年后，安哥拉修订了《私人投资法案》，以进一步促进私人投资。修订后将允许政府和投资者协商建立合同承包制关系，放宽临时经营许可的发放和向国外转移利润的法律限制，不再要求境外投资者必须使用安哥拉国内信贷。

最后是通过《私有化法案》[②] 并在 2019 年制订《私有化计划》（PROPRIV 2019—2022）。在新成立的国有资产管理局（IGAPE）的监督下，PROPRIV[③] 计划将 195 项国有资产转让给私营部门，包括 Sonangol 公司所有与核心业务无关的资产。

MSP 是一项财政调整政策，而 PRODESI 则是洛伦索政府提高安哥拉私营部门经济多元化能力的供给端战略。该计划旨在提高出口产品的附加值，促进进口替代，以降低对外部的依赖性。尽管以上种种，该计划没有任何明显的优先事项，因为其涵盖范围十分广泛，包括食品和农业、矿产资源、石油天然气、森林、纺织、土木工程、信息和电信技术、

[①] UNCTAD, *Economic and Social Impact of Covid-19 in Angola*, Washington: United Nations Conference on Trade and Development, 2022.

[②] Diário da República, Lei de Bases das Privatizações, *Assembleia Nacional*, 14 May 2019, https://www.ucm.minfin.gov.ao/cs/groups/public/documents/document/aw4x/mtcx/~edisp/minfin1171445.pdf, accessed 3 November 2022.

[③] Governo de Angola, Angola's Privatization Program 2019-2022, *PROPRIV*, 2019, https://www.bodiva.ao/media/propriv/20190818%20Privatization%20Program%20(EN).pdf, accessed 4 November 2022.

卫生、教育、科技、旅游和休闲。^① 但 PRODESI 的目标十分大胆，设想在 2022 年将安哥拉食品进口的外汇支出减少 15%，^② 非石油部门的外国直接投资增加 60%，安哥拉的营商环境指数排名提升 15 位。

PRODESI 计划拥有专门的配套资金方案。信贷支持计划（PAC）是一项由 20 多家国有商业银行和私人商业银行共同参与实施的融资机制。数字平台"国家生产者门户网站"（Portal do Produtor Nacional）已经建立，用以优化登记和信贷审批。还有一些其他监管措施，诸如将营业执照的办理时间从 36 天缩短到 24 小时，通过《破产和企业恢复法》，公司税减少 5%，土地登记证费用减少 91%，以及扩建信贷风险信息中心等。^③ 截至 2022 年 1 月，PRODESI 已经为 1043 个项目提供了 8790 亿宽扎的资金，^④ 遍及安哥拉所有省份。

因此，与安哥拉以往的改革相比，《国家发展计划（2018—2022）》构建了一套更加综合且具约束力的措施。人们期望外国投资和私营部门利用宽松的监管环境和低息贷款资金引领经济结构转型的进程。考虑到安哥拉私营部门的薄弱和后发工业化对发展型国家的重要性，该战略的可靠性还有待商榷。尽管如此，结构性改革议程的承诺还是带来了明显的短期效益。例如，IMF 执行董事会于 2018 年 12 月批准向安哥拉提供 37 亿美元的中期贷款（相当于安哥拉 SDR 份额的 361%）。

六、新冠肺炎疫情下的安哥拉：国家动员和社会经济脆弱性

新冠肺炎疫情的暴发影响了改革进展。由于医疗体系脆弱，安哥拉当局必须迅速采取措施控制病毒的传播。2020 年 3 月 20 日，在安哥拉

---

① PRODESI, Sobre o PRODESI, *PRODESI*, 2022, https://prodesi.ao/sobre, accessed in 7 November 2021.

② Lusa, "Angola corta importação de produtos da cesta básica para metade," *Diário de Notícias*, 24 July 2018, https://www.dn.pt/lusa/angola-corta-importacao-de-produtos-da-cesta-basica-para-metade-9629050.html, accessed 23 October 2022.

③ República de Angola, *Plano de Desenvolvimento Nacional* 2018-2022, p. 158.

④ Ana Paula, "PRODESI garante financiamento de 897 mil milhões de kwanzas," *Jornal de Angola*, 26 January 2022, https://www.jornaldeangola.ao/ao/noticias/prodesi-garante-financiamento-de-879-mil-milhoes-de-kwanzas-2/, accessed 10 November 2022.

出现首两例新冠肺炎病例的前一天，政府就已关闭陆地边境、禁止外国船只停靠和乘客下岸、禁止所有商业航班和私人飞机入境。[①] 3月23日，政府宣布学校、大学、教堂、餐馆和公共事务有关活动暂停15天。3月27日零时，总统宣布国家进入紧急状态。从即刻起，所有私人商业场所和公共场所都被关闭，城际和省际公共交通服务减少一半，摩的禁止上路，卫生部门有权关停存在高传染性风险的市场，餐馆营业仅限外卖和送餐上门。[②]

这些封控措施产生了效果。病毒传播速度放缓，大多数确诊病例被控制了罗安达。由于行政权高度集中，与其他撒哈拉以南非洲国家相比，安哥拉的疫苗接种表现也十分优秀。政府对疫苗冷链设施予以大力投入，并与NGO合作促进疫苗接种和打击虚假信息。同时，安哥拉的外交官们从国际合作伙伴那里获取援助。因此，截至2022年11月，安哥拉已为22%的人口进行了全面的疫苗接种，达到了非洲平均水平，并超过纳米比亚、肯尼亚、冈比亚、吉布提和乍得等许多国家。[③] 用世界卫生组织驻安哥拉代表贾米拉·卡布拉尔的话说："安哥拉政府从一开始就对疫苗的推广做出了承诺和努力，堪称典范。人员配置和技能培训到位、冷链物流完善、配套法规保障，这些充分的准备工作只是安哥拉成为非洲首批接收疫苗的国家之一的部分原因。"[④]

然而从经济上看，油价下跌和封锁措施的叠加影响在2020年的后三个季度造成了8.22%的GDP损失，政府的石油收入与2019年相比减少了30%。在2019年7月至2020年9月期间，宽扎兑美元汇率贬值40%，抑制了安哥拉的进口能力，并将2021年通货膨胀率推高至27%。政府债务占GDP的比重上升到131%，惠誉、标准普尔和穆迪都降低了

[①] Daniel Muondo e Cirlene Oliveira, "The new government reforms in time of COVID-19 in Angola in the current political and social context and the confrontation of social inequalities," *Katálysis* no. 24, v.1, 2021, pp. 66-75.

[②] UNCTAD, *Economic and Social Impact of Covid-19 in Angola*.

[③] AU, "Africa CDC COVID-19 Vaccine Dashboard," *African Union*, 2022, https://africacdc.org/covid-19-vaccination/, accessed 13 November 2022.

[④] Collins Boakye-Agyemang, "Inside Angola's 'exemplary' COVID-19 vaccination hubs," *World Health Organization*, 2 July 2021, https://www.afro.who.int/pt/node/14831, accessed 10 November 2022.

对安长期评级。^①大量非正规就业者遭受的冲击也很严重，60% 的非正规市场经营者声称损失巨大，40% 的人被迫减少食品支出。^②

面对公共卫生突发事件对社会经济产生的影响，需要评估政府财政是否能维持经济发展并保护 MPS 财政整顿措施的成果。因此，2020 年7 月 28 日，国民议会通过了总统提议的国家预算修正案，^③将一般支出削减 15%，而教育、卫生和社会支出占比从预算的 15% 增至 17%，经济事务支出占比从 4% 增至 7%。^④节流措施包括向国外债权人申请债务减免，并暂停所有非结构性支出、举借新债、招录和提拔公职人员。同时，削减非必要的公务出差，将 28 个部委合并重组为 21 个，将 559 个领导和管理职位缩减为 313 个。^⑤

腾出财政空间后，经济计划部宣布了针对企业和家庭的《综合经济重振计划》（Alívio Econômico）。面向企业，该计划对进口人道主义物资和捐赠物品免征增值税和关税；对用于生产 54 种基本商品的进口货物和原材料予以 12 个月税收减免；对社会保障缴款实行免息延付；对银行部门提供流动性支持；扩大对进口商的信贷额度。面向家庭农场和中小微企业，支持农业发展基金（FADA）投放了 150 亿宽扎的信贷额度，以 3% 的利息提供资金；安哥拉开发银行（ADB）投放约 380 亿宽扎信贷额度，风险投资主动策略基金（FACRA）投放了 70 亿宽扎融资额度。面向家庭，经济计划部宣布将 3% 的社会保障缴款直接转移至工资中，水电无论是否欠费照常供应，并拨付 3.15 亿宽扎用于发放肥皂、牛肉、

① Zahabia Gupta, *Angola*: *Deep Dive into Dept*.

② UNCTAD, *Economic and Social Impact of Covid-19 in Angola*.

③ Governo de Angola, Ministério das Finanças. Assembleia Nacional aprova OGE Revisto referente ao exercício econômico de 2020. *Ministério das Finanças*, 28 July 2020, minfin.gov.ao/PortalMinfin/#!/sala-de-imprensa/noticias/7955/assembleia-nacional-aprova-oge-revisto-referente-ao-exercicio-economico-de-2020, accessed 4 November 2022.

④ UNCTAD, *Economic and Social Impact of Covid-19 in Angola*.

⑤ Vera Daves de Souza, *Intervenção da Ministra das Finanças para Anúncio das medidas de revisão do cenário macroeconómico fruto do COVID-19 e choque petrolífero*, Luanda: República de Angola, Ministério das Finanças, 2020.

牛奶、米、豆类、鱼、糖及玉米面粉等生活必需品。^①

此外，新冠肺炎疫情的冲击促使政府优化、加快和扩大社会政策的实施。2020 年 9 月，劳动和社会保障部部长对《就业能力促进行动计划》（PAPE）的要点进行了微调，该计划起初较少关注能力建设，更多地关注就业岗位创造。PAPE 的获准预算为 220 亿宽扎，该计划将实施职业培训、发放自主创业工具包、向小企业提供小额信贷融资渠道以及促进雇用培训人员等措施，以驱动安哥拉年轻人创业。截至 2021 年 12 月，PAPE 创造了约 30000 个直接就业岗位和 45000 个间接就业岗位。^②2021 年 11 月 17 日，安哥拉启动了非正式经济重振计划（PREI），旨在一年内实现 200000 个非正规劳动者注册。在欧盟的融资支持下，该目标得以轻易实现。截至 2022 年 8 月，该计划登记了 246189 个就业岗位。^③

PAPE 和 PREI 计划面向城市，而《国家社会保护系统增强计划》则面向最脆弱的农村群体。该计划的外号为 Kwenda，在金邦杜语（Kimbundu）中是"行走"的意思，世界银行提供了融资和运营支持，社会行动、家庭和妇女赋权部（MSAFME）负责监督。Kwenda 于 2020 年 5 月 4 日启动，重点是将妇女登记为政府向个人提供补贴的受益人，由基层社区工作者和社会行动中心负责实施。截至 2022 年 1 月，Kwenda 登记家庭数量 502000 户，并为 14 个省的近 25 万个家庭提供每季度 25000 宽扎的转移支付。^④同样，"儿童赋权"（Valor Criança）计划进入第二阶段。在 MSAFME 的主持下，由安哥拉国家银行、联合国儿童基金会（UNICEF）和欧盟支持，截至 2021 年 10 月，该计划已为比耶

---

① República de Angola, Ministério da Economia e Planejamento, *Medidas de Alívio do Impacto Provocado pela Pandemia COVID-19 sobre as Empresas e Particulares*, Luanda: Ministério da Economia e Planejamento, 2020.

② Tatiana Costa, "Em dois anos, PAPE criou mais de 30 mil postos de trabalho directos," *Ver Angola*, 7 December 2021, https://www.verangola.net/va/pt/122021/Economia/28486/Em-dois-anos-PAPE-criou-mais-de-30-mil-postos-de-trabalho-directos.htm, accessed 10 November 2022.

③ PREI, "Dados Estatísticos," *Governo de Angola*, 8 August 2022, https://prei.ao/formalizacao-operadores-informais/, accessed 3 November 2022.

④ World Bank, "Q&A: How is Angola Reaching the Poor and Vulnerable During Covid-19?" *The World Bank Group*, 15 March 2022, https://www.worldbank.org/en/country/angola/brief/q-a-how-is-angola-is-reaching-the-poor-and-vulnerable-during-covid-19, accessed 1 November 2022.

省、莫西科省和威热省的 10512 个家庭提供了转移支付。[①]

总体而言，安哥拉国家在抗击疫情方面调动了大量社会资源，针对各种社会弱势群体采取公共政策，但在油价下跌和疫情封控的叠加影响下，这都不足以化解安哥拉国家能力过度集中、非正规经济体量庞大、粮食依赖进口和基础设施薄弱的结构性矛盾。失业率持续上升、外国直接投资保持低迷，2020 年资本投资达到历史最低点。[②] 更糟糕的是，在 2021 年 10 月至 2022 年 3 月期间，在已经面临长期干旱影响的南部威拉省、库内内省和纳米贝省，有 158 万人遭遇到严重的粮食危机。表面看来，市场力量和国际援助显然既不足以缓解这场危机对安哥拉人民生活条件的短期影响，也不足以推动中长期发展进程。

结　论

本文分析了为什么内战后安哥拉经济和社会仍极易受到新冠肺炎疫情和俄乌冲突等外部冲击的影响。我们认为，安哥拉在国家建设历史进程中形成了一个由城市精英统治的不对民众负责的政府，缺少政治和经济上的激励措施推动他们将国家基础设施拓展到沿海产油地区之外。为了展现维持这种社会结构的机制，我们讨论了总统权力下的石油收入集中化，以及安人运与传统权威的实效联合如何使该政权一再推迟基层自治选举的落实。

在第二部分，我们描述了若泽·爱德华多·多斯桑托斯执政时期制度化的非负责制治理形式所产生的一些后果。经过定量和定性指标的统筹分析，我们提出安哥拉存在二元的社会经济结构，其中精英阶层通过渗透到国家机器的庇护网络与资本密集型的采掘业绑定。同时，大部分

---

① Governo de Angola, "Programa Valor Criança," *Portal Oficial do Governo da República de Angola*, 4 October 2021, https://governo.gov.ao/ao/noticias/programa-valor-crianca/#:~:text=Mais%20 13.656%20crianças%20menores%20de,do%20programa%20"Valor%20Criança", accessed 13 November 2022.

② The Global Economy, "Angola: Capital investment, percent of GDP," *The Global Economy.com*, August 2021, https://www.theglobaleconomy.com/Angola/capital_investment/, accessed 14 November 2022.

人口依靠自给农业和非正式活动维持生计。除了严重的社会分化之外，由于国内的生产者群体处于脱节状态，日益增长的劳动力多数无法获得教育机会，这种二元性有效地阻碍了安哥拉生产力发展。

鉴此，本文作者认为，由于安哥拉政治、经济和意识形态二元性具有历史深度和广度，单凭经济紧缩措施可能永远无法让该国走上正确的发展道路。尽管目前在稳定宏观经济、吸引外国投资和加强国家私营部门方面所做的努力值得称赞，但安哥拉迫切需要增强国家的能力，推动制订以实现快速工业化、振兴农业、缓解贫困、国内生产基础多元化、普及公共产品和服务为目标的发展规划。正如东亚国家的成功发展所展现的那样，如果发展型国家没有能够起到引领作用的国家战略规划，就不会发生结构转型。

必须着重强调的是，本文主要通过安哥拉国内制度解释原因，而忽略了全球经济结构产生的变量，这一点同样重要。例如，冷战视角下的安哥拉内战是增加冲突和破坏程度的主要动因。大国一面谴责安哥拉的系统性腐败，一面推动自己庇护下的跨国公司、金融机构和避税天堂与安哥拉积极合作，如果没有这些因素，安哥拉石油和钻石产业的掠夺性特征是无法存在的。因此，我们认为对国际机制的分析将有助于重现安哥拉落后性和依赖性，是深化本研究课题的重要路径。

最后，尽管阻碍重重，但安哥拉丰富的矿产资源、大量的可耕地、广阔的绿色能源前景和日益增长的劳动力都是国家发展战略中可以发挥效用的禀赋。因此，当前亟须继续推进如下研究课题：安哥拉如何利用其潜在比较优势实现经济快速增长、提高劳动生产率和工业多样化？尽管落实权力下放改革至关重要，但不应将其视为万灵丹，而应将其作为增强国家能力的工具，以更好应对地方问题、确定发展机遇和实行公共政策。如果缺乏对以上目标所需的基础设施和人力资本进行长期投资的政治意愿，基层自治或许还会被庇护主义行为围剿，从而无法挽回阿戈什蒂纽·内图所召唤的神圣希望。

附：本篇英文

Farewell at the hour of departing: Angola's search for development in a turbulent world

Tiago Caungo Mutombo
Pedro Txai Leal Brancher[*]

Abstract: Inclusive development has yet to emerge in Angola two decades after the end of the Angolan Civil War. This chapter analyses the obstacles that have constrained Angola's economic development to take off and delimits the current administration's challenges to overcome them. The working hypothesis is that the core impediment to Angola's development has come from the structure of its political institutions. By examining the Angolan state-building historical process, we argue that the colonial and civil war legacies have formed an unaccountable centralized state apparatus resilient to institutional change. While incapable of effectively delivering development outcomes and providing public goods to the hinterland, the arrangement has been able to sustain institutional stability by leveraging oil revenues through clientelist networks and co-opting traditional authorities within countryside communities as a decentralized mechanism of social governance. This organizational form has perpetuated a dual socioeconomic structure in which the elites are tied to the capital-intensive extractive sector, while most of the population relies on agricultural subsistence and informal activities. Although the current efforts to macroeconomic stabilization, attract foreign investments, and strengthen

---

* Associate Professor at Universidade Metodista de Angola, Vice-Rector for the Area of Scientific Research, Post-Graduation and University Extension and Post-Doctorate. E-mail: mtiagocaungo@gmail.com. Post-Doctoral fellow at the Universidade Federal do Rio Grande do Sul (UFRGS) and at the Science and Technology National Institute for Public Policy, Strategy, and Development. Chair of the International Affairs Department at Universidade Metodista de Angola, E-mail: brancherpedro022@gmail.com.

the national private sector are necessary, they are insufficient to overcome historically entrenched dualities. There is an urgent need to reinforce the state's capacities to drive a developmental project aimed at rapid industrialization, agricultural revitalization, poverty alleviation, and public goods universalization. Thus, we suggest a research agenda concerned with the question: how can Angola leverage its latent comparative advantages to engender rapid economic growth, higher labour productivity, and industrial diversification?

Key Words: Angola; development; institutions; state capacity; dualism

Introduction

Antonio Agostinho Neto, Angola's national hero, was born in 1922 in the small village of Kaxikane, in the Icolo Bengo county, 60 km from Angola's capital Luanda. Son of the Methodist reverend Agostinho Pedro Neto and the teacher Maria da Silva Neto, Agostinho Neto was only four years old when Salazar's military dictatorship took power in Portugal and increased repression across colonial territories. As part of the black population categorized as civilized by colonial authorities, Agostinho was allowed to attend a respectable educational institution. By the age of 26, he moved to Portugal to study medicine. There, he not only started to describe Angola's society through the lens of literature and poetry but also began intense political activism for Angola's independence. In 1951, he created the Centre for African Studies along with several African colleagues, such as Amilcar Lopes Cabral and Mario Coelho Pinto de Andrade. In the following years, he would be arrested several times by Portugal's International and State Defence Police (PIDE) under accusations of separatism. In 1959, Neto returned to Luanda and became president of the People's Movement for the Liberation of Angola (MPLA). From 1962 forward, he commanded the People's Armed Forces of Liberation of Angola against the Portuguese forces during the Angola War of Independence. In 1975, Angola finally conquered its independency, and Agostinho became the first president of a young nation, a position he would occupy until he died in 1979.

In 2022, Agostinho Neto's birth centennial was intensely celebrated in

Angola and worldwide. Yet, in many ways, Angola has become fundamentally different from the one he left in the late 1970s. With one of the highest fertility rates in Africa, Angola's population increased from 8 million to 34 million between 1979 and 2021, while the urban population grew from 23 per cent to 67 per cent.[①] Endowed with natural resources unevenly distributed along its 1,246,700 km^2 territory and 1,650 km coastline, Angola's GDP rose from \$ 22.1 billion in 1980 to \$ 78 billion in 2020, when the country became the sixth largest[②] economy in Africa. Institutionally, Angola abandoned the Marxist-Leninist ideology and committed itself to construct a multiparty party-political system embedded in a private-led market economy. By choosing this path, former military enemies were transformed into political adversaries competing peacefully for the Angolan votes in general elections held every five years.

However, the economic underdevelopment and external dependence of Angola, extensively denounced by Neto, not only persisted but have been exacerbated in the last four decades. The diversified agricultural sector and the nascent light industry that emerged in late colonial times had given way to the lucrative oil economy that now constitutes most government revenues. The capital-intensive oil sector is densely connected with international markets but remains detached from the rest of Angola's economy, mainly agricultural subsistence and informal activities on which most of the population relies. This dual socioeconomic structure causes stark inequality and widespread poverty, which tend to increase severely whenever there is a fall in crude oil prices, making the Kwanza's value plumb and costs of food imports skyrocket. Therefore, development has yet to accompany Angola's urbanization, population rise, and economic growth.

The economic and social effects of the external shocks of the COVID-19

---

① World Bank, *Angola - Agriculture Support Policy Review: Realigning Agriculture Support Policies and Programs (English)*, Washington, D. C.: World Bank Group, 2021, http://documents. worldbank.org/curated/en/719131625036855154/Angola-Agriculture-Support-Policy-Review-Realigning-Agriculture-Support-Policies-and-Programs.

② Tatiana Costa, "Angola could become Africa's fourth-largest economy by 2050", *Ver Angola*, 20 July 2020, https://www.verangola.net/va/en/072020/Economy/21023/Angola-could-become-Africa's-fourth-largest-economy-by-2050.htm (accessed 10 November 2022).

pandemic outbreak and the onset of the Ukrainian War exasperated Angola's structural contradictions. Although the virus's lethality remained low, the pandemic reduced international oil demand, inducing an additional decline in the prices of the commodity that ensures a substantial influx of hard currencies into the country. Moreover, as a large part of Angola's labour force depends on the informal economy, the government-imposed lockdown measures induced an excessive reduction in per capita income in the most vulnerable population. Therefore, the lack of export diversification and high-level informality made the Angolan people over-vulnerable to the COVID-19 outbreak. Despite oil price recovery since the onset of the conflict in Eastern Europe, the disruptions in global chains brought to light the precarious position of a country that is a net importer of wheat, rice, palm oil, and fertilizers and has a low-productivity agricultural system.[1] Thus, the aliment and agricultural input inflation caused by the Ukrainian War aggravated the 1.6 million Angolans already suffering from food insecurity due to the onset of the worst drought in four decades in 2021.[2]

This chapter investigates why Angola has been incapable of overcoming the dualistic socioeconomic structure that makes it disproportionate vulnerable to external shocks two decades after the end of the Angolan Civil War. In other words, why did inclusive development and economic diversification fail to emerge in post-civil war Angola? Our work hypothesis is that the core obstacle to Angola's economic progress has come from the structure of its political institutions. By examining the Angolan state-building historical process, we argue that the colonial and civil war legacies have formed a centralized and externally oriented state apparatus ruled by an unaccountable[3] form of governance resilient to institutional change. While incapable of effectively

---

① Cedric Okou, John Spray, and Filiz Unsal, *Stable Food Prices in Sub-Saharan Africa. An Empirical Assessment*. IMF Working Paper, (New York: International Monetary Fund, 2022).

② Observador, "Quase 1,6 milhões sofrem de insegurança alimentar grave no sul de Angola, indica ONU", *Observador,* 4 May 2022, https://observador.pt/2022/05/04/quase-16-milhoes-sofrem-de-inseguranca-alimentar-grave-no-sul-de-angola-indica-onu/ (accessed 5 November 2022).

③ *See* Given Yurtseven, "State Failure or State Formation? Neo-patrimonialism and Its Limitations in Africa", *E-International Relations*, 29 June 2021, https://www.e-ir.info/2021/06/29/state-failure-or-state-formation-neo-patrimonialism-and-its-limitations-in-africa/ (accessed 10 November 2022).

delivering development outcomes and providing public goods to the hinterland, it has been able to politically leverage oil revenues through clientelist networks and co-opting traditional authorities within countryside communities as a decentralized social governance mechanism. Thus, the Angolan elites did not have the incentives to establish developmental capabilities to promote structural transformation or to genuinely commit themselves to institutionalize a dynamic market economy.

To consider an institutional arrangement resilient to change does not mean to assume its complete immobility. Similar to other resource-dependent countries, Angola's institutional change pattern is connected to the fluctuations of oil prices in international markets. The gradual political and economic liberalization that started with the downfall of oil prices in the late 1980s has created a path-dependence trajectory that has increased the pressures for reforms over the ruling party. Since 2014, the compound effects of another tumble in oil revenues, corruption scandals, and the COVID-19 pandemic have made Angola's socioeconomic contradictions almost unbearable for its people. Burden by the worst crisis since the end of the war and weak performance in the last two general elections, MPLA has committed itself to decentralizing state powers and implementing a structural adjustment program under the Monetary International Fund (IMF) guidance. Although it is an agenda with considerable limitations regarding short-term development outcomes, it is the first systematic attempt to transform Angola's state into a more efficient governance apparatus.

The chapter is structured in three sections, plus the conclusion. First, we discuss the challenges around the implementation of local authorities, the core element within the decentralization agenda in Angola, considering the country's state-building historical process and the influence of the crude oil export dependence on political dynamics. Second, we describe the harmful effects of Angola's dual economy on its productive powers, emphasizing the role of widespread poverty, poor infrastructure, and rigid inequalities as significant factors constraining the emergence of economic development. Third, we analyse the feasibility of the current administration's policy agenda in light of Angola's structural dualities and the vulnerabilities exposed by the COVID-19 pandemic crisis. Finally, we summarize the main arguments and consider paths for continuing the research agenda.

Institutional Dynamics of the Angolan State: centralization, traditional authorities, and autarchies

In the late 1960s, while Angola was still struggling against colonial rule, Agostinho Neto published a poetry book entitled "Sacred Hope". Among several poems, "Farewell at the hour of departing" became one of the most well-known for describing the angsts of a nation fighting for its freedom. Speaking with "all black mothers whose sons had left", the poet convenes a stand of performative hope, a gesture of becoming the future that has yet to come: "I no longer wait, I am the one that is expected, it's me, my mother, hope is us, your children, destined for a faith that feeds life."[①]

On 15 September 2022, Laurinda Cardoso, president of Angola's Constitutional Court, paraphrased Agostinho's words during the opening speech of the presidential nomination ceremony. Speaking directly at the president elected, Cardoso stressed that: "Angola cannot be delayed anymore. It is urgent that Angola not be simply a dream any longer. It must become a pleasurable reality even for the humblest of the Angolans." According to her, the electoral results unveiled the Angolan people's lack of hope for the future. Therefore, the new administration would have "to deal with the high levels of turnout abstention that the pool revealed, renewing the people's confidence in the state's capacity to conduct the matters and destines of the country. [②]

Cardoso's eloquent discourse exemplifies the Angolan judiciary autonomy concerning the Executive branch, a crucial institutional feature within the transition to a multiparty political system. On the other hand, the hurry in regaining people's trust in state guidance of public matters manifested by Cardoso is related to high poverty levels and essential service deprivation faced by most Angolans. In 2021, Angola was ranked 148th out of 190 countries on

---

① Agostinho Neto, *Sagrada Esperança*, (Lisbon: Sá da Costa, 1978), p. 10.

② Adéritco Casimiro, "'Angola não deve continuar a ser um mero sonho' – Laurinda Cardoso", *Correio da Kianda*, 15 September 2022, https://correiokianda.info/angola-nao-deve-continuar-a-ser-um-mero-sonho-laurinda-cardoso/ (accessed 5 November 2022).

the Human Development Index (HDI), with a life expectancy of 61 years, an average of 5.4 years of schooling,[1] and 48 per cent of the population without access to basic sanitation.[2]

In this underdeveloped context, political and academic actors conceive decentralization reforms as core mechanisms to improve public services and increase the political system's accountability. For instance, according to the National Permanent Secretary of Youth of the Social Renewal Party, Gaspar dos Santos Fernandes, "the institutionalization of municipal elections in Angola is the main lever for solving the main social problems."[3] For Clarice Beu, "the decentralization would improve public services and popular participation in political and economic issues." As for Nelson Pestana and Aslak Orre, decentralization is an instrument that would ensure "democratic participation, development, and civil and political security".[4]

Angola's constitution and MPLA's leaders agree with decentralizing the unitary state structure inherited from the war period. The 1992 Constitution brought the concept of local autarchies, locally elected territorial bodies with autonomous governance capacity and decision-making authority on local issues.[5] In the Angolan context, the local elected authorities would represent a territorial and democratic counter-influence to the customary traditional authorities, and the central government-appointed authorities. In 2010, the new

---

[1] UNDP, *Human Development Report 2021/2022 Overview. Uncertain Times, Unsettled Lives: shaping our future in a transforming world*, (New York: United Nations Development Program, 2022), https://hdr.undp.org/system/files/documents/global-report-document/hdr2021-22overviewenpdf.pdf (accessed 10 November 2022).

[2] World Bank, *People using at least basic sanitation services (per cent of population) - Angola*. The World Bank Group, 2022. https://data.worldbank.org/indicator/SH.STA.BASS.ZS?locations=AO (accessed 3 November 2022).

[3] Angola Telegraph, "Autarchy is the main lever for solving Luanda's social problems, says PRS youth leader", *Angola Telegraph*, 5 November 2022, https://angolatelegraph.com/politics/autarchy-is-the-main-lever-for-solving-luandas-social-problems-says-prs-youth-leader/ (accessed 7 November 2022).

[4] Nelson Pestana and Aslak Orre, "Para quando as autarquias em Angola", *Angola Brief*, v.4, no.8, (2014), p. 2.

[5] The term local autarchies have been used by Angolan government officials when referring to the decentralized institutional structures to be implemented in the country. In this article, we will employ the terms local autarchies and local elected authorities as synonyms.

Constitution not only defined local elected authorities' scope as the domains of education, health, energy, water, rural and urban equipment, culture and science, transport and communication, leisure and sports, habitation, social action, civil protection, environment and sanitation, consumer protection, promotion of social and economic development, territorial planning, municipal police, and decentralized cooperation but also stressed that they should have financial resources from the general budget of the State and from local taxes that are compatible with such tasks.[①] In 2014, during a speech for the MPLA's Central Committee, José Eduardo Santos stressed that "local authorities are fundamental for the country's development".[②]

Yet, despite constitutional provision and support from the ruling and opposition parties, in 2022, the leaders of Angola's 18 provinces, 164 municipalities, and 532 communes were still selected[③] by executive decrees. Why is that so? Why has it been so challenging to decentralize political and administrative power in Angola? Instead of the MPLA's power addiction hypotheses, we argue that the slow implementation of local authorities is better understood by contextualizing it on Angola's long-term state-building process. [④]

The modern Angolan state was born as a by-product of the Portuguese long-distance slave trade system established in the late fifteenth century. With the locus of economic activities turned to the Atlantic Ocean, Portuguese

---

① Lázaro Jaime, *O Conceito de Autarquias Locais na Constituição da República de Angola - o caso do Municípi*o, Dissertation, (Minho: Universidade do Minho, 2015).

② David Filipe, "Autarquias são fundamentais para o desenvolvimento do país, Eduardo dos Santos", *Novo Jornal*. 30 May 2014, https://novojornal.co.ao/politica/interior/autarquias-sao-fundamentais-para-o-desenvolvimento-do-pais-eduardo-dos-santos-3477.htm>l (accessed 1 November 2022).

③ Angola Telegraph, "Luanda governor appoints municipal administrators", *Angola Telegraph*, 8 November 2022, https://angolatelegraph.com/politics/luanda-governor-appoints-municipal-administrators/ (accessed 10 November 2022).

④ MPLA's power clinging hypothesis is generally advocated by members of the oppositional forces. It attributes the delay in decentralization reforms to the unwillingness of the ruling party to conceive a pluralistic governance arrangement. Although the agency of political players is a relevant variable for the understanding of institutional outcomes, we argue that historical and structural factors have greater explanatory strength to elucidate the long-term resilience of the centralized institutional arrangement even in the face of recurrent economic crises.

authorities did not concern with developing administrative infrastructure on the hinterland nor legitimate forms of taxation. For over three centuries, the colonial occupation was restricted to coastal enclaves and provision posts along major rivers, while alliances with local kingdoms and chiefs assured the slave influx from the interior. This configuration, with a highly lucrative ocean-oriented sector entangled with a traditional hinterland sector embedded in customary forms of domination, would be the first manifestation of the inseparable dualism that permeates Angola's economy until nowadays.

Until the end of the nineteenth century, Angola's territory remained divided into geographical blocks, each land homing people with particular political, linguistic, and cultural identities. The lack of social integration between different ethnic groups, which would be one of the sources of conflict after independence, would diminish only after the 1885 Berlin Conference, when Portuguese hinterland occupation efforts began amid territorial invasions from other European powers, such as Germany, France, and England. By then, an Afro-Portuguese slave trader elite had established rudimentary forms of administration in the surrounding areas of Luanda and Benguela. Along with Portuguese-sent troops, the Afro-Portuguese would militarily defeat traditional rulers in the Central Highlands areas, allowing for a gradual imposition of taxation at the beginning of the twentieth century. [1]

By late 1924, steam navigation along the Kwanza River and incipient railways leading to diamond extractives sites were set in place. In 1926, António Salazar's ascendency to power in Portugal renewed the impetus for the bureaucratization of the colonial society, which would be carried mainly by Portuguese staff stationed in Luanda and the marginalization of the Afro-Portuguese elite. Between 1950 and 1960, the number of whites living in Angola increased from 78,825 to 172,529. [2] Whereas Salazar's economic policies induced a slight industrialization surge and agricultural diversification, most of

---

[1] Malyn Newitt, "Angola in Historical Context", in Patrick Chabal and Nuno Vidal (eds.), *Angola The Weight of History*, (New York: Columbia University Press, 2008), pp. 19-92.

[2] Washington Nascimento, "Políticas coloniais e sociedade angolana nas memórias e discursos do escritor Raul David", *Anos 90*, v. 23, no. 44, (2016), pp. 265-289.

the native population remained subject to compulsory labour, and governance structures were designed to transform Angola's economy into an export platform that would provide surpluses for Portugal. [1]

Hence, during almost five centuries of colonial rule, most of the Angolan population was geographically separated from each other and excluded from formal education or participation in public governance. Nonetheless, two types of autochthones elites thrived in the interstices of the colonial social structure. The first was the traditional authorities, so-called *sobas*, which were local chiefs whose ruling power derived from hereditary and religious claims. [2] With knowledge of the territory and popular legitimacy, the *sobas* became fundamental allies of colonial bureaucracies, in charge of tax collection, labour recruitment, and political order at the community level. By operationalizing the *sobas's* bottom-up social acceptance, Portuguese authorities could project power widely without using significant contingents of soldiers and officials. [3]

Initially, MPLA tried to reduce traditional authorities' powers during the Angolan Civil War (1976-2002). After the conflict, however, considering the thinness of bureaucratic capacity and the low infrastructural reach of the new regime, President José Eduardo Dos Santos did not hesitate to bring *sobas* into the state apparatus. In the 2010 Constitution, traditional authorities' customary law was fully recognized, transforming Angola into a particular case of legal pluralism. By 2010, 31,845 traditional authorities with ruling power over communities of 200 to 300 people were registered within the Angolan state. [4] Aside from being entitled to public salary, *sobas* are often consulted by officials seeking community legitimacy to settle local disputes. As an institution whose attributions overlap with official authorities, the *sobas* represent a robust obstacle to establishing local bodies elected in competitive polls.

Alongside the *sobas*, the *assimilados* ("assimilated") were another native

---

[1]　Malyn Newitt, *Angola in Historical Context*, pp. 19-92.

[2]　*Soba* is the Portuguese translation of *sowa* from the native language, Kimbundo, spoken by the ethnolinguistic subgroup Ambundu which means the head of a particular region.

[3]　Malyn Newitt, *Angola in Historical Context*, pp. 19-92.

[4]　Santin Janaína and Carlos Teixeira, "Local Power and Traditional Authorities in Angola: challenges and opportunities", *Sequência*, no. 85 (2020), pp.136-172.

elite that emerged within colonialism. Unlike the *sobas*, the assimilated were Angolans, men that had received Portuguese education and had to display certain preconditioned behaviours to be considered civilized, a status that allowed them to escape compulsory work, occupy positions as civil servants, vote, travel the country, and get driver's licenses. To achieve civilized status, one had to master the Portuguese language, wear western clothes, become monogamous, abandon African traditions, adopt Christianity, prove an income level to sustain his family, and sit at dinner tables according to European costumes.[1]

By 1960, the assimilated represented 2.5 per cent of the Angolan population registered within the state. Like Agostinho Neto, Jonas Savimbi, Manuel Pedro Pacavira, Uanhenga Xitu, Jackques Arlindo do Santos, Adriano Sebastião, and Raul Mateus David, most of the first generation of Angolan writers and cadres of the nationalist movements were assimilated, having spent most of their lives in Luanda's surroundings and been educated on Protestant missions and European universities.[2]

In the post-civil war period, state-building was conditioned by the predominance of *sobas* and former assimilated within Angola's society. By co-opting the *sobas* into the state apparatus, the central government ensured low-cost administrative capillarity in distant areas through an institution whose authority is considered sacred by most of the countryside population. For Ricardo Soares de Oliveira and Susan Taponier, this *soba*-state relationship might be interpreted as a bifurcation of the Angolan state-building process, as "contrary to the modernizing discourse, the party-state is in effect building an archaic rural bubble".[3] As revealed by the Afrobarometer, in 2020, traditional authorities were Angolan's third most trustable institution, behind only religious leaders and the armed forces and ahead of the judiciary, police, and

① Iracema Dulley and Luísa Sampaio, "Accusation and Legitimacy in the Civil War in Angola", *Virtual Brazilian Anthropology*, no.17 (2020), pp. 1-20.

② Washington Nascimento, *Políticas coloniais e sociedade angolana nas memórias e discursos do escritor Raul David*, pp. 265-289.

③ Ricardo Soares de Oliveira and Susan Taponier, "'O Governo Está Aqui': post-war state making in the Angolan Peiphery", *Politique africaine*, n° 130, Jun, 2013, p. 179.

the presidency.[1] In other words, although there are no local elected bodies, the Angolan state has grassroots governance mechanisms that help it to sustain the political order without the necessity of public accountability.

In turn, although the promulgation of Nationality Law in 1975 ended the institutional divide between indigenous and assimilated Angolans, the economic, political, and cultural distance between urban educated elites and hinterland communities continued in post-colonial Angola. For example, "social prestige in MPLA society came to be associated with the mastery of the Portuguese-inflected deportment, speech patterns, and lifestyles of the central society; distance from it signified uncouth or un-Angolan parochialism".[2] Reinforcing this trend, during the Angolan Civil War, the destruction of the infrastructures connecting the national economy and the party's dependence on the oil-producing enclaves around Luanda's province as the financial lifeline of the war effort further alienated the regime's social base from the countryside. For instance, in 1985, only 12 out of the 628 that participated in the Second Party Congress were peasants.[3] With the end of the internal conflict, as the interior governance was guaranteed by *sobas*-state collaboration, most social ascendancy opportunities could remain concentrated within party members' networks and national capital boundaries, self-repeating the urban-rural divide inherited from the assimilated times.

Therefore, when peace came, such a composite of traditional authorities and Luanda base assimilated elites contributed to constraining the impetus for establishing local representative institutions. Still, the Angolan centralized and unaccountable state would not be as resilient to institutional change as it is if it did not have permanent access to the massive influx of international reserves

---

[1] Carlos Pacatolo and David Boio, "Religious leaders enjoy greater popular trust than other institutions in Angola, Afrobarometer survey shows", *Afrobarometer,* 25 June 2020, https://www. afrobarometer.org/articles/religious-leaders-enjoy-greater-popular-trust-other-institutions-angola/ (accessed 15 October 2022).

[2] Ricardo Soares de Oliveira and Susan Taponier, *"O Governo Está Aqui": post-war state making in the Angolan Periphery*, p. 171.

[3] Nuno Vidal, "The Angolan Regime and the Move to Multiparty Politics", in Patrick Chabal and Nuno Vidal (eds.), *Angola The Weight of History*, (New York: Columbia University Press, 2008), pp. 1-14.

pumped from oil exports.

From Crisis to Crisis: The Nexus Between Oil Export Dependency and Institutional Change

Angola's oil industry began in 1957 when Standard Oil and the Gulf Oil Company acquired the exclusive right to drill in Portuguese colonies.[1] By the late 1960s, oil had surpassed coffee as the most valuable export product, a trend that would endure during the war periods. As Angola's oil reserves are located in easily protected offshore enclaves in the north-western provinces of Luanda, Cabinda, and Zaire, they became MPLA's primary source of revenue[2] during the civil war. Sonangol, the state oil company established in 1976 through the nationalization of the Portuguese company ANGOL, would be isolated from internal political struggles and transformed into an enclave of bureaucratic excellence amid the state apparatus. The regime managed to keep most of the former companies' European employees by crafting a memorandum of understanding with former Portuguese executives in Lisbon. As stated by one of the staff who stayed after nationalization, "You see, through colonialism, foreign invasion, Marxist-Leninism and capitalism, I have not left the same building".[3]

In the first decade of the twentieth-one century, as the oil barrel prices increased from $ 32 to $ 187, Angola's oil production skyrocketed. In 2008, Angola overcame Nigeria as the major oil exporter in Sub-Saharan Africa, and in 2009, it became a member of the Organisation of the Petroleum Exporting Countries (OPEC). The high profitability attracted 87 per cent of Angola's FDI influx[4] to the oil and gas activities, overbalancing the public and private infrastructure investments toward the needs of the coastal regions to the detriment of the hinterland. As a result, the diversified agriculture and the

---

[1] Jorge Cacuto, "Angola Pós-Independente: Implicações Econômicas da Herança Colonial", *Economia e Pesquisa*, v.3, no.3, 2001, pp. 22-39.

[2] Eduardo Haddad et al, "Uneven Integration: the case of Angola. Research Paper", RP-20/02 (Riad: Policy Center for the New South 2020).

[3] Ricardo de Oliveira, *Magnificent and Beggar Land*, (London: Oxford University Press, 2015), p. 46.

[4] Eduardo Haddad et al, *Uneven Integration: the case of Angola*, 2020.

nascent manufacturing that emerged in the last decades of colonial rule gave way to a typical dual economy with an extractive sector tied to international markets but wholly disconnected from the rest of the subsistence economy on which most of the population is embedded.

The nexus between oil export dependency and Angola's institutional change dynamic is that oil revenues have been wholly concentrated under the President's control. In control of Sonangol's accounts, the presidency's inner circle could surpass international audits and engage in several extra-budget operations. This means that the head of the Executive branch held a mighty and discretionary source of resources that gave him leverage in domestic and international politics. On the one hand, as access to oil rents is the main form of personal enrichment, its distribution could be managed to accommodate allies or punish dissent. Rent-seeking practices linking clientelist networks with the presidency as the central hub became normalized, operating as the dominant form of elite reproduction and exclusion of the ordinary population.[1] On the other hand, oil revenues provided the state with financial resources to bargain with multinational corporations aiming to participate in the Angolan drilling fields and to resist international institutions' reform demands. In other words, its oil reserves granted Angola a larger policy space in the global economy compared to other developing countries.

The concentration of oil revenues in Angola's institutional arrangement creates a strong material basis for the resilience of the centralized mode of governance. In 2019, Sonangol's revenues were equivalent to 25 per cent of GDP, and its assets to 40 per cent.[2] With most of society living in multidimensional poverty and exhausted by decades of war, state elites would indulge themselves in the conspicuous consumption of luxury goods with no need for accountability or real institutional change. Furthermore, as the oil industry's control became vital to ensure political power at national and international levels, to lose the government's administration means to lose

---

[1] Nuno Vidal, *The Angolan Regime and the Move to Multiparty Politics*, 2008.

[2] World Bank, *Creating Markets in Angola. Opportunities for Development Through the Private Sector*, (Washington: International Finance Corporation 2019).

control of the clientelist networks. Thus, the economic centrality of the oil "pushes very high the stakes of political competition: the winner does take all".[1]

Therefore, similar to the effects of commodities prices on Latin American political cycles[2], Angola's institutional change pattern is connected to the fluctuations of oil prices in international markets. The amount of oil revenues passing through Sonangol's accounts is inversely related to the ruling party's need to accept a more decentralized state apparatus and a competitive multiparty political system.

For instance, Angola's oil economy benefited greatly from the Second Oil shock in 1979. The hike in international prices brought Western multinational corporations to participate in newly discovered blocks, including American Chevron, whose national government was officially committed to overthrowing MPLA's regime. Meanwhile, whereas most of the population had become dependent on international aid, foreigners and high public officials had access to exclusive shops where luxury imported goods were available. The favourable external scenario allowed the launching of recruitment campaigns that would enlarge MPLA's urban support base. In turn, the South African invasion of Angola's southern provinces in 1981 induced another round of power concentration around President Dos Santos's figure.[3]

In 1982, the upward trend inverted, causing a fall in government revenues and a climb in external debt. In the following year, MPLA's Central Committee approved the *Plano Global de Emergência* (Global Emergency Plan), which stressed the channelling of resources into the defence sector. However, another drop in oil prices in 1986 made Angola's external debt skyrocket, closing the doors of financial markets to the Angolan government. At this moment, the government aimed to establish ties with the IMF by introducing controlled privatization and timid market reforms within a financial adjustment program called *Programa de Saneamento Econômico e Financeiro* (Economic and

---

[1] Patrick Chabal, *"E Pluribus Unum*: Transition in Angola"*, in Patrick Chabal and Nuno Vidal (eds.), *Angola The Weight of History*, (New York: Columbia University Press, 2008), pp. 1-14.

[2] Daniela Campello, *The Politics of Market Discipline in Latin America*, (New York: Cambridge University Press, 2015).

[3] Nuno Vidal, *The Angolan Regime and the Move to Multiparty Politics*, 2008.

Finance Cleaning Program).[1] Still, the Kwanza's depreciation, the core measure required by the IMF, would be implemented only in 1992, when the collapse of the Soviet Union had turned Angola's external condition even worse. In 1991, under pressure from Washington and international financial institutions, MPLA agreed with the Bicesse Accords, which envisioned the realization of general elections by September 1992.[2]

The political and economic liberalization policy was forcefully reversed when the National Union for the Total Independence of Angola (UNITA) decided not to accept electoral results in 1992. The civil war would enter its most violent phase, which lasted until the death of UNITA's leader Jonas Savimbi in 2002. By then, oil prices had started to rise again, which, combined with the military victory, gave MPLA the confidence to bypass the resumption of the Lusaka protocol signed in 1994. The 2004 expected legislative election was postponed until 2008. Then, the presidential election envisioned for 2009 was delayed until 2012 due to the 2010 Constitution promulgation, which defined that the presidency would be in charge of the party's leader with the most extensive parliamentary bench.

With the influx of revenues restored, MPLA retook its membership recruitment policy nationwide, expanding its reach into UNITA's supporting bases, such as Bié, Huambo, and Huíla provinces, and started to bring the traditional authorities into its sphere of influence.[3] Thus, in 2012, with the MPLA ready to face a general election with minimal risks of losing power, the party obtained 71 per cent of the votes, ensuring an absolute majority of 175 deputies in the National Assembly and the permanence of Dos Santos as President.[4]

---

[1] Manuel Ferreira, "A política de recuperação econômica da RP de Angola", *Política Internacional*, No.1, v.l. no.1, (1990), pp. 1-26.

[2] Manuel Ferreira, "Performance Econômica em Situação de Guerra: o caso de Angola (1975-1992)", *África: Revista do Centro de Estudos Africanos*, v.16, no.1, (1994), pp. 135-156.

[3] Nuno Vidal, *The Angolan Regime and the Move to Multiparty Politics*, 2008.

[4] CNE, "Eleições – 2012", *Comissão Nacional Eleitoral*, 7 September 2012, https://www.cne.ao/elei%C3%A7%C3%B5es/2012 (accessed 10 September 2022).

Pushed by Crisis: A New Momentum for the Institutionalization of Local Autarchies

The post-war bonanza ended as soon as the upward trend in oil prices dramatically reversed. Between 2014 and 2020, the cost of Brent oil dropped from $ 100 per barrel to $ 21 per barrel, causing a loss of more than 40% in Angola's government revenues during the same period.[1] Once again, MPLA had to resort to austerity measures to ensure the confidence of the financial markets. Under the guidance of the IMF, the government launched a Macroeconomic Stabilization Plan (MPS) and a Privatization Program (PROPRIV). As a short-term measure to control the fiscal deficit, the government incurred external borrowing, which caused the Kwanza to depreciate by 38.9 per cent year-on-year and the government debt to rise from 83 per cent to 131 per cent between 2015 and 2020. The deterioration in terms of exchange reduced the import capacity, causing staple scarcity and increases in the costs of living.[2] By 2019, the unemployment rate got to 32 per cent in general and 56.5 per cent among the youth, 70 per cent of companies had halted their activities, and approximately 11 thousand firms were closed.[3]

Hence, when General João Lourenço ran for the presidency in 2017, the international environment had turned Angola's structural contradictions increasingly hard to manage. Aside from the economic crisis, national and foreign media widely exposed the clientelist system of the Dos Santos era as corruption scandals involving high-ranked individuals. The crisis engendered a robust drop in MPLA's popularity, and popular manifestations emerged in the larger urban areas.[4] The general perception was that Angola's golden age money

---

[1] República de Angola, *Plano de Desenvolvimento Nacional 2018-2022 v.1*, (Luanda: Governo de Angola 2018).

[2] Zahabia Gupta, *Angola: Deep Dive into Dept*, (Sydney: Standard & Poor's Financial Services, 2022).

[3] INE. *Indicadores de Emprego e Desemprego. Inquérito ao Emprego em Angola*, (Luanda: Instituto Nacional de Estatística, 2019).

[4] Zefanias Matsimbe and Nelson Domingos, "Angola's 2017 Elections and the Start of a Post-Dos Santos Era", *Journal of African Elections*, v.17, no.1, 2018, pp. 1-24.

had been appropriated into private hands to the detriment of the country's public services and economic development.

Differently from the late 1980s crisis, the effects of political liberalization during the previous decade had increased MPLA's electoral vulnerability. With the opposition gaining momentum, Lourenço's campaign promised to fight corruption and placed the institutionalization of local authorities at the centre of the agenda. In the last rally before the vote, Lourenço asked the MPLA for the courage to implement the decentralization reforms. According to him, with local authorities, the government would "solve those problems that affect the citizen in his municipality daily, without him having to leave his county".[1] Even so, MPLA voting decreased by 10 per cent compared with the 2012 election, which still granted it a qualified majority in the National Assembly but was a clear sign of MPLA's loss of societal support.[2]

Pressured by public opinion and the need to untangle the clientelist networks that supported President Dos Santos, Lourenço moved quickly to consolidate its power by replacing leaders of the Dos Santos era with cadres loyal to him[3] and advancing an anti-corruption campaign. In 2018, Lourenço launched the "2018-2022 Strategic Plan for the Prevention and Fight against Corruption", which guided the approval of several anti-corruption and anti-money laundering laws.[4] Between 2017 and 2021, the new legislation directed the opening of more than 1,500 corruption cases that recovered over $ 5.3 billion. Among the most renowned cases was the prosecution of the Dos Santos son, José Filomeno dos Santos, who was sentenced to five years in jail for stealing $ 500 million from the Angolan Sovereign Fund, and the charge of

① Confina Media, "Angola/Eleições: João Lourenço pede 'coragem' ao MPLA para implementar autarquias", *Cofina Media*, 19 August 2017, https://www.cmjornal.pt/cm-ao-minuto/detalhe/angolaeleicoes-joao-lourenco-pede-coragem-ao-mpla-para-implementar-autarquias?v=cb (accessed 29 October 2022).

② CNE, "Eleições – 2017", *Comissão Nacional Eleitoral de Angola*, 6 September 2017, https://www.cne.ao/elei%C3%A7%C3%B5es/2017 (accessed 30 October 2022).

③ Benjamin Augé, *Angola under Joao Lourenço: Who Are the New Players of MPLA State?* (Paris: Policy Center for the New South 2019).

④ Republica de Angola, "Plano Estratégico de Prevenção e Combate à Corrupção 2018-2022", *Procuradoria Geral da República*. 2017, https://dnpcc.pgr.ao/wp-content/uploads/2022/05/Plano-Estrategico.pdf (accessed 28 October 2022).

Isabel dos Santos, daughter of Dos Santos and former president of Sonangol, who had more than $ 1 billion in assets frozen.[①]

It is unlikely that Lourenço's anticorruption campaign will lead to immediate changes in Angola's entrenched mode of governance. Indeed, by 2020, 54 per cent of the Angolans considered the government's performance in the fight against corruption weak, and 39 per cent thought that it was being instrumentalized as a political tool to deal with opposition within the MPLA.[②] Still, by empowering prosecutors and shedding light on the extensiveness clientelist system, Lorenço's government is contributing to institutionalizing a more transparent and accountable public administration in the mid-long term.

On the other hand, the implementation of local autarchies progressed slower than expected. In 2018, Adão de Almeida, Minister of Territory Administration and State Reform announced the intention to hold local elections by 2020.[③] Yet, the stalemate between the government and the opposition concerning the Law on Local Authorities Institutionalization delayed the process. While MPLA advocated for a geographic gradualism implementation, UNITA and other opposition parties supported a functional gradualist approach. The first means that the process would begin only in some zones, which will serve as pilot projects to guide the later implementation across the country. The second is a phased process of transferring competencies from provincial authorities to local bodies. Whereas the debate was stuck in the National Assembly, the COVID-19 pandemic emerged. The sanitary crisis came as a perfect motive for the government undefinedly delaying the initiative, ending the hopes for local authorities' elections in 2022 and causing protests from opposition parties and civil society actors.

In 2022, campaigning for his second turn, once again, Lourenço renewed

① Voa Português, "Contas de sócios de Isabel dos Santos congeladas em Portugal", *VOA*, 3 May 2021, https://www.voaportugues.com/a/contas-de-s%C3%B3cios-de-isabel-dos-santos-congeladas-em-portugal/5875882.html, (accessed 28 October 2022).

② Carlos Pacatolo and David Boio, "Apesar dos ganhos, os angolanos mostram-se insatisfeitos com os esforços do governo no combate à corrupção", *Afrobarometer*. no.396, 9 October 2020.

③ Jornal de Angola, "Pacote sobre as autarquias apreciado hoje em Luanda", *Jornal de Angola*, 21 May 2018, https://www.jornaldeangola.ao/ao/noticias/detalhes.php?id=404952 (accessed 1 November 2022).

the intention to create local authorities. During a rally in Dundo, the capital of the province of Lunda Norte, the President stressed that "we must create the local authorities that will work at the municipal level [...], we feel more than anyone the need to bring power as close as possible to the citizen".[①] Nevertheless, Lourenço beat UNITA's leader Adalberto Costa Junior by 51.17 per cent against 43.95 per cent, the thinnest difference ever recorded. In the parliament, the outcome caused a 26 reduction in MPLA's caucus and an increase of 39 in UNITA's. Moreover, UNITA's sound victory in the province of Luanda, the largest electoral constituency in the country, and the lowest voting turnout in Angola's election history (only 44 per cent of the electorate voted) were clear signs that MPLA's rule is being contested as never before.[②]

After the tight election race, the government administration announced an inter-ministry commission to advance the local authorities' institutionalization and the construction of thirty-five municipal assembly facilities. In the parliament, the MPLA granted UNITA the presidency of the local authority power commission, a gesture interpreted as a manifestation of a possible agreement in the future.[③] Even so, there are still accusations from the opposition parties that the MPLA is deliberately stalling the discussions. This perception was reinforced in November when MPLA deputy Rui Falcao affirmed that local authorities' elections won't be held in 2023 but "only in 2024, in case the legislative package is resolved".[④]

---

① Novo Jornal. "Eleições: Presidente do MPLA garante a realização das eleições autárquicas no próximo ano", *Novo Jornal*, 3 August 2022, https://novojornal.co.ao/politica/interior/eleicoes-presidente-do-mpla-garante-a-realizacao-das-eleicoes-autarquicas-no-proximo-ano-109301.html (accessed 3 October 2022).

② CNE, "Edital referente às Eleições Gerais do dia 24 de Agosto de 2022", *Comissão Nacional Eleitoral*, 22 August 2022, https://www.cne.ao/storage/arquivos/EDITAL%20dos%20resultados%20definitvos%20do%20Apuramento%20Nacional,%20referente%20%C3%A0s%20Elei%C3%A7%C3%B5es%20Gerais%20do%20dia%2024%20de%20Agosto%20de%202022.pdf (accessed 3 November 2022).

③ Arão Ndipa, "Autarquias em Angola: Entre a expectativa e os receios da classe política e sociedade civil", *VOA*, 22 October 2022, https://www.voaportugues.com/a/autarquias-em-angola-entre-a-expectativa-e-os-receios-da-classe-pol%C3%ADtica-e-sociedade-civil/6801106.html (accessed 5 November 2022).

④ DW, "Angola: 'Não queremos acreditar que o PR tenha medo do poder local'", *DW*, 18 October 2022, https://www.dw.com/pt-002/angola-n%C3%A3o-queremos-acreditar-que-o-pr-tenha-medo-do-poder-local/a-63469269 (accessed 5 November 2022).

In sum, post-independence Angola's institutional change pattern has been driven less by the strategic goal of creating mechanisms to overcome the dualistic socioeconomic structure inherited from colonial times than by increases in the threat perception of the ruling party when it faces a crisis caused by reductions in oil prices. During boom periods, the articulation of oil revenues in the coastal-urban areas with the co-optation of the traditional authorities in the hinterland sustains the regime's legitimacy even without substantial improvements in the living conditions of most of the population. However, when the country is hit by external shocks such as the COVID-19 pandemic, Angola's growth model contradictions become explicit, as Angolans are obliged to face a disproportionate severe economic and social crisis. In these times, timid institutional reforms tend to flourish only to be delayed again as soon as the hike in oil prices is restored.

Even though the institutionalization of local autarchies should not be understood as a panacea, there is a growing literature suggesting the positive effects for public service delivery, agricultural productivity enhancement, and economic diversification of well-designed decentralization reforms in the African context.[1] Their institutionalization is becoming a pressing issue for the regime since, as the 2022 electoral outcomes revealed, MPLA's failure to reduce Angola's vulnerability to external shocks is increasing UNITA's voting base. In 2023, as oil prices will remain high due to the Ukrainian War, the question is whether the MPLA's weak electoral performance will be enough to retain João Lourenço's administration on the decentralization path praised during the electoral campaign.

The Duality of Angola's Social Economic Structure

On 11 November 1975, Agostinho Neto made a glorious speech announcing Angola's independence. Aside from praising the Angolan people's courage in the fight against colonialism, Neto stressed the two core challenges

---

[1]　See Jan Erk (ed.), *Decentralization, Democracy, and Development in Africa*, (New York: Routledge, 2017).

the new-born nation would face: first, he acknowledged that Angola was an underdeveloped country, which was palpable by the "image of the profound misery in that the Angolan people live"; Secondly, Neto perceived Angola as a dependent nation that gravitated "within the imperialist orbit". According to him, the interplay between these two characteristics explained the duality of Angola's socioeconomic structure, that is, the reasons why the national economy was "so profoundly distorted, with a traditional sector, alongside leading sectors and lagging regions surrounding the so-called development poles", as well as the motives of "the cruelty of unjust social relations".[1]

Almost four decades after Neto's speech, the dualism socioeconomic remains the essential challenge facing the Angolan nation. On the one side, the capital-intensive oil sector operates as an enclave embedded in the national economy. While it accounts for 33 per cent of the GDP and employs only 1.94 per cent of the workforce, the non-oil industry represented merely 4 per cent of the GDP in 2020.[2] Additionally, the oil sector has almost no forward or backward linkages with the rest of the economy. Even during the oil boom period, Angola had to import nearly 80 per cent of its oil derivatives due to low refinery capacity. In 2019, for instance, when state international currencies were diminished, the import dependency led to a two-week nationwide fuel shortage.[3]

As Africa's second major crude oil exporter, Angola is the world's fourth most prominent diamond producer, producing 9.3 million carats in 2021. Combined, the oil and diamond sectors form the material base that has sustained

---

① Agostinho Neto, "Discurso de Proclamação da Independência de Angola", *Nova Cultura*, 11 November 2021, https://www.novacultura.info/post/2021/11/11/discurso-de-agostinho-neto-na-proclamacao-da-independencia-de-angola (accessed 25 October 2022).

② CEDESA, "Um projeto de industrialização para Angola", 23 December 2020, *CEDESA*, https://www.cedesa.pt/2020/12/23/um-projeto-de-industrializacao-para-angola/, (accessed 6 November 2022).

③ Novo Jornal, "Combustíveis: João Lourenço toma em mãos problema da falha generalizada de gasolina e óleo em Luanda", *Novo Jornal,* 7 May 2019, https://novojornal.co.ao/sociedade/interior/combustiveis-joao-lourenco-toma-em-maos-problema-da-falha-generalizada-de-gasolina-e-gasoleo-em-luanda---o-pesadelo-dos-automobilistas-e-utilizadores-de-taxis-continua-70728.html (accessed 6 November 2022).

the Angolan bourgeoisie's conspicuous consumption of imported luxury goods.[①] Through the interplay of domestic clientelist networks with multinational wealth management offices, tax havens, corporate services providers, and consulting and accounting firms, Angolan elites can send their easy profits abroad instead of reinvesting in productive activities internally.[②] By participating in the circuits of international capital, the current Angolan upper class has become culturally and ideologically even more distant from the rest of the people as were the assimilated of colonial times.

Conversely, most of the population relies on the labour-intensive subsistence agriculture sector and informal activities. Subsistence agriculture accounts for 45 per cent of the workforce and 9.4 per cent of the GDP.[③] The main crops are cassava, corn, beans, potatoes, sweet potatoes, soy, banana, coffee, and rice. Small-scale family farms with rudimentary practices and undeveloped technologies account for 92 per cent of cultivated land. At the same time, a limited electrical grid in rural areas makes the use of agro-processing and irrigated agriculture unaffordable. Thus, agricultural output is not enough for national demands, with Angola having to import more than 50 per cent of its food and most of its agricultural inputs.[④]

In 2016, the multidimensional poverty rate in rural areas was 87.8 per cent, with most of the population deprived of appropriate cooking fuel, electricity, clean water, and public sanitation.[⑤] After the onset of the Ukrainian War, the dependence on external markets caused fertilizer shortages, double digits aliment inflation, and increased food insecurity.[⑥] To make things worse, climate change is already impacting Angola's agriculture. The country is facing the

---

① Claudia Gastrow, "Recycling Consumption: political power and elite wealth in Angola", in: Deborah Posel and Ilana Wyk. *Conspicuous Consumption in Africa*, (Johannesburg: Wits University Press, 2019), pp. 79-95.

② Nicholas Shaxson, *Oil and Capital Flight: the case of Angola*, (Berlin: Peri Working Paper Series, 2021).

③ World Bank, *Angola-Agriculture Support Policy Review*.

④ Ibid.

⑤ INE, *Pobreza Multidimensional em Angola*, (Luanda: Instituto Nacional de Estatística 2020).

⑥ WFP, *Implications of the Ukraine Crisis: food, fuel, fertilisers prices in the southern Africa region*, (Johannesburg: World Food Programme, 2022).

worst drought in 40 years, which might cause $ 749 in losses in the livestock and fisheries sectors.[1]

Angola's rural sector has already been different. In the last years of the colonial economy, Angola's fertile soils, freshwater abundance (Angola has 77 river basins and 43 hydrological basins), and favoured climate substantiated a highly productive rural economy, with the country achieving self-reliance on crops such as coffee, manioc, fruits, and maize. However, the 27 years of the civil war destroyed most of the infrastructure connecting production areas to markets, filled the countryside with landmines and unexploded bombs, and caused an intense rural exodus. Since the achievement of peace, production has increased considerably in products such as cereal, legumes, and poultry due to government investments and public policies. Yet, Angola's agricultural potential remains largely untapped, with only 7 per cent of the 45.7 per cent of the arable lands (almost the size of France) currently being farmed.[2]

In turn, Angola's informal economy is estimated to account for 39 per cent of the GDP and to be essential for 75 per cent of the Angolans. It includes various activities, from shoe shiners, merchants, and domestic services to transport and parallel currency exchange. The *zungueiras* are a particular feature of Angolan informality, women that spend their days walking through the streets selling different kinds of goods carried in huge baskets over their heads.[3] While seeking a complementary income in the face of elevated unemployment, informal workers are excluded from social protections, have limited access to finance, and are usually subject to extraneous long journeys.

Comparatively, in 2018, Angola's share of informal employment in total employment was 94.1 per cent, higher than SADC's (77 per cent) and Sub-Saharan Africa's (89.2 per cent) averages, as well as of countries such

---

① Izabela Leao, "Angola's agricultural sector could become Africa's powerhouse. Here's why", *World Bank*, 13 September 2022, https://www.weforum.org/agenda/2022/09/angola-agricultural-sector-powerhouse-of-africa/#:~:text=However%2C%20Angola%20may%20soon%20be,a%20variety%20of%20agricultural%20products (accessed 10 November 2022).

② World Bank, *Angola. Agriculture Support Policy Review.*

③ The Portuguese word *Zungueira* derives from the Kimbundo word *zunga*, which means surround, walk around, or circulate.

as Cameroon (90.9 per cent), Chad (94 per cent), and Congo 85.3 per cent. Informal employment is higher in agriculture (99.4 per cent) than in services (90.2 per cent), and industry (85.1 per cent).[1]

As the largest metropolitan area in the country, Luanda concentrates both the profitable services industries tied to the oil sector, and the largest share of informal workers, with an estimated 56 per cent (around 4 million people)[2] of its population engaged in informal activities. According to Luiekakio Afonso, Luanda's dualism is translated into a rigid social-spatial inequality among the living standards at the urban nucleus (*Baixa da Cidade)*, the semi-periphery (transition area), and the periphery. *Baixa Cidade*, which hosts 31 per cent of the population and includes neighbourhoods such as Ingombota, Maianga, and Sambizanga, is where not only the central government, national and multinational corporations' buildings are situated but also the majority of schools and hospitals.[3]

At the periphery, which comprises the Cazenga, Cacuaco, and Viana municipalities and is the home of 50 per cent of the population, there is a predominance of slums (*musseques*) with poor infrastructure and precarious services, as well as large open-air informal markets.[4] In the transition area, which covers the Talatona, Belas, and Kilamba Kiaxi municipalities and contains 15.5 per cent of the population, there is a coexistence among modern economic zones and luxury housing projects with oceans of poverty spread around the *musseques*. As the infrastructure and transportation services connecting the three areas are insufficient and scattered, the peripheral population is subjected to long hours in traffic jams in insecure and unlicensed vehicles (*candongueiros*) to get to and return from their jobs at the modern nucleus.[5]

---

[1] ILO, *Angola: Study on the migration from the informal economy for formal economy*, (Geneva: International Labour Organisation 2021).

[2] Luís Morais, *O Mercado Informal em Luanda*, Dissertação, (Lisboa: Universidade de Lisboa 2019).

[3] Luiekakio Afons, "Uma leitura da urbanização recente da cidade de Luanda partir da teoria dos dois circuitos da economia urbana", *PerCursos,* v. 23, no.51, 2022, pp. 167-210.

[4] The Portuguese word *musseque* also derives from the Kimbundo word – *mu seke -*, which means red sand, as were the color of the materials used in the first occupations in Luanda's suburbs.

[5] The Portuguese word *Candongueiro* is derived from the Kimbundo word *candonga*, which means illegal or small business.

At the same time, spatial asymmetries between provinces are significant. While the oil-producing provinces of Luanda, Cabinda, and Zaire accounted for 66.7 per cent of the GDP and merely 32 per cent of the population, the 15 other provinces with 68 per cent were responsible for only 33 per cent of GPD. The lack of infrastructural connectivity among coastal and hinterland areas constrains economic integration and further exacerbates regional inequalities. By 2020, Angola had one of the lowest total road networks in Southern Africa, much of which need to be repaired. Therefore, while for many developing countries such as Mexico, Egypt, and Colombia, the interregional trade aggregate values are higher than the international trade, Angola's international trade accounts for as high as 94 per cent of the GPD and interregional trade for only 29 per cent.[1]

Insufficient infrastructure and essential services deprivation help to explain why universal primary schooling is still a distant dream and secondary and tertiary education are privileges for the few. According to the last Integrated Survey on the Welfare of the Population, in 2009, 29 per cent of Angolan children had to walk more than 2 km to attend school, 26 per cent of children between 6-9 had never attended classes, secondary and tertiary education reached, respectively, 27 per cent and 9 per cent of the population, and 34 per cent of the population was illiterate.[2] Despite improvements, in 2020, 1.3 million children were outside the school, and 48 per cent of the population with 18 years or more did not have any education level concluded.[3]

Regarding high education, while the total number of students increased by 2.5 million to 10 million between 2002 and 2018, Luanda and Benguela still concentrated 72 per cent and 6.9 per cent of university enrolments in the country. Additionally, most universities struggle with deficient facilities,

---

[1] Eduardo Haddad et al, *Uneven Integration: the case of Angola*.

[2] INE, *Inquérito Integrado sobre o Bem-Estar da População*, (Luanda: Instituto Nacional de Estatística 2011).

[3] Onélio Santiago, "Mais de 30 por cento das crianças fora do sistema formal de ensino", *Novo Jornal*, 2021. https://novojornal.co.ao/sociedade/interior/mais-de-30-das-criancas-em-idade-escolar-fora-do-sistema-formal-de-ensino---estatisticas-de-julho-falam-em-quase-2-milhoes-105413.html (accessed 10 November 2022).

constrained funding, and the absence of structured professor careers.[1] During the COVID-19 pandemic, these gaps became even more prominent, as less than 36 per cent of the Angolan population has access to the Internet, and only 4 per cent could afford 1GB per month of a data package.[2]

The Angolan educational system conditions reflect the low priority of the sector in the state budget, which allocated only 2.4 per cent of GDP to education in 2021, compared to Namibia's 9.6 per cent, South Africa's 6.2 per cent, and Chad's 2.9 per cent. The same applies to social assistance and the health system. In 2020, the government allocated less than 0.1 per cent of the GDP to social assistance[3], while health expenditure (2.53 per cent of the GDP) remained well below Chad's (4.35 per cent), Namibia's (8.5 per cent), and South Africa's (9.11 per cent) in 2019. Thus, Angolan population remains vulnerable to outbreaks of diseases such as malaria, cholera, yellow fever, and Zika, with high child and maternal mortality rates.

The indicators above illustrate the dual socioeconomic structure that emerged from the historical reproduction of Angola's unaccountable state. Aside from an outstanding inequality, in which the wealthiest 1 per cent concentrated 58 per cent of the national income, while the bottom 50 per cent accounted for a share of only 9 per cent[4], these persistent imbalances positions the country at the bottom of most global rankings. For instance, Angola was ranked 128th out of 182 countries on the Global Quality Infrastructure Index[5] in 2020, 132nd out of 132 countries in the WIPO's Global Innovation Index[6] in 2022, and 101st out

---

[1] Angop, "Higher education teachers go on strike", *Angop*, 24 October 2022. https://www.angop. ao/en/noticias/educacao/professores-do-ensino-superior-em-greve/ (acessed 10 November 2022).

[2] AUC/OECD, *Dinâmicas do Desenvolvimento em África 2021. Transformação Digital e Empregos de Qualidade*, (Addis Ababa: AUC/OECD Publishing 2021).

[3] World Bank, *Angola Poverty Assessment*.

[4] WID, *Angola,* World Inequality Database, November 2022, https://wid.world/country/angola/ (accessed 10 November 2022).

[5] Juan Oteiza, "Global Quality Infrastructure Index 2020", *Tableau Software*, 2021, https://public. tableau.com/app/profile/juan.jos.oteiza/viz/GQII2020_public/MAP (accessed 13 November 2022).

[6] WIPO, *Global Innovation Index 2021 Tracking Innovation through the COVID-19 Crisis*, (Geneva: World International Property Organization, 2021).

of 113 countries on the Economist's Global Food Insecurity Index[1] in 2022.

The striking contrast between Angola's underdeveloped condition and its natural resource endowments should be interpreted as evidence of the concrete possibility of overcoming the challenges stressed by Agostinho Neto in 1975. The central institutional dilemma is channelling oil and diamond revenues toward development goals. In that regard, local authorities' institutionalization might play a positive role by increasing the state's capacities to "identify broad strategic areas in which their economies have latent comparative advantages" while providing the conditions for infrastructure and human capital improvements.[2]

As Angola ratifies its participation in the Southern African Development Community Free Trade Area and the African Continental Free Trade Area, industrial and agriculture productivity may benefit from opportunities for market expansion and lower cost of imported inputs. Finally, Angola is well-positioned to reap the benefits of the green transition. It has the second-largest installed hydropower generation capacity in Africa, even with only 5 per cent of its potential exploited, and is endowed with high and constant solar radiation, favourable wind corridors in the southwest, and robust potential for green hydrogen development.[3]

Angola Search for Development in João Lourenço Era

Under pressure from the ongoing economic crisis, João Lourenço's administration launched the National Development Plan (2018-2022 NDP) on 1st January 2018. As a medium-term planning instrument, the 2018-2022 NDP was supposed to be in line with the Long-Term Development Strategy for Angola

---

[1]　The Economist Newspaper, "The Global Food Security Index 2022", Economist Impact, 2022, https://impact.economist.com/sustainability/project/food-security-index/ (accessed 9 November 2021).

[2]　Justin Lin & Célestin Monga, *Beating the Odds. Jump-Starting Developing Countries*, (London, Princeton University Press, 2017), p. 4.

[3]　Energy Capital & Power, "Identifying Opportunities in Angola's Renewable Energy Sector", *Energy Capital & Power,* 21 July 2022, https://energycapitalpower.com/angola-opportunities-renewable-energy/ (accessed 1 November 2022).

2025[①] published in 2007. However, considering that Angola 2025 vision was produced amid the optimistic oil-boom period, the 2018-2022 NPD had to adjust some of its expectations. For instance, while the Angola 2025 Strategy envisioned achieving a relative poverty rate of 10 per cent by 2025, the 2018-2022 NDP reviewed the target to 25 per cent in 2022. Whereas the 2007 document projected an average annual rate of productivity growth of 4.1 per cent in 2025, the 2018-2022 NDP planned to reach 2.8 percent by 2022. While the Angola 2025 Strategy expected a 95 per cent nationwide water coverage, the NDP aimed to increase from 60 per cent in 2017 to 85 per cent in 2022.

The 2018-2022 NDP is a broad framework encompassing five-axis, twenty-five strategic policies, and eighty-three action programs. Specifically, just as the *Programa de Saneamento Econômico e Financeiro* (Economic and Finance Cleaning Program) aimed to function as an intentional letter to the IMF in the 1980s, the NDP 2018-2022 adopted an austerity line target to appraise international financial institutions. For example, it considered that the Angolan state would "assume, each time more, a regulatory, promoter, and coordinating role, progressively moving away from the economic operator figure".[②] Moreover, it envisioned resizing the entrepreneurial system through a broad privatization program focused on promoting the national private sector and attracting foreign investments. In other words, facing the decrease in oil revenues and an external debt stress situation, the plan embraced a neoliberal approach framed as a mechanism to improve the business environment and competitiveness.

2018-2022 NDP's strategic guidelines broke down into two core programs: the Macroeconomic Stabilization Program (MSP) and the Program to Support National Production, Export Diversification, and Import Substitution (PRODESI). The MSP, which the IMF would support through a Policy Cooperation Instrument (PCI) after Angola's Ministry of Finance request

---

① República de Angola, Ministério do Planejamento, *Angola 2025: Angola um país com futuro*, 2007, https://www.angonet.org/dw/sites/default/files/online_lib_files/angola_plan_2000-2025.pdf (accessed 17 October 2022).

② República de Angola, *Plano de Desenvolvimento Nacional 2018-2022*, p. 142.

in 2018, is focused on reducing state-led economic distortions, sustaining macroeconomic stability, and crowding out private investment.

One of the central distortions concerned Angola's exchange rate overvaluation, which diminished the competitiveness of export sectors, incentivized imports, and facilitated the emergence of black currency markets. Thus, by January 2018, Angola's Central Bank (Banco Nacional de Angola, BNA) abandoned the pegged exchange rate regime[1] and started a gradual transition toward a floating exchange rate determined by auctions organized by the BNA. Fiscal consolidation was another policy indicated by the MSP to be achieved by compressing primary expenditures, alienating state assets, eliminating subsidies, expanding non-oil revenues by introducing a value-added tax (VAT), and approving the Fiscal Responsibility Law. Finally, MPS defined the reduction of the debt-to-GDP ratio from 90 per cent in 2018 to 65 per cent by 2023 as the target anchoring the fiscal consolidation efforts.[2]

The austerity agenda received support in the parliament. In the following months, the National Assembly approved a package of pro-market legislation. In April 2018, it approved the Angolan Competition Act, which would be enforced by the recently created Competition Regulatory Authority (CRA). Inspired by the EU and Portuguese competition laws, the Angolan legal framework established the prohibition of anticompetitive practices, procedures to control mergers, and a state aid regime.[3]

Then, in June 2018, the National Assembly approved the Private Investment Law. The new legislation eliminated minimum values requirements for foreign investments, ended the need for partnerships with Angolan citizens or firms, created two more development zones, listed nine priority sectors with

---

[1] Almanas Stanapedis, "Angola: Kwanza slides in H1 amid controlled adjustment of the exchange rate regime", *FocusEconomics,* 20 August 2018, https://www.focuseconomics.com/countries/angola/news/exchange-rate/kwanza-slides-in-h1-amid-controlled-adjustment-of-the-exchange (accessed 10 November 2022).

[2] UNCTAD, *Economic and Social Impact of Covid-19 in Angola,* (Washington: United Nations Conference on Trade and Development, 2022).

[3] Neuza Dias, "Nova Lei da Concorrência em Angola", *LexAfrica,* 17 July 2018, https://www.lexafrica.com/pt/2018/07/nova-lei-da-concorrencia-em-angola/ (accessed 19 October 2022).

specific benefits, and instituted the Investment and Export Promotion Agency (AIPEX).[1] The Private Investment Law was amended[2] three years later to facilitate private investments further. It included a contractual system that would allow negotiations between state authorities and investors, easing the legal constraints for obtaining provisional licenses and transferring dividends abroad and removing the need to use internal credit by external investors.

The last steps were approving the Privatization Law,[3] and establishing the Privatization Program (PROPRIV 2019-2022) in 2019. Under the newly created Institute for Management State Assets (IGAPE) oversight, PROPRIV[4] planned to transfer 195 state assets to the private sector, including all Sonangol's assets unrelated to the company's core activities.

While the MSP was designed as a fiscal adjustment policy, PRODESI would be the Lourenço administration's supply-side strategy to boost Angola's private sector economic diversification capacity. The plan aimed to increase the value-added of exports and promote import substitution to reduce external dependence. Nonetheless, there are not any discernible priorities, as a broad range of sectors is included within the program scope: food and agriculture, minerals resources, oil and natural gas, forests, textile, civil construction, information, and telecommunication technologies, health, education, science, tourism, and leisure.[5] Still, PRODESI's goals are bold: it envisioned a 15 per cent[6] reduction in Angola's foreign currency expenditures with food supplies,

① Diário da República, "Lei n.º 10/18. Lei do Investimento Privado", *Assembleia Nacional*, 2018, https://icfml.org/wp-content/uploads/2021/05/LEI-N10-2018.pdf (accessed 5 November 2022).

② Diário da República, Lei que Altera a Lei nº 10/18 de 26 de Junho, Lei do Investimento Privado, *Assembleia Nacional*, https://www.ucm.minfin.gov.ao/cs/groups/public/documents/document/aw4x/mzg4/~edisp/minfin1388375.pdf (accessed 4 November 2022).

③ Diário da República, Lei de Bases das Privatizações, *Assembleia Nacional*, 14 May 2019. https://www.ucm.minfin.gov.ao/cs/groups/public/documents/document/aw4x/mtcx/~edisp/minfin1171445.pdf (accessed 3 November 2022).

④ Governo de Angola, Angola's Privatization Program 2019-2022, *PROPRIV*, 2019 https://www.bodiva.ao/media/propriv/20190818%20Privatization%20Program%20(EN).pdf (accessed 4 November 2022).

⑤ PRODESI, Sobre o PRODESI, *PRODESI*, 2022, https://prodesi.ao/sobre (accessed in 7 November 2021).

⑥ Lusa, "Angola corta importação de produtos da cesta básica para metade", *Diário de Notícias*, 24 July 2018, https://www.dn.pt/lusa/angola-corta-importacao-de-produtos-da-cesta-basica-para-metade-9629050.html (accessed 23 October 2022).

a 60 per cent increase in the foreign direct investment in non-oil sectors, and an elevation of 15 positions in Angola's rank in the Doing Business Index by 2022.

A specific program was created to finance PRODESI's projects. The Credit Support Program (PAC) is designed as a finance mechanism to be implemented by more than twenty public and private commercial banks. The digital platform *Portal do Produtor Nacional* (National Producer Portal) was formed to facilitate registration and credit approvals. Other regulatory measures included the reduction from 36 days to 24 hours for business licenses, the approval of the Insolvency and Corporate Recovery Law, a 5 per cent reduction in corporate taxes, a 91 per cent decrease in Land Registry Certificate's fees, and the expansion of the Credit Risk Information Centre.[1] By January 2022, PRODESI had already financed Kz 879 billion for 1043 projects in all of Angola's provinces.[2]

Thus, compared to Angola's previous reforms, the 2018-2022 NDP envisions a much more comprehensive and binding set of measures. The expectation is that, with regulatory liberalization and low-interest credit, foreign investments and the national private sector would lead a structural transformation economic process. Considering the weakness of Angola's private sector and the importance of a developmental state to late-coming industrialization, the soundness of the strategy is at least debatable. Still, commitment to the structural reform agenda brought noticeable short-term gains. For instance, in December 2018, Angola secured the approval of a $ 3.7 billion Extended Fund Facility (equivalent to 361 per cent of Angola's quota) from the IMF Executive Board.[3]

---

[1] República de Angola, *Plano de Desenvolvimento Nacional 2018-2022*, p. 158.

[2] Ana Paula, "PRODESI garante financiamento de 897 mil milhões de kwanzas", *Jornal de Angola*, 26 January 2022, https://www.jornaldeangola.ao/ao/noticias/prodesi-garante-financiamento-de-879-mil-milhoes-de-kwanzas-2/ (accessed 10 November 2022).

[3] IMF, IMF Executive Board Approves US$3.7 Billion Extended Arrangement Under the Extended Fund Facility for Angola, *IMF Press Release no. 18/463*, 7 December 2018, https://www.imf.org/en/News/Articles/2018/12/07/pr18463imf-executive-board-approves-extended-arrangement-under-the-extended-fund-facility-for-angola (accessed 9 November 2022).

Angolan responses to COVID-19: mobilization, vulnerabilities, and new delays in local autarchies institutionalization

The outbreak of the COVID-19 pandemic compromised the reform agenda schedule. With a precarious health system, Angolan authorities had to act swiftly to control the virus' spread. On March 20, one day before the first two cases of COVID-19 were registered in Angola, the government had already prohibited transit across the terrestrial borders, the docking and landing of vessels and passengers from abroad, and the entry of all commercial and private flights into the country.[1] On March 23, the government imposed a 15 days suspension of activities for schools, universities, churches, restaurants, and public events. At midnight on 27 March 2020, a Presidential Decree set the state of emergency into force. From then on, all private commercial establishments and public facilities were closed, urban and interprovincial public transport services were reduced to half of their capacity, moto-taxis were prohibited, health authorities could close formal or informal markets with a high risk of contagious, restaurants operation were restricted to takeaway and home delivery services.[2]

The containment measures were effective. The virus spread slowly, with most cases confined to Luanda. Considering the high level of administrative centralization, and compared to other Sub-Saharan African countries, Angola's vaccination also performed well. The government invested heavily in cold chain facilities and worked with several NGOs to boost vaccination and fight disinformation. Meanwhile, Angola's diplomacy staff could gather aid from international partners. Thus, by November 2022, Angola had fully vaccinated 22 per cent of its population, keeping up with the African average and above many countries such as Namibia, Kenya, Gambia, Djibouti, and Chad.[3] In the words of Djamila Cabral, World Health Organisation Representative in Angola: "the

---

[1] Daniel Muondo e Cirlene Oliveira, "The new government reforms in time of COVID-19 in Angola in the current political and social context and the confrontation of social inequalities", *Katálysis* no. 24, v.1 (2021). pp. 66-75.

[2] UNCTAD, *Economic and Social Impact of Covid-19 in Angola.*

[3] AU, "Africa CDC COVID-19 Vaccine Dashboard", *African Union*, 2022, https://africacdc.org/covid-19-vaccination/ (accessed 13 November 2022).

commitment and energy from Angola's government to get the vaccine rollout right was exemplary from very early on. Good preparation, including staffing and training needs, cold-chain logistics, and getting the regulations right, were just some reasons why Angola was one of Africa's first countries to receive vaccines."[1]

Economically, though, the compound effects of the oil prices decline and the lockdown measures produced an 8.22 per cent of GDP loss in the last three quarters of 2020, as well as a contraction of 30 per cent in government oil revenues compared to 2019. Between July 2019 and September 2020, the Kwanza lost 40 per cent of its value compared to the dollar, curbing Angola's import capacity and driving inflation to 27 per cent in 2021. Government debt to GDP increased to 131 per cent, making Fitch, Standard & Poors, and Moody's all lower the country's long-term ratings.[2] The negative impacts on the massive share of informal workers were also severe, with 60 per cent of informal market operators reporting very high losses and 40 per cent having to reduce their expenditures on food.[3]

The socioeconomic consequence of the sanitary emergency required a review of the government finances that would sustain economic activities while preserving the MPS' fiscal consolidation efforts. Thus, in July 28, 2020, the National Assembly[4] approved the revision of the state budget proposed by the presidency with a reduction of 15 per cent on general expenditures but an increase from 15 to 17 per cent on education, health, and social expenses, and a rise from 4 to 7 per cent on economic issues.[5] The contraction would come from debt reliefs granted by external creditors, as well as the suspension of all

---

[1] Collins Boakye-Agyemang, "Inside Angola's 'exemplary' COVID-19 vaccination hubs", *World Health Organization*, 2 July 2021, https://www.afro.who.int/pt/node/14831 (accessed 10 November 2022).

[2] Zahabia Gupta, *Angola: Deep Dive into Dept.*

[3] UNCTAD, *Economic and Social Impact of Covid-19 in Angola.*

[4] Governo de Angola, Ministério das Finanças. Assembleia Nacional aprova OGE Revisto referente ao exercício económico de 2020. *Ministério das Finanças*, 28 July 2020, minfin.gov.ao/ PortalMinfin/#!/sala-de-imprensa/noticias/7955/assembleia-nacional-aprova-oge-revisto-referente-ao-exercicio-economico-de-2020 (accessed 4 November 2022).

[5] UNCTAD, *Economic and Social Impact of Covid-19 in Angola.*

non-structural expenses, additional credits, admissions, and promotions in public functions, the decrease of governmental travel to essentials, the reduction of the number of ministries from 28 to 21, and of the leadership and management positions from 559 to 313.[1]

With a more significant fiscal space, the Ministry of Economy and Planning announced a comprehensive stimulus package (*Alívio Econômico*) for firms and households. For companies, it instituted exemptions on VAT and customs duties on imports of humanitarian goods and donations, a 12-month tax credit for imported goods and raw materials used to produce 54 essential goods in the basic basket, interest-free payment delays for social security contributions, liquidity support to the banking sector and extension of credit lines to importers. For family farming and micro, small and medium firms, the Fund for Support to Agrarian Development (FADA) established a credit line of Kz 15 billion to finance with 3 per cent interest, the Angola Development Bank (ADB) opened a credit line of approximately Kz 38 billion, and the Venture Capital Active Fund (FACRA) unlocked a credit line of Kz 7 billion. For households, the Ministry of Economy and Planning announced the transfer of 3 per cent of social security contributions directly to wages, the cancellation of cuts in electricity and water supply due to non-payment, and the disbursement of Kz 315 million for basic chest products distribution.[2]

Moreover, the COVID-19 shock propelled the government to adjust, accelerate and expand the implementation of social policies. In September 2020, the Minister of Public Administration Labour and Social Security fine-tuned the emphasis of the Employability Promotion Action Plan (PAPE), which began to focus less on capacitation and more on employment creation. With an approved budget of Kz 22 billion, the PAPE aims to boost the entrepreneurial spirit of young Angolans through measures such as vocational training, distribution

---

[1] Vera Daves de Souza, *Intervenção da Ministra das Finanças para Anúncio das medidas de revisão do cenário macroeconómico fruto do COVID-19 e choque petrolífero*, (Luanda: República de Angola, Ministério das Finanças, 2020).

[2] República de Angola, Ministério da Economia e Planejamento. *Medidas de Alívio do Impacto Provocado pela Pandemia COVID-19 sobre as Empresas e Particulares*, (Luanda: Ministério da Economia e Planejamento, 2020).

of self-employment kits, microcredit finance lines to small-business, and incentives for companies to hire trainees. By December 2021, PAPE had created approximately 30,000 direct jobs and 45,000 indirect ones.[1] On 17 November 2021, Angola launched the Informal Economy Reconversion Program (PREI), aiming to register 200,000[2] informal workers in one year. With financial support from the European Union, the target was easily achieved, with the program having licensed 246,189 jobs[3] by August 2022.

While PAPE and PREI target urban areas, the Strengthening the National Social Protection System Project was designed to reach the most vulnerable rural population. Informally known as *Kwenda*, which in the Kimbundu language means 'walking', the program has financial and operational support from the World Bank and is under the supervision of the Ministry of Social Action, Family and Women's Empowerment (MSAFME). Launched on 4 May 2020, Kwenda focused on registering women as beneficiaries of the government-to-person payments and is implemented alongside community workers and social action centres at the local level. By January 2022, Kwenda had written 502,000 families and delivered trimestral Kz 25,000 cash transfers for almost 250,000 families across fourteen provinces.[4] Likewise, the "Children Value" (*Valor Criança*) program was extended to a second phase. Under the auspices of the MSAFME and backed by the Angola National Bank, United Nations Children's Fund (UNICEF), and the EU, by October 2021, the program had made monetary

---

[1] Tatiana Costa, "Em dois anos, PAPE criou mais de 30 mil postos de trabalho directos", *Ver Angola*, 7 December 2021, https://www.verangola.net/va/pt/122021/Economia/28486/Em-dois-anos-PAPE-criou-mais-de-30-mil-postos-de-trabalho-directos.htm (accessed 10 November 2022).

[2] Expansão, "Programa de Reconversão da Economia Informal (PREI) conta com 14,5 milhões de euros da União Europeia", *Expansão*, 17 November 2021, https://expansao.co.ao/economia/interior/programa-de-reconversao-da-economia-informal-prei-conta-com-145-milhoes-de-euros-da-uniao-europeia-105498.html#:~:text=O%20PREI%20foi%20formalmente%20apresentado,operacionalização%20nos%20próximos%20nove%20meses (access 2 November 2022).

[3] PREI, "Dados Estatísticos", *Governo de Angola*, 8 August 2022, https://prei.ao/formalizacao-operadores-informais/ (access 3 November 2022).

[4] World Bank, "Q&A: How is Angola Reaching the Poor and Vulnerable During Covid-19?" *The World Bank Group*, 15 March 2022, https://www.worldbank.org/en/country/angola/brief/q-a-how-is-angola-is-reaching-the-poor-and-vulnerable-during-covid-19 (accessed 1 November 2022).

transfers for 10,512 families in Bié, Moxico, and Uíge provinces.[①]

In sum, the Angolan state achieved an impressive degree of mobilization to fight the pandemic, scaling up public policies that targeted different vulnerable social strata. Nonetheless, it was not enough to face the scale of Angola's structural contradictions – overcentralized state capacities, large informal economy, food import dependence, and poor infrastructure – and the compound effects of the downfall in oil prices and COVID-19 lockdowns. The unemployment rate kept rising, and foreign direct investment remained short, with capital investment reaching its record low in 2020.[②] Worse, in the southern provinces of Huila, Cunene, and Namibe, which were already facing the effects of prolonged droughts, 1.58 million people experienced high-level food insecurity between October 2021 and March 2022. On the face of it, it became clear that market forces and international aid would not be sufficient to mitigate the short-term effects of the crisis on Angolans' living conditions nor drive a mid to long-term development process.

Conclusion

This chapter analysed why post-civil war Angola's economy and society remain highly vulnerable to external shocks such as the COVID-19 pandemic and the Ukrainian War. We argued that Angola's historical state-building process fashioned an unaccountable state apparatus ruled by urban elites with few political and economic incentives to expand the infrastructural reach of the state beyond the oil-producing coastal areas. To illustrate the mechanisms that sustained this societal structure, we discussed how the centralization of oil revenues within the presidency and the MPLA's pragmatic alliance with the traditional leaders have allowed the regime to postpone the implementation of locally elected authorities recurrently.

---

① Governo de Angola, "Programa Valor Criança", *Portal Oficial do Governo da República de Angola*, 4 October 2021, https://governo.gov.ao/ao/noticias/programa-valor-crianca/#:~:text=Mais%2013.656%20crianças%20menores%20de,do%20programa%20"Valor%20Criança" (accessed 13 November 2022).

② The Global Economy, "Angola: Capital investment, percent of GDP", *The Global Economy.com*, August 2021, https://www.theglobaleconomy.com/Angola/capital_investment/ (accessed 14 November 2022).

In the second section, we described some consequences of the unaccountable form of governance institutionalized during President José Eduardo dos Santos's era. By systematizing quantitative and qualitative indicators, we showed that Angola has a dual socioeconomic structure in which the elites are tied to the capital-intensive extractive sector through clientelist networks that permeate state apparatus. At the same time, most of the population relies on agricultural subsistence and informal activities. Aside from the striking levels of inequality, this duality effectively hampers the development of Angola's productive powers, as domestic productive clusters remain disconnected and most of the growing labour force remains excluded from educational opportunities.

The authors, therefore, argue that a pure austerity agenda may never be enough to take the country to the appropriate path toward development due to the historical depth and extensive scale of Angola's political, economic, and ideological dualities. Although the current efforts to macroeconomic stabilization, attract foreign investments and strengthen the national private sector are laudable, there is an urgent need to enhance the state's capacities to drive a developmental project aiming at rapid industrialization, agricultural revitalization, poverty alleviation, domestic production base diversification, and universalization of public goods and services. As the successful development by countries in East Asia has demonstrated, there won't be structural transformation without a developmental state capable of leading a strategic national project.

It is important to stress that by focusing the explanation on domestic institutions, we left out the equally essential variables deriving from the global economic structure. For example, the overlay of Cold War dynamics into the Angola Civil War was the leading factor that increased the conflict extent and destruction level. Similarly, the predatory characteristic of Angola's oil and diamond sectors would not be possible without the active collaboration of multinational corporations, financial institutions, and tax havens that act under the protection of the same countries that condemn Angolan systemic corruption. Therefore, we indicate the analysis of the international mechanisms contributing to the reproduction of Angola's underdevelopment and dependent condition as a vital path for continuing the research agenda.

Lastly, despite immense obstacles, Angola's abundant mineral resources,

146

vast arable lands, broad green energy potential, and growing labour force are endowments that can be operationalized in a national development strategy. Hence, it is urgent to advance a research agenda concerned with the following question: how can Angola leverage its latent comparative advantages to engender rapid economic growth, higher labour productivity, and industrial diversification? For instance, although implementing decentralization reforms is crucial, it should not be conceived as a panacea but as a tool to enhance the state's capacities to respond better to local problems, identify development opportunities, and implement public policies. Without the political will to undertake the long-term investments in infrastructure and human capital needed to operationalize these goals, local authorities might as well be captured by clientelist practices and fail to recover the sacred hope summoned by Agostinho Neto.

非洲问题、非洲方案
与新自由主义治理困境

国际金融机构在非洲冲突、
复苏和过渡中的作用

——以埃塞俄比亚和苏丹为例

阿拉加·阿巴布·基夫勒　芬米·奥洛尼萨金著　董玳均译*

摘　要： 过去三年连续的冲击破坏了非洲以前的发展成果，阻遏了非洲与发达世界之间的经济融合。虽然这些冲击根源于非洲大陆以外，但在非洲大陆的内部条件下得以强化。因素之一就是冲突和不稳定，近一半的非洲国家不是脆弱就是受冲突的影响。尽管国际组织声称将支持非洲克服脆弱性和冲突，但他们应该如何与非洲接触仍然是一个主要的政策和学术问题。例如，国际金融机构（International Financial Institutions, IFIs）被要求帮助从经济面向解决脆弱性和冲突问题。然而，这些措施是否真正有帮助几乎没有共识。对于如何适应性地采取策略来纠正过去的错误，同时在广泛监测和研究的基础上试验新的帮助策略，国际金融机构本身就经常自相矛盾。对于这些国际金融机构的种种叙事及其背后的利益和议程，学术争论尚无定论。本文试图通过研究国际金融机构如何参与埃塞俄比亚和苏丹最近的冲突和过渡，为这些争论提供了崭新的实证依据。与此前的研究发现类似，本文认为，国际金融机构开出的发展处方的灵感仍然来自新自由主义经济愿景的核心本质，与对社会保障的关注具有不同程度的互补性，在两国产生的效果也不相同。在苏丹，社会保障支出缓慢地跟随着其他经济改革措施，后者的成功促进了

---

　　* 阿拉加·阿巴布·基夫勒（Alagaw Ababu Kifle），肯尼亚内罗毕非洲领导力中心（research fellow and head of fellowships at the African Leadership Centre）研究员和研究中心主任；芬米·奥洛尼萨金（Funmi Olonisakin），尼日利亚人，伦敦国王学院全球事务学院非洲领导力中心（Leadership and Development at the African Leadership Centre in the School of Global Affairs at King's College London）国际安全、非洲领导力与发展研究教授；董玳均，自由职业者，伦敦国王学院硕士毕业。

　　［注］本文由刘海方、王进杰进行中文翻译校对。

社会资源的支出，但当军方于 2021 年 10 月罢免了文官政府后，社会支出突然终止了，这严重影响了平民的生活。在埃塞俄比亚，两年战争期间，世界银行继续进行"以人为本"式的参与，然而国际货币基金组织却因为与冲突无关的原因暂停了该项目。因此，国际金融机构在苏丹发挥着积极协调的作用，但在埃塞俄比亚则充其量间接发挥了制止危机的作用。

关键词：埃塞俄比亚 苏丹 世界银行 国际货币基金组织 国际金融机构

引 言

非洲寻求社会经济进步的努力继续受到全球发展的影响。2019 年的新冠病毒大流行、俄乌战争和最近的全球经济动态（与国家层面的挑战相互作用）造成的冲击，继续侵袭着非洲的社会经济福祉，并逆转了过去几十年的进步。由于新冠肺炎大流行，2021 年非洲经济收缩了 1.6%，有 3000 万人陷入极端贫困。[①] 尽管 2021 年非洲出人意料地实现了快速复苏，增长率达到 4.7%，但俄乌战争的爆发（与全球经济趋势、冲突和不稳定以及气候变化的相互作用）减缓了这一复苏趋势，使复苏变得困难，甚至引发了其他宏观经济问题。[②] 在冲突刚开始时，小麦、化肥和能源的价格分别上涨了 28%、22% 和 20%，然而通货膨胀率高达 40%。[③] 物价上涨又使 1500 万人陷入极端贫困。[④] 据估计，约有 1.4 亿非洲人面临着严重的粮食不安全问题，如果不给予应有的重视，社会紧张和冲突可能会加剧。[⑤]

[①] AfDB, *African Economic Outlook 2022: Supporting Climate Finance and a just Energy Transition in Africa*. Abidjan, Côte d'Ivoire: African Development Bank, 2022.

[②] IMF, *Regional Economic Outlook*: *Sub-Saharan Africa*: *Living on the Edge*, Washington DC: International Monetary Fund, 2022.

[③] AfDB, *African's Macro-Economic Performance and Outlook*. Abidjan: *African Development Bank*, 2023.

[④] 同上。

[⑤] AUDA-NEPAD, *Annual Report*: *African Union Development Agency-Nepad. Johannesburg*: AUDA-NEPAD, 2022.

因此，尽管对社会保护支出的需求仍然很高，非洲同样面临着财政空间有限的限制，无法提供更多支出。抵御大流行所需的社会支出已经使非洲国家的财政状况紧张，而目前发达和中等收入经济体经济放缓以及随之而来的金融收紧，进一步置非洲国家财政于窘境。[①] 非洲国家获得外部融资的渠道有限，即使有，也只能以高利率获得——结果使得非洲债务问题进一步恶化，接近一半的非洲国家要么陷入债务危机，要么面临债务困难的高风险。[②] 越来越不确定的外部环境对大多数非洲国家产生了负面影响，同时社会政治冲突和气候变化等非洲内部因素正变为另一组阻碍增长和损害福祉的挑战。因此，非洲的复苏对策既要针对外部冲击源，也要针对具有弹性的内部决定因素。

由于非洲的问题具有全球根源，国际行为体在帮助其解决经济问题方面往往具有重大利益和贡献。国际金融机构作为国际组织和行为体生态系统中的一个组成部分，在帮助非洲从外部冲击中复苏和解决经济危机以及贫困的内部根源方面发挥着关键作用。例如，国际货币基金组织宣称，疫情发生以来，已向撒哈拉以南非洲国家紧急拨款 270 亿美元，并批准新增了 230 亿美元特别提款权。[③] 它还在其紧急贷款工具中引入了一个新的粮食冲击窗口，用以支持因为粮食价格上涨引起的国际收支问题。同样，WB 声称，已经提供了 2000 多亿美元来帮助发展中国家克服疫情的影响。[④]

更重要的是，从本文的角度来看，国际金融机构声称将针对非洲国家具体的冲突、政治动荡挑战提供量身定制的支持，以大力支持这些国家解决内源性社会经济问题。暴力和不安全因素显著增加，已经掣肘若干非洲国家社会经济发展，所以国际金融机构对脆弱和冲突局势的关注，的确是受欢迎的新动态。WB 确定的"脆弱和受冲突影响的国家"

---

① IMF, *Regional Economic Outlook*: *Sub-Saharan Africa*: *Living on the edge*.

② Kassahum, Bitsat Yohannes, "One Year Later: The impact of the Russian conflict with Ukraine on Africa," *Africa Renewal*, 13 February 2023, https://www.un.org/africarenewal/magazine/february-2023/one-year-later-impact-russian-conflict-ukraine-africa.

③ IMF, *Regional Economic Outlook*: *Sub-Saharan Africa*: *Living on the edge*.

④ WB, *How the World Bank Group is helping countries address COVID*-19 (*Coronavirus*), 2022.

（fragile and conflict affected states，FCS）名单中，有近一半来自非洲。[①]
从全球趋势和区域观察来看，脆弱和受冲突影响的非洲国家数量可能会
增加：暴力冲突达到了30年来的最高水平，被迫流离失所的人数将达
到有史以来的最高水平；在2023年和2024年，有多达30个非洲国家可
能会经历与选举相关的政治风险。[②]因此，对非洲脆弱性和受冲突影响
的国家的关注，不仅是由于其数量的增加以及国家所占比例过高，还有
这些国家特殊的发展需求。脆弱性和受冲突影响国家与低收入国家表现
出同样的经济问题，也面临着其他额外的挑战，因此特别需要适合其情
况的发展支持。

在脆弱性和受冲突影响中，发展行为体必须学习如何在不安全的环
境中履行其使命，并致力于减少暴力和战争，然而安全干预必须具有明
确的发展意识。WB和IMF确实开始认识到不仅需要与FCS国家合作，
而且需要以与非FCS不同的合作方式让他们参与其中。WB和IMF原本
参与并主导冲突后国家的经济重建及宏观经济政策，现在则是越来越多
地卷入并试图习惯针对这种过渡和恢复性国家。然而，他们自身对于参
与过渡和冲突充满了分歧，而且并非一成不变，至少在言论上如此。虽
然这些机构自称有足够的适应能力来帮助FCS国家，但也有很多人指出
他们导致冲突加剧并损害了民生福祉。

本文重新梳理了这些IFIs最近在应对脆弱和冲突局势上的战略转变
方面的争论，以正在进行过渡的埃塞俄比亚冲突和苏丹为案例，讨论非
洲最近的发展。本文还详细讨论了IFIs在战略上的转变程度，以及它们
在促进和平与发展方面的前景和挑战。处于极具地缘政治影响力之地的
埃塞俄比亚和苏丹，分别于2018年和2019年开始过渡，过渡过程和挑
战都具有相似的特点。[③]当2020年底埃塞俄比亚陷入战争时，苏丹的过
渡也仍然处于漫长的煎熬中。在WB最新战略（IMF也协同一致）中，

---

① WB, *List of Fragile and Conflict Affected Situations*, 2022, https://thedocs.worldbank.org/en/
doc/9b8fbdb62f7183cef819729cc9073671-0090082022/original/FCSList-FY06toFY22.pdf.

② WB, *World Bank Group Strategy for Fragility, Conflict, and Violence* 2020-2025 (*English*).
Washington Dc: World Bank; AfDB, Africa's Macro-Economic Performance and Outlook, 2020.

③ Aly Verjee, "Political Transitions in Sudan and Ethiopia: An Early Comparative Analysis,"
Global Change, Peace & Security 33, no.3, 2021, https://doi.org/10.1080/14781158.2021.1961703.

埃塞俄比亚被定义为一个受冲突影响的国家，而苏丹则是一个脆弱型的国家。因此，观察 IFIs 对这两个国家的参与情况，将有助于了解 IFIs 和 FCS 国家关系的变化及其连续性。这也揭示了 IFIs 与这些国家政治当局之间的权力动态关系。IFIs 的发展和过渡愿景与这些国家社会之间的协调程度，也将是本次讨论的一个重要问题。

本文分为六个部分，引言之后的第二部分叙述了 IFIs 在参与 FCS 方面的演变，这些机构的政策文件和报告中都有相关内容。随后，第三部分讨论了学者们对 IFIs 参与 FCS 的争议和看法。第四部分简要介绍了 IFIs 在埃塞俄比亚的参与情况，第五部分详细分析了 IFIs 在苏丹的情况。最后，第六部分就本文讨论中出现的问题提出了一些总结意见，并就中国参与非洲事务提出了一些政策建议。

一、IFIs 自身对其参与 FCS 的叙事

IFIs 认为，他们对不断变化的环境有足够的适应能力，并不断制定出一系列措施，旨在帮助各国从冲突中恢复重建。[1] 例如，WB 声称，它们对受冲突影响的国家和脆弱国家的参与，已经从关注冲突后重建发展到了对冲突全过程的参与和应对，这是根据 WB 2011 年题为《冲突、安全与发展》研究报告以及 2018 年与联合国共同编写的《和平之路研究》报告做出的调整。[2] 报告称，其新的《脆弱国家战略》（2020—2025）将前一份报告中强调的安全、正义和发展之间的联系与后者呼吁更加重视冲突的预防进行了更好的整合。WB 声称，这一新战略对 WB 思维和运作的多个方面进行了创新。根据这项新战略，WB 现在关注冲突的所有过程，即使在冲突情况下也要参与其中，以"保护机构能力和人力资

---

[1] WB, *World Bank Group Strategy for Fragility, Conflict, and Violence* 2020-2025 (*English*), 2022. IMF, *IMF Strategy for Fragile and Conflict Affected States* (*FCS*), https://www.imf.org/en/Topics/fragile-and-conflict-affected-states#:~:text=Therefore%2C%20the%20IMF%20is%20stepping%20up%20its%20engagement,promote%20sustainable%20and%20inclusive%20growth%2C%20and%20exit%20fragility.

[2] WB, *World Bank Group Strategy for Fragility, Conflict, and Violence* 2020-2025 (*English*).

本"，并增加对脆弱国家和受冲突影响国家的支持数量和类型。[①]该战略规定，WB 将通过预防冲突、支持难民和收容社区、解决基于性别的暴力、支持各国向冲突后国家过渡以及继续参与冲突局势，来支持脆弱和受冲突影响的国家。

IMF 也同样声称，其对支持脆弱和受冲突影响国家的优先关注和承诺，越来越适应其经验、教训和不断发展的知识。[②]在此基础上，IMF 认为，它试行的国家参与战略，是基于对脆弱和冲突的驱动因素的识别以及对各国政治和经济背景的了解。因此它寻求整合基金的监督、能力发展和贷款实践；增加为脆弱国家和受冲突影响国家提供优惠性支持的数量和灵活性；还建立了一个新的复原力和可持续性信托基金（Resilience and Sustainability Trust Fund, RST），以应对低收入国家的结构性长期挑战。[③]根据 IMF 的说法，这些不同的措施累积到一起，就是最终在 2022 年推出的脆弱和受冲突影响国家新战略。

在这项新战略中，IMF 承认脆弱国家和受冲突影响国家的特殊需要，认识到在这些国家的发展干预无法成功地按照"常规发展"的方式进行。[④]认识到脆弱和冲突局势对这些国家宏观经济的关键作用，并试图通过调整其方法来执行在这些国家的任务，"考虑到每个国家的脆弱因素、政治经济动态和改革的具体限制"[⑤]。IMF 声称，将采纳参与 FCS 的新原则，承认有必要根据其脆弱性和冲突情况调整其方法、为 FCS 制定国家参与战略、扩大伙伴关系以扩大其比较优势，并调整其参与方式以满足 FCS 的需求。在这方面，它通过具有环境敏感性的检测和分析、扩大实践参与以及灵活设计的贷款安排来实现这一点，这些安排根据脆弱和冲突状态的实际情况来调整程序设计和条件性。[⑥]因此，WB 和 IMF 都将各自作用描述为与受脆弱性和冲突影响的国家和社会高度相关。尽管如此，学术界对于 IFIs 在改善社会福利和加强促进增长的宏观经济框

---

① WB, *World Bank Group Strategy for Fragility, Conflict, and Violence* 2020-2025 (*English*).

② IMF, *IMF strategy for fragile and conflict affected states (FCS)*.

③ 同上。

④ 同上。

⑤ 同上。

⑥ 同上。

架方面仍有很大争议。

二、学者观察与争论

关于 IFIs 在低收入国家的参与，特别是在 FCS 的参与，本文注意到主要有两种学术争鸣：第一种质疑了 IFIs 存在的首要理由，而第二种则审视了 IFIs 是否以及如何导致（不）安全和（欠）发展。根据其基本前提，WB 致力于消除极端贫困并促进共同繁荣，而 IMF 则旨在确保宏观经济增长，并为经济增长创造条件。然而，这两个机构的行为所依据的利益、动机和意识形态，以及它们（未能）贡献的社会成果，与它们公开宣称的有所不同。一些学者认为，IMF 的目的是通过支持存在严重外汇短缺和国际收支问题的国家来应对经济崩溃。[①] 从这个角度来看，借款国签署 IMF 的条件，要么是因为它们希望将自己困在可能不受欢迎的政策措施中，要么是因为它们缺乏外汇并减少了外汇储备。[②] 然而，其他人认为，IFIs 利用国家的经济和政治脆弱性将新自由主义制度化，而不考虑其措施的社会和经济结果。Dolan-Evans 认为，WB 利用战争发生的机会，通过新自由主义的和平建设行动来建立新自由主义社会。[③] 根据这一观点，在 IMF 开始提倡诸如货币贬值、削减公共开支、经济自由化和放松管制等紧缩措施的同时，WB 也在推动同样的自由主义政策，即加强私有化、竞争力和增长。[④]

根据证据的多寡和可能的意识形态倾向，学者们对 IFIs 最近对社会支出和社会包容的重视给予了不同的评价。一些人认为，即使强调了

[①] James Raymond Vreeland, "Why Do Governments and the IMF Enter into Agreements? Statistically Selected Cases," *International political science review* 24, no. 3, 2003, https://doi.org/10.1177/0192512103024003003.

[②] Vreeland, James Raymond, "Why do Government and the IMF Enter into Agreements? Statistically Selected Cases," *International Political Science Review* 33, no. 3, 2003, pp. 321-343, https://doi.org/10.1177/0192512103024003003.

[③] Elliot Dolan-Evans, "Making War Safe for Capitalism: The World Bank and its Evolving Interventions in Conflict," *Security dialogue* 53, no. 6, 2022, https://doi.org/10.1177/09670106221091382.

[④] Dolan-Evans, "Making War Safe for Capitalism: The World Bank and its Evolving Interventions in Conflict."

这些方面，其核心仍然是私有化和自由化的自由主义经济正统，其目的是"新自由主义制度、消除贸易壁垒、减少劳工保护，并将受冲突影响的国家和全球资本循环联系起来"[1]。国家行动因此倾向于被"重新定向、甚至加强"，以支持最全球化的金融部门，以及资本对社会和劳工权利的攻势。[2] Reinold 还认为，尽管 IMF 公开承诺为经济增长、社会保护和良好治理创造必要条件，但当地的工作人员却优先考虑宏观经济的稳定。[3] 根据 Kentikelenis 等人的说法，[4] 54% 的案例没有遵守 IMF 设定的社会支出下限，这使得 IMF 关于社会保护的说法要不就是夸夸其谈、装腔作势，要不就是虚与委蛇、华而不实，那些最需要社会保护的人仍然是受紧缩措施影响最大的人。

因此，从这些学者的角度来看，问题在于，当这两个目标发生冲突时，IMF 会首先考虑债务可持续性问题，而不是受援国所受的社会影响。Eichengreen 和 Woods 强调了这一因素，他们认为，促进经济增长的需求可能不同于退出 IMF 计划之所需。[5] 其他来自批判性政治经济学传统的观点从根本上挑战了 IFIs 在冲突后国家开展业务所依据的理念。Cohn 和 Duncanson 认为，IFIs 以市场为导向的方法认为，人类的生殖保健和维持生计的劳动以及外部环境的性质，对于市场的正常运作并不重要；[6] 基于这种错误的假设，IFIs 将战后恢复等同于 GDP 的增长和世界

① Dolan-Evans, "Making War Safe for Capitalism: The World Bank and its Evolving Interventions in Conflict."

② João Márcio Mendes Pereira, "Recycling and expansion: an analysis of the World Bank agenda (1989-2014)," *Third world quarterly* 37, no. 5, 2016, https://doi.org/10.1080/01436597.2015.1113871.p. 825.

③ Theresa Reinold, "The Path of Least Resistance: Mainstreaming 'Social Issues' in the International Monetary Fund," *Global society: journal of interdisciplinary international relations* 31, no. 3, 2017, https://doi.org/10.1080/13600826.2016.1203764.

④ Alexander E. Kentikelenis, Thomas H. Stubbs, and Lawrence P. King, "IMF conditionality and development policy space, 1985-2014," *Review of international political economy: RIPE* 23, no. 4, 2016, https://doi.org/10.1080/09692290.2016.1174953.

⑤ Barry Eichengreen and Ngaire Woods, "The IMF's Unmet Challenges," *The Journal of economic perspectives* 30, no. 1, 2016, https://doi.org/10.1257/jep.30.1.29.

⑥ Carol Cohn and Claire Duncanson, "Whose recovery? IFI prescriptions for postwar states," *Review of international political economy: RIPE* 27, no. 6, 2020, https://doi.org/10.1080/09692290.2019.1677743.

经济的融入，而事实上应该是重建战争造成的破坏，解决战争带来的任何新挑战，并改变整个战争时期的政治经济格局。[①] 另一些人则认为，IFIs 可能没有充分考虑这些不同目标之间实际上可能相互冲突，甚至相互抵消。[②]

第二种学术争论的重点是 IFIs 在 FCS 中对和平与冲突所采取措施产生的影响，以及产生这些结果的机制。一些研究直接反对这些自相矛盾的措施，比如 Casper 认为，接受 IMF 条件的领导人比那些没有接受条件的领导人更容易遭到政变的威胁。[③] IMF 的安排往往会削弱领导人分配租金的能力，从而削弱领导人维持联盟完整性的能力。因此，那些被排除在租金分配过程之外的精英成员会密谋发动政变。[④] Hartzell 等人同样认为，IMF 强加的结构调整方案增加了内战的风险，因为它产生了输家和赢家，同时破坏了国家克服分布式冲突的能力。[⑤] 这些学者认为，要想摆脱贫困和冲突，就必须要在 IMF 的自由化之路以外另辟蹊径。Dolan-Evans 还认为，WB 的干预加剧了不公正、不平等和暴力。[⑥] Cohn 和 Duncanson 同样认为，IFIs 在冲突后通过资源开采实现和平的战略，既没有认识到"解决战争造成的破坏、混乱和扭曲"所需要的东西，也没有支持"可持续和平所需的过渡"，而是制造了最容易引发战争和经济不平等的社会因素。[⑦] 同样，Reinsberg 等人认为，IMF 的方案往往会

[①] Carol Cohn and Claire Duncanson, "Whose recovery? IFI prescriptions for postwar states," *Review of international political economy: RIPE* 27, no. 6, 2020, https://doi.org/10.1080/09692290.2019.1677743.

[②] Thomas Edward Flores and Irfan Nooruddin, "Financing the peace: Evaluating World Bank post-conflict assistance programs," *Review of International Organizations* 4, no. 1, 2009, https://doi.org/10.1007/s11558-008-9039-0.

[③] Brett A. Casper, "IMF Programs and the Risk of a Coup d'état," *The Journal of conflict resolution* 61, no. 5, 2017, https://doi.org/10.1177/0022002715600759.

[④] Casper, "IMF Programs and the Risk of a Coup d'état."

[⑤] Caroline A. Hartzell, Matthew Hoddie, and Molly Bauer, "Economic Liberalization via IMF Structural Adjustment: Sowing the Seeds of Civil War?" *International organization* 64, no. 2, 2010, https://doi.org/10.1017/S0020818310000068.

[⑥] Dolan-Evans, "Making war safe for capitalism: The World Bank and its evolving interventions in conflict."

[⑦] Cohn and Duncanson, "Whose recovery? IFI prescriptions for postwar states," 1215.

加剧人类的不安全感。[1]

尽管以上这些学者争论大多强调了 IFIs 并没有取得成果，但也有少数例外。Flores 和 Noooruddin 认为，不管被干预的国家再次发生冲突还是经济得以复苏，都与 WB 的干预没有关系。[2]另一方面，Vadlamannati 等人认为，在其他因素不变的情况下，IMF 的方案是倾向于促进民族和平。[3]根据这些作者的观点，当一个国家具备更加细分的族群版图时，IMF 的方案会促进族际和平；但当族群存在两极分化时，其干预往往会加剧冲突。

因此，IFIs 的干预是否带来安全和福利效应既没有定论，关于其背后的利益、议程以及借款人扮演角色的争论也没有停止。这些争论和争议大多是基于 IFIs 过去的行为，尚且没有充分反映其最近在战略上的转变。此外，应该先了解支撑这些争论的假设，因为他们往往不去质疑除了 IFIs 提出的方案外，还有什么其他的替代方案。正如 Vadlamannati 等人所建议的那样，任何对 IMF 的批评都需要考虑，如果自动实施紧缩政策会产生怎样的后果，通常会是经济崩溃。[4]因此，在强调 IFIs 以推动宏观经济稳定和经济增长的名义所扮演的恶化冲突的角色时，专家也需要避免总是简单地将借款人描述为无辜受害者。许多调整后产生的经济和社会问题，可能与导致这种 IMF 调整的问题一样多。接下来的两个部分将基于埃塞俄比亚和苏丹最近的过渡和动荡来反思这些学者的争论及其不足之处。

---

① Bernhard Reinsberg, Daniel O. Shaw, and Louis Bujnoch, "Revisiting the security–development nexus: Human security and the effects of IMF adjustment programmes," *Conflict management and peace science*, 2022, https://doi.org/10.1177/07388942221111064.

② Flores and Nooruddin, "Financing the peace: Evaluating World Bank post-conflict assistance programs."

③ Krishna Chaitanya Vadlamannati, Gina Maria G. Østmoe, and Indra de Soysa, "Do IMF programs disrupt ethnic peace? An empirical analysis, 1985-2006," *Journal of peace research* 51, no. 6, 2014, https://doi.org/10.1177/0022343314538478.

④ Vadlamannati, Østmoe, and de Soysa, "Do IMF programs disrupt ethnic peace? An empirical analysis, 1985-2006."

三、IFIs 与 2018 年后埃塞俄比亚的过渡

埃塞俄比亚人民革命民主阵线（1991—2018）领导下的埃塞俄比亚政府，对 IFIs 建议的某些自由化措施是非常抵制的。政府在许多场合多次呼吁货币贬值、电信和银行部门等国有企业私有化、金融部门自由化和土地所有权私有化，但实际上只按照自己的节奏实施了某些方面的建议。由于该国录得了强劲的经济增长指数，加上埃塞俄比亚在地缘政治上的重要性，该政权的这些行为并没有导致 IFIs 与政府之间的关系恶化。因此，尽管如上述论断所说，IFIs 持续推动自由主义经济范式，证明其核心上仍是促进自由经济政策，但毕竟还是有其能动力边界的。他们不得不承认各国都有其经济愿景，并拥有其所获发展援助的主事权。[①]

然而，埃塞俄比亚政府的发展模式并非毫无瑕疵——其增长主要是由政府对基础设施的投资和国有企业推动的。国有企业和与党派掌控的禀赋在许多方面都优先于私营部门，无论是获得外汇还是获得土地和信贷。[②]更令人担忧的是，政府对于有生产力的国有企业和那些寻租者、浪费者，已经失去了分辨的能力。其结果是债务不断增加，因为在多数情况下，这种投资并不是在充分的成本效益分析基础上进行的。[③]由于出口不足以抵销进口，国际收支问题进一步恶化了债务情况。[④]随着对外汇需求的增加，加上实行爬行钉住外汇汇率制度，导致正式汇率和平行汇率之间的差距越来越大。

尽管存在这些经济问题，但党内的共识是，这些问题将在发展型国

---

① Stephen Brown and Jonathan Fisher, "Aid donors, democracy and the developmental state in Ethiopia," *Democratization* 27, no. 2, 2020, https://doi.org/10.1080/13510347.2019.1670642.

② Christopher Clapham, "The Ethiopian developmental state," *Third world quarterly* 39, no. 6, 2018, https://doi.org/10.1080/01436597.2017.1328982.

③ FDRE, "A Homegrown Economic Reform Agenda: A Pathway to Prosperity," 2020. extension://elhekieabhbkpmcefcoobjddigjcaadp/https://www.mofed.gov.et/media/filer_public/38/78/3878265a-1565-4be4-8ac9-dee9ea1f4f1a/a_homegrown_economic_reform_agenda-_a_pathway_to_prosperity_-_public_version_-_march_2020-.pdf.

④ FDRE, "A Homegrown Economic Reform Agenda: A Pathway to Prosperity."

家模式下得到解决。然而，随着阿比－艾哈迈德的崛起，以及随后他的繁荣党和提格雷人民解放阵线（TPLF）之间紧张关系的升级，一个重新审视发展模式的关键时刻出现。阿比政府和 IFIs 开始建立比以前更紧密的联系。尽管很难确定双方对于拉近这一密切关系各自发挥的作用，但双方似乎都将这一时期的关键事件解释为推动各自议程的好时机。IFIs 似乎已经预见到形势已经成熟，可以引导该国的发展议程从发展主义转向其他大多数非洲国家正在实行的新自由主义。阿比似乎也需要他们的支持来巩固其权力。他很快宣布，他将推动国有企业私有化，包括利润最高、全球知名的埃塞俄比亚航空公司。① 紧密仰仗 IFIs 和其他多边顾问，埃塞俄比亚政府提出了一个"本土创制的"经济改革计划，据一位观察员说，这个计划与 IMF 模板中的方案没有任何区别。② 这种对私有化和自由化的追求，进一步扩大了 TPLF 和政府之间的分歧，加上其他因素，最终导致了 2020 年 11 月的全面战争。

IFIs 在冲突期间的参与

战争爆发后，根据其最近的战略，WB 继续与埃塞俄比亚政府合作。虽然 WB 的参与是基于之前制定的国家伙伴关系框架，但随着冲突的爆发，WB 声称它向"以人为本"的发展方向做了一些调整。③ WB 还声称，根据 FCS 战略，在埃塞俄比亚爆发多次冲突期间，它仍然在开展业务，旨在通过关注人类基本需求、健康、粮食安全、营养和教育来解决该国脆弱性和冲突的根源。④ 的确，如表 1 所示，即使在两年的冲突期间，WB 在埃塞俄比亚批准的项目数量和投资金额看起来都非常可观。

---

① Aaron Maasho, "Ethiopia opens up telecoms, airline to private, foreign investors," *Reuters* (2018), https://www.reuters.com/article/us-ethiopia-privatisation-idUSKCN1J12JJ.

② Alemayehu Geda, "Ethiopia's 'Homegrown' Reform: If the diagnosis is not right, it may end-up a Wish List," 2019, https://www.researchgate.net/publication/335972270_Critique_of_Ethiopia's_PM_Abyi's_new_Homegrown_Policy_2019; Ayele Gelan, "Ethiopia's 'Homegrown' Economic Reform: An Afterthought," *Fotune* 2019, https://addisfortune.news/ethiopias-homegrown-economic-reform-an-afterthought/.

③ WB, *Strategy*, 1 January 2023, https://www.worldbank.org/en/country/ethiopia/overview#2.

④ 同上。

表1　世界银行在埃塞俄比亚的项目

	2018	2019	2020	2021	2022
世行批准的项目数量	8	4	9	11	7
金额：百万美元	2546	1125	3711.60	1680	1590

资料来源：根据世界银行埃塞俄比亚网页数据整理，Projects (worldbank.org)

　　然而，（WB）FCS战略中的许多建议在埃塞俄比亚并没有得到执行。首先，它对该国冲突程度的分类缺乏准确性。埃塞俄比亚2020年时还不属于FCS国家，可能是因为在WB对国家的地位进行了分类后，战争才爆发；2021年，WB将该国划分为中等烈度冲突地区，这是很成问题的。根据WB的定义，中等烈度冲突是指冲突绝对死亡人数超过250人（根据ACLED[①]），或者超过150人（根据UCDP[②]）；冲突死亡人数与人口数量之比为每10万人有1—2人死亡（根据ACLED），或者有0.5—1人死亡（根据UCDP），而且与前一年相比，伤亡人数至少增加了100%。另一方面，根据ACLED和UCDP，高烈度冲突是指冲突死亡的绝对人数超过250人（根据ACLED）和150人（根据UCDP），而且每10万人超过10个（根据ACLED和UCDP）以上。[③]根据这一衡量标准，2021年的埃塞俄比亚实际上应该被归类为高烈度冲突地区，却被归类为中等强度冲突地区，直至2022年，才被视为高烈度冲突地区。

　　其次，尽管FCS要求WB在此基础上进行风险和复原力评估，并进行基准干预，但现有的资料显示，这一点可能并没有做到。WB在上述领域为解决该国冲突的源头而进行干预，充其量可以说乏善可陈。提格雷和该国其他地区的冲突，主要是由于权力斗争和对国家未来方向缺乏共识，这不可能简单地通过对上述领域的干预来解决。最

---

　　① 在美国注册的非政府组织"武装冲突地点事件数据项目"（Armed Conflict Location & Event Data Project, ACLED），参见其官网相关介绍，https://acleddata.com/acleddatanew/wp-content/uploads/dlm_uploads/2021/11/ACLED-History_v2_February_2022.pdf。——译者注
　　② 瑞典乌普萨拉冲突数据项目（The Uppsala Conflict Data Program, UCDP），有约40年历史，详情参见其官网相关介绍，https://www.pcr.uu.se/research/ucdp/。——译者注
　　③ WB, *World Bank Group Strategy for Fragility, Conflict, and Violence* 2020-2025 (*English*).

后，尽管埃塞俄比亚本可以从国际开发协会（International Development Association, IDA）为 FCS 国家提供的三套方案中的任意一套获得支持，以补充其基于绩效的捐助，但事实并非如此。不可否认，如果国际开发协会认为有关当局致力于克服脆弱性和冲突的根源，就会在这些方案下提供支持；也就是说，实际上 WB 认为埃塞俄比亚当局没有致力于结束冲突。

IMF 同样欢迎 2018 年后埃塞俄比亚的政治和经济自由化努力。2019 年，IMF 通过其优惠性的扩展信贷机制和非优惠性的扩展融资机制提供了创纪录的 29 亿美元贷款，为期 3 年。埃塞俄比亚政府被要求采取一系列自由化和改革措施，这些措施通常都是 IMF 向发展中世界提起的。此外，IMF 指出，这些经济改革措施的实施，绝不以牺牲为减少贫困而提供的社会保护为代价。优惠贷款的条件之一是"重组"埃塞俄比亚与债权人之间的讨论。由于埃塞俄比亚未能与债权人就债务重组达成协议，该国提取了 3.186 亿美元后，扩展信贷机制于 2021 年 9 月中止。[1] 尽管半途而废并不是因为国内冲突的骤然爆发，但观察家们认为，冲突可能会削弱债权人的信心，从而使得债务重组协议难以达成。IMF 在 2021 年 8 月还向该国提供了 4.06 亿美元的特别提款权，正如同时也向其他受大流行病影响的发展中国家提供的一样。因此，从表面上看，IMF 似乎继续以对待所有其他国家的方式对待该国，没有因为冲突而调整其运行。

然而，也有观察家认为，IMF 拒绝谈判新的安排是由于美国实施的经济和贸易制裁，在美国制裁没有解除的情况下，IMF 不太可能恢复谈判。[2] 无论怎样，在二十国集团债务框架未能取得成功的情况下，IMF 似乎不会向该国启动任何新的信贷机制。即使埃塞俄比亚已经签署了和平协议，其经济学家们的看法是，如果埃塞俄比亚不同意将其外汇制度从有管理的浮动汇率转变为由市场汇率决定，IMF 就不会与埃塞俄比亚

---

[1]　Fortune, "IMF Credit Facility Expires as Debt Rework Faces Delay," 2021, https://addisfortune. news/imf-credit-facility-expires-as-debt-rework-faces-delay/.

[2]　IHS, *Country Executive Summary-Ethiopia*, 2 November 2022.

重启谈判。政府先前已经同意逐步贬值货币，以控制货币贬值的通货膨胀效应，当然 IMF 倾向于快速和急剧贬值。[1] 由于埃塞俄比亚政府金融需求越来越大，大大削弱了其议价能力，可能除了接受 IMF 的条件之外别无选择。该国的外债接近 300 亿美元，偿债是政府最高的支出之一。

既有经济学文献对于货币贬值给发展中国家经济增长和福利造成的影响尚无定论。有些作者认为，贬值对经济产出并没有影响；而另一些人则认为，这种影响取决于经济的规模和结构。[2] 然而，其他关注农产品出口的人则认为，这对出口的影响是积极和重大的。[3] Momodu 和 Akani 认为，虽然货币贬值在短期内会促进经济增长，但其长期影响是负面的。[4] 还有人认为，在指出其潜在的紧缩影响时，也很难捕捉到贬值对整个经济的影响。一位埃塞俄比亚的分析人士认为，目前埃塞俄比亚的经济问题是结构性的，货币贬值不是万能药。相反，这将加剧已经达到两位数的通胀。因此，即使货币贬值有好处，也必须与其他措施相结合才能实现，而这些措施并不能简单地以"权宜之计"的方式来实现。除非有大量的外部资金注入，否则贬值的通货膨胀效应肯定会发生。根据埃信华迈（IHS Markit，一家风险咨询公司）的说法，埃塞俄比亚至少需要 60 亿美元的储备，才能使得货币大幅贬值而不至于出现通货膨胀的失控。将储备量增加到这一水平需要数十亿美元，短期内不太

---

① IMF, *2019 Article IV consultation and request for three-year arrangement under the Extended Credit Facility-press release and staff report*, 2020. https://www.imf.org/en/Publications/CR/Issues/2020/01/28/The-Federal-Democratic-Republic-of-Ethiopia-2019-Article-IV-Consultation-and-Requests-for-48987." (2020).

② Florence Bouvet, Roy Bower, and Jason C. Jones, "Currency Devaluation as a Source of Growth in Africa: A Synthetic Control Approach," *Eastern economic journal* 48, no. 3, 2022, https://doi.org/10.1057/s41302-022-00211-4; Joseph Odionye and Jude Chukwu, "The asymmetric effects of currency devaluation in selected sub-Saharan Africa," *Ekonomski anali* 66, no. 230, 2021, https://doi.org/10.2298/EKA2130135O.

③ Halit Yanikkaya, Huseyin Kaya, and Osman Murat Kocturk, "The effect of real exchange rates and their volatility on the selected agricultural commodity exports: A case study on Turkey, 1971-2010," *Agricultural economics* (Praha) 59, no. 5, 2013, https://doi.org/10.17221/122/2012-AGRICECON.no. 5 (2013).

④ Austin A. Momodu and Fynface N. Akani, "Impact of Currency Devaluation on Economic Growth of Nigeria," *AFRREV IJAH* 5, no. 1, 2016, https://doi.org/10.4314/ijah.v5i1.12.

可能获得。①

即使获得外部资金注入，即由于 IMF 实施其新的脆弱性框架，重新调整了他们以前的支持方式来支持埃塞俄比亚的战后重建进程并且完成了债务重组协议，其对冲突驱动因素的影响可能并不明显。在宏观层面上，这种资金注入将有助于政权稳定宏观经济，而宏观经济只有在特定情况下才会促进社会福利。如果没有这样大量的资金，通货膨胀的上升将是贬值过程中最有可能出现的结果，并产生多方面的负面影响。

无论如何，在短期内，几乎没有证据表明 IFIs 的参与是对冲突的敏感回应，并有助于解决冲突的根源。即使是 WB 和 IMF 都提供支持富有成效的安全网计划形式的社会支出，他们对社会包容性的积极贡献也受到其他一系列措施的影响。例如，针对最弱势群体的燃油补贴的合理化，随着不断上升的通货膨胀，反而会使那些不那么弱势群体的资产贬值。以中低收入贫困率指数（3.65 美元）来衡量，该国的贫困人口占总人口的 65%，这意味着绝大多数人都勉强生活在贫困线水平，生计来源上任何微小的变化都很容易影响他们。

四、IFIs 与苏丹 2019 年后的过渡

2019 年苏丹爆发推翻长期独裁者奥马尔·巴希尔（Omar Ai-Bashir）的革命之前，IFIs 并没有足够的参与度，这主要是由于巴希尔统治下的苏丹所累积的欠款，以及美国将苏丹列为了"支持恐怖主义的国家"。在巴希尔下台后，军民混合过渡政府的成立并拥抱包容性和平、经济改革以实现包容性增长，苏丹开始了融入国际经济和政治体系的进程，IFIs 将苏丹的过渡视为将其转变为民主繁荣国家的千载难逢的机会。因此，他们开始思考如何让苏丹和过渡政府合作，进行宏观经济改革，从而解决债务拖欠问题，并使苏丹走上民主和包容性增长的道路。到 2020 年 7 月，IMF 启动了 29 亿美元的人员监督方案。该计划试图通过帮助苏丹在财政政策、货币政策以及结构和体制改革领域进行改革，以帮助苏

---

① IHS, "Executive Summary Ethiopia, Country Risk Profile," 30 November 2022.

丹参与重债穷国倡议所必需的几项改革。[1]该计划推出时，苏丹正处于无休止的经济危机中，高额的财政赤字导致通货膨胀、货币贬值和通过货币化筹备赤字融资的循环。[2]

根据 IMF 的人员监督方案，苏丹同意实行汇率自由化、调动更多财政、扩大社会安全网、取消能源补贴并进行结构改革，以实现包容性增长和更大的竞争力。[3]因此，燃料补贴从 2019 年占 GDP 的 10.5% 降到了 2020 年占 GDP 的 3.8%，电价提高了 500%；在大规模贬值后，2021 年 2 月统一了正规和平行汇率，这是苏丹转向市场决定汇率变化的一部分。[4]到了 2020 年底，苏丹被美国从支持恐怖主义国家的名单中除名，这有助于苏丹偿还部分贷款，特别是拖欠非洲开发银行和 WB 的债务，这帮助苏丹继续获得了这些机构的财政支持。IMF 表示，这些措施的实施应该不设时间表，而是满足以下条件，即在汇率自由化之前建立必要的货币框架和加强银行体系、在取消补贴和汇率改革之前建立社会安全网并开展大规模沟通活动，以确保人们接受这些措施。[5] IMF 稍晚的报告指出，这项建议并没有得到采纳，其他措施早在扩大社会安全网之前就开始实施，甚至几乎没有与之同步——正如 IMF 所承认的那样，这造成了社会压力。[6]事实上，在此期间，公众对取消补贴的抗议已经非常普遍。

然而，这具有欺骗性，很容易将责任从 IMF 转移到苏丹政府身上。IMF 规定，苏丹获得外部资源的条件是进行人员监督方案（SMP）中标出的改革，而包括安全网方案在内的一些改革将首先需要外部资源。在

---

[1] IMF, *Sudan. 2019 Article IV Consultation-Press Release; Staff Report; and Statement by the Executive Director for Sudan*, 2020. https://www.imf.org/en/Publications/CR/Issues/2020/03/10/Sudan-2019-Article-IV-Consultation-Press-Release-Staff-Report-and-Statement-by-the-Executive-49254.

[2] 同上。

[3] 同上。

[4] IMF, *Sudan: Enhanced Heavily Indebted Poor Countries Initiative-decision point, IMF Country Report Number 21/144*, 2021.

[5] IMF, *Sudan: 2019 Article IV Consultation-Press Release; Staff Report; and Statement by the Executive Director for Sudan*.

[6] IMF, *Sudan: Enhanced Heavily Indebted Poor Countries Initiative-decision point, IMF Country Report Number 21/144*, 2021.

外部资金付诸阙如的情况下，苏丹政府能做的事情是实施 SMP 中那些不需要大量外部资金的内容，这将使他们能够获得渴望已久的外部支持，即使这在短期内意味着广大民众利益的受损。无论如何，IMF 认为这一进展令人满意，苏丹于 2021 年 6 月底达到了重债穷国的决策点。在 SMP 期间，通货膨胀率仍然高得离谱，在 2021 年 2 月达到了 412.75%，陷入贫困的人数显著增加。在 2021 年 2 月被解除支持恐怖主义的国家名单之后，苏丹才随着慢慢获得外部资金而开始了社会保护的扩展，证明对不断扩大的经济困难收益不大，当局和 IFIs 将其轻描淡写为"调整的痛苦"。

在达到重债穷国的决策点后，苏丹得到了减免债务的承诺，与 IMF 签署了另一份扩展信贷协议。该协议试图巩固 IMF 前一时期的"宏观经济收益"，同时认识到由于改革进程的脆弱性，宏观经济问题可能会继续存在。根据这一安排，苏丹同意进行关键改革，其中包括针对国有企业和安全部门的治理，这似乎最终招致了 10 月的政变（稍后讨论）。此外，苏丹还同意增加资源调动、进一步减少补贴、加强社会安全网计划和金融体系，并加强国有企业的治理和透明度。[1] 在这些措施中，最后一项措施似乎对塑造此后整个国家发生的事件特别是军队行为具有关键作用。IMF 的《治理诊断》报告的初步发现认为，国有企业（尤其是国防部门的企业）缺乏财政透明度，其采购系统缺乏监管和监督的独立性，数据存在严重缺陷；[2] 不透明的自然资源治理和反腐败法律框架、多重税收优惠以及缺乏司法独立等，也是其治理问题。因此，WB 风险和复原力评估认为，改革进程的下一阶段是要翻转安全部门俘获国家的问题，因为这是苏丹脆弱性和冲突的动因。[3]

---

[1] IMF, *Sudan: Request for a 39 month arrangement under the extended credit facility-press release, staff report, and statement by executive director for Sudan. IMF report number 21/142*, 2021, https://www.imf.org/en/Publications/CR/Issues/2021/06/30/Sudan-Request-for-a-39-Month-Arrangement-Under-the-Extended-Credit-Facility-Press-Release-461358.staff report, and statement by executive director for Sudan. IMF report number 21/142," (2021).

[2] 同上。

[3] WB, *Sudan: Country Engagement Note for the period FY21-FY22*, 2020. extension://elhekieabhbkpmcefcoobjddigjcaadp/https://documents1.worldbank.org/curated/en/879871602253859419/pdf/Sudan-Country-Engagement-Note-for-the-Period-FY21-FY22.pdf.

2020 年 7 月 IMF 签署 SMP 之后，WB 随即于 2020 年 9 月签订了重新参与的战略文件。怀揣着脆弱性战略，WB 走在确定苏丹的脆弱性和冲突来源问题的前列。根据其《风险和复原力评估》报告，WB 将精英勾结的排他性治理、功能失调和精英控制经济、区域失衡以及缺乏机构能力，视为苏丹脆弱性的主要结构性动因。[①] 苏丹的改革进程特别需要使"苏丹的安全实体部门摆脱其不透明的收入来源"，包括他们在"石油、阿拉伯树胶、芝麻、武器、燃料、小麦、电信、银行、房地产和黄金以及一系列与消费品有关的部门"的收入。[②] 为此，WB 寻求两个关键目标，一是帮助苏丹偿还债务，二是帮助其从 WB 的脆弱性战略中受益，并有助于重建社会契约、包容性和公民参与。为了实现这些目标，WB 提议开展一些活动，包括提供技术援助，开展分析和诊断工作，设计苏丹家庭支持计划并为其调动资源、促进经济机会、改善服务的提供以及建设国家能力。如果苏丹在困厄中达到了国际货币基金苛刻的条件，这可以视为衡量银行成功的标准，那么可以说 WB 的支持的确至关重要。一旦苏丹还清了国际开发协会的欠款，就能通过 WB 的"脆弱性"方案获得财政支持。WB 能够通过该方案中的转向拨款（Turn Around Allocation，TAA）获得资金，补充其常规的基于绩效的拨款，受益于 WB 20 亿美元的拨款，以"巩固和平、释放该国的生产潜力、支持私营部门，并为 WB 的双重目标作出贡献"[③]。

然而，在全面实施 IMF 的扩展信贷机制和 WB 的支持方案前，由军方领导的苏丹主权委员会于 2021 年 10 月罢免了该国的文职领导人，并推翻了过渡政府时期出台的一些措施。其中，军方解散了为收回公共资产而设立的委员会，任命巴希尔时代的人物进入司法机构和安全机构，并任命军政府领导人布尔汗的盟友进入了主权委员会。[④] IFIs 和捐助方

---

① WB, *Sudan: Country Engagement Note for the period FY21-FY22*.

② 同上。

③ WB, *IDA 20 Special Theme: Fragility, Conflict and violence*, 2021. extension://elhekieabhbkpmcefcoobjddigjcaadp/https://documents1.worldbank.org/curated/en/164221625067263643/pdf/IDA20-Special-Theme-Fragility-Conflict-and-Violence.pdf.3.

④ US, *Sudan's Imperiled Transition*: *U. S. Policy in the Wake of the October 25th Coup*: *Hearing Before the Committee on Foreign Relations*, *U. S. Senate*, http://foreign.senate.gov., Feb. 1st 2022.

立即做出反应，暂停对该政权的所有财政援助和承诺的支持。因此，超过45亿美元的援助被暂停，巴黎俱乐部也暂停了对苏丹190亿美元债务减免的讨论。美国向IFIs施压并要求其暂停援助，其解释是，军政府虽然不会受到这些措施的直接影响，但"这一大规模援助的搁置会导致苏丹经济崩溃，（军队）的商业利益也会被淹没殆尽"[①]。

苏丹货币随之大幅贬值，国际收支迅速恶化，而俄乌战争进一步影响了苏丹的经济。在社会方面，贫困率预计将从2014年的18.4%上升到2022年的29.1%，预计到2022年秋季，39%的人口将因为粮食不安全陷入贫困状态。[②]苏丹公民抱怨说，许多苏丹人的生活条件已经达到了"屈辱"的程度，人道主义者遗憾地表示，他们必须做出"令人痛心的决定"，即支持谁、离开谁。[③]暂停援助虽然对人民有重大影响，但似乎已达到了预期的效果，即迫使军政府就其向文职过渡的条件进行谈判。2022年12月，一份组建文官政府的框架协议得以签署，最终协议近在咫尺。[④]

因此，IFIs与其他行为体协调、参与苏丹的过程似乎在很大程度上是有效的。他们意识到应该尝试找出导致该国冲突的主要动因，在必要时不回避使用财政惩罚措施。WB的解释是，当局准备好合作时，就会恢复援助，帮助该国摆脱脆弱性的新战略；当局背弃承诺时，援助就会退出。这些进程的唯一挑战便是对社会支持方案的承诺不够充分，这可能在某种程度上会激发新的冲突。考虑到苏丹2019年的革命最初正是因为面包价格的上涨，没人能够保证未来经济困难时不会再继续引发类似事件。甚至在文官政府被军方推翻之前，公众就已经明显地因为经济

---

① US, *Sudan's Imperiled Transition*: *U. S. Policy in the Wake of the October 25th Coup*: *Hearing Before the Committee on Foreign Relations*, *U. S. Senate*, http://foreign.senate.gov., Feb. 1st 2022.

② WB, *Sub-Saharan Africa*: *Macro Poverty Outlook*: *Country-by-Country analysis and projection for the developing world*, 2022, Washington, D. C.: World Bank Group.

③ Dabanga, "Living conditions in Sudan 'humiliating'," 2022, https://www.dabangasudan.org/en/all-news/article/living-conditions-in-sudan-humiliating.

④ Dabanga, "FFC-CC: 'Sudan Final Agreement imminent'," 2023, https://www.dabangasudan.org/en/all-news/article/ffc-cc-sudan-final-agreement-imminent#:~:text=January%2019%2C%202023%20The%20Central%20Council%20of%20Sudan%E2%80%99s,on%20%28transitional%29%20justice%2C%20which%20was%20scheduled%20last%20week.

困难对其提出抗议。尽管政府制订了苏丹家庭支助方案来预防和抵消这种情况，但因为太过于迟缓，而且其他改革措施也不能同步进行，这证明了 IFIs 沾沾自喜的社会保护方案还是过于自负了。

结　语

IFIs 在脆弱和受冲突影响的国家推行的政策具有很强的连续性，虽然也有一些明显的变化。尽管识别了导致脆弱性和冲突的独特环境，并对预算范围和交付方式进行了一些调整建议，但其建议的普遍政策措施仍然是收紧货币监管、限制政府开支、动员广泛社会资源（尽管脆弱和冲突环境中几乎没有采取这些措施的余地），以及放宽汇率，也意味着货币贬值。这些措施被认为能够实现宏观经济的稳定，从而为依赖私营部门的包容性增长奠定了有利的基础。虽然社会支出和解决最弱势群体的需求得到了承认，并被纳入了 IFIs 的方案中，但在这方面取得的进展差强人意，而且似乎 IFIs 并不要求受援国下一阶段将其提升为必需的。然而，如果不能解决对普遍大众特别是弱势群体的实际需求，就会引起民众的消极反应，并可能使政府陷入进一步的不稳定。可以理解的是，WB 增加了对脆弱和受冲突影响国家的资源分配，并继续参与冲突局势，然而，其举措在解决冲突和脆弱性驱动因素方面的贡献程度是有差异的。在埃塞俄比亚，冲突的原因与 WB 的发展干预之间几乎没有直接联系，而在苏丹，WB 试图根据脆弱性和冲突的主要驱动因素进行干预。IMF 最近推出了脆弱性战略，是否开启与之前不同的行动方式仍有待观察。虽然 IFIs 在冲突和脆弱局势中的作用并不理想，但问题也源于这些政府的不当行为，正是这些行为首先导致了他们的国家陷入冲突和脆弱的局势。这就提出了早期干预以防止冲突升级为大规模暴力的重要性，这也是联合国通过其维护和平（Sustaining Peace）议程一直在努力解决的问题。要把各种国际干预框架联系起来，为受冲突影响的人们的生活带来真实的价值，仍有许多工作要做。

本文讨论了 IFIs 在过去四年对埃塞俄比亚和苏丹的参与，能够为中国和非洲国家的交往提供哪些政策建议呢？在这方面，我们有三点看法和经验可供中国参考。长期以来，中国一直在 IFIs 认为脆弱和受冲突影响的国家开展业务，因此，IFIs 承认即使在困难的环境下也需要继续参与的事实，可以证明中国在非洲参与的前提是无可争议的。此外，由于长时间的参与，中国已经积累了在这种情况下应对和平挑战与机遇的经验和诀窍，基于此，中国至少可以避免对这些国家造成伤害。

其次，中国要继续在许多被称为 FCS 的国家中进行强有力的参与，进一步融合发展和安全考量可能才是明智之举。中国的非洲和平理念被广泛认为是以发展为导向的，即发展领域的成功有助于和平和稳定。虽然总的来说，发展有助于和平，但在过渡时期，仅靠发展合作本身可能还不足以防止危机。正如埃塞俄比亚的案例所表明的那样，这种冲突会使以前以发展为导向的合作所取得的收益发生逆转。因此，中国可能会考虑在关键时刻进行积极的政治参与，以维护发展成果和由此带来的和平。在这方面，中国最近任命的非洲之角特使确实是一个受欢迎的举措，但可能需要进一步制度化，例如建立一个加强版的合格技术支持团队。其他合作安排，如中国与埃塞俄比亚政府就保护"一带一路"倡议下的项目达成的安全协议，可能也需要超越技术支持层面，同时针对更深层次威胁这些项目的不安全因素进行讨论。

最后，在经济领域，非洲国家过去的发展成果，特别是 FCS 国家，正在被非洲不断增加的债务所破坏。在这方面，中国可以通过帮助推动二十国集团债务重组框架来提供支持。人们担心，二十国集团框架仍然非常缓慢，对支持非洲国家债务问题的紧迫性反应不足，而且这一债务减缓进程可能受制于地缘政治对抗和紧张局势。随着地缘政治对抗和竞争的加剧，专注于短期收益的诱惑可能会很强烈，中国需要抵制。唯此，中国才能尽自己的所长防止以牺牲非洲弱国和穷国为代价的极端全球战略对抗和竞争。

新泛非主义与非洲能动性

——多重危机背景下非洲的和平安全治理

托　马*

摘　要: 非洲大陆多年来面临多重错综复杂的和平与安全挑战,相比其他地区呈现出一定程度的脆弱性。新冠疫情和俄乌冲突作为两大全球性冲击性危机,加剧了非洲大陆几乎所有国家的安全风险,也使得其原本就有的多因素交织互动、跨国跨区域性质更加恶性循环、相互叠加。但是,与外来观察家悲观的预测不同,不管是针对新冠疫情的治理还是对于俄乌冲突的应对,非洲大陆都显现出巨大的自主性和韧性,其能动性治理成果斐然可观:从大陆、次地区到国家层面都在致力于寻求本土化自主性的解决方案,与此同时在全球治理中贡献出非洲方案。这种致力于实现自主性的过程,可以概括为新泛非主义性的团结原则和集体安全治理模式。本文通过盘点非洲大陆整体和各个次区域近几年面临的主要安全风险与挑战,研判了新冠疫情和俄乌冲突作为重大全球性转折事件如何恶化了其多重危机,也概要梳理和剖析了非洲在这样背景下如何自主性应对风险、维护和平与安全,并指出了其特征与不足之处。

关键词: 和平与安全　恐怖主义　非洲能动性　集体安全治理　(新)泛非主义

引　言

近年来,许多非洲国家安全问题加剧,其背后的原因很复杂,既有长期的历史遗留下来的问题,也有因为当前全球政治环境恶化大背景下

---

*　托马(Donglona Adawa Thomas),北京大学国际关系学院博士候选人。

非洲所面临的诸多政治、经济、社会和气候变化相互叠加的现实挑战。在新冠疫情和俄乌冲突的全球背景下，这些挑战尤为突出。正如联合国秘书长安东尼奥·古特雷斯所说，新冠疫情和俄乌冲突给人类带来了三重危机，即粮食危机、能源危机和财政危机；[①] 这些危机对脆弱的国家具有不可估量的后果，对非洲地区影响尤甚。

疫情冲击之下，非洲各国面临更大结构性压力，特别是体系薄弱、经济发展不平衡的非洲国家陷入资源供应严重欠缺、分配更加不均衡的紧张态势；这些结构性困境又直接或间接以各种形式反映到社会各阶层，成为社会和族群之间冲突的主要根源。尼日利亚、喀麦隆、乍得、尼日尔、马里、布基纳法索、索马里等国，都出现严重的社会冲突（族群冲突、农民与牧民冲突等），其导致的受害者居多。在政府对此治理不力、不能提供有效保护的背景下，族群往往被迫"自我武装"起来，而恐怖组织也因此有机可乘，导致思想极端化或青年群体被诱引加入恐怖组织。2022年春季俄乌冲突以来，全球能源和粮食价格上涨的效应，已经传导到非洲，很多国家原有的族群冲突、农民与牧民冲突大有愈演愈激烈之势，特别是西非地区、萨赫勒地区、大湖地区和中非地区的冲突呈现持续上升态势，受害平民也越来越多。

非洲虽然在应对新冠疫情时刻可圈可点，[②] 但因为存在诸多结构性的因素，在后疫情时代和来自域外的俄乌冲突面前，却显现出巨大的和平安全危机。只有先了解非洲的历史，才能更深入研判当下正在经历多重危机的非洲大陆和平安全挑战加剧的根由，也是观察和理解非洲和平安全治理的起点。

---

① Nations Unies, "La « triple crise » en Afrique est aggravée par la guerre en Ukraine, déclare Guterres en visite au Sénégal," *ONU Info*, 1 mai 2022, https://news.un.org/fr/story/2022/05/1119262, accessed December 21, 2022.

② 刘海方：《新冠肺炎全球大流行下非洲的抗疫和中非合作》，《国际政治研究》2020年第3期，第12—17页。

一、非洲和平安全的历史与现状

1. 历史视角下非洲的和平安全

非洲国家的安全形势虽然各有其特殊性，但是安全轨迹存在或多或少的共同特点。非洲安全威胁的起点可以追溯到前殖民时代，因为人口的迁徙和流动持续存在，该时代的特点是迁移群体与其所进入社区的原有群体间为争夺生产和生活资料往往会爆发冲突，并大多以和解的方式结束。这种相对的和平与安宁随着欧洲殖民者入侵而终结，非洲人的不安全感前所未有地增加，生产和生活都随时处在各种暴力剥削压迫威胁之下，暴力殖民统治成为非洲人不安全的主要根源。殖民反过来激发了城市和农村地区非洲人的斗争，直至大规模反帝反殖民和追求独立自主民族国家的斗争轰轰烈烈爆发——双重激荡下，内部冲突成为非洲安全问题的主要特征。

20 世纪 50 年代非洲国家先后独立至今，非洲安全局势的特点仍然是罕有国家间冲突，这明显与西方中心主义视角下的以"国家间斗争"为预设的安全概念大相径庭。但是，这并不意味着新生的非洲国家没有安全挑战。根据 1964 年非洲统一组织通过的《非洲国家间边界争端的开罗决议》(Cairo Resolution on Border Disputes between African States)，[①] 新生非洲大陆政治版图直接继承了殖民时代"瓜分非洲"和民族分裂统治的格局，即殖民统治前缺乏共同政治生活经历的近万个大大小小的人类共同体单元被挤压分割为 50 多个殖民地基础上生成的国家。这意味着每一个国家都存在数十数百个这样的酋长国、部落，甚至小的血亲家族整合为一个民族国家，国族认同建立的过程不可能一蹴而就，大多数民众还是习惯之前历史形成的认同。这导致政权要么就是合法性不足，要么就是治理能力有限，或者具有明显的脆弱性，派系、族群、宗教等分野都在竞争政权，抑或直接就是争夺生产生活资源——伴随着国家内部

---

① 张春:《化边缘为中心: 非洲的跨境安全研究》,《国际政治研究》2022 年第 3 期, 第 9--35 页。

冲突和内战的增加，国家机器本身越来越成为其统治下公民不安全的根源。[①]与其他地区相比，非洲自 2001 年以来暴力事件的数量增加最多；[②]互联网和社交媒体上，非洲的暴力和非暴力性骚乱案件被关注，也被无限放大，俨然成为非洲的代名词。

2. 混合型和平与安全挑战

国家建构绝非一朝一夕之功，非洲以外的世界其他国家和地区也都需要长期的完善过程。独立至今，非洲各国普遍存在着国内政权能力不足、治理不完善基础上的和平安全挑战。事实上，疫情与俄乌冲突前，这种根源性的安全挑战在非洲地区已经演化成混合型和平与安全问题，即不同类型安全挑战交织在一起、互相作用（见图 1），呈现出错综复杂的局面。具体而言，一直困扰非洲的和平与安全表现为国内各种冲突（如族群冲突、农牧民冲突等）、政局动荡导致的政变、恐怖主义、有组织犯罪、贩卖人口、气候变化、粮食安全等诸多方面；也就是说，关系政权稳定的政治性安全叠加着世界其他地区也同样面临的各类非传统安全，而且更重要的是，以上几乎所有单一类型的安全挑战都具有复杂的跨国性。[③]这些各类安全问题不仅相互作用，并且存在一定程度的恶性循环或多重恶性循环，即具有 A 导致 B，而 B 反过来可能引发 A，或 A 导致 B、C 等的因果关系。比如，气候变化会导致冲突，恐怖主义战争、政治动乱等各种形式的冲突会加剧环境的破坏和气候变化。正如张海滨所说，"环境压力既是政治紧张局势和武装冲突的起源，也是它们的结果"[④]。

---

① Júlia Palik, Aas Rustad Siri and Methi Fredrik, "Conflict trends in Africa, 1989-2019," *Peace Research Institute Oslo (PRIO)*, 2020, https://reliefweb.int/report/world/conflict-trends-africa-1989-2019, accessed March 13th 2023.

② 同上。

③ 张春：《化边缘为中心：非洲的跨境安全研究》，《国际政治研究》2022 年第 3 期。

④ 张海滨：《环境与国际关系：全球环境问题的理性思考》，上海人民出版社，2008 年，第 174 页。

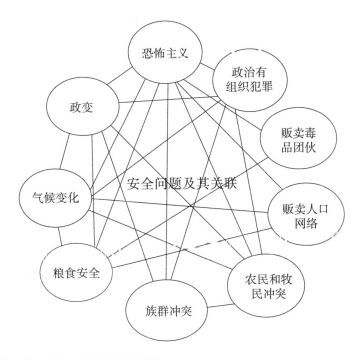

图1　非洲当前各类安全问题及其相互关联

来源：笔者自制

实际上，多年来非洲面临着气候变化带来的严峻冲击，此冲击不仅影响着粮食安全，也直接或间接成为导致各种冲突的主要原因之一。值得关注的是，学界和政界一般将导致非洲国家冲突的原因归咎于政治、经济、社会、宗教等，鲜有从气候变化角度分析其对人类安全造成的威胁与影响的。譬如，自20世纪50年代以来，苏丹一直处于内战状态，联合国安理会多次派遣维和部队和研究专家前往该国控制局面以及研究导致冲突的原因，然而很多报告都得出结论说，导致冲突、内战和2011年分裂为南、北苏丹的根本原因是阿拉伯人和黑皮肤的非洲族群之间的差异性和紧张关系，①直到2007年时任联合国秘书长潘基文（Ban Ki Moon）才提出，"我们几乎总是用一种方便的军事和政治术语来讨论达尔富尔，普遍性认为是部族武装与黑人叛乱分子、农民与牧民之间

---

① Silke Marie Christiansen, *Climate Conflicts: A Case of International Environmental and Humanitarian Law*, Springer, 2016, pp.31-32.

的种族冲突。追溯冲突的根源，我们会发现更复杂的动态，即在各种社会和政治原因中，达尔富尔冲突源于生态危机，至少部分是由气候变化引起的"[1]。此后，苏丹内战被定性为"第一次气候战争"（the first climate war）。

二、疫情和全球动荡加剧非洲安全挑战：恐怖活动升级

恐怖主义组织在非洲升级是疫情和全球动荡作为催化剂外在因素恶化非洲安全局势的最明显表现。如图2所示，2012年以来，伊斯兰马格里布基地组织（Al Qaeda in the Islamic Maghreb，AQIM）、博科圣地（Boko Haram，BH）及其西非地区伊斯兰国（Islamic State in West Africa，ISWA）分支、索马里武装组织"青年党"（AL Shabaab）、先知的信徒组织（Ahlu Sunnah Wal Jama'a，ASWJ），以及原名为"大撒哈拉伊斯兰国"（Islamic State in the Greater Sahara，ISGS）的萨赫勒地区伊斯兰国（Islamic State Sahel Province，ISSP）等伊斯兰国恐怖组织分支与派别，逐渐在大陆散点到密集扩张的趋势非常明显（见图2）。这些组织对非洲大陆方方面面具有极大的破坏性冲击，使其受影响地区陷入泥潭一般的安全困境，长期胶着，难以摆脱。

如图2所示，恐怖主义已经成为非洲安全局势最主要的破坏性力量。根据联合国开发计划署新发表的报告，2021年，全球死于恐怖主义的人当中近一半来自非洲地区，其中三分之一以上来自索马里、布基纳法索、尼日尔和马里4个国家——全球范围内来看，疫情以来恐怖主义活动明显增加了国别。[2]据《2022年全球恐怖主义指数》（Global Terrorism Index）的报告，全球范围18个受恐怖主义影响最多的国家当中（报告涉及全世界163个国家），8个为非洲国家，即尼日尔、马里、刚果民主共

---

[1]　Ban Ki Moon, "A Climate Culprit In Darfur," Washington, 2007, https://www.washingtonpost.com/wp-dyn/content/article/2007/06/15/AR2007061501857.html, November 29, 2022.

[2]　UNDP, "Journey to extremism in Africa: Pathways to recruitment and disengagement," *Reliefweb*, https://reliefweb.int/report/world/journey-extremism-africa-pathways-recruitment-and-disengagement, 2023, p. 14.

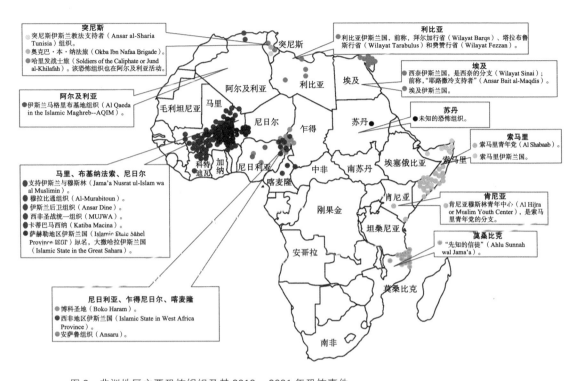

图 2　非洲地区主要恐怖组织及其 2012—2021 年恐怖事件

资料来源：笔者根据《非洲战略研究中心》（*Africa Center for Strategic Studies*）的图表编译[1]

和国、布基纳法索等国[2]（其他国家见表 1）。疫情期间，恐怖主义不但增加了其袭击活动（见图 3），而且已经逐渐渗入大陆的不同区域，连长期和平安宁的南部非洲也不放过。同时，根据联合国开发计划署最新的报告，恐怖主义组织往往利用各国的脆弱性（如恶劣的社会环境包括失业问题、粮食危机），或通过宗教传播手段，诱惑大量当地青年人加入恐怖组织，而被疫情影响以及俄乌冲突导致的粮食危机正好给这些恐怖组织提供了机会。[3]

---

① Africa Center for Strategic Studies, "Surge in Militant Islamist Violence in the Sahel Dominates Africa's Fight against Extremists," January 24, 2022, https://africacenter.org/spotlight/mig2022-01-surge-militant-islamist-violence-sahel-dominates-africa-fight-extremists/, accessed December 5, 2022.

② Institute for Economics & Peace, "Global Terrorism Index 2022: Measuring the Impact of Terrorism," Sydney, March 2022, http://visionofhumanity.org/resources, accessed October 18, 2022.

③ UNDP, "Journey to extremism in Africa: Pathways to recruitment and disengagement."

表1　撒哈拉以南非洲国家恐怖主义指数排名
及2011—2021年分值变化

国家	分数	排名	2011—2021年的变化	2020—2021年的变化
索马里	8.398	3	0.502	−0.091
布基纳法索	8.270	4	8.270	0.148
尼日利亚	8.233	6	0.753	−0.188
马里	8.152	7	3.804	0.230
尼日尔	7.856	8	4.027	0.441
喀麦隆	7.432	11	4.247	−0.193
莫桑比克	7.432	13	6.923	−0.399
刚果（金）	6.733	17	0.935	0.713
乍得	6.379	19	2.861	−0.281
肯尼亚	6.166	20	0.388	−0.192
坦桑尼亚	4.530	36	3.351	−0.300
布隆迪	4.310	42	4.310	0.026
乌干达	4.271	43	−1.073	1.158
埃塞俄比亚	4.106	45	−1.136	4.106
贝宁	3.759	49	−0.978	3.164
塞内加尔	3.164	53	3.164	1.261
多哥	1.580	70	−1.235	−0.527
卢旺达	1.243	73	−2.701	−0.490
南非	1.243	73	0.351	−0.490
毛里塔尼亚	1.243	73	1.243	1.243
安哥拉	0.509	84	−3.389	−0.318
加蓬	0.291	86	−2.648	−0.218
博茨瓦纳	0.291	86	0.291	−0.218
刚果共和国	0.000	93	0.000	0.000
科特迪瓦	0.000	93	−4.610	−2.464
吉布提	0.000	93	0.000	0.000

国家	分数	排名	2011—2021 年的变化	2020—2021 年的变化
赤道几内亚	0.000	93	0.000	0.000
厄立特里亚	0.000	93	−3.734	0.000
斯威士兰	0.000	93	0.000	0.000
冈比亚	0.000	93	0.000	0.000
加纳	0.000	93	0.000	0.000
几内亚	0.000	93	0.000	0.000
几内亚比绍	0.000	93	0.000	0.000
莱索托	0.000	93	−2.273	−2.028
利比里亚	0.000	93	0.000	0.000
马拉维	0.000	93	0.000	−0.158
纳米比亚	0.000	93	0.000	0.000
塞拉利昂	0.000	93	−1.179	0.000
南苏丹	0.000	93	−0.227	0.000
赞比亚	0.000	93	0.000	0.000
津巴布韦	0.000	93	−1.201	0.000
毛里求斯	0.000	93	0.000	0.000
马达加斯加	0.000	93	0.000	0.000
中非共和国	0.000	93	0.000	0.000
地区平均			0.433	0.004

资料来源：*Global Terrorism Index* 2022, p. 44

据苏赛克斯大学 Clionadlı Raleıgh 教授建立的《武装冲突地点和事件数据项目》发布的最新数据显示，2019 年至 2022 年末，非洲地区面临的安全风险持续上升，爆炸事件、战争、暴乱事件、针对平民的暴力事件等不安全事件的数量越来越多（见图 3）。不同地区和国家经历或遭受影响的程度有所不同，但大陆几乎每天会发生恐怖事件、有组织的政治暴力活动、绑架案等，无数人死亡或流离失所。另外，可以证实新冠疫情全球大流行以来，非洲安全形势恶化明显，根据美国国防部支持的非洲战略研究中心（Africa Center for Strategic Studies）[①]公布的数据，2021年非洲大陆恐怖主义事件比 2020 年增加了 10%，有关事件与活动超过5500 次。[②]

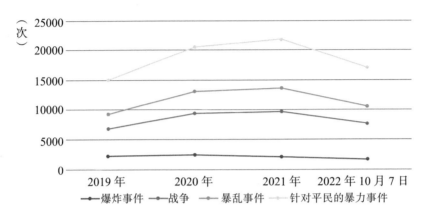

图 3　2019—2022 年非洲不安全事件

资料来源：《武装冲突地点和事件数据项目》（*The Armed Conflict Location & Event Data Project—ACLED*），https://acleddata.com/dashboard/#/dashboard（2022 年 10 月 17 日）

　　一系列传统与非传统安全问题交织在一起，导致非洲很多国家的局势出现恶性循环的局面；更糟糕的是，疫情以来越来越多的非洲人面临着前所未有的饥饿问题。根据世界粮食计划署的统计，世界上 60% 的饥饿人口生活在受战争和暴力影响的地区。[③]根据联合国粮农组织（FAO）的数据，2010—2019 年，全球受饥饿影响人数有 6 亿多；但是 2019—2021 年跃增到 7.679 亿人，其中 2.78 亿（约五分之一、占总人口的 20.2%）为非洲人。[④]此外，愈演愈严峻的安全问题导致了不计其数的难民、流

---

　　① 该中心 1998 年由美国白宫宣布成立，1999 年正式成立并开始运营。

　　② Africa Center for Strategic Studies, "Surge in Militant Islamist Violence in the Sahel Dominates Africa's Fight against Extremists," January 24, 2022, https://africacenter.org/spotlight/mig2022-01-surge-militant-islamist-violence-sahel-dominates-africa-fight-extremists/, accessed December 5, 2022.

　　③ World Food Programme, *A Global Food Crisis*, https://www.wfp.org/global-hunger-crisis?_ga=2.190687595.1924369741.1669457709-1642116799.1669457709, accessed November 26, 2022.

　　④ FAO, IFAD, UNICEF, WFP and WHO, *The State of Food Security and Nutrition in the World 2022: Repurposing food and agricultural policies to make healthy diets more affordable*, Rome, FAO, 2022, pp.10-12, https://www.fao.org/documents/card/en/c/cc0639en, accessed November 26, 2022.

离失所者和寻求庇护者。据不同机构的数据显示，非洲大陆拥有 3000 万以上难民、境内流离失所者和寻求庇护者，占世界总数的一半以上，其中来自西非和中非地区的占 11%，东非与非洲之角及大湖地区占 20%，南部非洲地区为 9%，来自北非和中东地区的总数为 17%。[①] 俄乌冲突爆发已经一年多的时间，目前还没有完整数据显示粮食安全恶化的情况，但飞涨的粮价和能源价格，必定会是雪上加霜，让非洲大陆安全形势由此受到更多直接或间接的影响。

三、各次地区安全局势盘点

尽管非洲大陆的安全轨迹存在共同特点，但不同次地区和个别国家面临的具体问题与挑战的程度与深度不大一样，其表现特征也有所不同。下文将根据地理特征、安全问题特征及其关联性，宏观性概述与各次地区面临的安全问题与挑战包括其趋势。

1. 西非、中非和萨赫勒地区

西非和萨赫勒地区是安全形势最恶劣的地区，传统与非传统安全因素盘根错节、相互掺杂，各种恐怖主义组织形成了非常庞大的恐怖网络（见图 2 和图 4）、跨国犯罪组织、族群冲突、农民和牧民冲突等，加之成为地区政治特征的政变一应俱全，使得该地区安全局势日益严峻。如上所述，这些恐怖组织相互联系，并且与全球基地组织和伊斯兰国有直接联系，他们跨境渗透能力强大，博科圣地自 2014 年以来就控制着乍得湖地区，不断对尼日利亚、乍得、喀麦隆和尼日尔境内发动恐怖袭击；2021 年萨赫勒地区几乎每天发生恐怖主义事件，暴力事件增加约 70%，特别是马里、布基纳法索和尼日尔境内，[②] 而且更糟糕的是，恐怖分子逐

---

① UNHCR, *Africa*, https://www.unhcr.org/en-us/africa.html?query=Africa, accessed January 3, 2023; Africa Center for Strategic Studies, *Record 36 Million Africans Forcibly Displaced*, July 19, 2022, https://africacenter.org/spotlight/record-36-million-africans-forcibly-displaced-is-44-percent-of-global-total-refugees-asylum/, accessed January 3, 2023; UNHCR, *Global Report 2021: The Stories Behind the Numbers*, p. 11.

② Africa Center for Strategic Studies, *Surge in Militant Islamist Violence in the Sahel Dominates Africa's Fight against Extremists*, January 24, 2022, https://africacenter.org/spotlight/mig2022-01-surge-militant-islamist-violence-sahel-dominates-africa-fight-extremists/, accessed December 12, 2022.

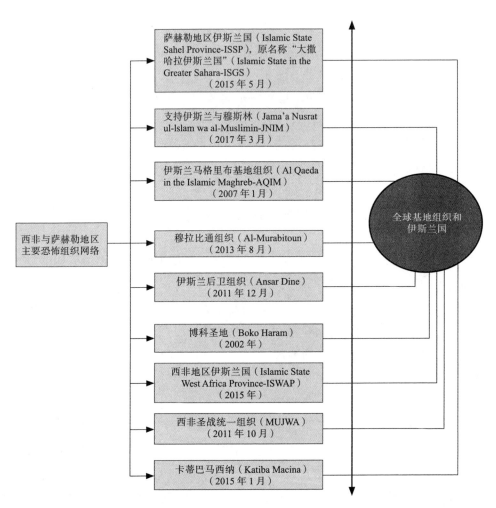

图 4　西非与萨赫勒地区主要恐怖组织网络

资料来源：笔者自制①

渐蔓延至其他长期和平安宁的西非国家，如加纳、科特迪瓦、多哥、贝宁等。

　　此外，近三年来，西非和萨赫勒地区（包括紧邻的中部非洲）政局比较动荡，发生了一系列武装政变更迭政府事件。文官政府既然治理无

---

　　① 笔者根据收集阅读的材料，针对西非和萨赫勒地区的主要恐怖组织，包括他们之间的联系及其与基地组织和伊斯兰国的联系，画出此图。

能，政变或者军队干政，就容易成为政治传统。实际上自独立以来，马里、布基纳法索、乍得、中非共和国、几内亚等国家都出现过两次以上的政变。不管政变的出发点是什么，背后一定存在着某种政治利益，而且对和平和安全的破坏性是不可否认的。

值得一提的是，萨赫勒地区也是受气候变化影响最大的地区之一，据联合国人道主义事务协调办公室 2022 年报告显示，2020 年 15 个全球受气候变化影响最大的国家中，12 个为非洲国家，其中大部分是西非和萨赫勒地区国家，包括了上文提到的动荡最为明显的马里、布基纳法索、苏丹、乍得、尼日尔等国。[①]气候变化因素，多大程度上与上文提到的其他安全挑战相互作用、激化和叠加产生更多的安全风险，还有待进一步的实证调研。

2. 非洲之角、东部非洲与大湖地区

非洲之角、东部非洲与大湖地区同样面临着多重错综复杂的安全问题与挑战，各种不安全因素交织在一起，使得安全局势越来越严峻。埃塞俄比亚的内战加上厄立特里亚因素、苏丹多年以来的内战危机、与基地挂钩的恐怖主义组织武装组织"索马里青年党"、南苏丹政局不稳等传统与非传统安全问题，对此地区造成了很大的隐患与困扰。2022 年底，埃塞俄比亚内战由非盟周旋，在南非签订了和平条约，终于宣告了两年内战的结束，但厄立特里亚因介入埃塞俄比亚内部冲突而使地区秩序与和平存在变数。2020 年 11 月埃塞俄比亚内战爆发后，厄立特里亚政府出兵协助埃塞俄比亚政府攻打提格雷，然而 2022 年年底交战双方签署和平条约之时，厄立特里亚没有被邀请出席。和平条约签署不久，厄立特里亚于 2022 年 11 月仍然向提格雷进攻，使此和平条约蒙上了阴影。实际上，厄立特里亚与提格雷之间敌意的渊源可以追溯到 20 世纪 70 年代，分别在 1998 年和 2000 年提格雷解放军（Tigray Peoples' Liberation Force）和厄立特里亚解放军（Eritrea Peoples' Liberation Force）之间的交战便是此不良好关系的后果。此外，多年来索马里青年党不仅

---

① United Nations Office for the Coordination of Humanitarian Affairs (OCHA), *Global Humanitarian Overview 2022*, p. 22, https://www.unocha.org/sites/unocha/files/Global%20Humanitarian%20Overview%202022.pdf .

不断制造恐怖主义袭击、破坏索马里本土的和平安宁，而且不断扩散和外溢到非洲之角和东部非洲，成为破坏地区安全的主要因素之一。截至目前，该恐怖主义组织不但在埃塞俄比亚、苏丹、肯尼亚、坦桑尼亚等国制造恐怖袭击，而且在该地区招兵买马、散布宗教极端化思想，同时开始在其他国家成立其分支，如肯尼亚伊斯兰青年中心（Al Hijra）。[①] 有智库也认为，自2019年7月以来莫桑比克北部境内比较活跃的恐怖主义组织，也是索马里青年党或全球性的基地组织的分支。[②]

近年来，反政府武装"M23运动"（March 23 Movement）不断在刚果（金）东部发动的袭击活动，已经导致大批平民死亡和流离失所，成为影响大湖地区，甚至是非洲整个大陆和平安全局势的最大威胁。更糟糕的是，刚果（金）政府多次谴责卢旺达对M23的支持，使得双方关系陷入僵局，2022年3月两国暂停了外交往来，导致大湖地区紧张局势愈演愈烈。卢旺达则以牙还牙，总统保罗·卡加梅于2023年1月9日提出卢旺达从此拒绝接受来自刚果（金）的难民。[③]根据联合国难民署（UNHCR）的数据，截至2022年6月，非洲之角、东非和大湖地区大约有495万难民和寻求庇护者，[④]大部分难民来自刚果（金）、埃塞俄比亚、索马里、苏丹、南苏丹、布隆迪等。卢旺达2022年接受了总数近14万的难民，其中55%来自刚果（金）。[⑤]其实，M23的来历可以追溯到20世纪90年代，多年以来反反复复地进行叛乱活动，总是以政府不履行

[①] Christopher Anzalone, "Kenya's Muslim Youth Center and Al-Shabab's East African Recruitment," October 2012, Volume 5, Issue 10, https://ctc.westpoint.edu/kenyas-muslim-youth-center-and-al-shababs-east-african-recruitment/, accessed January 9, 2023.

[②] Eric Morier-Genoud, "The jihadi insurgency in Mozambique: origins, nature and beginning," *Journal of Eastern African Studies*, 2020, Vol. 14, No. 3, pp.396-412; Tore Refslund Hamming, "The Islamic State in Mozambique," *Lawfare Institute*, https://www.lawfareblog.com/islamic-state-mozambique, accessed January 9, 2023.

[③] RFI, "President Kagame says Rwanda can accept no more refugees from DR Congo," https://www.rfi.fr/en/africa/20230110-president-kagame-says-rwanda-can-accept-no-more-refugees-from-dr-congo, accessed January 17, 2023.

[④] UNHCR, *East and Horn of Africa, and the Great Lake Region*, April-June 2022, p. 2.

[⑤] UNHCR, *Rwanda*, https://reporting.unhcr.org/rwanda?year=2023#toc-latest-updates, accessed January 16, 2023.

和平协定为由与国家正规军队开战。[①]

3. 南部地区

相比其他次地区，南部非洲的安全局势一直相对稳定；从上文图1来看，该地区各国的恐怖主义指数和排名也相对较低。不过，目前威胁到地区安全的主要因素是上文提到的莫桑比克北部德尔加多角省内自2019年开始活跃起来的恐怖主义组织，刚果（金）的叛乱组织的活动对该地区也有外溢效应，包括刚果（金）与卢旺达之间的紧张局势。尽管南部非洲发展共同体以及其他行为体一直积极协助莫桑比克抗击恐怖组织，但依然存在恐怖主义渗入该地区其他国家的风险。当然，除了宏观的安全问题之外，各国家也面临着许多微观的安全威胁，比如贫困问题、极端不平等、党派斗争等，也使在南部非洲国家各种民众生活在阴影下，特别是偷盗、打砸抢劫等社会治安层面的风险挑战频发，本文不展开讨论。

近几年来南非政局呈现出紧张的态势，加之被疫情加剧的失业、贫困、不平等、仇外心理、种族主义等问题，都是影响安全局势的客观与潜在因素。有学者认为，这些因素是南非未来将面临的主要安全问题与挑战。[②]此外，2021年中旬开始，斯威士兰（eSwatini）境内兴起了一系列反对君主制并提倡民主化的抗议活动。斯威士兰是非洲唯一拥有绝对君主专制的国家，也是当今世界少有此制度的国家之一。自1986年18岁的姆斯瓦蒂三世（King Mswati III）[③]执政以来，拥有至高无上的绝对权力，对司法、行政、议会等主要政府机关具有绝对权力，成为当今

---

① Furaha Umutoni Alida, "Do They Fight for Us?" Mixed Discourses of Conflict and the M23 Rebellion Among Congolese Rwandophone Refugees in Rwanda," *African Security*, 2014, volume 7, issue 2, pp.71-90; TV Monde, "RDC: qui sont les rebelles du M23 et pourquoi sont-ils source de tensions avec le Rwanda?" https://information.tv5monde.com/afrique/rdc-qui-sont-les-rebelles-du-m23-et-pourquoi-sont-ils-source-de-tensions-avec-le-rwanda, accessed January 17, 2023; Africa Center for Strategic Studies, "Rwanda and the DRC at Risk of War as New M23 Rebellion Emerges: An Explainer," June 29, 2022.

② Jakkie Cilliers, "South Africa's security sector is in crisis – reform must start now," *The Institute for Security Studies*, July 21, 2021, https://issafrica.org/iss-today/south-africas-security-sector-is-in-crisis-reform-must-start-now, accessed March 17, 2023.

③ 台湾地区译作恩史瓦蒂三世。

世界上少数拥有绝对权力的国家领导。然而，2021年6月该国民众开始了针对其绝对权力、呼吁民主化改革的示威浪潮。尽管南部非洲发展共同体（SADC）政治、国防和安全合作机构主席和南非总统西里尔·拉马福萨（Cyril Ramaphosa）于同年11月出面协调并促使全国对话，但至今为止，斯威士兰君主还没做出推行任何民主化举措。虽然这些政治、经济与社会问题是当事国的国内问题，但如果处理不好会成为影响地区安全局势的因素。更值得注意的是，这些动乱很大程度上有可能会被无孔不入的恐怖主义组织利用，并成为它们渗入该地区的机会。

4. 北非地区

整体而言，北非地区也面临着错综复杂的安全问题，许多安全威胁与挑战交织在一起，如跨国安全威胁（恐怖主义、跨国犯罪、非法交易、贩卖人口、毒品贩卖等）、国内族群冲突、叛乱、国家间摩擦等，使得安全环境较紧张。与此同时，该地区与西非及萨赫勒地区的安全问题有着关联。目前，萨赫勒地区的安全问题也外溢成为威胁北非安全的主要因素，特别是涉及与全球基地和伊斯兰国有千丝万缕联系的不同恐怖组织。

阿拉伯之春（Arab Springs）发生至今12年时间，其衍生和余绪在北非依然强大，尤其是利比亚。2011年穆阿迈尔·卡扎菲政权被推翻后，利比亚不但陷入内乱，周边地区与国家安全遭受了很大的破坏，特别是西非和萨赫勒地区。自此事件以来，利比亚的政治、社会与安全局势日益恶化，如打开了潘多拉盒子，一夜之间释放出各种不法分子、恐怖组织、各种冲突、毒品和武装交易、贩卖人口、非法移民等现象。客观而言，利比亚持续的政治动荡与其经济挑战也密不可分，不同阶层与外来行为体对石油资源的争夺、政治暴力的持续循环等因素，阻碍着减贫政策实施、经济不平等的解决、社会福利提供等努力。疫情和俄乌战争，双双加剧本来就糟糕的政治与经济形势，^①和平安全似乎更是遥不可及。

相比于利比亚，其他北非国家的安全环境较稳定，尽管埃及、突尼

---

① International Peace Institute, *The Situation in Libya: Reflections on Challenges and Ways Forward*, June 29, 2022, https://www.ipinst.org/2022/06/the-situation-in-libya-reflecting-on-challenges-and-ways-forward, accessed January 19, 2023.

斯和阿尔及利亚也都存在潜在和零星的恐怖组织。阿拉伯之春后，北非国家都调整或进行了政治（制度）改革，政局一直相对平稳，即便出现过抗议运动如摩洛哥（2016—2017）和阿尔及利亚（2019），也是小规模而已。值得一提的是，摩洛哥与阿尔及利亚长久以来关系不睦，一旦关系恶化会影响北非地区的秩序、和平与安全。

四、多重危机下非洲安全治理中的能动性与韧性

1. 多重危机对非洲经济的影响

2019年末疫情暴发后，无数观察家从对非洲的刻板印象出发，预测非洲大陆将拖累人类走出疫情的脚步。但事实相反，非洲没有像其他地区那样快速地"沦陷"为新冠疫情重灾区，而是在非盟和非洲成员国家共同努力下，实现快速预警和检疫能力培训与布防，尽可能斩断疫情扩散链条，并且深入社区，通过提高警戒意识、传播必要防疫知识，最大程度地减少了疫情初期对民众的伤害、降低了其对经济和社会的冲击，从而被国际公共卫生专家视为"非洲奇迹"。[1]难怪针对2022年6月宣称要讨论解决"全球战争、粮食短缺、能源价格震荡和通货膨胀问题"的七国集团（G7）峰会，并未受邀参加的时任肯尼亚总统肯雅塔以公开信的形式，建议七国集团向非洲学习如何应对多重危机的经验——"集体性思考并行动、非洲以投资未来的方式应对已经在发生的重大挑战"[2]。非洲应对新冠疫情这种非传统安全的方式，恰恰体现了这种集体性的力量，也是肯雅塔总统向富国喊话的底气。

然而疫情对于非洲社会经济的影响依然明显，在大多数非洲国家，卫生医疗条件的局限和非正式就业形态使得民众在疫情之下的生活更为艰难。[3]作为重要创汇来源的旅游业停摆，非洲经济遭遇半个世纪以

---

① 刘海方：《变动世界秩序中的非洲》，《世界知识》2023年第1期，第12—17页。
② 刘海方：《被忽视的自强大陆——多重危机中的非洲能动性》，《文化纵横》2022年第4期，第43—53页。
③ 刘海方：《新冠肺炎全球大流行下非洲的抗疫和中非合作》，《国际政治研究》2020年第3期，第12—17页。

来最严重的衰退，2020 年非洲 GDP 萎缩了 2%；2021 年，在大宗商品价格反弹和社交限制逐步放宽的加持下，撒哈拉以南非洲经济有所复苏反弹；[①] 但 2022 年非洲大陆实际 GDP 增长（4.1%）明显低于 2021 的 6.9%，不同国家的经济表现差异也很大，疫情的长期影响和俄乌冲突被认为是非洲经济增速放缓的重要原因。[②]

尽管困难重重，从全球来看，2022 年非洲经济增长速度仍然取得了第二位的好成绩，仅次于亚洲（见图 5）。根据非洲发展银行的预测，2023—2024 年期间，非洲 GDP 增长将保持稳定，平均增长率约为 4%。[③]

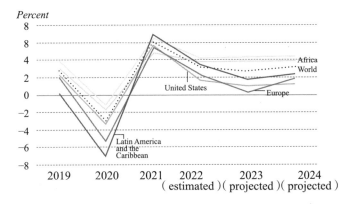

图 5　2019—2024 年非洲与世界其他地区 GDP 增长情况

资料来源：African Development Bank Group, "Africa's Macroeconomic Performance and Outlook, January 2023," p. 9

2. "新泛非主义" 的大陆治理模式

能够取得这样的成就，不能不提被非洲本土学者称作"新泛非主义"的大陆治理模式，即面对当前非洲国家的新任务和新挑战，如气候变化问题、粮食安全问题、安全与发展关联的问题，在承认各个成员国

---

①　姚桂梅：《新冠肺炎疫情下非洲地区形势特点与中非合作展望》，《当代世界》2022 年第 5 期。

②　王进杰：《非洲经济发展的机遇和挑战》，《北大非洲电讯》第 516 期，2022 年 10 月 26 日，https://mp.weixin.qq.com/s/kDFhF-0zqRLLjJC8RSm6gw。

③　African Development Bank Group, "Africa's Macroeconomic Performance and Outlook, January 2023," p. 9.

主权独立完整的基础上，推进非洲国家各方面合作，实现集体发展。①
疫情暴发不久，面对各国市场小、难以在国际市场上快速采购到防疫设
备和物资的困难，非盟迅速召集成立了大陆统一的防疫物资和疫苗集体
采购系统；2022 年 1 月，泛非支付和结算系统正式上线，非洲大陆自贸
区内部跨境交易得以实现，而且减少了对第三方货币的依赖。乌克兰危
机爆发突然带来全球供应链中断、大部分非洲国家的粮食和能源采购困
难显现后，非洲进出口银行与非洲大陆自贸区合作，设计开发了农业产
品采购系统，促进非洲本土的卖家和买家直接在系统中实现信息对接和
通过系统进行交易。②此外，大力发展农业也是针对粮食危机非洲各方
力量采取的重要应对措施，正如非洲开发银行行长所说："非洲人不要被
施以饭食，而要田里有粮——非洲人要学习机械种植收割足够养活自己
的粮食，骄傲地端着自己的饭碗。"③

　　除了政治经济领域的危机干预措施，一整套集体治理的理念也正在
军事安全领域形成，即在非盟里组建常备军，在次区域组织框架下建设
各区域的常备军。面对国内的动荡局势，非洲国家领导人采用国内对话
方式，与不同阶层的相关方（包括武装分子，甚至恐怖组织，如上文的
M23）进行对话协商、和平谈判，埃塞俄比亚、马里、布基纳法索和刚
果（金）等热点国家都在自主协商，或者由代表非盟和次地区组织的其
他非洲国家资深政治家斡旋。同样，国家间的摩擦也在有关国家由第三
方或多方斡旋对话下趋向达成共识解决争端，比如马里与布基纳法索关
于不明身份军队问题、刚果（金）与卢旺达关于 M23 的争端问题（截至
2023 年 3 月尚未解决）。

　　在进行集体安全治理的过程中，有鉴于多重混杂的安全问题以及地
区性安全关联，非洲不同地区尤其是安全局势较恶劣的地区（西非、萨
赫勒地区和中非地区），往往成立了多个相应的组织、机制和倡议，而

① Michael Amoah, *The new pan-Africanism: globalism and the nation state in Africa*, I. B. Tauris, 2019.

② 刘海方：《变动世界秩序中的非洲》，《世界知识》2023 年第 1 期。

③ "African Development Bank Board approves $1.5 billion facility to avert food crisis," *African Development Bank Group*，转引自刘海方：《被忽视的自强大陆——多重危机中的非洲能动性》。

此前既有的其他功能的地区组织也往往在其框架内将安全议题纳入战略与决策，并增设了新的和平与安全管理机构（见图6）。[1] 虽然机构众多、叠床架屋，给成员国带来沉重的义务和经济负担（也难免增加了对国际社会或发达国家在财政和军备上的依赖），[2] 这些组织、机制和倡议也并非全部得到非盟的认可或支持，但它们的宗旨毕竟是为了解决地区性的安全挑战所做的努力。

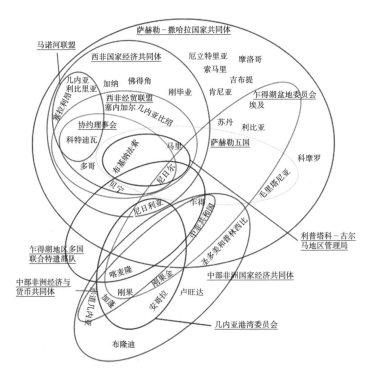

图6 非洲有关安全管理的组织与机制

资料来源：朱伟东、王婷：《非洲区域经济组织成员身份重叠现象与消解路径》，《西亚非洲》2020年第1期，第96—117页[3]

---

① 由于非洲大陆涉及安全管理的组织与机制的多样性，本文只选择了安全局势较恶劣的地区。

② 有关组织成员身份重叠研究，请参见朱伟东、王婷：《非洲区域经济组织成员身份重叠现象与消解路径》，《西亚非洲》2020年第1期，第96—117页。

③ 英文同类图示可以参见 Amandine Gnanguênon, "Mapping African regional cooperation: How to navigate Africa's institutional landscape," *European Council on Foreign Relations*, 29 *October* 2020, https://ecfr.eu/publication/mapping-african-regional-cooperation-how-to-navigate-africas-institutional-landscape/。

3. 集体行动中的韧性

疫情不但没有蔓延扩散，并且相比其他地区与发达国家，非洲大陆在地区和次地区层面号召所有国家团结一致，携手共同应对疫情。尽管在抗疫的道路上困难重重，但非洲国家非常清楚集体行动的重要性，并且它们的努力是建立在实现自主性决心的基础之上。实现自主性走向一体化是非洲大陆多年以来向往的发展道路与愿景，不管面临何种挑战，非洲行为体始终不懈地推进此政策。也就是说，疫情期间，非洲国家在应对多重危机的过程中，集体行动凸显了非洲能动的韧性与泛非主义精神。尽管面临着全球和地区性的各种挑战，非洲地区呈现出了一定程度的韧性。

"新泛非主义"思想基础上的集体安全治理，与传统泛非主义一样鼓励非洲国家相互之间的团结（solidarity）——也就是说，成员国可以超越组织和机制既定的范围开展行动，比一般集体安全治理走得更远。非盟承认八个次区域组织，这些次区域组织成立的主要目的是促使区域经济合作，进而推动大陆一体化；由于安全问题的迫切性，这些组织在非盟和联合国的授命下（但不完全是）可以在本地区展开安全治理行动。非洲的集体安全治理使得次区域组织的行动常常超越本地区、超越政治和经济利益，它建立在非洲伦理与泛非主义哲学思想基础之上的团结原则。本着实现大陆安全化的决心，非洲国家团结友爱、相互支持，很多国家往往在自身经历困难之际、挺身帮助其他冲突中的国家。例如，2022 年 12 月 28 日，南苏丹宣布在东非共同体行动框架下派遣 750 名士兵协助刚果（金）抗击叛军（目前已经在行动中），此前已有乌干达、肯尼亚和布隆迪派遣部队前往刚果（金）东部展开维和行动——这是基于成员国的高度共识，即刚果（金）东部叛乱武装的种种行动构成整个东非地区的安全挑战。南苏丹自身正在经历各种传统与非传统安全挑战，安全局势堪忧，而且水灾之后又面临着严重的饥荒，却不顾自身要为此承担的经济重负，自愿派遣部队支持地区性的行动。类似地，2021 年卢旺达也跨区域派遣部队协助莫桑比克抗击恐怖主义，2020 年还派遣部队协助中非共和国政府攻打叛军，该行动是双边协议下的，不在联合国框架下。^①同样的例子还有索马里，一个安全局势长期严峻的国家，但是 2018 年在区域行动框架下向南苏丹派遣了部队，并表示没有任何理由可以阻止它参与非洲地区的安全治理。^②

　　有关研究也认为，非洲国家在力图实现自主性道路上，集体治理逐渐成为安全治理的重要模式。挪威国际事务研究所联合国与全球治理中心研究教授塞德里奇·德·科宁（Cedric de Coning）、安德鲁（Andrew E. Yaw Tchie）和 Anab Ovidie Grand 在一篇文章中采用了"临时安全倡议"（ad-hoc security initiatives）概念，讨论非洲地区安全治理机制（萨赫勒五国集团、乍得湖地区多国联合特遣部队等），认为它们是集体安全治理的新模式。他们提出，临时安全倡议是一种新兴的机制安排，将国家置于寻找安全解决方案的中心；同时与邻国合作，通过跨区域合作应对跨国威胁，使受影响的国家能够通过采用联合跨境行动（joint cross-border operations）在其境内和跨境开展行动。^③ Baldaro Edoardo 和 Elisa Lopez Lucia 也提出，"非盟（AU）、西非国家经济共同体（ECOWAS）和萨赫勒五国集团为治理困扰该地区的安全问题，提供了不同的空间尺度，创新了替代性干预空间和安全治理技术，共同参与安排地区的新安全治理，并为非洲大陆以外的全球其他地区定义了新的安全治理模式。"^④

　　在疫情和俄乌冲突双重外来挑战之下，非洲国家确实面临多重安全挑战与威胁，国际社会并没有能够系统性提供帮助和解决方案，非洲国家之间的团结更为明显与坚固、实现自主治理的紧迫性更为凸显，集体行动中的团结无比重要。同样，针对全球性的挑战与危机，非洲的能动性也日益显现，非洲的声音和非洲方案也逐渐进入全球治理中，

---

　　① Brendon J. Cannon and Federico Donelli, "Rwanda's Military Deployments in Sub-Saharan Africa: A Neoclassical Realist Account," *The International Spectator*, 2022, pp.1-19.

　　② Mohammed Yusuf, "Somalia Says Ready to Send Troops to S. Sudan for Security," *Voice of America*, September 19, 2018, https://www.voanews.com/a/somalia-says-ready-to-send-troops-to-south-sudan-for-security/4578700.html, accessed February 9, 2023.

　　③ Cedric de Coning, Andrew E. Yaw Tchie, and Anab Ovidie Grand, "Ad-hoc Security Initiatives, an African response to insecurity," *African Security Review*, 2022, Vol. 31, No. 4, pp. 383-398.

　　④ Baldaro Edoardo and Elisa Lopez Lucia, "Spaces of (in-)Security and Intervention: Spatial Competition and the Politics of Regional Organizations in the Sahel," *Territory, Politics, Governance*, 2022, p. 2.

比如针对俄乌冲突，非洲方面一直提倡和平的解决方案，即对话与和平谈判。①

<h2 style="text-align:center">结　语</h2>

本文以疫情及俄乌冲突为全球性转折事件，概述了此前就存在大量安全问题的非洲大陆，是如何应对更具挑战性的多重危机的，同时重点剖析了非洲在传统和非传统安全领域的新型治理模式。客观而言，多年以来非洲大陆面临的传统与非传统安全因素交织在一起，相互作用呈现出错综复杂的局面，这种安全问题的属性是结构性的，根源于长期的历史根源和独立以来的恶性循环。面对新冠疫情以及俄乌冲突的冲击，大陆的安全局势更为恶劣，恐怖主义袭击、族群冲突（包括农民与牧民冲突）、跨国犯罪等问题越来越严重。不同恐怖组织与伊斯兰国等全球性恐怖组织勾连在一起，不仅从西非、萨赫勒地区和东非逐渐渗入其他地区，还利用恶劣的社会环境、围绕经济的冲突（资源分配、失业等问题）诱惑他人加入恐怖组织，尤其是青年群体。疫情削弱了各国的经济发展和财政能力，俄乌冲突导致的能源危机及粮食供应严重欠缺，又一次为恐怖组织提供了浑水摸鱼甚至发展壮大的机会，不同安全问题因此加剧了恶性循环，安全局势更为复杂，解决这些问题需要不同行为体的努力与团结，特别是针对地区性或跨区域性的安全挑战、发展和安全相互关联性的挑战等等。

在应对措施方面，本文认为，非洲已经开始探索的"新泛非主义"基础上的集体安全治理模式，经验越来越丰富，呈现向成熟模式发展的积极态势。近几年来，非洲国家在安全治理方面不断努力探索本土化可持续的方案，在这个过程中集体行动是实现自主性最主要的因素。当

---

① Institut Montaigne, "Senegal: The 'Voice' of Africa in the Russian-Ukrainian Crisis," July 1, 2022, https://www.institutmontaigne.org/en/analysis/senegal-voice-africa-russian-ukrainian-crisis, accessed February 9, 2023; African Press Agency, "Russia-Ukraine war: Ecowas chair pushes for peace," October 26, 2022, http://apanews.net/en/news/russia-ukraine-war-ecowas-chair-pushes-for-peace/, accessed February 9, 2023.

然，集体安全治理并非始于疫情期间和俄乌冲突，但自上述两件全球性事件发生以来，非洲行为体的集体行动加快，也体现出了更为坚定的团结路线图。疫情和俄乌冲突固然转移了国际社会的注意力，并导致非洲的安全挑战与威胁在全球问题中再度被边缘化，但非洲国家弱而不怯，勇于面对挑战和风险，并由此推进更具自主性、能动性的集体治理，这种其他区域或大陆罕见的团结原则，不但为解决非洲问题发挥更大作用，同时为全球治理注入了新的启发和治理路径。

全球地方化：疫情之下非洲公立大学的"转型"危机

——以博茨瓦纳大学罢工为例

陈　亮　刘乃菁[*]

摘　要： 非洲大学在 2022 年经历了一系列罢工事件。本文以全球地方化视角透视博茨瓦纳大学于 2022 年底发生的罢工事件，试图呈现新冠疫情和新自由主义改革在非洲高等教育界产生的在地后果。笔者通过对罢工活动的参与观察和法律文本分析，辅以对相关人员的访谈，认为新冠疫情引发的经济下行引发了以涨薪为主要诉求的罢工，但罢工形式体现出博茨瓦纳的地方性制度色彩，也是对抵制该校自二十年前引入的新自由主义改革的延续。通过对新自由主义在欧美和非洲高等教育界的流布及后果的梳理和经验研究，笔者认为教育界的新自由主义以审计文化为内核，导致了威权主义的抬头。这一经验观察构成了对笃信市场主义的新自由主义的批判。

关键词： 新自由主义　疫情　非洲高等教育　审计文化　罢工　博茨瓦纳

引　言

博茨瓦纳大学（The University of Botswana，简称 UB）位于博茨瓦纳首都哈博罗内，是博茨瓦纳的最高学府，也是 2005 年前博茨瓦纳唯一的公立大学。2022 年 11 月，UB 发生了为期两周的罢工。发动罢工的

---

　　* 陈亮，澳大利亚国立大学人类学博士，博茨瓦纳大学人文学院中国研究系讲师；刘乃菁，澳大利亚国立大学亚太学院博士生。

两个工会分别是教研人员和高级教辅人员工会①"乌巴苏"（UBASSSU）和职工工会"乌布苏"（UBSU）。罢工教师和教辅人员打着"UB员工受到薪资歧视"的旗帜，高举"UB不能再恶化下去了！""挽救UB，校长下台！"的标语牌，一路用博茨瓦纳语唱着"我们要钱，你们（校方管理层）讲故事"，迈着传统舞步，结队在校园里游行。队伍到了校门口集合地点，数位罢工召集人依次发表演讲，罢工人员高喊："谁分裂我们，我们就分裂谁！""UB所有的事情我们都知道，只有一个人不知道！""校长下台！下台！"

因为罢工正逢圣诞节前的期末考试月，学校管理层如临大敌，通过召开院系会议，指派系主任为"核心人员"，监督没有参加工会的教研人员在教辅人员罢工的情况下，严格执行考试纪律，确保试卷分发回收到位，以不影响考试成绩和学位证书。博茨瓦纳当地媒体多次报道这次罢工，罢工者一度要求教育部长参与对话，但教育部长并未如期出现在罢工者的面前。一位参与罢工的领导告诉笔者，如果罢工诉求得不到满足的话，次年的期中考试，还会发起新的罢工。②

UB的教职员工与校方的紧张关系并非孤例。非洲大学罢工潮在新冠疫情逐渐缓和之时却逐步高涨。2022年2月，大津巴布韦大学（GZU）教师罢工要求涨薪。③加纳大学教师联盟于2022年11月发动全国15所高校罢工，要求涨薪60%以应对通胀。④最严重的乃是尼日利

---

① "教辅人员"英文为support staff。因为这一具有历史意义的称谓涉及UB先前的改革，笔者采取"教辅人员"的译法而不采用中国高校普遍的"行政人员"的说法。下文将会进一步讨论。

② 这位工会领导也是一位教授，在参加笔者所在院系的院长组织同乡好友和UB的同事的聚会时告诉笔者继续罢工的意图。2023年2月中旬，UB教职员工果然再次举行了为期一周的罢工。

③ "GZU Lecturers Join Incapacitated Colleagues, Announce Strike," *New Zimbabwe*, 24 Feburary 2022, https://www.newzimbabwe.com/gzu-lecturers-join-incapacitated-colleagues-announce-strike/.

④ "UTAG strike continues as govt fails to meet demands of striking lecturers," *GhanaWeb*, 30 November 2022, https://www.ghanaweb.com/GhanaHomePage/NewsArchive/UTAG-strike-continues-as-govt-fails-to-meet-demands-of-striking-lecturers-1672178.

亚公立大学的教职员工罢工，导致学生8个月无课可上。[①] 尼日利亚大学教师抗议学校设施经费不足；教师工资低廉（教授的工资一个月只有1000美元）；政府不断投资兴建新的私立大学，政府官员却将子女送往欧美高校。有报道指出，尼日利亚的公立大学在过去的23年之内已经历了17次罢工。[②] 非洲大学工会组织的罢工运动显示出非洲高等教育界面临的危机，也与世界范围内的大学罢工遥相呼应。[③]

这种危机是由新冠疫情所引起的经济衰退所触发，还是由席卷全球乃至非洲教育界的其他因素所导致？抑或有一些本土性的制度文化在起作用？本文以博茨瓦纳大学2022年的罢工潮为案例，以全球地方化（glocalization）视角为分析框架，试图剖析这一现象背后的制度成因。本文首先介绍此次罢工参与方的动员过程，以及罢工方与学校管理层的矛盾。其次，在全球地方化的框架下讨论新自由主义的发源和在非洲高等教育界的扩张和落地机制。最后，将罢工事件置于博茨瓦纳高等教育变迁之中，揭示此次罢工体现出的高校转型危机中的新变化。

一、大学罢工："转型"危机与罢工同盟

博茨瓦纳位于非洲南部，毗邻南非、津巴布韦和纳米比亚。因为在1966年独立之初发现了钻石资源，并将钻石资源成功地国有化，避免了非洲国家常见的"资源诅咒"，经济年增长率在数十年内保持9%以上。博茨瓦纳从1960年代世界倒数的穷国变为中等以上收入国家（2021年

---

① "Nigeria's public university lecturers suspend strike after eight months," *Reuters*, 14 October 2022, https://www.reuters.com/world/africa/nigerias-public-university-lecturers-suspend-strike-after-eight-months-2022-10-14/.

② "17 strikes in 23 years: a unionist explains why Nigeria's university lecturers won't back down," *The Conversation*, 8 September 2022, https://theconversation.com/17-strikes-in-23-years-a-unionist-explains-why-nigerias-university-lecturers-wont-back-down-190170.

③ 例如2013年1月，英国也爆发了席卷150所高校的教职员工罢工。参考大学与学院联盟网页，https://www.ucu.org.uk/article/12671/2023。

博茨瓦纳人均 GDP 达到 6367 美元）[①]，成为非洲的"例外"和"奇迹"。[②]
博茨瓦纳大学在 2005 年之前是博茨瓦纳唯一的公立大学，其前身是罗马天主教会在巴苏陀兰（今莱索托）设置的宗教性质浓厚的庇护十二大学。[③] 因为博茨瓦纳国库相对充裕，保证了公立大学教育经费预算的充足拨付。2010 年以来，博茨瓦纳大学每年的预算在 1.5 亿美元左右。因为 UB 的工资薪酬等级表不公开，笔者只能估计大学讲师／高级讲师的年收入约 40 万到 60 万普拉（1 美元＝ 12.8 普拉）。

在新冠肆虐期间，博茨瓦纳于 2021 年的 3、4 月份和 7、8 月份经历了两次大的疫情冲击，[④] 并于 2022 年 12 月首次报告发现了奥米克戎变种。该国 GDP 在 2020 年下降了 10.6%，不过在 2021 年因为全球钻石市场的复苏而回弹。[⑤] 通胀率从 2022 年初的 2% 上升到 12 月的 12.4%，仅交通运输业贡献的通胀率就达到了 6.8%。[⑥] 俄乌战争更是引发了博茨瓦纳油价上涨，哈博罗内的小巴司机于 2022 年 5 月举行了全市罢工，抗议政府不顾民生上调油价，导致入不敷出。[⑦]

单从经济角度而言，参加罢工的博茨瓦纳教员和行政人员或教辅人员所受疫情的影响稍有不同。由新冠与俄乌战争引发的经济下行带来的交通费用、房租上涨，对教辅人员的冲击更大，因为他们的合同中没

---

① 数据来源：https://tradingeconomics.com/botswana/gdp-per-capita，查询时间：2023 年 1 月 15 日。

② J. Clark Leith, *Why Botswana Prospered* (McGill-Queen's Press, 2005). 经济学家 Leith 将博茨瓦纳的高速发展归因于对钻石资源的掌控与初期的基础设施建设，并且认为博茨瓦纳的传统文化包含了相当民主的因素，对经济发展有促成作用。但也有批评者认为 Leith 有意识避免讨论博茨瓦纳内部发展计划的失败：投资数十亿普拉只能做到肉鸡自给自足、银行呆账坏账、对南非经济的绝对依赖，以及过重依赖钻石资源造成的经济单一与不平等（博茨瓦纳的基尼系数在 2023 年为全球倒数第 10 位）。参考 Ian Taylor, "Revtewed Wεrk(s): Why Botswana Prospered by J. Clark Leith," *International Affairs*, Vol. 82. No. 3, 2006, pp. 603-604.

③ 庇护十二天主教大学（Pius XII Catholic University）是于 1946 年在莱索托成立的以罗马教宗命名的高等教育机构。

④ 参考维基百科"博茨瓦纳新馆疫情"条目。https://en.wikipedia.org/wiki/COVID-19_pandemic_in_Botswana.

⑤ 博茨瓦纳新冠疫情期间的 GDP 如下：2019 年 167 亿美元，2020 年 149.3 亿美元，2021 年 176.1 亿美元，180 亿美元（2022 年预计）。

⑥ 数据来源：博茨瓦纳统计局，https://tradingeconomics.com/botswana/inflation-cpi，查询时间：2023 年 1 月 14 日。

⑦ https://www.mmegi.bw/news/commuters-stranded-due-to-transporters-strike/news.

有交通和住房补贴。对教研人员而言，他们的工资与公立大学的预算直接相关。最常听到的抱怨是他们的工资在 5 年之内都没有增加，反因通胀缩水。教职员工原先有年度教学考核优秀的奖金（半个月到一个月工资），在新冠后也被取消了。

与教职工利益更相关的是 UB 现任校长（vice chancellor）自 2017 年上任推行的"转型"（transformation）改革。"转型"是在政府拨款削减、招生规模扩大的背景下提出来的，目的是推动 UB 从非盈利型大学"转型"为盈利型的大学，并完成从教学型大学向科研型大学、国立大学向国际化大学的转变。在 2011 至 2012 年间，博茨瓦纳大学总预算为 1.45 亿美元，其中 77% 来自政府拨款，21.5% 是学生学费。[1] 疫情前的 2018 至 2019 年，UB 的总预算约 1.48 亿美元，其中 59.3% 为政府拨款，28.0% 为学生学费。[2] 2019 年员工成本高达总预算 1.45 亿美元的 70.5%。[3] 可以看出，总预算持平，政府拨款在 7 年里下降了 18%，而学费收入上涨了 8%。

在 2022 年 2 月新校监（chancellor）就职的全校员工会议上，校长在演讲中继续强调学校的"转型"和盈利，并宣布为"转型"所设立的多个委员会和咨询、论证、实施的路线图。笔者入职参加的教研人员培训，均围绕着"转型"展开，这些"转型"的文件和演示文稿不乏各种柱状图、折线图、韦恩图和"战略""创新""利益相关者"等管理学和各种成功心理学词汇（如"走出舒适区"），但与实际教学和科研无关。

"转型"对公立大学教员更切身的冲击是合同临时化、课时增多、科研经费减少，但科研发表压力不减。至少从 2019 年开始，UB 与教职员工的合同开始大规模临时化，无论是新招募讲师还是老教师，合同多为两到三年，依据年度绩效管理系统（Performance Management System，简称 PMS）考核成绩，决定是否续签，并且在续签时人力资源部会放出招聘广告，需要续聘人员与新招募人员竞争上岗。"转型"的另一个目的是在各种评估以后进行裁员（retrenchment）或遣散（layoff），这成了悬

---

① Richard Tabulawa and Frank Youngman, "University of Botswana: A National University in Decline?" In Damtew Teferra eds. *Flagship Universities in Africa*. Palgrave Macmillan, 2017, p. 37.

② 博茨瓦纳大学 2018—2019 年报告。

③ 同上。

在所有教研人员（特别是固定期合同人员）头上的一把"达摩克利斯之剑"。教辅人员在上述2月份全校会议上表示，长期缺乏各种基础设施（如网络）和设备维护的资金，无法实现硬件上的升级，"转型"丝毫不解决眼前的问题。一位教授则针锋相对地指出"转型"之下的各种措施都是可望而不可行的"梦想清单"（wish list），用于"转型"的资金更是见不到踪影。

在博茨瓦纳，教研人员和教辅人员的不满有合法的组织化表达渠道——工会和罢工。博茨瓦纳继承了英国的劳资关系制度。在法律框架下，学校工会的权利几乎与校方平齐。依据"乌巴苏"（教研人员和高级教辅人员工会）和校方签订的协议，自由结社是工会的基础，校方不得干涉和威胁工会办公人员、工会成员；而工会办公成员、工人代表、工会成员也不得干涉和威胁学校雇员。集体工资协商和罢工也要遵循法律程序。谈判破裂后，工会才可以发动罢工或"劳工行动"（industrial action）。

工会正是在这样的法律框架下发动了罢工。2022年10月时值博茨瓦纳大学40年校庆，"乌巴苏"（教研人员和高级教辅人员工会）号召会员抵制校庆。从10月开始，在该工会领导的推动下，工会化的进程加速了，包括敦促每位工会会员招募5个新会员、要求各系选举工人代表（shop steward）、向工会成员和非工会人员转发相关法律文件如《集体劳工协议》等。与此同时，两个工会"乌巴苏"和"乌布苏"向大学所在的区劳动局（district labor office）提请与校方就涨薪进行仲裁。仲裁被工业法庭判无效后，于11月先后发起了长达两周的罢工。

从这份内容颇为翔实的仲裁报告可以看出工会和校方争议的具体内容和工会的斗争策略。仲裁申请人（applicant）是工会主席和总书记，被告（respondent）是大学的人力资源总监。工会认为UB校长财务状况不透明，要求学校涨3%—5%的工资，以应对博茨瓦纳近年来通胀带来的后勤人员的薪资缩水，而仲裁结果明显倾向于支持工会。首先，被告校方曾以案件复杂为由，申请法律人员代表校方，但申请人（工会）认为引入法律代表是歧视工会，因为工会会费有限，无法支付引入法律代表的相关费用。仲裁员认为，根据《行业争议法》，事件本身并不复杂，法律代表的引入确实对工会不公平，因此驳回校方的请求，支持工会。第二个争议在于教辅人员的服务是否属于"必要服务"（essential services）。校方认为教研人员才是大学的核心，教辅人员的服务不属于"必要服务"。仲裁员再次援引《行业争议法》，认为教辅人员的教学服务必要，他们的服务属于"必要服务"。第三，UB 雇员的工资是否与博茨瓦纳政府挂钩？校方多次表示，大学理事会一直以来主张 UB 的薪资并不与政府工资级别挂钩。仲裁人驳回了校方的主张，因为大学理事会从法律顾问得到的意见一直是校长的工资等同于博茨瓦纳教育部常设秘书的，并且依据博茨瓦纳《关于收入、雇佣、价格和利润的国家政策修正案》（2005 年）条款，博茨瓦纳大学作为一所"半官方非赢利性机构"（non-profit parastatal）仍然从政府接受资助。仲裁员认为，虽然博茨瓦纳大学在内部薪资上可以保持一定自主权，但这并不意味着校长工资与政府脱钩。第四，关于工会要求 3%—5% 工资的要求，因为双方没有充分共享相关信息，仲裁员建议工会次日向 UB 申请公开 2021—2022 年的预算，后者 10 月 25 日回复后，双方将于 11 月 3 日再次进行协商。

就工会合法斗争的策略而言，可以看到运动的矛头指向了校长，并且通过将政府工资—校长工资—教员工资—教辅人员工资链接挂钩，论证教研人员和高级教辅人员的薪水必然随着政府涨薪而上涨。笔者在第三部分还会谈到这一点。

不过，博茨瓦纳工业法庭 11 月 10 日便推翻了"乌巴苏"与校方的仲裁决议，称其缺乏法律基础。11 月 11 日，一封工会发送给院系的邮件显示，"乌布苏"（职工工会）与校方的调解陷入僵局，"乌布苏"主席与校方人力资源总监合签罢工声明，决定依照法律率先于 11 月 14 日—18 日举行罢工。紧接着，"乌巴苏"也宣布罢工。

实际罢工动员过程表明了教辅人员和教研人员结成了牢固的同盟。首先，就罢工破坏性而言，罢工的时间点选在了期末考试期间，教辅人员参加罢工的直接后果是考试有可能无法进行。教辅人员包括教学管理人员，也包括电工、木匠、IT 人员、教学秘书以及学校专设的监考人员。依照学校规章制度，监考人员会在考试开始前四十分钟到考场，摆放时钟，从一个密封袋中拿出考试卷分开放在课桌上，然后与提前半小时来的两位教职工（多为本门课程的教师）交接。开考前，监考人员查验学生证，然后留守在考场外一小时。在考试结束的半个小时前，返回考场，回收准考证和多余的试卷。因此，监考人员的缺场，就会影响到期末考试的正常进行；而期末考试成绩更关联到学生学位的授予。其次，在话语层面，工会强调两类人员的团结，反对校方的分裂。校方为了应对罢工，通过学院施压，让教研人员代行监考职责，并由作为"管理层"的系主任监督。但工会领导在院系应对罢工的紧急会议上提出反对意见，主张教研人员代行职责是在法律上"破坏罢工、破坏团结"。

不过，笔者认为，教辅人员和教研人员的同盟只是罢工的策略，而非基于日常的工作关系。根据笔者的观察，在大学日常教研活动中，教学设备（如投影设备、音箱）等常常功能不全，从南非购入的教学管理系统常常出现漏洞，但IT人员要么缺席，要么无法解决问题。办公室的空调无法制冷，校方维修工人上门七八次仍然无法修好，最后笔者被告知维修材料费不足，申请往往动辄数月，因此每次上门维修多少带有完成任务的表演色彩。许多行政秘书等办公室人员往往在大学任职长达数十年，常常因为病假或事假不来办公室。这些服务部门的低效无能已经成为不向外人公开但内部人皆知的秘密，或人类学家赫兹菲尔德所言的"文化亲密性"（cultural intimacy）。[①] 当我向本地的教职员工抱怨这一现象时，他们向我解释这种低效或"无能"的原因：政府和大学的行政职位多为永久性质。"许多人在办公室里一坐便是二三十年，已经把办公室当成自己家一样，办不完事就明天再来。"而新来的领导想有任何改变，往往被老员工以老资历训斥。

以上在博茨瓦纳大学观察到的不同机构在日常运行时互相掣肘、罢工时却走向联合的悖论，需要对下文所述的新自由主义改革在非洲高等教育界的扩散及其后果有所了解，并且熟悉地方性制度结构和人们（公开的和非公开的）的关注点，才能进行有效的"深描"（格尔茨语）。笔者在下文中将采用"全球地方化"（glocalization／glocal）框架透视这一

---

① Michael Herzfeld, *Cultural Intimacy: Social Poetics and the Real Life of States, Societies, and Institutions*, London and New York: Routledge, 2016.

现象。"全球地方化"的概念实际上源于 1980 年代日本的索尼公司，用以指导在全球不同市场针对当地需求调整广告策略。Featherstone 将这种"日本化"即"一种全球战略，它不寻求强加标准产品或形象，而是根据当地市场的需求量身定制"提炼为"全球地方化"。[①] Victor Roudometof 进一步梳理了全球地方化的概念谱系和演变。[②] Richard Tabulawa 提出，全球和地方在世界日益交融的现实中，往往是一种现象的两个侧面，全球和地方因素的互动往往会产生无法预料的后果。[③] 通过全球地方化的分析框架，笔者将在下文梳理新自由主义的发源、表现形式和在非洲高校的扩散，然后再次回到对本次罢工的讨论上来。

二、新自由主义、审计文化和非洲大学

新自由主义（neoliberalism）被广泛认为是以华盛顿共识为基础、以市场力量代替国家力量的意识形态和实践，在过去的半个世纪里，从欧美以一种全球性的强势力量扩散到全世界范围，产生重大的政治、社会、文化影响。新自由主义在撒哈拉以南非洲国家的政治经济影响集中体现在结构调整政策（Structural Adjustment）。从 1960 年代开始，独立运动和去殖民化席卷非洲大陆，独立的非洲国家试图切断与前宗主国的政治经济联系，但在 20 世纪 70 年代末发生了经济危机。从 1980 年代开始，世界银行、国际货币基金组织等机构以挽救经济危机为名，提供了结构调整方案，开始主导非洲大陆的政治社会进程。结构调整的要旨在于减少非洲国家的公共支出、教育和服务，依赖于市场和私有经济的力量，实现经济的复苏。然而，结构调整的实施结果不尽如人意，相对于

[①] M. Featherstone, *Undoing culture: Globalization, postmodernism and identity*, London: SAGE, 1995.

[②] Victor Roudometof, "The glocal and global studies," *Globalizations*,12.5, 2015, pp. 774-787.

[③] Richard Tabulawa, "Global Influences and Local Responses: The Restructuring of the University of Botswana, 1990-2000," *The International Journal of Higher Education and Educational Planning* 53. No. 4, 2007, pp. 457-482.

同时期崛起的中国和东南亚地区，非洲经历了近 20 年的经济停滞。[1] 工业制成品不得不依赖西方进口。[2]

那么，新自由主义对非洲的大学教育产生了何种作用？如果公共支出、教育和服务是国家或公共部门的必要组成部分，新自由主义如何在教育领域体现？为了回答这些问题，有必要将新自由主义和非洲高等教育的关系放在一个更长的历史脉络中进行讨论。

独立以前的非洲高等教育相对世界其他地区比较薄弱，且高度依赖于前宗主国的利益和意识形态。独立前的非洲大学教育多为殖民宗主国提供资金，但模式各有侧重。例如，英国的高等教育强化巩固宗主国—殖民地的政治经贸关系，法国侧重文化同化，而比利时强调基础教育和神学教育。[3] Ochewa-Echel 认为这些殖民地的高等教育系统多少受到起源于欧洲中世纪的大学"象牙塔"神学传统影响，与殖民地本身的社会需求严重脱节。[4] 这种脱节状况直到独立运动之后才得到改善，但经济危机发生之后，非洲对高等教育的本土需求再次被以世界银行为代表的国际组织所忽略。

事实上，世界银行早在 1960 年代便提出了"基本需求"纲领（basic needs approach），认为高等教育并非基本需求而是奢侈品，通过基础教育培养经济所需的人才便足够非洲国家发展需要。因为新自由主义笃信个体化的选择，个人和机构会依据"回报率"来做出决策，个人是否上大学便不应由公有部门决定，而纯属于私域事务。因此，世行无意在非洲高等教育上进行投资或援助。在 1980 年代的结构调整计划中，这一"基本需求"纲领继续得到体现：高等教育应该交给私有经济部门而

[1] Paul Collier and Jan Willem Gunning, "Why Has Africa Grown Slowly?" *Journal of Economic Perspectives*, Vol 13. No. 3, 1999, pp. 3-22.

[2] 有趣的是，经济发展的差距与隔绝造成了 21 世纪的新现象：随着中国成为"世界工厂"，开始有大批来中国香港和中国内地采买商品的非洲客商，引起了学术界的广泛关注。其中不少商人之前也是政府工作人员（离职经商可以类比为中国 20 世纪八九十年代的"下海"）。这也可以视为新自由主义在非洲产生的意料之外的后果。

[3] Ajayi, J. F. A., Goma, L. K. H. and Johnson, G. A., *The African experience with higher education*, Athens: Ohio University Press, 1996.

[4] James R. Ochwa-Echel, "Neoliberalism and University Education in Sub-Saharan Africa," *SAGE Open*, 2013, pp. 1-8.

非国家运营。不过，大学走市场化路线办学在非洲并非没有成功案例，例如乌干达的马凯雷雷大学出现了"马凯雷雷奇迹"，[1] 甚至被称为"非洲的哈佛"。该大学通过扩大招生，改善了教学条件，教职员工和院系的福利也得到了改善。然而，批评者指出个人选择论和高等教育不属于"基本需求"的命题，现实世界中高等教育只能由有钱的家庭负担，事实上剥夺了穷人受高等教育的权利。即便在马凯雷雷大学，高回报率的受益者实际上是教师这一行业，而不是教育本身。扩招的后果是师生比增加很快，虽然教师工资因此上涨，但学生更得不到充足指导；扩招后引入统一学位标准，课程设置忽略本土情况而一味标榜欧美标准，造成教育供给与就业市场错配，学生在这样的错配下被推入就业市场，往往结局惨淡，而高校对改变这种不充分就业的情况有心无力。这类私有化办学在非洲增长很快，造成了学位泛滥、学历贬值的现象。[2]

新自由主义提倡不依赖政府而大力推行私有化办高等教育，其运作机制离不开日益引发学者关注的"审计文化"（audit culture）。[3] 审计文化源于英国首相撒切尔夫人当政时期。从1980年开始，在新自由主义指引下，英国政府大力推行国有资产私有化，售卖英国石油（British Petroleum）、新城发展集团公司（New Town Development Corporation）、区域水务局（Regional Water Authority）、大英航天（British Aerospace）等国有企业。从1982年开始，从四大会计事务所（例如普华永道）抽调人员组成审计署，不仅以"质量""效率""绩效""物有所值"（value for money）等名义审计公共部门的财务，并且通过评级进行实际上的监管。1992年，英国成立了教育、儿童服务和技能标准化办公室（Office for Standards in Education, Children's Services and Skills，简称 OFSTED），对地方教育局、教师课程和教育相关研究进行审计，并扩大到英国的

---

① A. Sawyerr, "Challenges facing African universities: Selected issues," *African Studies Review* 47(1), 2004, pp. 1-59.

② "African universities recruit too many students: Over-recruitment is a continent-wide problem," *The Economists*, 12 April 2017.

③ Cris Shore and Susan Wright, "Audit Culture and Anthropology: Neo-Liberalism in British Higher Education," *The Journal of the Royal Anthropological Institute*, Vol. 5, No. 4, 1999, pp. 557-575.

大学。①

Cris Shore 和 Susan Wright 认为，新自由主义名义上奉行市场至上，实际上遮蔽了权力的运作——依据社会学家福柯的说法，被掩盖的权力，往往是最有效的权力。②在英国，政府通过赋予第三方的审计公司以审查权，权力关系转移到审查者和被审查者之间，实际上加强了政府对被审计对象的控制，并且悖论性地在实践中导致某种程度上的反市场威权主义抬头。例如，英国在 1990 年代成立高等教育资助评议会，由高级学术人员和行政人员构成，给每个系打分。如果没有满意的结果，就会撤销对院系的资助，并且砍掉不吸引学生的课程。同一时期，英国高校人类学系推行研究评估（Research Assessment Exercise）和教学质量评估（Teaching Quality Assessment）。在实施的第一阶段，教职员工尚能互相提议，营造改进研究和教学的气氛，到了第二阶段，因为引入了惩罚落后者的措施，并将院系排名和所获资助挂钩，大学教员的"共同治校"（collegiality）氛围受到了严重损害。换言之，审计文化表面上看起来是客观的管理，但离不开惩罚性的威权主义行为。同时，审计文化把难以量化的教学科研活动量化，那些无法量化的活动变得没有丝毫价值，大学员工职业发展在量化目标的指挥棒下变得碎片化。人们因为怕落后而感到恐惧，而教师也变成了只对自己负责、自我激励、按照考评监督自己行为的个体。③但是人们很难去反对这一制度，只能通过力争上游在制度中行事，反而强化了这一制度。

与英国的经验相比，新自由主义在非洲如何落地生根？在乌干达马凯雷雷大学，新自由主义改革实际造成的后果往往被遮蔽在经济数字之下。Mahmood Mamdani 曾在 1980 年代担任该校社会科学学院院长和学术人员联合工会主席，后担任非洲社会科学研究发展委员会（CODESRIA）主席。在《市场中的学者：1989—2005 年马凯雷雷大学新自由主义改革两难》一书中，他认为从学校预算上看，2003—2004 年

---

① Cris Shore and Susan Wright, "Audit Culture and Anthropology: Neo-Liberalism in British Higher Education," *The Journal of the Royal Anthropological Institute*, Vol. 5, No. 4, 1999, pp. 557-575.

② 同上。

③ 同上。

度公共预算分摊到每个学生身上的费用为 300 万乌干达先令（折合 1530 美元），而私人资助分摊到每个学生身上的费用为 120 万乌干达先令（折合 612 美元），但是人们总觉得学校的财源来自后者。这种错觉实际上是由学校财政分配方式造成的：公共预算通过学校行政机构进行分配，构成固定雇用职员的基本工资和收入；而教学单位的收入则来自自费生学费，构成教学人员的绩效。[①] 换言之，人们更关注经济蛋糕的增量，而忽略经济蛋糕的存量。然而，新自由主义的激励导致教员极力扩大自费生人数。在话语层面上，大学教员主张大学属于为其工作的人，在院系"分权"的名义下取得教学和财政上的独立，打破了原有的院系教学合作。一些非市场职业导向的服务性的学科如教育学的课程没有兄弟院系的老师交叉授课（例如文学教育方向的学生需要学习文学类课程）；即使授课，也往往推迟提交阅卷结果——有时长达半年，危及学生毕业，或仅仅因为该系学生"不是我们的学生"而给出低分。[②] 更多的混乱是由大学评议会成员（senate）决策造成的。1995 年教育学院为了盈利，开设了与文科教育学士日间课程平行的夜班课程。3 年之后，因为要保证教学质量，开始要求日校和夜校采取统一标准，并规定文学院对夜校进行指导。但吊诡的是，此时文学院的课程已经完全市场导向了，何来保证夜校的教育水准？其他院系如宗教学系、文学系也乱象迭出，大多出自学院管理层在保证教学质量和盈利之间摇摆不定。

Chris Willott 在尼日利亚东南部的一所高校进行的人类学研究揭示了在大学教职员工内部产生的宗派主义和对立。[③] 这所学校的社会政策系分为两派，他们之间的对立可以追溯到 1960 年代冷战引发的意识形态上的对立。一派可称为自由派，另一派可称为马克思主义派、信仰社会主义，参与工会活动。两派各有一位学术领军人物。1970 年代尼日利亚石油一度因石油丰产而繁荣，但 1980 年代该国进行了结构调整，引

① Mahmood Mamdani, *Scholars in the Marketplace*: *The Dilemmas of Neo-Liberal Reform at Makerere University* 1989-2005, South Africa: HSRC press, 2007, p. vi – vii.

② 同上注，第 59 页。

③ Chris Willott, "Working Factionalism and Staff Success in a Nigerian University: A Departmental Case Study," In Bierschenk, T. and de Sardan, eds., *States at Work*, Brill, 2014, pp. 91-112.

发了社会震荡，尼日利亚货币奈拉急剧贬值，教职员工收入大幅缩水。有一些教职员工便想方设法在打法律的擦边球获取额外收入。两派在意识形态上的对立淡化，但在"挣外快"的态度上产生新的对立：自由派赞成挣外快，而秉持左翼传统的人则由于贬抑自我逐利行为，而持反对态度。在学生培养上，左翼传统派对学生评分大体依照学生的学业表现，而自由派则大多卷入了所谓的"排序"（sorting）行为，即与学生进行金钱交易，帮助后者获得高学分。"自由派"挣外快的途径还包括出租大学场地、售卖讲义、操弄考试等。2005年后，新上任的校长提拔了一位"自由派"成员当系主任，自由派的行为得到了机构性的支持，两派的对立加剧，尤其在另一个关系到教师实际利益的领域——教职晋升上产生了白热化的竞争。不出所料，倾向于谋取经济利益的一派在晋升上占了上风。Willott认为意识形态对立在这一新的条件下有继续淡化的趋势，因为马克思主义派常在院系会议上为经济利益争吵，并且也谋求"大佬"的支持以通过考核和获得晋升。

同为非洲国家的博茨瓦纳的情况又如何呢？博茨瓦纳大学的Motsomi Marobela教授认为，与其他高负债运作而接受世界银行结构调整的其他非洲国家相比，博茨瓦纳得天独厚的矿产资源让政府免于累积债务，因此新自由主义政策如私有化、竞标、就业合同化、灵活就业在博茨瓦纳的表现非常不一致。[1] 换言之，政府和公共服务部门不会因为濒临破产而不得不接受结构调整的方案。但是Marobela认为，新自由主义的鼓吹者如世界银行和外国顾问通过提拔培训一部分高级经理和主管并且保证他们的利益不受损害，而侵蚀了博茨瓦纳的公共服务部门。无独有偶，Richard Tabulawa在回溯博茨瓦纳大学1998年的一次改革及其后果时，聚集于学校外方高级职员和中层管理者。[2] Tabulawa认为，与其他国家被强加结构调整相比，博茨瓦纳对外来的经济概念的吸收是通

---

[1] Motsomi Ndala Marobela, *Political Economy of Botswana Public Sector Management: From Imperialism to Neoliberalism*, VDM Verlag Dr. Müller, 2010.

[2] Richard Tabulawa, "Global Influences and Local Responses: The Restructuring of the University of Botswana, 1990-2000," *The International Journal of Higher Education and Educational Planning* 53 (4), 2007, pp. 457-482.

过外国顾问来实现的，但与既有的治理结构发生作用，却起到了相反的后果。外来理念在本土推行过程中事与愿违，效率不增反减，这正反映了"全球地方化"过程中的全球和地方之间的缠杂关系。下文将详细介绍这一大学改革。

1998 年 UB 的改革背景如下：从 20 世纪 70 年代到 80 年代，世界经济衰退，博茨瓦纳钻石收入下降，到了 1990 年初，政府投入资源减少，必须自负盈亏，开始提倡"效率"和"实效"。1996 年以后，世界银行把博茨瓦纳列为中高收入国家，富国的捐助〔如美国国际开发署（USAID）〕急剧减少，但学生入学数量有增多趋势。这便构成了 1998 年大学改革的外部挑战：需要用更少的资源，管理更多的学生和庞大的机构。

就地方结构性因素而言，Tabulawa 认为博茨瓦纳大学的行政组织可以被刻画为"共同治校"和行政科层的混合体。前者是一种"水平"或"横向"组织，后者是一种"垂直"或"纵向"组织。根据《博茨瓦纳大学法律（1982）》，博茨瓦纳大学的校监（chancellor）由总统或副总统兼任，下设校长（vice chancellor）①、大学理事会（University Council）、学术评议会（Senate），下面是一些主任委员会（directorate）和院系（faculties and departments）。这一架构沿袭了英国的大学制度，学术评议会尤其承载着"共同治校"（collegiality）的功能。共同治校指的是大学教职员工在学术上分工协作、共同承担责任。教职员工有浓厚的协商民主传统，达成共识之后开展行动。然而，这种协商耗时耗力，因此成为强调效率和执行的最高管理层的开刀对象。

然而，在职的第二任校长汤姆士·格乌教授（一位博茨瓦纳的历史

---

① 博茨瓦纳总统与博茨瓦纳大学有直接的关系。2008 年法律规定校长职位不一定由总统担任，但总统仍然有权力任命校长。2011 年，任命的新校长不是理事会推荐的，而是总统的政治盟友。2012 年，理事会包括总统的一个兄弟和商业伙伴。2013 年，理事会主席是总统的律师。后来教育部部长可以任命校长。在校长之下，院长由校长任命，通过院会议推荐。系主任需要在咨询系成员之后，再向校长推荐，而不是通过选举。但是 1990 年代以后，院长由选举产生的传统就终止了。参考 Richard Tabulawa and Frank Youngman, "University of Botswana: A National University in Decline?" In Damtew Teferra eds, *Flagship Universities in Africa*, Palgrave Macmillan, 2017, pp. 17-55。

学家）的改革只进行到主任委员会、尚未触及院系教师，便遭到了行政集团的抵制。他推行的"职业化"改革要求员工有正式的认证才能上岗，这损害了那些只有大学学历或者没有学历但通过经年累月工作提拔到中层管理岗位的人员。这些行政人员跟校长开了很多会，表达了不满，并且游说有权的政治人物进行干涉。事实上，大学理事会中也常有总统指定的政治盟友，甚至不按照法律规定由大学理事会任命校长，而是由总统直接指定人选。^①当改革向下不顺畅，向上传导到国家最高领导层，大学理事会便决定由莎朗·希沃特教授（一位美国女性）来担任校长，继续改革。Tabulawa猜测，因为外人不知道机构内部的矛盾，有可能治愈因前任校长改革而造成的组织惰性甚至半瘫痪状态。

第三任校长在上任之初便采取强力措施：重大决定由校长咨询几位副校长（deputy vice chancellor）之后作出，由下层执行。这一高度自信的姿态呈现出雷厉风行的效率和执行原则，但关系到中层管理者时，校长放弃了之前的强制裁员和遣散方案，而采取了"调配"（redeployment）政策，优先考虑那些资质和经验兼有的人员上岗，对缺乏资质和经验的人提供合适的培训以提高组织的效率和实效。改革的最后结果是没有人丢掉工作，但管理层变得膨胀，并产生了至少两个纵向的行政组织。第一个纵向组织是高级管理团队，包括新任命的3个常务副校长，分管行政/财务、学术和学生，直接对校长负责，加强了校长的权力。第二个纵向组织是中层的主任办公室。此次改革涌现出17名主任，包括研发、学生福利、人力资源等部门。

组织的膨胀影响了教学活动的实施。以学术发展中心（Centre for Academic Development，简称CAD）这一主任办公室（directorate）为例，CAD可以由一个副教授以上职称的人领导，但是主任必须倚重非学术背景的下属。这个机构是制定评估、课程发展，以及新教学方法推广、出台关键性政策的机构。政策提议一般由该办公室提出，再征求教研人员的意见。因此，教研人员有关学术和科研的决策被转移到这个部门。不

---

① Richard Tabulawa and Frank Youngman, "University of Botswana: A National University in Decline?" In Damtew Teferra eds, *Flagship Universities in Africa*, Palgrave Macmillan, 2017, pp. 17-55.

过，这类机构也面临新自由主义改革的压力。这些主任科室的中层管理层采用合同制，因为新自由主义相信合同制与"生产力"有直接关系，合同工比拥有永久职位的人更具有生产力，并且合同制加强了决策层（executive）的权力（特别是任免续聘权力）。所以，这些中层管理人员的压力也增大了，更加强了执行的力度，而削弱了协商的传统。这类非学术人员占据管理决策位置引起了学术人员的严重不满，因此非学术人员（non-academic）被校方更名为教辅人员，以表示这部分员工对于大学业务不可或缺的作用，从而合理化此次改革。

与此同时，作为"共同治校"重要载体的大学评议会（senate）也被管理层稀释了。1998 年之前是有学术背景的人员（各院院长、系主任和教授）构成了学术评议会的成员，但是学术评议会机构在改革者看来过于臃肿，议事过程冗长，严重影响效率。1998 年以后，系主任被减掉，代之以每个学院派 2 个代表，其中之一必须是教授或者副教授。同时加入了一些主任（包括研发部、学术服务部以及各中心的常务主任），这导致所谓的"学术行政人员"的比例增加了。第二任校长看似雷厉风行的改革，实际造成组织膨胀，加强了大学的官僚化，对大学后续治理产生了重要影响。

三、对大学"转型"和罢工的再审视

如果说博茨瓦纳大学 20 年前已经有过类似的改革，那么，现任校长倡导的"转型"和先前的改革有何异同？引发的大学职工反应包括罢工是否是历史的重复？回答这些问题有助于我们理解抽象的新自由主义的在地发展和新的结构性矛盾。

若对博茨瓦纳大学 20 年前经历的改革和当下的改革作一比较，便可以发现教研人员和行政人员的位置有微妙的变化。20 年前的改革针对大学教员治校的效率低下，但改革首先向非教研人员（non-academics）开刀。第二任校长的"半截子改革"之后，非教研人员被管理层定义为"教辅人员"，以合理化这部分员工对大学的贡献。20 年后，校长试图动用行政力量对教研人员进行改革，但教研人员主动联合教辅人员。从工会与校方的仲裁决议文本来看，"教辅人员"的服务被"乌巴苏"（教研人员和教辅人员工会）定义为"必要服务"，体现出两部分员工之间的联动和认同。显然，这种认同有现实的利益基础。首先，自 2019 年以来，大学的教学岗位和非教学岗位均在推行短期合同化（固定期合同为两到三年）。其次，新冠疫情之下的通货膨胀和物价上涨是两类人员共同面临的压力。

笔者认为，两者联合的基础更基于博茨瓦纳社会长久以来形成的社会心理预期和被改革对象的"互保"。工会将教辅人员和教研人员的工资与校长的工资挂钩、将校长的工资与政府资金挂钩的层层绑定，体现出学校职员——无论教研人员还是"教辅人员"（即行政人员）——对隶属于国有部门的公立大学的依赖心理。

大学员工对体制的依赖也可以看成是博茨瓦纳社会的缩影。据博茨瓦纳劳工部门统计，直到 2011 年，博茨瓦纳仍然是以公有制经济为主，中央政府仍然是最大的雇主，占到就业人员 64 万人的 26.3%；地方政府占 20.8%，半官方占 4.4%，而私有经济雇员占 48.5%。[①] 政府部门或大学的工作享有声望，是人们羡慕的对象。博茨瓦纳大学的许多毕业生宁愿在政府领取低微的实习工资（约 1600 普拉 / 月，合人民币 840 元），也不愿去企业工作。[②] 相当部分正如尼日利亚的案例所揭示的那样，早期意识形态色彩在高等教育界发生了淡化。博茨瓦纳大学工会罢工虽然由左翼组织发动，但是并不将矛头直接指向新自由主义带来的反效果，即扩张的行政部门的掣肘造成的学校治理效率低下。

值得注意的是，博茨瓦纳大学除了雇用白人担任高等职位和教师，也有雇用津巴布韦、赞比亚等非洲国家教师和印度教师的传统。博茨瓦纳大学希望到 2022 年外籍教职员工达到 30%，以弥补国内教职员工资质不足的短板。UB 在教职员工的构成上，既有少量工作多年、已经上升到高级教职和管理职位的牛津剑桥毕业生，也有相当数量没有获得博

---

① 数据来源：博茨瓦纳人力资源发展理事会，https://hrdc.org.bw/?q=public-sector。

② 在政府部门工作享有更高声望，导致青年宁愿待业也不愿找工作的现象也出现在其他非洲国家。参考 Daniel Mains, *Hope is Cut: Youth, Unemployment, and the Future in Urban Ethiopia*（Temple University Press, 2011）一书中对埃塞俄比亚青年的分析。

士学位便担任讲师的教员。那些在英联邦国家或其他国家获得博士学位的外籍教员便构成了对师资的补充。这些新来的外籍教师均签订两到三年的合同。① 大学的临时工化（casualisation）在世界范围内并非新现象。2023 年初在英国爆发的卷涉 150 所高校和 70000 名大学员工的罢工主要针对合同短期化导致的职业焦虑和通货膨胀的压力。② 与英国类似，澳大利亚大学教员的临时工化也非常突出。③ 并且，学校大量招募全世界的研究人员，通过提高发表量提高学校排名，吸引国际学生，提高学费收入。2014 年到 2019 年澳大利亚大学的国际学生学费翻了三倍，而大量学生的教学工作则交给临时教师。

那么，博茨瓦纳这部分合同临时化的国际员工是否积极参加罢工、他们有何利益诉求呢？笔者采访的员工福利办公室主任表示，此次改革相当不透明，似乎只有几位高层在策划雇员"比例缩减"（scale down），但领养老金的本地员工除非有过错否则不会被轻易裁撤，而合同工的风险就更大一些。两位分别来自巴基斯坦和津巴布韦的外籍讲师告诉笔者，本地人占据行政管理岗位，让新招募的外籍教师承担院系大量的教学工作。这些课程的学生动辄几十人至一两百人，教学量极大，但系里的发表论文工作往往也依赖这些外籍教师。在如此重担下，他们连参与罢工的时间都是匮乏的。

在第一部分中，笔者已经述及在转型引发的罢工危机中的管理层和工会成员的矛盾。那么，在教学活动中，这种矛盾是否有所体现？在

---

① 博茨瓦纳雇用外籍专家短期服务的传统，至少可以追溯到 1970 年代。参考 "Botswana: In the Shadow of Pretoria," *The Atlantic*, August 1978, https://www.theatlantic.com/magazine/archive/1978/08/botswana-in-the-shadow-of-pretoria/661843/。"GZU Lecturers Join Incapacitated Colleagues, Announce Strike," *New Zimbabwe*, 24 February 2022, https://www.newzimbabwe.com/gzu-lecturers-join-incapacitated-colleagues-announce-strike/。

② 参考英国大学与学院联盟网页，https://www.ucu.org.uk/article/12680/Universities-to-be-hit-with-18-days-of-strike-action-before-April。

③ Joe McCarthy 认为，澳大利亚国立大学通过将教学时间工时化，雇用大量临时讲师（casual lecturer）和临时教师（casual tutor）以降低终身教职员工的工资成本。该校 2019 年临时讲师和临时教师的折算全职工时（Full Time Equivalent，FTE）是 2010 年的 5 倍，而讲师以上的职务折算全职工时几乎没有变化。参考 "The Concern over Rising Academic Casualisation: An Interview with Joe McCarthy," *Woroni*, 19 March 2021, https://www.woroni.com.au/news/the-concern-over-rising-academic-casualisation-an-interview-with-joe-mccarthy。

笔者所在的院系，这种矛盾是通过 Marobela 所揭示的机制而内化的。Marobela 认为，在博茨瓦纳早期的新自由主义改革中，是通过提拔培训一部分高级经理和主管，并且保证他们的利益不受损害而推行的。前任外籍系主任离职后，由院长指派一位本地讲师担任系主任。这位新系主任没有博士头衔，因此可算是破格提拔，领取系主任的津贴。新系主任上任后，在考试中严密监督其他教员的监考，确保考试完全不受罢工影响。在随后的工作中，严格执行其他支持性部门的指导文件（如上述学术发展中心提供的 CAD 测试考评指导），而不顾教学活动的实际规律和实际需求。在有教员反映 CAD 向学生提供的学术训练缺乏针对性时，新系主任也并不愿意做出相应的调整。具有讽刺意味的是，新主任给学生的考试评分相当宽松，并且鼓励其他教员效法，因为学生对教师的反馈也是教师考评的重要参考之一。无论是 CAD 的教学指导意见，还是学生给教师的评分和教师给学生的评分，都体现了博茨瓦纳大学从上到下行政化控制的强化。上述案例虽然是个案，但反映了在博茨瓦纳大学的地方性语境中，内部的审计文化和威权主义正因此次罢工的冲击而有所加强。显然，这种"执行力"的加强是以大学同仁协商精神的削弱为代价的。而这和英国 1990 年代审计文化所导致的负面后果[1]如出一辙。

结　语

本文在全球地方化的框架下，通过博茨瓦纳大学这一公立大学的罢工活动，讨论疫情和新自由主义对非洲高等教育的影响。本文认为，发源于欧美的新自由主义一直是应对经济下行的对策，但成为一种放之四海而皆准的意识形态。此次新冠疫情和俄乌战争诱发的经济下行构成了新自由主义重新抬头的条件，即重新以提高效率和生产力为名对大学特别是公立大学进行改革。

然而，根据新自由主义发源地（如英国）和在全世界推行的后果来

---

[1]　Cris Shore and Susan Wright, "Audit Culture and Anthropology: Neo-Liberalism in British Higher Education," *The Journal of the Royal Anthropological Institute*, Vol. 5, No. 4, 1999, pp. 557-575.

看，新自由主义往往导致其倡导的市场主义出现相反后果，即权力的加强、效率的降低等。这些出人意料的后果如全球地方化理论所揭示的那样，是当地原有的制度文化与全球性的新自由主义的复杂作用而产生的。从乌干达、尼日利亚和博茨瓦纳的案例可以看出，乌干达、尼日利亚公立大学院系的新自由主义主要体现在高校教师教学行为的市场化，包括教职员工以分数交换经济利益的行为，以及围绕考核与竞争形成的教职员工之间的派系。博茨瓦纳大学 20 世纪之初自上而下的"减员增效"改革，反倒引起了行政层反弹和改革半途而废，引起了行政中层权力扩张，在高层（大学评议会）和基层横向层面稀释了教职员工的"同仁治校"权力。相较而言，博茨瓦纳公立大学的预算财源也许更为宽松。乌干达、尼日利亚公立大学的市场化和逐利行为更为露骨，而博茨瓦纳大学的行政科层化更为严重。前者损害学生利益，而后者在改革压力下所产生的权力重构和机构性内耗，均与新自由主义鼓吹者所笃信的市场化可以提高效率、生产力和"物有所值"的预设不相符：在乌干达和尼日利亚，学生的毕业证书失去价值而不是"物有所值"；在博茨瓦纳，大学的治理效率和教学质量也并没有提高。

最后，通过对博茨瓦纳大学新近罢工和内部治理变化的分析，本文认为罢工既有博茨瓦纳的法律传统，也有基于博茨瓦纳社会对公有经济和雇佣稳定性的心理依赖和对市场化的抵制。而面临罢工压力的校方通过加强审计文化对教学活动加强控制，日常教学活动中的威权主义也有抬头趋势。远在非洲教育界发生的全球地方化过程，同样值得全球其他地区包括中国高校参考。首先，面对新冠疫情和俄乌冲突以及不确定的未来，高等教育体制机制改革应该与社会经济发展的各阶段需求相适应，在面对短期经济波动时依然要以前瞻性的眼光培育以及储备人才，在云谲波诡的形势变化中保持定力。其次，笔者以为在潜在的危机中，高校应弱化量化指标的"指挥棒"功能，坚守教学、研究和以知识服务社会之使命，回归高校作为汇聚、创造与传播知识的载体。

发展转型及其内生动力

人口转型下的非洲农业发展之路：
农民合作社的作用

峯阳一　兰加里拉伊·加文·穆切图著　李明儒译[*]

摘　要： 在未来一百年里，生活在非洲和亚洲的人口将占据世界总人口的百分之八十。尽管非洲人口急剧增长，但其生育率实则已经开始下降。随着被抚养人口的减少，劳动年龄人口在非洲总人口中的比例将有望增加。除了目前由COVID-19和全球政治不稳定而导致的壁垒之外，这种所谓的人口红利可能会对非洲劳动密集型产业的发展做出重大贡献。然而，如果非洲农村地区资本密集型粮食生产开始自上而下的加速，那么，大量的剩余人口将会被释放出来，这就可能导致无法控制的城市化。非洲有很多富有弹性的农民社会，自殖民时代以来，他们一直在抵制并在可能的情况下逆转了土地剥削。因此，通过形成多种农民合作社，有意识地走农民路线，就可以有效缓解人口转型和农民阶层分化带来的冲击。此外，可以期待，非洲的农业合作社不仅能够发挥其经济功能，还有教育功能，从而唤醒农村群众的社会政治意识，以及实现该群体思想的去殖民化。本文首先对全球情况进行综述，然后以津巴布韦合作社为案例展开研究。

关键词： 人口学　农业　农民之路　恰亚诺夫　合作社

---

　　* 峯阳一（Yoichi Mine），现任日本同志社大学全球研究院教授；兰加里拉伊·加文·穆切图（Rangarirai Gavin Muchetu），现任萨姆·莫约非洲农业研究所（the Sam Moyo African Institute for Agrarian Studies）研究员；李明儒，现为日本同志社大学全球研究院博士候选人。
　　［注］本文由刘海方、王进杰进行中文翻译校对。

引言：悲观主义与乐观主义

在关于非洲的论述中，悲观主义与乐观主义的论调始终贯穿于殖民时代、独立时代和后殖民时代。悲观主义者认为非洲大陆将成为全球政治不稳定的来源，而乐观主义者则认为，非洲（特别是其丰富的自然资源）将为当地和全球经济带来巨大利益。然而，上述极端的观点并非源自非洲内部；其大多数都是非洲以外的观察者为了在知识或政策市场上获得更大利益而提出的论调。

在 21 世纪的首个十年里，非洲资源出口型国家的高增长率使得"崛起的非洲"这一形象在国际上传播开来；然而，非洲的外向型发展模式随后被证明是不可持续的，因此，诸如此类开发性的乐观主义论调也随之开始减弱。[①] 在原殖民宗主国人的心中，深埋着对不驯服的"深色民族"的恐惧，种族对立在某些方面类似于正义："它也许会沉睡，但绝不会消亡"[②]。事实上，对非洲自主发展的可能性持悲观主义和怀疑态度的论述已经形成当代西方讨论非洲的基调。

然而，随着一个新的因素——全球人口变化——在政策讨论中凸显，近来，这种极化的关于非洲的讨论又开始加剧。[③] 在未来一百年内，非洲的人口可能会大幅增长。根据联合国经济和社会事务部（UNDESA）人口司的预测，基于非洲地区相对较高的生育率以及卫生条件的改善，该地区的人口将在 21 世纪增加 5 倍（基于中位变量的预测）（如图 1）。

---

① Sam Moyo and Yoichi Mine, "Introduction: African Potentials for Conflict Resolution and Transformation," in Sam Moyo and Yoichi Mine (eds.), *What Colonialism Ignored*: *"African Potentials" for Resolving Conflicts in Southern Africa*, Bamenda, Cameroon: Langaa RPCIG, 2016. As for the Africa-rising discourses, see the IMF conference, "Africa Rising: Building to the Future," organised in Maputo in May 2014. http://www.africa-rising.org/ (accessed 20 January 2022).

② Vijay Prashad, *The Darker Nations*: *A People's History of the Third World* (New York: New Press, 2007); Raymond Leslie Buell, "Again the Yellow Peril," *Foreign Affairs* 2, no. 2, 1923, p. 295.

③ As for balanced and comprehensive overviews, see the following. David Canning, Sangeeta Raja, and Abdo S. Yazbeck (eds.), *Africa's Demographic Transition*: *Dividend or Disaster?* Washington, D.C.: World Bank, 2015; Clifford O. Odimegwu and Yemi Adewoyin (eds.), *The Routledge Handbook of African Demography*, London: Routledge, 2022.

这就意味着在未来一百年内，非洲和亚洲人口将各占世界总人口的 40% 左右，从而构成总和约 80% 的主要群体。鉴于这种数量上的优势，亚洲人和非洲人之间对话的程度和质量关乎未来世界的样貌。①

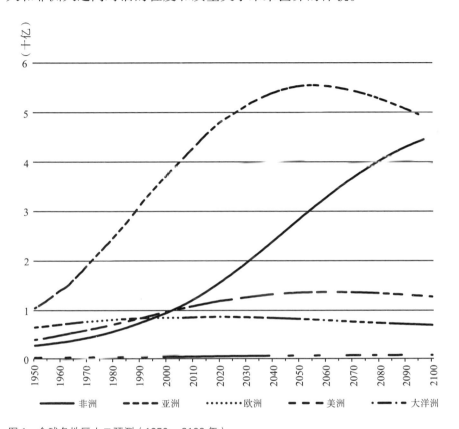

图 1　全球各地区人口预测（1950—2100 年）

资料来源：United Nations Department of Economic and Social Affairs (UNDESA), Population Division, *The 2022 Revision of World Population Prospects*. https://population.un.org/wpp/ (accessed 20 January 2023)

在本文中，我们首先概述全球人口转型的情况，然后讨论未来非洲农村的社会景观；接下来，将追溯全球人口转型的趋势，并着重讨论农村 / 城市关系的重要性；随后，将介绍非洲农业积累的三种历史轨迹，并指出它们可能通过剥夺土地而最终趋于一致；鉴于非洲政治经济的矛

---

① Yoichi Mine, *Connecting Africa and Asia*: *Afrasia As a Benign Community*, London: Routledge, 2022.

盾加剧，我们认为，通过走劳动密集型的农民路线就可以有效地解决剩余人口和贫困化的问题；最后，以津巴布韦为例，着重讨论农业合作社在基于技能培训以及其成员的社会政治意识形成方面的作用。尽管现阶段大力发展基础设施建设以满足非洲大陆强劲的需求仍是中国对非援助的主要特点，但技术转让和人力资源的开发将会在未来几十年内变得越来越紧迫。除对个人进行培训外，为机构建设和集体行动提供支持同样至关重要。例如，正常运转的乡村组织是灌溉渠等公共产品维护不可或缺的机构。然而，农民组织必须是本土的，由农民自发组织和拥有。在这一点上，农业合作社具有巨大潜能。多年来，中国始终秉承"自力更生"的原则与非洲开展外交往来，这使中国在调动非洲农民的积极性以及推进农村组织可持续发展方面具有比较大的优势。同时，非洲农业合作社拥有丰富的历史，我们认为尝试研究当地合作社的经验对中国发展机构来说具有重要意义。

一、人口统计学：过去与现在的经验教训

对非洲持极端的悲观主义源自种族偏见。虽然我们理应果断排斥诸如此类的歪曲言论，但还是会有人将生活在非洲大陆的人们视为等待施舍的被动受害者，并且强调他们的脆弱性而非韧性。当然，我们也需要谨慎对待这些有关脆弱性的观点，毕竟其中也有不乏善意的。

当全球新冠疫情暴发之初，卫生系统不健全的非洲被预计将会受到巨大的冲击。然而，尽管缺乏精确的数据，但毋庸置疑的是，非洲新冠感染的死亡人数大大低于西方国家。目前对这一现象产生的原因有诸多猜测，但值得注意的是，在以年轻人为主要人口组成群体的非洲，青壮年在感染新冠病毒后出现重症的可能性很低，并且很多非洲人生活在广袤的农村地区，人与人之间的接触不像城镇那样密切[①]。此外，我们不可

① As for Africa's unique survivability against COVID-19, see, for example, Joseph Waogodo Cabore et al., "COVID-19 in the 47 Countries of the WHO African Region: A Modelling Analysis of Past Trends and Future Patterns," *The Lancet Global Health* 10, Issue 8, 2022; Binta Zahra Diop et al., "The Relatively Young and Rural Population May Limit the Spread and Severity of COVID-19 in Africa: A Modelling Study," *BMJ Global Health*, 2020;5:e002699.

否认，非洲通过应对例如艾滋病与埃博拉等严重的、突发的以及普遍的公共卫生危机时，已经积累了大量的实战经验。

2022 年爆发的俄乌冲突是一场复杂的危机，它将削弱世界上每个角落的能源安全以及粮食安全。然而，非洲的石油生产国从上涨的自然资源价格中获益。在非洲，只有像索马里等少数饱受战争摧残并严重依赖粮食援助的国家，才会受到由于国际谷物价格上涨而带来的重击。[①] 我们需要充分了解非洲正在面临的挑战，也要认清其所具备的优势：一方面，非洲地区粮食生产的多样性——如玉米、水稻、木薯、香蕉等——使其比只生产一种主食的国家更能抵御粮食危机；另一方面，非洲当前粮食危机的主要原因是萨赫勒地区及其他干旱地区由气候变化而导致的持续干旱，而不是国际粮食价格的波动。所有工业化国家都应该对"人类世"中存在的这种威胁承担责任。[②]

上述事例表明，非洲大陆对近年来爆发的全球危机的应对，与非洲的人口特征以及其农业经济的自我修复能力密切相关。让我们重新回到人口长期转型的问题上，几乎所有人口学家都科学地预测，在 21 世纪后半叶非洲将出现大量劳动力。[③] 长远来说，这对非洲乃至世界其他地区是福还是祸？

与马尔萨斯（Malthusian）关于人口无止境增长的假设相反，许多发达国家都将在不久的未来遭遇严峻的人口短缺。一位不遗余力批评中国全球实力的美国评论家霍华德·佛伦奇（Howard French），刻意地拿美国"吸引全球移民的蓬勃未来"与中国社会迅速老龄化的"凄凉远景"进行对比。[④] 他明确指出，应阻止其他国家与中国进行交易往来，中国的影响也将大幅减少。然而，中国的人口转型意味着该国的人口构成正

---

① All wheat imports of Somalia have been from Russia and Ukraine. Tim G. Benton et al., *The Ukraine War and Threats to Food and Energy Security: Cascading Risks from Rising Prices and Supply Disruptions*, Research Paper, Chatam House, 13 April, 2022, p. 9.

② Mine, *Connecting Africa and Asia*, pp. 40, 99.

③ Mine, *Connecting Africa and Asia*, chaps. 1 and 2.

④ Howard W. French, *Everything under the Heavens: How the Past Helps Shape China's Push for Global Power*, New York: A. A. Knopf, 2017. Canadians massively accept foreign migrants based on their calculation of national interests. Darrell Bricker and John Ibbitson, *Empty Planet: The Shock of Global Population Decline*, New York: Crown Publishers, 2019.

在接近当代欧洲和日本的水平。如果有人建议我们不要与情况越来越像欧洲的中国交往，那么，我们是否也不应该与欧洲交往呢？

除了大国之间的竞争，中国适龄劳动人口供应的放缓也会对世界经济的前景产生重大影响。古德哈特（Charles Goodhart）与普拉丹（Manoj Pradhan）预测，东亚劳动力供应的萎缩将诱发通货膨胀并推高全球利率。他们认为，虽然印度和非洲在理论上有可能取代中国，但考虑到非洲市场的分散性以及人力资本的匮乏，我们不能乐观期待非洲劳动力供应快速抵消全球的老龄化。[1]

然而，回顾历史，19世纪西方国家人口扩张的速度和规模也与20世纪的东亚和21世纪的非洲一样巨大。[2]1859年，德国的总生育率（TFR）为5.17，美国为4.48，英格兰与威尔士的总生育率在1775年不低于5.87。[3]这些比率都高于当代非洲的平均生育率，即2021年的4.31。伴随着劳动力的急剧增长，西方国家经历了资本密集型工业的快速扩张。19世纪也标志着大西洋奴隶贸易的终止和欧洲列强对非洲殖民地的瓜分。欧洲的崛起就是交战国招募青年加入常备军、互相残杀的过程，这将世界拖入了20世纪上半叶的两次毁灭性战争。在历史上，欧洲始终扮演着问题制造者的角色，在国内外到处掠夺和破坏人力资本。

二、人口过剩与土地问题

截至2022年11月15日，世界人口总数已经达到80亿。纵观各个地区人口的变迁，这个过程看起来就像几个形状相似的波浪一个接一个地涌向海岸。然而，改变经济发展进程的并不是人口的绝对规模，而是适龄劳动人口在总人口中的比例。图2显示了亚非地区几个人口大国适龄劳动人口随时间变化的比率，尽管20世纪下半叶该比例开始萎缩，但非洲的人口大国将在同期开始出现明显的青年人口激增。仔细观察，

---

[1]　Charles Goodhart and Manoj Pradhan, *The Great Demographic Reversal: Ageing Societies, Waning Inequality, and an Inflation Revival*, Cham: Palgrave Macmillan, 2020.

[2]　Paul Morland, *The Human Tide: How Population Shaped the Modern World*, London: John Murray, 2019.

[3]　Massimo Livi-Bacci, *A Concise History of World Population*, 6th Edition, Chichester: Wiley Blackwell, 2017, chap. 4.

我们会发现，埃及与南非的年龄构成在整个时期并没有明显变化，但适龄劳动人口在尼日利亚和刚果民主共和国等国家预计将急速增加。在这些国家，由于人口年龄结构的变化，人口红利对国内生产总值的贡献可能是非常巨大的（这点将在关于恰亚诺夫的章节中再次讨论）。[①]

卡尔·马克思在《资本论》中区分了相对过剩人口和绝对过剩人口，后者对应的是几十年来没有太大波动的（自然）人口增长，而马克思则更关注前者，即在资本积累过程中产生并不断被排挤出资本主义体系的激增失业人口。相对过剩人口不仅在资本密集型工业化发展时期增加，同时也在资本向农村地区扩张时期增加。因此，罗莎·卢森堡认为，资本主义的延续，有赖于一个非资本主义形态的边缘地带的支持。马克思称之为资本原始积累的阶段"仍在继续"[②]。

假设像种植园农业这种类型的资本密集型农业不断扩大，农村对家庭劳动力的需求就会降低。一般来说，非洲的农民都是小农户。如果他们在农村没有了工作，年轻的农村人就会离开他们的村庄到城镇去。如果城镇不能够吸纳被排挤出村庄的人口，那么，这些人将无家可归。事实上，资本主义创造出了一支愿意以更低工资工作的队伍，从而加剧了剥削并阻碍了发展。举个例子，一个村庄的粮食产量有可能从过去的100吨增加到200吨，而这个村庄的农业工人数量却由于技术的进步而直接从100人减少到20人。由此，这个村庄的人均产出量将提高10倍。但是，如果在农村失去工作的这80个人无法在其他地方找到工作，他们就可能会因饥饿而死。萨米尔·阿明（Samir Amin）认为，忽视就业保障的农业技术革新将导致半数人类的灭绝，英国经济史上的圈地运动将在南方国家无情地重演。[③] 否则，粮食增产的一大部分就理应免费分配给他们（如果生产是基于合作社，利润可能会通过成员分红的形式重新

---

① "Declines in child mortality, followed by declines in fertility, produce a 'bulge' generation and a period when a country has a large number of working-age people and a smaller number of dependents. Having a large number of workers per capita gives a boost to the economy provided there are labor opportunities for the workers" Canning et al., *Africa's Demographic Transition*, p. 1.

② Rosa Luxemburg, *The Accumulation of Capital*, translated by Agnes Schwarzschild, London: Routledge, 2003, p. 420.

③ Samir Amin, *Ending the Crisis of Capitalism or Ending Capitalism?* translated by Victoria Bawtree, Cape Town: Pambazuka Press, Dakar: CODESRIA, Bangalore: Books for Change, 2011, p. 124.

分配回社区）。强调就业机会的观点得到了马克思主义与非马克思主义经济学家的认同，简而言之，"衡量一个国家是否成功地将青年人口膨胀转化为人口红利的一个基本指标就是青年人口的就业（失业）率"①。

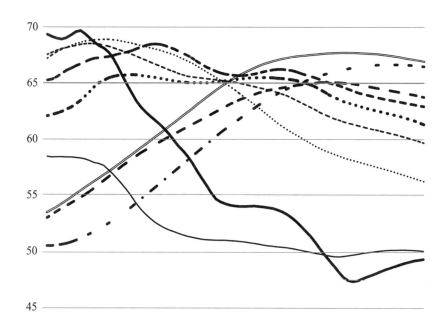

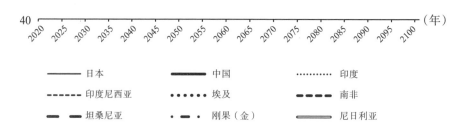

图 2　全球劳动年龄人口的比例预测（2020—2100 年）
资料来源：UNDESA, Population Division, *The 2022 Revision of World Population Prospects*

---

①　Justin Yifu Lin, "Youth Bulge: A Demographic Dividend or a Demographic Bomb in Developing Countries?" 5 January 2012, https://blogs.worldbank.org/developmenttalk/youth-bulge-a-demographic-dividend-or-a-demographic-bomb-in-developing-countries, accessed 20 January 2023.

正如 20 世纪 50 年代末曾经出任加纳国父恩克鲁玛（Kwame Nkrumah）经济顾问的刘易斯（W. A. Lewis）所主张的，农业革命当始终先于工业革命。在他看来，所有经济部门，包括生产和制造业，都应该同时扩大。然而，极具讽刺意味的是，农村停滞的局面因加纳拥有相对良好的教育而加剧，那些受过教育的年轻人带着很高的期望离开农村地区前往城市中心。因此，刘易斯优先考虑的不是全国性的基础教育，而是成人教育，包括农业推广服务——这对保持农业和工业之间的平衡以及遏制农村人口大规模流向城市至关重要。[1]

一些经济学家和人口学家试图研究非洲未来可以在多大程度上享受人口红利。大多数观点强调了资本短缺的问题。伊斯特伍德（Robert Eastwood）与李普顿（Michael Lipton）曾发出告诫，他们认为低储蓄率会阻碍非洲的资本形成。[2] 在一篇题为《非洲崛起：抓住人口红利》的文章中，德拉蒙德（P. Drummond）等人认为，为了充分利用非洲丰富的劳动力资源，非洲有必要从农业走向制造业。[3] 艾哈迈德等人（Ahmed et al.）从统计学的角度强调了教育作为附加值的意义。[4] 克利夫兰（J. Cleland）与町山和代（Machiyama）列举了妨碍人口红利的因素，并对制造业中几乎没有增长的就业率表示惋惜。[5] 虽然侧重点不同，但上述思辨大多都是以工业化的成功作为前提，鲜少关注农村群众的困境。这种反农业的政策偏见是很危险的。

---

[1] Yoichi Mine, "The Political Element in the Works of W. Arthur Lewis: The 1954 Model and African Development," *The Developing Economies* 44, no. 3, 2006, pp. 329-355.

[2] Robert Eastwood and Michael Lipton, "Demographic Transition in Sub-Saharan Africa: How Big Will the Economic Dividend Be?" *Population Studies* 65, no. 1, 2011, pp. 9-35.

[3] Paulo Drummond, Vimal Thakoor, and Shu Yu, "Africa Rising: Harnessing the Demographic Dividend," *IMF Working Paper* 14, no.143, 2014.

[4] S. Amer Ahmed, Marcio Cruz, Delfin S. Go, Maryla Maliszewska, and Israel Osorio-Rodarte, "How Significant Is Sub-Saharan Africa's Demographic Dividend for Its Future Growth and Poverty Reduction?" *Review of Development Economics* 20, 2016, pp. 762-793.

[5] John Cleland and Kazuyo Machiyama, "The Challenges Posed by Demographic Change in Sub-Saharan Africa: A Concise Overview," *Population and Development Review* 43, 2017, pp. 264-286.

三、三条轨迹

在过去几个世纪的欧洲殖民统治时期，非洲出现了三种不同类型的农业结构。[①] 第一种模式是在欧洲人定居的殖民地中出现的"劳动力储备"政治经济，以南非、纳米比亚、津巴布韦和肯尼亚高原最为典型。在历史上，欧洲移民剥夺了当地农民的土地，垄断了自然资源和基础设施。这种殖民者的积累方式，是把廉价劳动力再生产的重担置于被隔离的"公社"地区的农民特别是农村妇女的肩上，以满足采矿业和城市经济的需要。第二种模式是为开采农业和矿产资源而设立的"特许飞地"。这种模式最鲜明的演绎就是在中非，跨国资本直接控制那里的种植园和矿山，强迫经营。第三种模式是西非和东非的贸易经济，在那里，貌似自主的农民被动员起来为全球市场生产配额，这些特定商品如棕榈油、可可和棉花。[②]

这三种类型都不是静态的结构，而是动态的轨迹，其过程由阶级斗争的复杂性和殖民统治的模式决定。尽管这些历史模式对当代政治经济产生了深远的影响，但如今这些模式也逐渐走向趋同，究其原因正是世界资本主义危机通过非洲的土地剥削产生了新一轮的资本积累浪潮。当津巴布韦的小型农户们在努力开垦土地的同时，整个非洲却正在建立新的资源开采飞地。西方和亚洲的外国资本与当地盟友勾结进行土地掠夺，有媒体报道中国也参与其中，虽然也不乏夸大之嫌。[③]

非洲社会经历了飞速的变化。正如历史学家约翰·伊利夫（John Iliffe）在《非洲穷人》（*The African Poor*）一书结尾处所指出，20 世纪的南部非洲，由于大面积的土地被白人定居者（现如今被当地权贵以及外国

---

① Moyo and Mine, "Introduction," pp. 15-19.

② The French term, *traite*, means milking (getting milk from an animal like a cow). People keep them alive, feed them, and exploit them.

③ Deborah Brautigam, *Will Africa feed China*? New York: Oxford University Press, 2015. We are still not very sure if a genuine class of African capitalists are born out of such a process（我们仍然不能够确定在这样的过程中是否会诞生真正的非洲资本家阶层）. John Iliffe, *The Emergence of African Capitalism*: *The Anstey Memorial Lectures in the University of Kent at Canterbury*, 10-13 May 1982, London: Macmillan, 1983.

资本）征用而开始被结构性贫困所笼罩，表现为低收入家庭的世代自我复制。我们目睹的非洲部分地区因土地稀缺而陷入结构性贫困，与欧洲和亚洲的情况相似。从某种意义上来说，大量的失地穷人将会在未来失去获得资源的机会。[①]历史上，农民的生产能力受到保存的地方，就会出现土地集中；在土地被剥夺达到临界点的地方，农民反抗就会再掀高潮。纵观整个非洲大陆的趋势，民主土地改革的关键在于农民动员的程度和复原力。

　　鉴于目前矛盾的激烈程度，关于未来的发展政策有两点必须要强调。第一，应牢记要优先考虑在农村创造就业机会（合作社可以帮助实现这一目标）。图3和图4展示了对非洲持续增长人口居住地的预测，由于农村的总生育率往往较高，这两个图之间的差异表明，在未来几十年

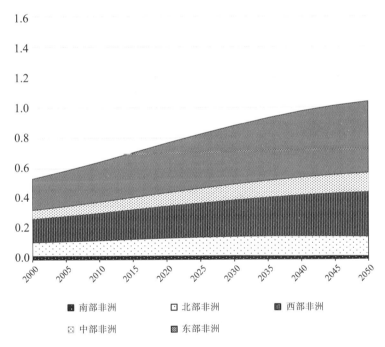

图 3　非洲的农村人口（2000—2050 年）

资料来源：UNDESA, Population Division, *The 2018 Revision of World Urbanization Prospects*. https://population.un.org/wup/ (accessed 20 January 2023)

---

① John Iliffe, *The African Poor: A History*, Cambridge: Cambridge University Press, 1987, chap. 14.

里，非洲可能会有大量人口从农村流向城市和城镇。忽视农民需求的政策会把他们推向城市，而城市人口又会去寻求对他们有利的政策。事实上，俄乌冲突对非洲最大的影响或许不是普通意义上的粮食短缺，而是可能导致城市中由食品价格上涨而引发的"食品暴动"。尽管政客们出于政治稳定的考量听取了城市公民的心声，但他们对农村群众的反应在政治上往往具有选择性。[①] 除非采取适当的政策解决农村失业问题，否则恶性循环就可能会在非洲生根发芽。

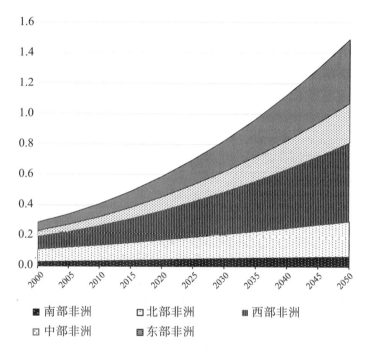

图4　非洲的城市人口（2000—2050 年）

资料来源：UNDESA, Population Division, *The 2018 Revision of World Urbanization Prospects*

第二，劳动力的质量比数量更重要，非洲大量的年轻劳动力应当面向"高质量增长"。加雷思·奥斯汀（Gareth Austin）对人口增长持积极

[①]　Robert H. Bates, *Markets and States in Tropical Africa*: *The Political Basis of Agricultural Policies*, Berkeley: University of California Press, 1981. Assem Abu Hatab, "Africa's Food Security under the Shadow of the Russia-Ukraine Conflict," *The Strategic Review for Southern Africa* 44, no. 1, 2022, pp. 37-46.

态度，他强调了过去非洲在人类发展特别是教育和卫生领域的成就。[①]
根据联合国经济和社会事务部（UNDESA）的数据集显示，非洲的平均
预期寿命在 2021 年达到了 61.7 岁，已经超过了 1973 年东亚的平均水平
（61 岁），这就意味着非洲大陆在健康和营养方面取得了令人瞩目的进
步。然而，非洲大众受教育的水平参差不齐。如图 5 所示，在撒哈拉以
南的非洲，尽管各个国家的表现有所不同，完成小学教育的人口比例仍
保持在 70% 左右。优质劳动力意味着创造性的劳动，因为被动、顺从的
劳动力的生产率并不会很高。工人管理在"泰勒制度"和"福特制度"
下可能很有效，但当把机械任务交由机器人工作时，生产效率就会更
高。因此，在人类参与劳动过程的地方，就有必要培养每个工人的积极
性。作为群众学习集体性与独立性思考、组长们学习管理技能的天然学
校，城乡合作社有着巨大的潜力。

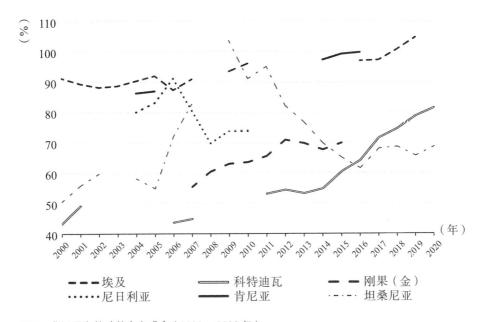

图 5　非洲国家基础教育完成率（2000—2020 年）

资料来源：World Bank Data. https://data.worldbank.org/topic/4 (accessed 20 January 2023)

---

① Gareth Austin, "Labour Intensity and Manufacturing in West Africa, c.1450-c.2000," in Gareth
Austin and Kaoru Sugihara (eds.), *Labour-Intensive Industrialisation in Global History*, Abingdon, Oxon:
Routledge, 2013.

四、重审合作社与农民路线

虽然合作社的生活方式深深植根于非洲社会经济体制中，并构成大多数非洲社会不可或缺的一部分，但正规的农业合作社是由殖民当局引入的。[①] 从某种程度上说，它们的历史与我们在上文讨论的非洲社会形成的三种轨迹的农业结构相关。在 20 世纪初的英国殖民地，乌干达的棉花生产商、乞力马扎罗山的咖啡生产商和加纳的可可生产商建立了运作良好的合作社，属于西部和东部非洲贸易经济的范畴。这些合作社的成立意在避免中间环节的剥削，并合法地被纳入殖民框架。相比之下，法国当局选择直接干预，建立了具有系统性和强制性的合作社；比利时殖民地天主教传教士在建立合作社方面发挥了至关重要的作用；而在非洲葡语国家，合作社只是推广工作的一个附属品。另一方面，在南部非洲的种族隔离时期，农民被系统性地剥夺了土地，大型合作社由白人农场所建并为其服务。在殖民时代，尽管非洲农民的经历因地而异，但他们始终没有把自己当作这些合作社的主人。

更讽刺的是，大多数非洲国家在独立后都继承了傲慢的合作式发展，继续对农村社会进行经济控制并确保政治统治。废除这种自上而下的（控制）方式，仍然是非洲合作社发展面临的最大挑战之一。在 20 世纪 80 年代至 90 年代，国际货币基金组织和世界银行强加给南方债务缠身国家的结构调整计划（SAP），对非洲合作社的性质产生了复杂的影响，即合作社不得不同时面对在新自由主义的竞争市场中存活下来，并更好保护其成员的责任。[②]

很难搞清楚非洲合作社活动的规模。根据世界合作社监测（WCM），

---

① The following description is adapted from Patrick Develtere, "Cooperative Development in Africa up to the 1990s," in Patrick Develtere, Ignace Pollet and Fredrick Wanyama (eds.), *Cooperating out of Poverty: The Renaissance of the African Cooperative Movement*, Geneva: International Labour Office, 2008; Jürgen Schwettmann, *Cooperatives and Employment in Africa*, Geneva: ILO, 1997.

② Develtere, "Cooperative Development in Africa."

全球有 4575 个合作社，其中只有 8 个合作社来自非洲。[①]联合国估计，在 2014 年全球至少有 10 亿人从属于 260 万个合作社，并且有 1 亿人受雇于这些合作社。合作社每年创造大约 3 万亿美元的收入，[②]这相当于法国经济活动的规模。定期进行全面的调查对于丰富非洲合作社的数据至关重要。根据国际劳工组织（ILO）的调查，在 2003 至 2005 年，佛得角、埃及、埃塞俄比亚、加纳、肯尼亚、尼日尔、尼日利亚、南非、卢旺达、塞内加尔和乌干达等 11 个非洲国家的合作社成员总数达到 3000 万，普及率（合作社成员占总人口的比例）达到 7%。如果我们把这个比率作为既定值，"通常每户只有一个合作社成员，假设平均家庭规模为六人，那么，'合作社密度'就超过总人口的百分之四十"[③]。

近年来，全球对合作社和农民小规模种植越来越感兴趣。联合国宣布 2014 年为国际家庭农业年。由于东亚以及卢拉总统领导下的巴西在支持农民改革方面相对成功，人们重新对农民生产道路产生了兴趣。再往前回顾，联合国还将 2012 年定为合作社年，强调了合作社和农民运动之间的相互联系。2019 年，联合国秘书长发布了一份关于《社会发展中的合作社》的报告，强调了合作社在实现可持续发展目标（SDG）方面的作用。[④]农业合作社恰恰是农民经济与合作社这两个领域中重叠之处。在以市场为导向的经济中，市场失灵的主要原因是国家、市场和社区之

① See the website of the International Cooperative Alliance. https://www.ica.coop/en/our-work/world-cooperative-monitor, accessed 20 January 2023.

② Dave Grace and Associates, *Measuring the Size and Scope of the Cooperative Economy: Results of the 2014 Global Census on Cooperatives*, Madison, WI: Dave Grace and Associates for the United Nation's Secretariat, Department of Economic and Social Affairs, Division for Social Policy and Development, 2014.

③ Patrick Develtere and Ignace Pollet, "Renaissance of African cooperatives in the 21st century: Lessons from the field," in Patrick Develtere, Ignace Pollet and Fredrick Wanyama (eds.), *Cooperating out of Poverty: The Renaissance of the African Cooperative Movement*, Geneva: International Labour Office, 2008; Schwettmann, *Cooperatives and Employment in Africa*, p. 6.

④ *Cooperatives in Social Development*, Report of the United Nations Secretary-General, A/74/206, 22 July 2019.

间或内部信息的不对称性。[1] 如果农民一直处于无组织状态，他们的声音在政策制定和实施的前、中、后期都会被忽视。那么，可以采取哪些措施来组织农村基层的心声以及赋予农民权利呢？在此，我们想强调合作社的独特作用。

我们可以通过几种方式将农村集体行动概念化。新兴机构包括劳工管理的公司，劳工所有的公司、集体，储蓄和信贷合作社（SACCO）以及各种形式的合作社。在 20 世纪 80 年代至 90 年代，激进的学者们普遍认为，任何形式的农村集体行动都不可能在资本主义框架下被设想出来。[2] 然而，在学术和政策界认识到家庭农业的重要性后，反思社会组织在发展中的作用就变得极为必要。[3] 人们对合作社的诉求仍然强大。

那么，合作社是如何构成的？它与公司或资本主义农业企业又有什么不同？俄罗斯农业经济学家亚历山大·恰亚诺夫借鉴了杜冈-巴拉诺夫斯基（M. I. Tugan-Baranovskii）与帕基特诺夫（K. Pazhitnov）的思想，将合作社与其他形式的组织区分开来。关注合作社运动是为了培养自助（self-help）、民主、公平、平等和团结的价值观，这些价值观可通过遵循国际合作社联盟（ICA）在 1937 年、1966 年和 1995 年制定的合作社原

[1] Keijiro Otsuka and Kaliappa Kalirajan (eds.), *Community, Market and State in Development* (Basingstoke: Palgrave Macmillan, 2011). The critical dimension of community cohesion is missing in G. F. Ortmann and R. P. King, "Agricultural Cooperatives I: History, Theory and Problems," *Agrekon* 46, no. 1, 2007, pp. 18-46.

[2] Michael Reich and James Devine, "The Microeconomics of Conflict and Hierarchy in Capitalist Production," *Review of Radical Political Economics* 12, no. 4, 1981, pp. 27-45; Daniel Egan, "Toward a Marxist Theory of Labor-Managed Firms: Breaking the Degeneration Thesis," *Review of Radical Political Economics* 22, no. 4, 1990, pp. 67-86. See also Zhanping Hu, Qian Forrest Zhang, and John Donaldson, "Why Do Farmers' Cooperatives Fail in a Market Economy? Rediscovering Chayanov with the Chinese Experience," *Journal of Peasant Studies*, September 29, 2022, pp. 1-31.

[3] Rangarirai Gavin Muchetu, "Family Farms and the Markets: Examining the Level of Market-Oriented Production 15 Years after the Zimbabwe Fast Track Land Reform Programme," *Review of African Political Economy* 46, no. 159, 2019, pp. 33-54; Carlos Guanziroli, Antonio Buainain, and Alberto Sabbato, "Family Farming in Brazil: Evolution between the 1996 and 2006 Agricultural Censuses," *The Journal of Peasant Studies* 40, no. 5, 2013, pp. 817-843; Food and Agriculture Organization (FAO) and the International Fund for Agricultural Development (IFAD), *United Nations Decade of Family Farming* 2019-2028. *Global Action Plan*, Licence: CC BY-NC-SA 3.0 IGO, Rome: FAO and IFAD, 2019.

则而实现。与资本主义性质的机构以追求盈利为目标不同，合作社并不受这一终极目标的驱动。合作社拥有扎根于基层集体行动的民主结构，具有保护其成员的潜力，不仅可以防范新自由主义的矛盾和市场失灵，还可以防范掠夺性国家本身的侵害。[①]

合作社可能想有效地利用资本资源并在其成员之间重新分配收益，或者它们可能试图通过利用其组织力量来解决社会经济和政治弊病（后者的目标可能包括实现阶级和谐，以及将农民从经济束缚中解放出来）。抑或，他们会同时追求两者。恰亚诺夫关于合作社的理念极具吸引力，因为他是通过农民的能动性和企业家精神的视角来定义合作社的。恰亚诺夫式合作社代表了小规模家庭农场主享受大规模利益的机会，同时又不失去其个性以及自己对生产过程的控制。那么，哪些是恰亚诺夫式合作社中的重要内容？它与非洲又有什么联系？在本文的剩余部分，我们将基于恰亚诺夫的理论，讨论合作社在人口变化和非洲家庭农业复原力方面的重要性。

五、恰亚诺夫、农民与合作社

在恰亚诺夫看来，任何成功的合作倡议（或任何其他农村社会政策或发展计划）的先决条件是首先了解农村地区的现实情况。[②]为此，在为农民面临的挑战提供任何类型的解决方案之前，他花时间尝试了解俄罗斯的农村。一般而言，我们试图从两个角度考虑恰亚诺夫的理论与合作社组织的相关性。

首先，在农村地区阶级分化加深的同时，农民对合作社的态度也开始出现分歧。随着资本主义关系的渗透，尽管其速度没有列宁所假设的

---

① Karin Wedig and Jörg Wiegratz, "Neoliberalism and the Revival of Agricultural Cooperatives: The Case of the Coffee Sector in Uganda," *Journal of Agrarian Change* 18, no. 2, 2018, pp. 348-369; See also James Scott, *Seeing Like a State: How Certain Schemes to Improve the Human Condition Have Failed*, New Haven: Yale University Press, 1998.

② Chayanov, *The Theory of Peasant Co-Operatives*; Alexander Chayanov, "On Differentiation of the Peasant Economy," *Russian Peasant Studies* 4, no. 4, 2019, pp. 6-21.

那样快，农民的两极分化却不断在俄国农村推进。[1] 类似的趋势在非洲也很明显：非洲农民不是一个单一的阶级，而是由几个阶级或子阶级组成的。[2] 在土地和农业改革的过程中，这种差异化可能会变得更加明显，从而使恰亚诺夫式的合作社变得更为重要。恰亚诺夫观察到了六个农民阶层——贫困、贫穷、中贫、中等、中富和富有（尽管恰亚诺夫并没有使用这些术语），他们加入合作社的动机和资源各不相同。有些人很富有，而有些人很贫困，不能参与合作社活动。因此，适当了解这些群体在农业社会中的配置就显得至关重要。[3] 在非洲的农业结构中，贫穷到中等阶层的农民往往占大多数，这被认为是民众参与合作社的理想选择。中等到中富者可以在没有政府的帮助下参与，而贫困人群可能需要国家提供一些扶持来提高生产力和参与度。富裕阶层往往是与合作社对立的。"中等阶层"民众强大的参与感为非洲合作社的发展提供了肥沃的土壤。

农民家庭主要受到使用价值（粮食安全）的驱动，而非交换价值（市场销售）。一般来说，这样的家庭往往只有很少的资本密集型技术，并主要依靠家庭劳动力。由于忽略了这些事实，非洲在殖民和独立时期实施的大多数农业政策都鼓励出口作物生产，其结果是家庭层面上的粮食长期不安全。与此同时，农民经济并不完全与市场经济隔离。他们不是自给自足的，而是买卖的，因此是"半"商业化的。[4]

现在，我们转向第二个视角。尽管在某种程度上参与市场交易，但农民经济的生产和消费是以家庭为单位，这就使合作社具有明显的分散性质。恰亚诺夫认为，农民家庭的生产力可以与家庭规模成正比。这种

---

[1]　Henry Bernstein, "V. I. Lenin and A.V. Chayanov: Looking Back, Looking Forward," *Journal of Peasant Studies* 36, no. 1, 2009, pp. 55-81.

[2]　Sam Moyo, Praveen Jha, and Paris Yeros, "The Classical Agrarian Question: Myth, Reality and Relevance Today," *Agrarian South*: *Journal of Political Economy* 2, no. 1, 2013, pp. 93-119.

[3]　Chayanov, *The Theory of Peasant Co-Operatives*, chap. 2.

[4]　Chayanov's understanding seems to apply not only to labour-scarce but also to labour-abundant economies（恰亚诺夫的理解似乎不仅适用于劳动力稀缺的经济体，也适用于劳动力丰富的经济体）. Philip C. C. Huang, "Is 'Family Farms' the Way to Develop Chinese Agriculture?" *Rural China*: *An International Journal of History and Social Science* 11, 2014, pp. 189-221.

关系之所以如此，是因为家庭农场主的劳动力是由家庭成员免费提供的，而资本主义农场主则会雇佣非家庭劳动力。家庭劳动力是根据生存的需要和工作的劳繁程度（苦役）来提供的，这表现为消费者 / 劳动者（consumer/worker，下文简写为 C/W）的比率。家庭劳动力供应增加到其产出的边际效用等于劳动的边际负效用。在这个等式中，要考虑到家庭的代际结构，因为在一个大家庭中，并不是每个人都能提供劳动力。这其中有被扶养人（消费者而并非生产者——老人和小孩）和劳动力提供者（既是生产者又是消费者——成年人和 15 岁以上的青少年），这些家庭成员的比例决定了家庭的生产力。比例越小（15 岁以上的青少年越多），每个成员为实现家庭消费的工作量就越少，为市场剩余生产释放出更多的劳动时间。

在通常情况下，生育率逐渐下降（低龄儿童数量的减少）将导致 C/W 比率的下降。例如，一个有两份工作的成年人和两个被抚养子女的家庭，其 C/W 比率为 4/2=2，而一个有两份工作的成年人和两个工作年龄的子女（因上学而各提供一半劳动时间）的家庭，其 C/W 比率为 4/（2+0.5+0.5）=1.33。家庭结构决定了其生活水平的上限和下限以及生存所需的经济活动程度。[1] 这就意味着，随着家庭规模的扩大，农民家庭可用的劳动力也在增加，从而提高了每户的农业生产力。因此，人口红利将使农民受益，并且由家庭农民组成的村庄有望在人口和工业转型期间吸收过剩劳动力方面发挥重要作用。

农民经济的这种性质也对合作社的组织方式产生了重大影响。虽然家庭和亲属关系的形式因地区而异，但联合生产和消费的家庭单位不

---

[1] A. V. Chayanov, *The Theory of Peasant Economy*, edited by Daniel Thorner, Basile Kerblay, and R. E. F. Smith, Manchester: Manchester University Press, 1986, pp. 57-59. Lal Thilakarathne and Youkichi Yanagita, "The Chayanov Concept of a Peasant Farm Economy," *Research Bulletin of the Faculty of College of Agriculture Gifu University* 61, 1996, pp. 45-59. Chayanov hypothesise a big family with up to nine children (which is not so common in African families). See also our Table 1.

可能这么大 [①]。只要构成合作社的单位是自主家庭（作为决策单位），合作社的治理就会以协调为基础，而不是通过自上而下的控制。当然，家庭有理由参加合作社。随着家庭劳动力的增加，生存需求将很快得到满足，更多劳动力可以转而从事以市场为导向的生产和非农活动，或者从事其他农场的工作。然而，如果农民在市场上以及在与有时是剥削性政府的关系中被孤立，他们就会处于不利地位。因此，农民需要被联合起来，同时保持他们的自主权 [②]。

六、非洲农民合作社的前景：基于津巴布韦的案例研究

在本部分中，我们将简要讨论农民合作社在 21 世纪非洲社会经济发展中的作用。在激烈的人口转变和重新寻求农民路线的背景下，国家政府和其他利益相关者应该为合作社创造什么样的计划和环境支持？到目前为止，我们已经在抽象的层面上探讨了恰亚诺夫的理论，但他的思想在当代非洲农业结构中的分量有多重？

以津巴布韦为例，在那里，激烈的土地改革导致了由 A1（小规模）、A2（大规模）和 CA（公共区域）组成的土地结构的出现。A1 和 A2 代表自 2000 年以来不同农民群体重新安置的地区，而 CA 则代表了殖民时期划定的贫困的自给农区。在关于三条轨迹的部分中，我们指出，非洲大陆的土地掠夺和农民的抵抗可能会导致泛非土地结构向南部非洲的模

[①] While we do not assume that a larger kin unit can be an effective unit of decision-making in terms of labour allocation, production, and consumption, we agree that more empirical research is needed especially about the mechanism of intra-family decision-making（虽然我们不认为较大的亲属单位可以成为劳动分配、生产和消费方面的有效决策单位，但我们认同实证研究的必要性，特别是关于家庭内部的决策机制）. E. A. Hammel, "Chayanov Revisited: A Model for the Economics of Complex Kin Units," *The Proceedings of the National Academy of Sciences* (*PNAS*) 102, no. 19, 2005, pp. 7043-7046. Chayanov, *The Theory of Peasant Co-Operatives*, pp. 3-5.

[②] Along with the demographic transition of African society, the C/W ratio is expected to decrease up to a point at which capital becomes the primary limiting factor of rural development. This gives scope for savings and credit cooperative organisations (SACCOs) together with production cooperatives［随着非洲社会的人口转型，C/W 比率预计将下降至资本成为农村发展的主要限制因素的程度，这就为储蓄和信贷合作组织（SACCOs）以及生产合作社提供了空间］. See more in Lal and Yanagita, "The Chayanov Concept of a Peasant Farm Economy," 1996, pp. 48-49.

式靠拢，在那里，土地问题会引起公众的强烈关注。从这方面讲，津巴布韦的情况可能是相关的，而且在某种程度上是有代表性的。

萨姆·莫约非洲农业研究所（Sam Moyo African Institute for Agrarian Studies，SMAIAS）2015 年进行的基线调查发现，89.7% 的津巴布韦农民利用自己的家庭劳动力在农场从事劳动，这意味着大多数津巴布韦小农户被视为农民。[①] 基于 2018 至 2019 年进行的后续调查研究，该机构试图检验恰亚诺夫农村分化理论在津巴布韦的适用性。对家庭数据的聚类分析表明，在土地改革后的津巴布韦，出现了五个农民阶层——贫困、贫穷、中等、中富和富有。集群的主要决定因素包括出售和雇用临时（非长期）劳动力的做法、非农业收入的规模以及土地利用的范围。换句话说，农民的特征和分组取决于他们对土地和家庭劳动力的密集利用程度。较高的商业化程度和较大的家庭规模往往是一致的：从贫穷（3.84）、中等（3.98）到中富（4.52）。[②]

根据五个年龄集群的分类显示，贫穷和中等集群的儿童（表 1 中的 0—9 岁和 10—19 岁）不仅在绝对数量上而且在相对数量上，都是巨大的。这些集群中的农民往往依靠家庭劳动力，集约化耕种自己的土地，从而为公平的合作活动提供了肥沃的土壤。关于 C/W 比例的讨论实质是，农户中的工人数量越多，可用于维持生计的劳动力就越多，最终甚至有助于农场以外的创收活动。因此，恰亚诺夫注意到青少年（尤其是 15—19 岁年龄组）在课余时间给予的辅助工作的作用。10—19 岁年龄组的密度（占总数的 24.6%，占贫困户的 26.0%）就是一个典型的例子。

[①] In the same study, a trimodal agrarian structure at the national level was highlighted, while a later study confirmed the persistence of this trimodal structure at local and regional levels. Sam Moyo, Walter Chambati, Freedom Mazwi, and Rangarirai Gavin Muchetu, "Inter-District Household Survey: Follow up to the Baseline Survey," Harare, Zimbabwe, 2015 (mimeo); Freedom Mazwi, Rangarirai Gavin Muchetu, and George T. Mudimu, "Revisiting the Trimodal Agrarian Structure as a Social Differentiation Analysis Framework in Zimbabwe: A Study," *Agrarian South*: *Journal of Political Economy* 4, no. 10, 2021, pp. 60-73.

[②] Rangarirai Gavin Muchetu, *After Radical Land Reform*: *Restructuring Agricultural Cooperatives in Zimbabwe and Japan*, Bamenda: Langaa RPCIG, 2021, chap. 7; The discussion of this section is based on the questionnaire survey targeting eight agricultural cooperatives in Goromonzi District, Zimbabwe. The survey was conducted by Muchetu in 2018 and 2019.

表1　合作社成员家庭的年龄结构

年龄范围（岁）	农民分类											
	贫困		贫穷		中等		中富		富有		总和	
	数量	%	数量	%	数量	%	数量	%	数量	%	数量	%
0—9	10	15.4	42	14.4	44	16.7	19	13.6	1	5.0	116	14.9
10—19	17	26.2	76	26.0	64	24.3	31	22.1	4	20.0	192	24.6
20—29	8	12.3	55	18.8	48	18.3	23	16.4	3	15.0	137	17.6
30—39	7	10.8	42	14.4	28	10.6	14	10.0	2	10.0	93	11.9
40—49	5	7.7	22	7.5	30	11.4	18	12.9	4	20.0	79	10.1
50—59	10	15.4	22	7.5	24	9.1	18	12.9	3	15.0	77	9.9
60—69	7	10.8	17	5.8	16	6.1	10	7.1	2	10.0	52	6.7
70—	1	1.5	16	5.5	9	3.4	7	5.0	1	5.0	34	4.4
总和	65	100.0	292	100.0	263	100	140	100	20	100.0	780	100.0

资料来源：SMAIAS 2018 至 2019 年调研数据

非洲农民的退休年龄因国家而异。通常只要该地区农民在身体和精神上能够完成耕作所需的任务，他们就会继续工作。据表1显示，70岁以上人口占总人口的4.4%，而0至10岁人口占总人口的14.9%。在生产力（人均产量）相对较高的情况下，津巴布韦农村的C/W比率应该保持很低。[①]不了解非洲农村的人，有时会提出毫无根据的主张——例如，有人提出，非洲的大问题并非人口爆炸，而是农村老龄化；但事实上，非洲农村人口的重心仍然是年轻人，[②]津巴布韦的情况也不例外。另一方面，比较0—9岁和10—19岁这两个年龄组的规模，我们便可以发

[①]　We can simulate changes in the C/W ratio for all households, taking into account fertility and mortality rates (the effect of technological change is difficult to calculate). Results will be presented in a separate paper.

[②]　Felix Kwame Yeboah and T S Jayne, "The Myth of Africa's Ageing Farmers," *Rural* 21: *The International Journal of Rural Development* 54, no. 03/20, 2020, pp. 39-41.

现，就津巴布韦农村而言，无止境的人口扩张也是一个神话。30—39 岁年龄组的减少表明应该有大量人口迁出农村，而合作社有望成为吸引年轻村民留在乡村的一块吸铁石。

虽然关于合作社的讨论在学术界和政策制定者中仍存在分歧，但非洲的合作社在日常农业活动中证明了它们的实用性。虽然许多合作社仍未注册，但津巴布韦改革后的农业促使合作社增加。正如穆切图所指出的那样，国家、非政府组织甚至私营部门在与农民打交道时，都利用了某种形式的集体方案来降低交易成本。[1] 如图 6 所示（基于 2018 至 2019 年收集的田野调查数据），津巴布韦农民创建或加入合作社以期改善他们的生计（34%），增强自己的能力以对抗剥削（22%）、解决市场失灵（16%），以及增加产量（15%）。

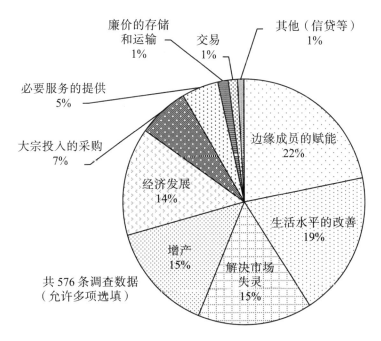

图 6 建立合作社的动机

资料来源：2018 至 2019 年调研数据

---

① Muchetu, *After Radical Land Reforms*.

通过近期的土地改革进程，合作社运动在重新安置区似乎焕发出新的生命力。表 2 中的数据显示，在安置区（A1），合作社是由农民自己组建的（98%），而在自给区（CA），64% 的合作社是在非政府组织的指示和指导下组建的——即便在 CA，人们仍然可以感受到国家的存在，那里大约 20% 的合作社是根据一些国家计划或倡议成立的。同时，那些已经加入合作社的成员发现了明显的好处，比如在 A1 中，更好地解决市场失灵（21.7%）和增加产量（19.9%）；在 CA 中的益处是赋能（25.3%）和更好的经济发展，如增加收入（23.0%）（见图 7）。虽然自下而上的合作社运动为津巴布韦及其他地区的合作社带来了发展潜力，但它们仍然需要国家（政策框架）和私营部门的支持（公平和真正的"自由"市场）。

表 2　合作社的发起者

	安置区		自给区		总和	
	数量	%	数量	%	数量	%
政党	1	1.1	0	0.0	1	0.5
推广人员	0	0.0	1	1.0	1	0.5
非政府组织	1	1.1	64	64.0	65	33.9
当地权威	0	0.0	4	4.0	4	2.1
当地政治领袖	0	0.0	4	4.0	4	2.1
当地农民或合作社成员	90	97.8	7	7.0	97	50.5
地区发展基金（政府）	0	0.0	20	20.0	20	10.4
总和	92	100.0	100	100.0	192	100.0

资料来源：2018 至 2019 年调研数据

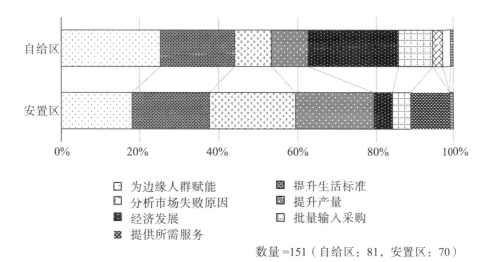

图 7　从合作社中获益

资料来源：2018 至 2019 年调研数据

　　穆切图利用社区－国家－市场的框架，提出了对国家、农民和合作社结构本身进行社会经济和政治改革的建议（见表 3）。该研究发现并非基于抽象的、理想化的新制度主义模型，而是源于仔细考察了非洲社会基层的合作实践，特别是在津巴布韦，人们聚沙成塔，汲取集体的力量。[①] 每个角色在非洲农业发展中都扮演着至关重要的作用，政府则为长期的国家发展创造宏观条件。正如在肯尼亚、乌干达和津巴布韦的案例研究中所显示的那样，最重要的是需要确保领导者具有政治意愿。[②] 一旦有了这样的意愿，实施其他的工作（如政策改革、农民认证和有效的补贴）就会变得更容易管理，当然，并不是所有的事情都能够自动生成。

[①]　As for organisational ingenuity utilising local knowledge and resources at hand, see Ellen Mangnus and Mirjam Schoonhoven-Speijer, "Navigating Dynamic Contexts: African Cooperatives as Institutional Bricoleurs," *International Journal of Agricultural Sustainability* 18, no. 2, 2020, pp. 99-112.

[②]　Wedig and Wiegratz, "Neoliberalism and the Revival of Agricultural Cooperatives"; Muchetu, *After Radical Land Reform*; Francis Fanuel Lyimo, *Rural Cooperation*: *In the Cooperative Movement in Tanzania*, Dar es Salaam: Mkuki Na Nyota Publishers and African Books Collective, 2008.

表3　如何为合作发展创造有利环境

国家	农民	合作框架
· 经济环境	· 社会经济行为改革	· 新三级会员制
· 政治环境	· 从依赖综合到自我	· 强大且独立的国家/区域联邦
· 政策工具	解放	· 叠加式/阶段式合作开发
· 国家补贴	· 管理提升	· 合作身份
· 农业培训和教育政策	· 农业培训	· 储蓄和信用合作社的重要性和合
· 农民和合作证书		作银行

资料来源：Muchetu, *After Radical Land Reform*, pp. 318-343

　　在合作社的发展过程中，农民成员有望发挥举足轻重的作用。除了长期以来提倡通过教育和技能培训提高管理技能的建议外，合作社成员还应该改变他们的思维方式，培养自助的意识，以便合作社成员克服依赖综合征——这是通过各种补贴计划持续推行养成的一种殖民心态，被丹比萨·莫约认为是农村发展的主要障碍之一。[①] 合作社及其成员应该确保选举出能够推动组织发展的诚信度高的领导人。穆切图在他的著作中为非洲合作社的有效重组提出了一系列建议。除了发展储蓄和信贷合作社（SACCOs）和合作银行外，他还引入了叠加式、多阶段合作社发展模式（从单一用途合作社开始逐渐发展为多功能合作社），以及通过三级会员制将合作社的利益分配给社区中的非会员的想法。[②]

　　有大量证据表明，在坦桑尼亚和日本等国，妇女参与合作社的程度很高，[③] 在一些不分性别的合作社中，妇女成员比例分别高达65%和95%。[④] 在非洲，除了这些普通合作社以外，妇女还有她们自己的合作社，以消除不平等与社会排斥、解决与性别相关的农业问题（包括土地

---

　　① Dambisa Moyo, *Dead Aid*: *Why Aid Is Not Working and How There Is a Better Way for Africa*, New York: Farrar, Strause and Giroux, 2009.

　　② See more in Muchetu, *After Radical Land Reform*, chap. 8.

　　③ The Japanese consumer cooperatives are predominantly run by women as they seek to purchase safe quality food directly from the farmers. The majority of them are urban women.

　　④ Frederick O. Wanyama, *Cooperatives and the Sustainable Development Goals*: *A Contribution to the Post*-2015 *Development Debate*: *A Policy Brief*, Brussels: International Co-operative Alliance, Geneva: Cooperatives Unit, Enterprises Department, International Labour Organization, 2014, p. 7.

所有权和获得教育、技能、信息和资金的不平等）。在上述所有方面，合作社都可以在赋予妇女权利方面发挥重要作用，从而消除持续存在的性别不平等现象。合作社有巨大的潜力，可以进一步将妇女带到农业斗争的前线，并提升妇女的能动性。[①]

结　语

如果印度在中国之后进入人口减少阶段，非洲人口的转型对全球经济来说将会是一个巨大的福音，即持续供应劳动力。然而，如果不断增长的工业劳动力无法获得相对廉价的消费品（如食品），那么工资成本就会极度增加，非洲将无法与其他地区展开竞争。工业化的前提是提高农业生产率，特别是粮食生产。虽然整个 21 世纪非洲的人口预计将继续增长，但生育率会逐渐下降，随之而来的是劳动年龄人口在非洲劳动力中所占的比例将增加。如果制度条件得到改善，个体农户就会摆脱温饱阶段，农村地区就有可能进入一个良性循环的繁荣期。

尽管如此，随着资本对农业投资的推进和机械化的发展，过剩人口就会以一种社会无法接受的规模产生。那么，是否有可能通过推广劳动密集型的家庭农业，而非资本密集型的大型农场，让人才留在乡村、保护环境资源，并为城市居民提供充足的食物？我们是否能够在逐步提高农业生产率和精心培育社区使用价值的同时，确保公众的参与和为妇女赋权呢？

在本文中，我们已经看到了合作社活动的巨大潜力，农民永远不会消亡。在 21 世纪下半叶，合作的村庄或许能够吸纳年轻有为之士，从而遏制失控的城市化进程，因为农民并不仅仅是一个临时阶级联盟的有用对象。农民路线体现出一种强大的解放思想，是从马克思、恩格斯、考茨基、恰亚诺夫、列宁，到毛泽东、法农、加布拉尔和莫约的思想中一

---

① Cooperative Facility for Africa (COOP AFRICA), *Empower Rural Women – End Poverty and Hunger: The Potential of African Cooperatives*, ILO Office for Kenya, Somalia, Tanzania, 2007. https://www.ilo.org/global/docs/WCMS_174990/lang--en/index.htm, accessed 20 January 2023.

步一步演变而来。[①] 以农民为中心的思想已经深入人心。通过学习非洲农民的智慧，尊重他们的自主权和自我组织经验，可以使中国和非洲其他亚洲发展伙伴在非洲开展的项目更具可持续性，还能深化他们在非洲人民心中"真朋友"的形象。

在高举去殖民化的崇高理想大旗的同时，非洲的农业合作社将作为致力于正义、公平和效率的自治组织而不断壮大和发展。2018 年，作为国际合作社联盟（ICA）的组成部分，非洲农业合作联盟组织（Alliance Africa Agricultural Cooperative Organisation，AAACO）成立，有望成为一个有效的泛非洲合作社联合会。[②] 借助农民的复原力，联合合作社将必须应对农业家庭企业当前面对的各种长期和短期的挑战。

长期挑战包括如何从战略上应对人口结构转型和传统与新兴援助国在非洲日益增长的参与度，以及这些捐助国时而在非洲展开的激烈竞争。短期挑战包括如何组织农村人口有效地应对突发的、关键的、普遍的威胁（如新型冠状病毒）。尽管联合国秘书长在 2021 年的报告中强调了合作社在从疫情中"更好重建"后疫情时代中的作用，但社交距离和其他限制措施制约了农业合作社的复原力。对于农村领导人来说，想要向他们的成员伸出援手变得非常困难。[③] 然而，只要农民家庭怀有组织起来的动机和愿望，农业合作社就会一次又一次地绝地重生。

---

① Moyo et al., "The Classical Agrarian Question," p. 105.

② https://icaafrica.coop/en/alliance-africa-agricultural-cooperative-organisation-aaaco, accessed 20 January 2023. Cooperatives are expected to contribute to "Social Solidarity Economy" in Africa. See the research conducted in Cameroon, Morocco, Senegal, South Africa, and Tunisia. International Labour Organization (ILO), *Social and Solidarity Economy: Social Innovation Catalyst in Africa?* Geneva: ILO, 2022.

③ *Cooperatives in Social Development*, Report of the United Nations Secretary-General, A/76/209, 22 July 2021; Nicola Francesconi, Fleur Wouterse, and Dorothy Birungi Namuyiga, "Agricultural Cooperatives and COVID-19 in Southeast Africa: The Role of Managerial Capital for Rural Resilience," *Sustainability* 13, no. 3, 2021, 1046. Surveys about COVID-19 were conducted in Madagascar, Malawi, Rwanda, and Uganda.

附：本篇英文

Africa's Agrarian Development Paths under Demographic Transition: The Role of Peasant Cooperatives

Yoichi Mine　Rangarirai Gavin Muchetu[*]

Abstract: People living in Africa and Asia will account for 80 per cent of the world's population in the next hundred years. Although Africa's population growth is noticeably dramatic, its fertility rate has already begun to decline. As the dependent population shrinks, the share of the working-age population in the total population of Africa is expected to increase. This so-called demographic dividend may contribute significantly to labour-intensive development in Africa beyond the current setback caused by COVID-19 and global political instability. However, if capital-intensive food production in rural areas accelerates top-down, massive surplus populations will be unleashed, which may lead to uncontrollable urbanisation. Africa abounds in resilient peasant societies that have resisted – and when possible reversed – land dispossession since colonial times. The shocks of rapid demographic change and class differentiation of the peasantry can be alleviated by deliberately pursuing the peasant path through various forms of cooperatives. Moreover, the agricultural cooperatives in Africa are expected to perform not only economic but also educational functions, thereby awakening socio-political consciousness among rural masses and decolonising the mind of people. The paper begins with a global overview and concludes with a case study of Zimbabwean cooperatives.
Key Words: demography; agriculture; peasant path; Chayanov; cooperatives

---

　　* Yoichi Mine is Professor at the Graduate School of Global Studies, Doshisha University, Kyoto, Japan. Rangarirai Gavin Muchetu is Research Fellow at the Sam Moyo African Institute for Agrarian Studies (SMAIAS), Harare, Zimbabwe.

Introduction: Pessimism vs Optimism

Throughout the colonial, independence, and post-colonial eras, the discourses on Africa have diverged into pessimism, according to which the continent would become a source of global political insecurity, on the one hand, and optimism, according to which Africa, especially its rich natural resources, would bring a substantial benefit to the local and global economy, on the other. However, such extreme ideas and opinions have not emanated within Africa; these are mostly the discourses presented by outside observers seeking to gain additional influence in the intellectual or policy marketplace.

While the image of "rising Africa" was disseminated by the high growth rates of resource-exporting countries in Africa during the first decade of the twenty-first century, such exploitative optimism started to wane as the pattern of extroverted development in Africa turned out to be unsustainable.[1] The fear of the defiant "darker nations" is deeply embedded in the mind of the people of the former colonial powers. "Racial antagonism resembles justice in one respect if in no other: it may sleep but it never dies".[2] Indeed, pessimism and scepticism about the possibility of autonomous development seem to form the keynote of the contemporary Western discourses on Africa.

More recently, however, the polarised views about Africa's future have begun to intensify again as a new factor, global demographic change, comes to the fore in the policy discourses.[3] It is highly probable that Africa's population

---

[1] Sam Moyo and Yoichi Mine, "Introduction: African Potentials for Conflict Resolution and Transformation", in Sam Moyo and Yoichi Mine (eds.), *What Colonialism Ignored: "African Potentials" for Resolving Conflicts in Southern Africa* (Bamenda, Cameroon: Langaa RPCIG, 2016). As for the Africa-rising discourses, see the IMF conference, "Africa Rising: Building to the Future", organised in Maputo in May 2014. http://www.africa-rising.org/ (accessed 20 January 2022).

[2] Vijay Prashad, *The Darker Nations: A People's History of the Third World* (New York: New Press, 2007); Raymond Leslie Buell, "Again the Yellow Peril", *Foreign Affairs* 2, no. 2 (1923), p. 295.

[3] As for balanced and comprehensive overviews, see the following. David Canning, Sangeeta Raja, and Abdo S. Yazbeck (eds.), *Africa's Demographic Transition: Dividend or Disaster?* (Washington, D.C.: World Bank, 2015); Clifford O. Odimegwu and Yemi Adewoyin (eds.), *The Routledge Handbook of African Demography* (London: Routledge, 2022).

will grow substantially in the coming one hundred years. As projected by the Population Division, the United Nations Department of Economic and Social Affairs (UNDESA), Africa's population is expected to increase fivefold (based on the medium-variant projection) in the twenty-first century due to relatively high fertility rates and improvements in health conditions in the region (Figure 1).

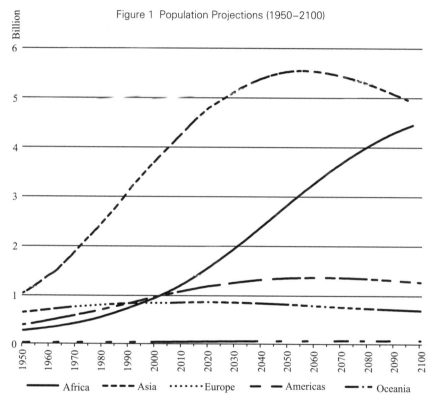

Figure 1 Population Projections (1950–2100)

Source: United Nations Department of Economic and Social Affairs (UNDESA), Population Division, *The 2022 Revision of World Population Prospects*. https://population.un.org/wpp/ (accessed 20 January 2023)

This means that Africans and Asians will each form more or less 40 per cent of the world's population, thereby constituting about an 80 per cent majority in combination, within the coming hundred years. Given this numerical preponderance, the future shape of the world will be determined primarily by the extent and quality of dialogue between Asians and Africans.[①]

In this paper, we start with a macro view of global population transformation and then proceed to discuss the future social landscape of the African countryside. In the next section, we trace the trends of global demographic transformation and underscore the significance of rural/urban relations. Then, we present three historical trajectories of agrarian accumulation in Africa and indicate their possible convergence through land dispossession. Given the intensified contradictions of the African political economy, we demonstrate that the question of surplus population and pauperisation could be effectively addressed by pursuing the labour-intensive peasant path. Finally, drawing on the case of Zimbabwe, we focus on the role of agricultural cooperatives in terms of not only skill training but also socio-political awareness of their members.

While Chinese aid to Africa has been characterised by the development of large-scale infrastructure to meet strong demand on the continent, the priority of technology transfer and investment in human resources is expected to be much higher in the coming decades. In addition to training individuals, it will be critically important to provide support to institution-building and collective initiatives; for example, functioning rural organisations are indispensable for maintaining public goods such as irrigation canals. However, peasant organisations must be indigenous and owned by peasants themselves. It is at this point that agricultural cooperatives have great potential. Having approached Africa with the principle of self-reliance for many years, China may have a comparative advantage in motivating African villagers and making rural organisations sustainable. As agricultural cooperatives in Africa have their own rich history, we believe that attempts to examine local experiences of cooperatives may be of no small significance to Chinese development agencies.

Demography: Lessons from the Past and the Present

Behind the extreme pessimism about Africa lies racial prejudice. While

---

① Yoichi Mine, *Connecting Africa and Asia: Afrasia As a Benign Community* (London: Routledge, 2022).

such distortions should be immediately rejected, some others see the people living on the continent as passive victims waiting for handouts and stress their vulnerability rather than their resilience. We need to be cautious, as this attitude involves good intentions.

When COVID-19 first spread, the damage was expected to be colossal in Africa, where health systems were not well developed. However, despite the paucity of accurate statistics, it is clear that deaths from the infection have been considerably lower in Africa than in the West. While there is much speculation as to the reasons for this phenomenon, it is essential to note that in Africa, the majority of the population is made up of younger people who are less likely to develop severe symptoms when infected with COVID-19, and that many Africans live in vast rural areas where physical contact between people is not as dense as in towns.[①] It also cannot be underestimated that Africa has amassed practical lessons through its responses to serious, sudden, and pervasive health crises such as HIV/AIDS and Ebola.

The war in Ukraine, which began in 2022, is a complex crisis that will undermine both energy security and food security in every corner of the world. However, the oil-producing countries of Africa benefit from the rising prices of natural resources. Only some war-torn countries, such as Somalia, which are heavily dependent on food aid, will be hit particularly hard by the rise in international grain prices.[②] We need to recognise both the advantages that Africa enjoys and the challenges it faces. On the one hand, the diversity of foods produced by African regions – maize, rice, cassava, banana, and others – makes them more resilient to food crises than countries with only one staple food. On the other hand, the major cause of the current food crisis in Africa is

---

① As for Africa's unique survivability against COVID-19, see, for example, Joseph Waogodo Cabore et al., "COVID-19 in the 47 Countries of the WHO African Region: A Modelling Analysis of Past Trends and Future Patterns", *The Lancet Global Health* 10, Issue 8 (2022); Binta Zahra Diop et al., "The Relatively Young and Rural Population May Limit the Spread and Severity of COVID-19 in Africa: A Modelling Study", *BMJ Global Health,* 2020;5:e002699.

② All wheat imports of Somalia have been from Russia and Ukraine. Tim G. Benton et al., *The Ukraine War and Threats to Food and Energy Security: Cascading Risks from Rising Prices and Supply Disruptions,* Research Paper, Chatam House, 13 April, 2022, p. 9.

the persistent droughts in the Sahel and other arid regions due to climate change rather than fluctuations in international food prices. All industrialised countries should bear responsibility for this threat in the Anthropocene.[1]

These examples show that Africa's demographic characteristics and the resilience of its agrarian economies have been closely related to the responses of the continent to the recent global crises. Let us revert to the subject of long-term transformation. All demographers scientifically predict a massive supply of labour force in Africa in the latter half of the present century.[2] Is this a blessing or a curse for Africa and the rest of the world in the long term?

Contrary to the Malthusian assumption of the endless proliferation of the human race, many developed countries will face serious underpopulation in the near future. A relentless American critic of China's global power, Howard French, neatly contrasted the buoyant future of the United States that would accept global migrants with the dismal future of China which would suffer a rapid greying of society.[3] His argument explicitly discouraged the actors outside China from transacting business with China, whose numerical presence is expected to wane considerably. However, China's demographic transition means that the population composition of the country is approaching the level of contemporary Europe and Japan. If we are advised not to engage with China, which is increasingly resemblant to Europe, should we not associate with Europe either?

Beyond competition between big powers, the slowing down of the supply of the working-age population in China may significantly impact on the outlook of the world economy. Charles Goodhart and Manoj Pradhan predicted that the shrinking labour supply in East Asia would induce inflation and push up the interest rate globally. According to them, while it is theoretically possible for India and Africa to substitute as China, we cannot be optimistic about the effect of a rapid labour supply in Africa offsetting global ageing, given the fragmentation of the

---

[1] Mine, *Connecting Africa and Asia,* pp. 40, 99.

[2] Mine, *Connecting Africa and Asia,* chaps. 1 and 2.

[3] Howard W. French, *Everything under the Heavens: How the Past Helps Shape China's Push for Global Power* (New York: A.A. Knopf, 2017). Canadians massively accept foreign migrants based on their calculation of national interests. Darrell Bricker and John Ibbitson, *Empty Planet: The Shock of Global Population Decline* (New York: Crown Publishers, 2019).

market and the poor quality of human capital on the continent.[1]

However, in hindsight, the pace and size of demographic expansion of Western countries in the nineteenth century were also as colossal as those of twentieth-century East Asia and twenty-first-century Africa.[2] In 1859, the total fertility rates (TFR) were 5.17 for Germany and 4.48 for the United States of America. The TFR of England and Wales was no less than 5.87 in 1775.[3] Those rates were higher than the TFR of contemporary Africa: 4.31 in 2021. Along with a dramatic increase in the workforce, the Western countries went through rapid capital-intensive industrial growth. The nineteenth century also marked the termination of the Atlantic slave trade and the partitioning of African colonies by the European powers. The growth of Europe was the process in which belligerent countries recruited the youth to the standing army and ferociously attacked each other, dragging the world into devastating wars two times in the first half of the twentieth century. Europe was historically a great trouble-maker, plundering and ruining human capital at home and abroad.

Surplus Populations and the Agrarian Problem

On 15 November 2022, the world population reached 8 billion. Looking at the shifts in population by region, the process looks as if several waves in similar shapes are surging towards the shore one after another. However, it is not the absolute size of the population but the share of the working-age population in the total population that would change the course of economic development. Figure 2 shows the changing ratios over time in several populous countries in Afrasia; while the working-age population will shrink in Asian countries in the second half of the twentieth century, the big African nations will begin to enjoy a significant youth bulge in the same period. In a closer look, the age compositions

---

[1]   Charles Goodhart and Manoj Pradhan, *The Great Demographic Reversal: Ageing Societies, Waning Inequality, and an Inflation Revival* (Cham: Palgrave Macmillan, 2020).

[2]   Paul Morland, *The Human Tide: How Population Shaped the Modern World* (London: John Murray, 2019).

[3]   Massimo Livi-Bacci, *A Concise History of World Population,* 6th Edition (Chichester: Wiley Blackwell, 2017), chap. 4.

in Egypt and South Africa do not change much throughout the period, but the working-age population in countries such as Nigeria and the Democratic Republic of the Congo is expected to increase sharply. In these countries, the demographic dividend, the addition to GDP due to the changing composition of generations, can be huge (this point is taken up again in the agrarian contexts in the section on Chayanov).[①]

In *The Capital,* Karl Marx distinguished the relative surplus population from the absolute surplus population. While the latter corresponds to the (natural) population increase that progresses over decades without much fluctuation, Marx drew more attention to the former, the upsurge of jobless masses created in the process of capital accumulation and continuously expelled out of the capitalist system. The relative surplus population increases not only when capital-intensive industrialisation evolves but also when capitalism reaches out to rural areas. In this connection, Rosa Luxemburg argued that the survival of capitalism depends on the sustenance of non-capitalist peripheries. The stage of Marx's primitive accumulation "is still going on".[②]

If capital-intensive (labour-saving) agriculture such as plantation farming expands, family labour will be less needed in the countryside. Typically, African farmers are smallholders. Without jobs in rural areas, young people will leave their villages for towns and cities. If the urban industry cannot absorb the surplus people pushed out of the villages, there will be no place for them to go. Indeed, capitalism creates a reserve army of labour willing to work for less, heightening exploitation and underdevelopment. Here is an illustration. Food production in a village may increase from 100 tons to 200 tons, with the number of agricultural workers in the same village decreasing from 100 persons to 20 persons due to technological progress. Then, the output per capita will be ten times higher. But if the 80 workers who lost their jobs in the village could not

---

① "Declines in child mortality, followed by declines in fertility, produce a 'bulge' generation and a period when a country has a large number of working-age people and a smaller number of dependents. Having a large number of workers per capita gives a boost to the economy provided there are labor opportunities for the workers" (Canning et al., *Africa's Demographic Transition,* p. 1).

② Rosa Luxemburg, *The Accumulation of Capital,* translated by Agnes Schwarzschild (London: Routledge, 2003), p. 420.

find employment elsewhere, they would starve to death. Samir Amin argued that innovations in agricultural technology that neglect job security would lead to "the genocide of half of humanity" and that the Enclosure in British economic history would be mercilessly repeated in the South.[1] Otherwise, a large part of the increased harvest should be distributed to them for free (if production is based on cooperatives, profits may be redistributed back to the community through member dividends). The view that emphasises job opportunities is shared by Marxist and non-Marxist economists. Simply put, "one basic measure of a country's success in turning the youth bulge into a demographic dividend is the youth (un)employment rate".[2]

As advocated by W. A. Lewis, who served as the Economic Advisor to Ghana's Kwame Nkrumah in the late 1950s, the agricultural revolution should always precede the industrial revolution. According to him, all economic sectors, including food production and manufacturing, should expand simultaneously. It was a big irony that the problem of rural stagnation was exacerbated by the relatively good education enjoyed by Ghana, where the educated youth with high expectations left rural areas for the urban centres. Thus, Lewis prioritised not so much nationwide primary education as adult education, including agricultural extension services. It was thought to be essential to keep the balance between agriculture and industry and stem the tide of the mass exodus from rural areas to cities.[3]

Several economists and demographers have tried to examine the extent of the demographic dividend that could be enjoyed by future Africa. Most arguments emphasise capital shortages. R. Eastwood and M. Lipton cautioned

---

[1] Samir Amin, *Ending the Crisis of Capitalism or Ending Capitalism?* translated by Victoria Bawtree (Cape Town: Pambazuka Press, Dakar: CODESRIA, Bangalore: Books for Change, 2011), p. 124.

[2] Justin Yifu Lin, "Youth Bulge: A Demographic Dividend or a Demographic Bomb in Developing Countries?" 5 January 2012, https://blogs.worldbank.org/developmenttalk/youth-bulge-a-demographic-dividend-or-a-demographic-bomb-in-developing-countries (accessed 20 January 2023).

[3] Yoichi Mine, "The Political Element in the Works of W. Arthur Lewis: The 1954 Model and African Development", *The Developing Economies* 44, no. 3 (2006), pp. 329-355.

Figure 2 Ratio of Working-Age Population (2020-2100)

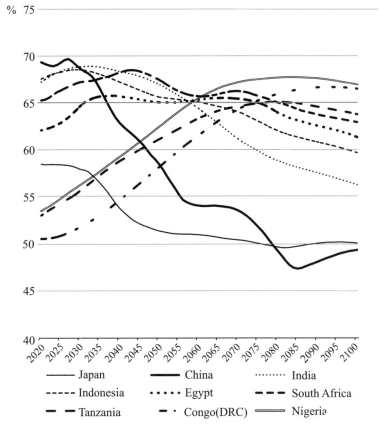

Source: UNDESA, Population Division, *The 2022 Revision of World Population Prospects*

against low savings rates that would hinder capital formation in Africa.[1] In an article titled "Africa Rising", P. Drummond et al. argued that a shift from agriculture to manufacturing was necessary to take advantage of plenty of labour in Africa.[2] Ahmed et al. statistically underlined the significance of education as

[1] Robert Eastwood and Michael Lipton, "Demographic Transition in Sub-Saharan Africa: How Big Will the Economic Dividend Be?" *Population Studies* 65, no. 1 (2011), pp. 9-35.

[2] Paulo Drummond, Vimal Thakoor, and Shu Yu, "Africa Rising: Harnessing the Demographic Dividend", *IMF Working Paper* 14, no.143 (2014).

value-added.[1] J. Cleland and K. Machiyama enumerated factors that militated against the population dividend and lamented that there was little sign of growing employment in manufacturing.[2] While the emphasis is put differently, most of the debate is predicated on the success of industrialisation, and little attention is paid to the predicament of the rural masses. This policy bias against agriculture is dangerous.

Three Trajectories

In the course of European colonial domination in Africa in the past centuries, three distinct types of agrarian structures emerged.[3] The first pattern is the "labour reserve" political economies that emerged in settler colonies, typically in South Africa, Namibia, Zimbabwe and the Kenyan highland. Historically, the white settlers dispossessed the land of the peasantry and monopolised natural resources and infrastructures. This settler mode of accumulation placed the heavy burden of reproduction of cheap labour-power for the mining and urban economy on the shoulders of the peasants, especially women, in the segregated "communal" areas. The second is the "concession enclaves" set up for the extraction of agricultural and mineral resources. This modality evolved in noticeably coercive ways in Central Africa, where the plantations and mines were directly controlled by the transnational capital. The third is trade economies, or *économie de traite,* in West and East Africa, where seemingly autonomous peasants were mobilised to produce quotas of specific commodities such as palm oil, cacao and cotton for the global market.[4]

These are not static structures but dynamic trajectories whose courses

---

[1]　S. Amer Ahmed, Marcio Cruz, Delfin S. Go, Maryla Maliszewska, and Israel Osorio-Rodarte, "How Significant Is Sub-Saharan Africa's Demographic Dividend for Its Future Growth and Poverty Reduction?" *Review of Development Economics* 20 (2016), pp. 762-793.

[2]　John Cleland and Kazuyo Machiyama, "The Challenges Posed by Demographic Change in Sub-Saharan Africa: A Concise Overview", *Population and Development Review* 43 (2017), pp. 264-286.

[3]　Moyo and Mine, "Introduction", pp. 15-19.

[4]　The French term, *traite,* means milking (getting milk from an animal like a cow). People keep them alive, feed them, and exploit them.

have been determined by the complexity of class struggles and the patterns of colonial domination. Although these historical patterns cast a long shadow on the contemporary political economy, there is also a tendency today for these patterns to converge, as the crisis of world capitalism has produced a new wave of accumulation through land dispossession in Africa. While smallholders have struggled to reclaim the land as witnessed in Zimbabwe, new resource-extractive enclaves are being established throughout Africa. There is a collusion between Western and Asian foreign capital and their local allies for land grabbing, even though field reports suggested that Chinese involvement could be somewhat exaggerated.[①]

African society undergoes rapid change. As the historian John Iliffe noted at the end of *The African Poor,* Southern Africa in the twentieth century began to be haunted by structural poverty in the form of low-income families being reproduced across generations as vast tracts of land were expropriated by white settlers (and now by local African dignitaries as well as foreign capital). We witness the emergence of structural poverty caused by land scarcity in parts of Africa, similar to those in Europe and Asia. The shape of African society in the future may therefore become closer to that of today's India in the sense that legions of landless poor are denied access to resources, if we let things ride.[②] Where the productive capacity of peasants has historically been preserved, land concentration is underway. Where land dispossession has reached a critical point, peasant resistance resurges. Looking at trends across the continent, the key to democratic agrarian transformation lies in the strength and resilience of peasant mobilisation.

Given the intensity of the current contradictions, two aspects of future development policies must be specifically underlined. First, it must be remembered that the job creation effort in the countryside should be prioritised (cooperatives can help achieve this). Figures 3 and 4 show projections about the places where the growing population in Africa are expected to reside. Given that

---

① Deborah Brautigam, *Will Africa feed China?* (New York: Oxford University Press, 2015). We are still not very sure if a genuine class of African capitalists are born out of such a process. John Iliffe, *The Emergence of African Capitalism: The Anstey Memorial Lectures in the University of Kent at Canterbury 10-13 May 1982* (London: Macmillan, 1983).

② John Iliffe, *The African Poor: A History* (Cambridge: Cambridge University Press, 1987), chap. 14.

Figure 3 Rural Population in Africa (2000-2050)

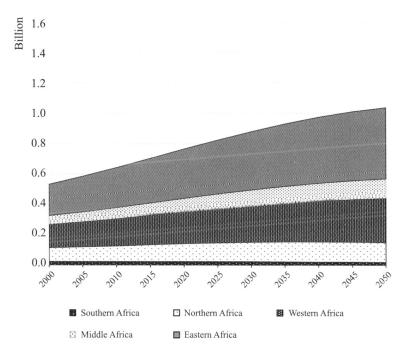

Source: UNDESA, Population Division, *The 2018 Revision of World Urbanization Prospects*. https://population.un.org/wup/ (accessed 20 January 2023)

TFR tends to be higher in the countryside, the difference between these two figures indicates that a mass exodus from the countryside to cities and towns is likely in Africa in the coming decades. Policies neglecting the needs of peasants push them into cities, and the urban population then seek policies favourable to them. In fact, the most pressing impact of the Ukraine War on Africa may not be food shortages in general but rising food prices that may lead to "food riots" in cities. While politicians heed the voices of urban citizens for the reason of regime security, their reaction to the grievances of rural masses tends to be politically selective.[1] Unless appropriate policies addressing rural unemployment

---

[1] Robert H. Bates, *Markets and States in Tropical Africa: The Political Basis of Agricultural Policies* (Berkeley: University of California Press, 1981). Assem Abu Hatab, "Africa's Food Security under the Shadow of the Russia-Ukraine Conflict", *The Strategic Review for Southern Africa* 44, no. 1 (2022), pp. 37-46.

Figure 4 Urban Population in Africa (2000–2050)

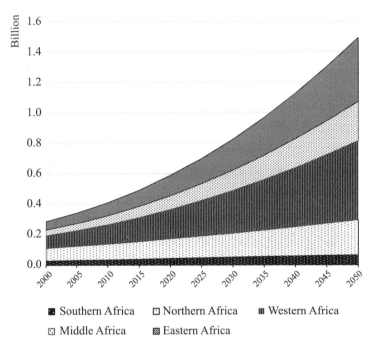

■ Southern Africa   ☐ Northern Africa   ⊞ Western Africa
☑ Middle Africa   ▨ Eastern Africa

Source: UNDESA, Population Division, *The 2018 Revision of World Urbanization Prospects*

are taken, a vicious circle may take root.

Second, the quality rather than the quantity of the workforce matters. The abundant young African labour should be geared to "quality growth". Taking a positive view of the population growth, Gareth Austin underscores the past achievements in human development in education and health in Africa.[1] According to the UNDESA dataset, the life expectancy at birth in Africa reached 61.7 years in 2021, already more extended than the level of East Asia in 1973, 61.0 years, indicating an impressive advance in health and nutrition on the continent. However, the educational attainment is mixed: as shown in Figure 5, the ratio of those who have completed primary education remains around 70

---

[1] Gareth Austin, "Labour Intensity and Manufacturing in West Africa, c.1450-c.2000", in Gareth Austin and Kaoru Sugihara (eds.), *Labour-Intensive Industrialisation in Global History* (Abingdon, Oxon: Routledge, 2013).

per cent in sub-Saharan Africa, though the country-level performances vary. Quality labour means creative labour, as the productivity of the passive, obedient workforce cannot be very high. Worker discipline may have worked under the Taylor and Ford systems, but mechanical tasks are performed more efficiently when relegated to robots. Where human beings are involved in the labour process, it is necessary to foster the motivation of each worker. As a school for the masses to learn to think collectively and independently, and for group leaders to acquire managerial skills, rural and urban cooperatives will have great potential.

Figure 5 Primary Education Completion Rate (2000–2020)

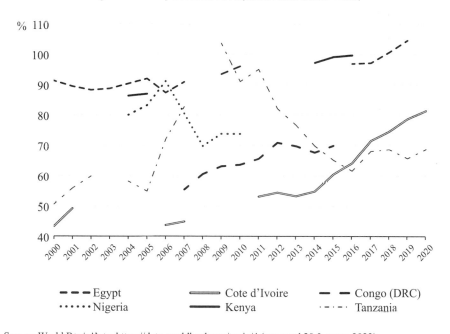

Source: World Bank Data. https://data.worldbank.org/topic/4 (accessed 20 January 2023)

Cooperatives and the Peasant Path Revisited

Although the cooperative way of life was deeply embedded in African socio-economic institutions and formed part and parcel of most African societies, formalised agricultural cooperatives were only introduced by the colonial authorities.[①] To some extent, their history is related to the three trajectories of agricultural structures we discussed in the previous section. In the British colonies, at the beginning of the 20th century, cotton producers in Uganda, coffee producers in Kilimanjaro, and cocoa producers in Ghana established functioning cooperatives, which correspond to the category of trade economies in West and East Africa. These cooperatives were formed to avoid intermediate exploitation and were to be legally integrated into the colonial framework. In contrast, the French authorities opted for direct intervention, giving systematic and coercive character to the cooperative initiatives. In the Belgian territories, Catholic missionaries played essential roles in setting up cooperatives, while in Lusophone Africa, the cooperative was just an adjunct to extension work. On the other hand, in Southern Africa, where peasants were systematically dispossessed of their land, large cooperatives were established by and for white farms during the apartheid era. In colonial times, even though their experience varied from region to region, African peasants did not regard themselves as the owners of cooperative institutions.

Ironically, after independence, most African states inherited the hubris approach to cooperative development to maintain the control of the rural social economy and secure political domination. Dismantling the top-down approach remains as one of the biggest challenges to cooperative development in Africa. In the 1980s and 1990s, the Structural Adjustment Programs (SAP), which was imposed by the International Monetary Fund (IMF) and the World Bank on debt-ridden countries in the South, had a mixed effect on the nature of African cooperatives, which had to survive in a neoliberal, competitive market and at the same time were forced to be more accountable to their members.[②]

It is not easy to specify the scale of cooperative activity in Africa. On a global scale, the World Cooperative Monitor (WCM) show data about 4,575 cooperatives worldwide, to which only 8 cooperatives contributed from

---

① The following description is adapted from Patrick Develtere, "Cooperative Development in Africa up to the 1990s" in Patrick Develtere, Ignace Pollet and Fredrick Wanyama (eds.), *Cooperating out of Poverty: The Renaissance of the African Cooperative Movement* (Geneva: International Labour Office, 2008); Jürgen Schwettmann, *Cooperatives and Employment in Africa* (Geneva: ILO, 1997).

② Develtere, "Cooperative Development in Africa".

Africa.[①] The United Nations estimated that in 2014, at least 1 billion people were members of 2.6 million cooperatives, and 100 million were employed by them globally. Cooperatives generated 3 trillion dollars in revenue per year,[②] which is comparable to France's economic activity. Conducting regular and comprehensive surveys is indispensable to enriching data on cooperatives in Africa. According to an ILO survey, in 2003/05, the total cooperative members in eleven African countries, Cabo Verde, Egypt, Ethiopia, Ghana, Kenya, Niger, Nigeria, South Africa, Rwanda, Senegal, and Uganda, amounted to thirty million, and the penetration rate (the ratio of cooperative members to the total population) reached 7 per cent. If we take this rate as given, as " there is usually only one cooperative member per household, and assuming an average household size of six persons, the 'cooperative density' exceeds 40% of the total population".[③]

The interest in cooperatives and small-scale peasant farming has been growing globally in recent years. The United Nations declared the year 2014 as the International Year of Family Farming. The renewed interest in peasant production was occasioned by the relative success of pro-peasant reforms in East Asia and more recently in President Lula's Brazil. Earlier, the United Nations had also celebrated the year 2012 as the Year of the Cooperatives, highlighting the interlinkages between the cooperative and peasant movements. In 2019, the United Nations Secretary-General issued a report on "Cooperatives in Social Development", highlighting cooperatives' role in achieving the Sustainable

---

① See the website of the International Cooperative Alliance. https://www.ica.coop/en/our-work/world-cooperative-monitor (accessed 20 January 2023).

② Dave Grace and Associates, *Measuring the Size and Scope of the Cooperative Economy: Results of the 2014 Global Census on Cooperatives* (Madison, WI: Dave Grace and Associates for the United Nation's Secretariat, Department of Economic and Social Affairs, Division for Social Policy and Development, 2014).

③ Patrick Develtere and Ignace Pollet, "Renaissance of African cooperatives in the 21st century: Lessons from the field", in Patrick Develtere, Ignace Pollet and Fredrick Wanyama (eds.), *Cooperating out of Poverty: The Renaissance of the African Cooperative Movement* (Geneva: International Labour Office, 2008); Schwettmann, *Cooperatives and Employment in Africa,* p. 6.

Development Goals (SDGs).[1] Agricultural cooperatives are situated where the two areas, the peasant economy and cooperatives, overlap. The main reason for market failure in a market-led economy is the asymmetry of information within or between the state, market, and community.[2] If peasants remain disorganised, their voices will be ignored before, during and after policy formulation and implementation. Then, what steps can be taken to organise grassroots voices in the countryside and empower the peasants? Here, we would like to emphasise the unique role of cooperatives.

We may conceptualise rural collective action in several ways. Burgeoning institutions include labour-managed firms, labour-owned firms, collectives, savings and credit cooperative societies (SACCOs), and various forms of cooperatives. In the 1980s and the 1990s, radical scholars held a common view that any form of rural collective action could not be envisaged in the capitalist framework.[3] However, the recognition of the importance of family farming in academic and policy circles has necessitated the rethinking of social organisations in development.[4] The cooperative appeal seems to remain steadfast.

---

[1] *Cooperatives in Social Development,* Report of the United Nations Secretary-General, A/74/206, 22 July 2019.

[2] Keijiro Otsuka and Kaliappa Kalirajan (eds.), *Community, Market and State in Development* (Basingstoke: Palgrave Macmillan, 2011). The critical dimension of community cohesion is missing in G. F. Ortmann and R. P. King, "Agricultural Cooperatives I: History, Theory and Problems", *Agrekon* 46, no. 1 (2007), pp. 18-46.

[3] Michael Reich and James Devine, "The Microeconomics of Conflict and Hierarchy in Capitalist Production", *Review of Radical Political Economics* 12, no. 4 (1981), pp. 27-45; Daniel Egan, "Toward a Marxist Theory of Labor-Managed Firms: Breaking the Degeneration Thesis", *Review of Radical Political Economics* 22, no. 4 (1990), pp. 67-86. See also Zhanping Hu, Qian Forrest Zhang, and John Donaldson, "Why Do Farmers' Cooperatives Fail in a Market Economy? Rediscovering Chayanov with the Chinese Experience", *Journal of Peasant Studies,* September 29, (2022), pp. 1-31.

[4] Rangarirai Gavin Muchetu, "Family Farms and the Markets: Examining the Level of Market-Oriented Production 15 Years after the Zimbabwe Fast Track Land Reform Programme", *Review of African Political Economy* 46, no. 159 (2019), pp. 33-54; Carlos Guanziroli, Antonio Buainain, and Alberto Sabbato, "Family Farming in Brazil: Evolution between the 1996 and 2006 Agricultural Censuses", *The Journal of Peasant Studies* 40, no. 5 (2013), pp. 817-843; Food and Agriculture Organization (FAO) and the International Fund for Agricultural Development (IFAD), *United Nations Decade of Family Farming 2019-2028. Global Action Plan,* Licence: CC BY-NC-SA 3.0 IGO (Rome: FAO and IFAD, 2019).

What then constitute a cooperative, and what make it different from a corporation or a capitalist farming enterprise? Drawing on the works by M. I. Tugan Baranovskii and K. Pazhitnov, the Russian agrarian economist, Alexander Chayanov, distinguished cooperatives from other formations.[1] To focus on the cooperative movement was to foster the values of self-help, democracy, equity, equality, and solidarity achievable through the adherence to the cooperative principles as later set down by the International Cooperative Alliance (ICA) in 1937, 1966, and 1995. Unlike profit-making in the case of capitalist organisations, cooperatives are not driven by one ultimate goal. Cooperatives with democratic structures rooted in grassroots collective action have the potential to protect their members not only from neoliberal contradictions and market failures but also from the predatory state itself.[2]

Cooperatives may want to utilise capital resources efficiently and redistribute gains among members, or they may try to fix socio-economic and political ills by taking advantage of their organisational power (the objective of the latter may include the realisation of class harmony in addition to the liberation of the peasantry from economic bondage). Otherwise, they may seek both at the same time. The ideas of Chayanov on cooperatives are appealing because he defined cooperatives through the lenses of the agency and entrepreneurship of peasants. The Chayanovian cooperative represents a chance for small-scale family farmers to enjoy large-scale benefits without losing their individuality and control of their own production process. So, what is important in the Chayanovian cooperative, and how is it relevant to Africa? In the rest of this paper, drawing on his theory, we discuss the significance of cooperatives in the context of demographic change and the resilience of family farming in Africa.

---

[1] Alexander Chayanov, *The Theory of Peasant Co-Operatives,* translated by David Wedgwood Benn (Columbus: Ohio State University Press, 1991), p. 14.

[2] Karin Wedig and Jörg Wiegratz, "Neoliberalism and the Revival of Agricultural Cooperatives: The Case of the Coffee Sector in Uganda", *Journal of Agrarian Change* 18, no. 2 (2018) pp. 348-369; See also James Scott, *Seeing Like a State: How Certain Schemes to Improve the Human Condition Have Failed* (New Haven: Yale University Press, 1998).

Chayanov, Peasants, and Cooperatives

Chayanov pointed out that a prerequisite for any successful cooperative initiative (or any other rural social policy or development program) was to understand the reality of the rural areas first.[①] For this purpose, he spent time trying to understand the Russian countryside before proffering any type of solutions to the challenges peasants faced. In generic terms, let us consider the relevance of Chayanov's theory to the organisation of cooperatives from two perspectives.

First, while class differentiation deepens in rural areas, peasants' attitude towards cooperatives begins to diverge. With the penetration of capitalist relationships, the polarisation of the peasantry proceeded in the Russian countryside, even though its pace was not as quick as hypothesised by V. I. Lenin.[②] A similar trend is also evident in Africa; the African peasantry is not a homogenous class but consists of several classes or sub-class categories.[③] In the course of land and agrarian reforms, such differentiation may become more visible, thereby making the Chayanovian cooperatives even more relevant. Chayanov observed six peasant classes with different motivations and resources to join the cooperative – penury, poor, poor-middle, middle, middle-rich and rich (though Chayanov did not use these terms). Some were too rich, while others were too poor to participate in cooperative activities. Therefore, an appropriate understanding of the configuration of these groups in agrarian society is critically important.[④] In the African agrarian structure, the poor to the middle stratum tend to be a majority, which is considered ideal for popular participation in cooperatives. The middle to the middle-rich can participate without

---

① Chayanov, *The Theory of Peasant Co-Operatives;* Alexander Chayanov, "On Differentiation of the Peasant Economy", *Russian Peasant Studies 4,* no. 4 (2019), pp. 6-21.

② Henry Bernstein, "V. I. Lenin and A. V. Chayanov: Looking Back, Looking Forward", *Journal of Peasant Studies* 36, no. 1 (2009), pp. 55-81.

③ Sam Moyo, Praveen Jha, and Paris Yeros, "The Classical Agrarian Question: Myth, Reality and Relevance Today", *Agrarian South: Journal of Political Economy* 2, no. 1 (2013), pp. 93-119.

④ Chayanov, *The Theory of Peasant Co-Operatives,* chap. 2.

government help, while the poor may require some enabling subsidy from the state for them to be productive and participate. The rich tend to be antagonistic to cooperatives. The strong presence of the "middle" provides fertile ground for the growth of cooperatives in Africa.

Peasant households are mainly motivated by the use value (food security) rather than the exchange value (market sales). Typically, such a household has limited capital-intensive technologies and predominantly relies on family labour. Being neglectful of these facts, most agricultural policies implemented in the colonial and independence era in Africa have encouraged export crop production. The result has been chronic food insecurity at the level of households. At the same time, peasant economies are not totally insulated from the market economy. They are not autarkic but sell and buy, and as such are "half" commercialised.[①]

Let us now move to the second perspective. While engaging in market transactions to some extent, the unit of production and consumption of peasant economies is a family household, which gives cooperatives distinctively decentralised characteristics. Chayanov argued that the productivity of the peasant household could be proportional to the size of the family household. The relationship is so because the labour for the family farmer is provided for free by the household members as opposed to the capitalist farmer that would hire non-family labour. Family labour is furnished according to the function of the necessity of subsistence and the tiresomeness of work (drudgery), which is expressed as the consumer/worker (C/W) ratio. The domestic labour supply increases up to a point where its marginal utility of output equals the marginal disutility of work. In this equation, the generational structure of the family should be taken into consideration, as not everyone can provide labour in a large family. There are dependents (consumers but not producers – small children and the elderly) and labour providers (both producers and consumers – adults and working-age children), and the ratio of these family members determines the

---

① Chayanov's understanding seems to apply not only to labour-scarce but also to labour-abundant economies. Philip C. C. Huang, "Is 'Family Farms' the Way to Develop Chinese Agriculture?" *Rural China: An International Journal of History and Social Science* 11 (2014), pp. 189-221.

productivity of the households. The smaller becomes the ratio (more working-age children – theoretically from 15 years old), the less each member should work to achieve household consumption, releasing more labour hours for surplus production for the market.

Generally, the gradual fertility decline (the shrinkage of small children) will conduce to a decline in the C/W ratio. For example, a family of two working adults and two dependent children will have a C/W ratio of 4/2 = 2, while a family of two working adults and two working-age children (providing half labour hours each because of school) will have a C/W ratio of 4/(2+0.5+0.5) = 1.33. The family structure determines its lower and upper living standards and the degree of economic activity required for survival.[①] This means that as the size of the family increases, so is the labour available to the peasant family, thereby increasing the agricultural productivity per household. Thus, the demographic dividend will benefit the peasantry, and villages made up of family farmers are expected to play a significant role in absorbing excess labour during the demographic and industrial transition.

This nature of peasant economies also has significant implications for the organisation of cooperatives. While the forms of family and kinship vary from region to region, family units in which consumption and production are jointly carried out cannot be so large.[②] As long as the unit that constitutes a cooperative is the autonomous family (as a decision-making unit), governance of cooperatives will be based on coordination rather than through top-down control. There are reasons for families to participate in cooperatives. As family labour increases, subsistence needs will soon be met, and more labour can be redirected

---

① A. V. Chayanov, *The Theory of Peasant Economy,* edited by Daniel Thorner, Basile Kerblay, and R.E.F. Smith (Manchester: Manchester University Press, 1986) pp. 57-59. Lal Thilakarathne and Youkichi Yanagita, "The Chayanov Concept of a Peasant Farm Economy", *Research Bulletin of the Faculty of College of Agriculture Gifu University* 61 (1996), pp. 45-59. Chayanov hypothesise a big family with up to nine children (which is not so common in African families). See also our Table 1.

② While we do not assume that a larger kin unit can be an effective unit of decision-making in terms of labour allocation, production, and consumption, we agree that more empirical research is needed especially about the mechanism of intra-family decision-making. E. A. Hammel, "Chayanov Revisited: A Model for the Economics of Complex Kin Units", *The Proceedings of the National Academy of Sciences (PNAS)* 102, no. 19 (2005), pp. 7043-7046. Chayanov, *The Theory of Peasant Cooperatives,* pp. 3-5.

to market-oriented production and non-farm activities or to the work on other farms. However, farmers are at a disadvantage if they remain isolated both in the market and in their relations with the sometimes exploitative government. Peasants need to be federated while maintaining their autonomy.[①]

Prospects for Peasant Cooperatives in Africa: The Case of Zimbabwe

In this section, we briefly discuss the role of peasant cooperatives in the 21st-century socio-economic landscape of Africa. Against the backdrop of radical demographic transition and the renewed prospects for a peasant path, what sort of programs and enabling environment should the national governments and other actors create for cooperatives? We have explored the theory of Chayanov at an abstract level so far, but how much do his ideas weigh in the contemporary African agrarian structures?

Let us give an example of Zimbabwe, where a drastic land reform gave rise to the emergence of an agrarian structure comprising A1 (small-scale), A2 (large-scale), and CA (Communal Area). A1 and A2 represent the areas resettled by various groups of peasants, mainly in 2000, while CA represents impoverished subsistence farming areas demarcated during the colonial era. In the section on three trajectories, we indicated that continental land grabbing and peasant resistance might lead to a pan-African convergence of agrarian structure towards a Southern African pattern, where land issues attract keen attention from the public. The case of Zimbabwe may be pertinent and to some extent representative in this regard.

The 2015 baseline survey conducted by Sam Moyo African Institute for Agrarian Studies (SMAIAS) found that 89.7 per cent of the Zimbabwe farmers utilised their own family labour for manual work on the farm, which means that

---

① Along with the demographic transition of African society, the C/W ratio is expected to decrease up to a point at which capital becomes the primary limiting factor of rural development. This gives scope for savings and credit cooperative organisations (SACCOs) together with production cooperatives. See more in Lal and Yanagita, "The Chayanov Concept of a Peasant Farm Economy", 1996, pp. 48-49.

a majority of Zimbabwean farmers were considered peasants.[1] A subsequent research based on a follow-up survey conducted in 2018/19 attempted to test the applicability of the Chayanovian theory of rural differentiation to the case of Zimbabwe. The cluster analysis of the household data demonstrated the emergence of five peasant classes in post-land reform Zimbabwe – penury, poor, middle, middle-rich and rich. Major determinants of clustering included the practice of selling and hiring casual (non-permanent) labour, the size of non-agricultural income, and the extent of land utilization. In other words, farmers were characterised and grouped depending on their intensive use of land and family labour. The higher degree of commercialisation and the larger size of households tend to coincide: from poor (3.84), middle (3.98) to middle-rich (4.52).[2]

The age classification of five peasant clusters reveals a big presence of children (0-9 and 10-19 in Table 1) in poor and middle clusters in not only absolute but also relative terms. Peasants in these clusters tend to rely on family labour and cultivate their own land intensively, thereby providing a fertile ground for equitable cooperative activities. The essence of the discussion about the C/W ratio was that the more the number of workers in a peasant household, the more the labour available for subsistence, which eventually contributes to income-generating activities even beyond the farm. In this regard, Chayanov noted the role of supporting work given by children after school (especially the 15-19 age group). The thickness of the 10-19 age group (24.6 per cent of the total and 26.0 per cent of the poor households) is a case in point.

---

[1] In the same study, a trimodal agrarian structure at the national level was highlighted, while a later study confirmed the persistence of this trimodal structure at local and regional levels. Sam Moyo, Walter Chambati, Freedom Mazwi, and Rangarirai Gavin Muchetu, "Inter-District Household Survey: Follow up to the Baseline Survey," Harare, Zimbabwe, 2015 (mimeo); Freedom Mazwi, Rangarirai Gavin Muchetu, and George T. Mudimu, "Revisiting the Trimodal Agrarian Structure as a Social Differentiation Analysis Framework in Zimbabwe: A Study," *Agrarian South: Journal of Political Economy* 4, no. 10 (2021), pp. 60-73.

[2] Rangarirai Gavin Muchetu, *After Radical Land Reform: Restructuring Agricultural Cooperatives in Zimbabwe and Japan* (Bamenda: Langaa RPCIG, 2021), chap. 7; The discussion of this section is based on the questionnaire survey targeting eight agricultural cooperatives in Goromonzi District, Zimbabwe. The survey was conducted by Muchetu in 2018 and 2019.

Table 1 Age Structure of Cooperative Members' Households
(Goromonzi, Zimbabwe)

Age Range	Classification of the Peasants										
	Penury		Poor		Middle		Mid-dle-Rich		Rich		Total	
	No.	%	No.	%	No.	%	No.	%	No.	%	No.	%
0-9	10	15.4	42	14.4	44	16.7	19	13.6	1	5.0	116	14.9
10-19	17	26.2	76	26.0	64	24.3	31	22.1	4	20.0	192	24.6
20-29	8	12.3	55	18.8	48	18.3	23	16.4	3	15.0	137	17.6
30-39	7	10.8	42	14.4	28	10.6	14	10.0	2	10.0	93	11.9
40-49	5	7.7	22	7.5	30	11.4	18	12.9	4	20.0	79	10.1
50-59	10	15.4	22	7.5	24	9.1	18	12.9	3	15.0	77	9.9
60-69	7	10.8	17	5.8	16	6.1	10	7.1	2	10.0	52	6.7
70-	1	1.5	16	5.5	9	3.4	7	5.0	1	5.0	34	4.4
Total	65	100.0	292	100.0	263	100	140	100	20	100.0	780	100.0

Source: 2018/19 survey data

The retirement age for farmers in Africa varies from country to country. Mostly, African peasants continue working as long as they are able to physically and mentally perform the tasks required for farming. In Table 1, the group of people aged over 70 is 4.4 per cent of the population, while the 0-10 group is 14.9 per cent. The C/W ratio of rural Zimbabwe should remain very low with relatively high productivity (production per capita).[①] People without knowledge of rural Africa sometimes make ungrounded claims. In place of a population explosion, it is argued that rural ageing is becoming a big problem in Africa. In fact, however, the centre of gravity of Africa's rural population continues to

---

① We can simulate changes in the C/W ratio for all households, taking into account fertility and mortality rates (the effect of technological change is difficult to calculate). Results will be presented in a separate paper.

be the youth,[1] and the case of Zimbabwe is no exception. On the other hand, comparing the size of the two age groups, 0-9 and 10-19, we can notice that an endless population expansion is also a myth as long as rural Zimbabwe is concerned. The shrinkage of the 30-39 age group should indicate a massive migration out of villages. Cooperative activities are expected to serve as a magnet to attenuate the young villagers' urge to leave for towns.

While debates over cooperatives continue to divide opinions in academia and policy-makers, African cooperatives prove their usefulness in everyday farming activities. The post-reform agriculture in Zimbabwe resulted in a rise in cooperative formations, albeit many remain unregistered. As Rangarirai Gavin Muchetu found, the state, NGOs and even the private sector utilise some forms of group approaches when engaging with the peasants to cut transaction costs.[2] As shown in Figure 6 (based on the field survey data collected in 2018/2019), Zimbabwean peasants created or joined cooperatives to improve their livelihoods (34 per cent), empower themselves against exploitation (22 per cent), address market failures (16 per cent), and increase production (15 per cent).

The cooperative movement in the resettled areas seems to have been given a new life by the process of the land reform that continued until recently. Data presented in Table 2 reveals that cooperatives were formed by peasants themselves (98 per cent) in the resettled areas (A1), and 64 per cent of the cooperatives were formed under the instruction and guidance of NGOs in CA, the subsistence areas. The presence of the state was still felt in CA, where around 20 per cent of the cooperatives were formed under some state programs or initiatives. And, those who had joined the cooperative realised significant benefits after joining them in the form of better addressing market failures (21.7 per cent) and increased production (19.9 per cent) in A1 and in the form of empowered members (25.3 per cent) and better economic development like increased income (23.0 per cent) in CA (Figure 7). While the cooperative movement from below presents a potential for genuine cooperatives in

---

① Felix Kwame Yeboah and T S Jayne, "The Myth of Africa's Ageing Farmers", *Rural 21: The International Journal of Rural Development* 54, no. 03/20 (2020), pp. 39-41.

② Muchetu, *After Radical Land Reforms.*

Zimbabwe and beyond, they still require state support (policy frameworks) and private sector support (equitable and genuinely "free" markets).

Figure 6 Motivation for Establishing Cooperatives

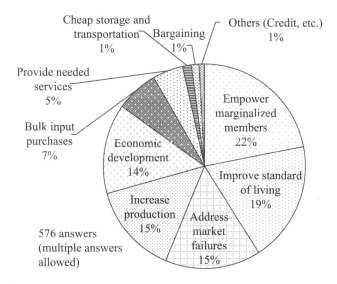

Source: 2018/19 survey data

Table 2 Initiator of Cooperatives

	A1		CA		Total	
	No.	%	No.	%	No.	%
Political party	1	1.1	0	0.0	1	0.5
Extension officer	0	0.0	1	1.0	1	0.5
NGO	1	1.1	64	64.0	65	33.9
Local authority	0	0.0	4	4.0	4	2.1
Local political leader	0	0.0	4	4.0	4	2.1
Local farmers or coop members	90	97.8	7	7.0	97	50.5
DDP (Government)	0	0.0	20	20.0	20	10.4
Total	92	100.0	100	100.0	192	100.0

Source: 2018/19 survey data

Figure 7 Benefit from Cooperatives

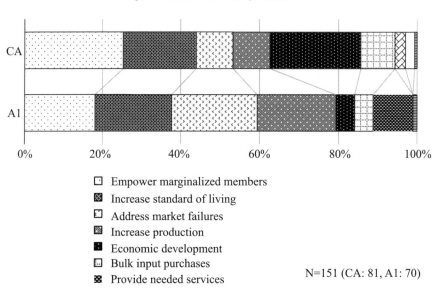

☐ Empower marginalized members
▨ Increase standard of living
☒ Address market failures
▨ Increase production
■ Economic development
▣ Bulk input purchases
✖ Provide needed services

N=151 (CA: 81, A1: 70)

Source: 2018/19 survey data

Utilising the community-state-market framework, Muchetu proposed socio-economic and political reformation of the state, the peasantry, and the cooperative structure itself (see Table 3). This is not derived from an abstract, idealistic neo-institutional model but based on a close examination of grassroots cooperative attempts, particularly in Zimbabwe, to draw power from *bricolage*.[①] Each of the three plays a crucial role in agrarian development in Africa, with the government creating macro conditions for long-term national development. On top of the list, as shown in the case studies on Kenya, Uganda, and Zimbabwe, there is the need to secure the political will on the part of the leaders.[②] Once such a will is established, implementing the rest (policy reform, farmer certification, and effective subsidies, for example) becomes much more

---

[①] As for organisational ingenuity utilising local knowledge and resources at hand, see Ellen Mangnus and Mirjam Schoonhoven-Speijer, "Navigating Dynamic Contexts: African Cooperatives as Institutional Bricoleurs", *International Journal of Agricultural Sustainability* 18, no. 2 (2020), pp. 99-112.

[②] Wedig and Wiegratz, "Neoliberalism and the Revival of Agricultural Cooperatives"; Muchetu, *After Radical Land Reform*; Francis Fanuel Lyimo, *Rural Cooperation: In the Cooperative Movement in Tanzania* (Dar es Salaam: Mkuki Na Nyota Publishers and African Books Collective, 2008).

Table 3 Creating an Enabling Environment for Cooperative Development

State	Peasantry	Cooperative Structure
· Economic environment · Political environment · Policy instrument · State subsidies · Agricultural training and education policy · Farmer and cooperative certification	· Socio-economic, behavioural reform · Self-emancipation from the dependency syndrome · Improvement in management · Agricultural training	· New 3-tier membership structure · Strong and independent national/regional federation · Stacked/staged cooperative development · Cooperative identity · Importance of SACCOs and the cooperative bank

Source: Muchetu, *After Radical Land Reform*, pp. 318-343

manageable, though all things cannot be added automatically.

In the cooperative development process, the peasant members are expected to play a pivotal role. In addition to the age-old recommendation of improving management skills through education and skills training, the cooperative members should also change their mindsets. Nurturing the sense of self-help will help cooperative members overcome the dependency syndrome, one form of colonial mentality perpetuated through various subsidy programs, which Dambisa Moyo identified as a major impediment to rural development.[①] Cooperatives and their members should be able to ensure the election of high-integrity leaders who can move the organisations forward. In his book, Muchetu made a set of suggestions for the effective restructuring of African cooperatives. In addition to developing SACCOs and cooperative banks, a suggestion was made to introduce stacked, multi-stage cooperative development (start as a single-purpose cooperative and then gradually develop into a multi-purpose cooperative), as well as the idea of distributing cooperative benefits to non-members in the community through a three-tier membership system.[②]

---

① Dambisa Moyo, *Dead Aid: Why Aid Is Not Working and How There Is a Better Way for Africa* (New York: Farrar, Strause and Giroux, 2009).

② See more in Muchetu, *After Radical Land Reform,* chap. 8.

There is an abundance of evidence that shows high women participation in cooperatives in countries such as Tanzania and Japan,[1] with women's membership in some non-gender-specific cooperatives reaching as high as 65 per cent and 95 per cent, respectively.[2] In Africa, in addition to these general cooperatives, women have their own cooperatives to fight inequality and social exclusion, which address gender-related agrarian questions, including inequalities in land ownership and access to education, skills, information and finance. In all these respects, cooperatives can be instrumental in empowering women so that persistent gender inequalities are eradicated. There is enormous potential for the cooperatives to bring women further to the front line of the agrarian struggle and promote their agency.[3]

Conclusions

If the labour supply in Africa increases when India, following China, enters a phase of depopulation, Africa's demographic transition would be a magnificent blessing for the global economy. However, if the ever-growing industrial workforce does not have access to relatively cheap wage goods (food), then wage costs will desperately increase, and Africa will be unable to compete with other regions. A precondition for industrialisation is to raise the productivity of agriculture, especially of staple food. While Africa's population is expected to grow throughout the 21st century, fertility rates will gradually decline, and concomitantly, the proportion of the working-age population in the workforce will increase in Africa. If institutional conditions improve, individual peasant households will escape the stage of bare survival and, rural areas may enter a

---

① The Japanese consumer cooperatives are predominantly run by women as they seek to purchase safe quality food directly from the farmers. The majority of them are urban women.

② Frederick O. Wanyama, *Cooperatives and the Sustainable Development Goals: A Contribution to the Post-2015 Development Debate: A Policy Brief* (Brussels: International Co-operative Alliance, Geneva: Cooperatives Unit, Enterprises Department, International Labour Organization, 2014), p. 7.

③ Cooperative Facility for Africa (COOP AFRICA), *Empower Rural Women – End Poverty and Hunger: The Potential of African Cooperatives,* ILO Office for Kenya, Somalia, Tanzania, 2007. https://www.ilo.org/global/docs/WCMS_174990/lang--en/index.htm (accessed 20 January 2023).

virtuous circle of prosperity.

Nevertheless, as capital investments in agriculture advance and mechanisation progresses, a surplus population can be generated on a socially unacceptable scale. Would it be possible to keep the talented people moored in the countryside, conserve environmental resources, and provide ample food for urban residents by promoting labour-intensive family farming rather than capital-intensive gigantic farms? Can we not gradually increase agricultural productivity and carefully nurture the use value in communities, while ensuring popular participation and empowering women?

In this paper, we have seen that the activities of cooperatives have enormous potential in this regard. Peasants will never perish. In the second half of the twenty-first century, cooperating villages may be able to accommodate young aspirant women and men, thereby checking the pace of unruly urbanisation, as the peasantry is not just a useful object of a temporary class alliance. The peasant path embodies a powerful liberatory idea that has evolved from Marx, Engels, Kautsky, Chayanov and Lenin to Mao, Fanon, Cabral, and Moyo.[1] The endurance of the idea of the centrality of peasants is impressive. By learning from the wisdom of African peasants and respecting their ownership and experience of self-organisation, China and other Asian development partners of Africa can make their projects sustainable and strengthen their presence as true friends of the African peoples.

While holding high ideals to decolonise the mind of people, agricultural cooperatives in Africa will grow and flourish as autonomous organisations committed to justice, equity, and efficiency. In 2018, the Alliance Africa Agricultural Cooperative Organisation (AAACO) was established as a part of the ICA, with the expectation of becoming an effective pan-African federation of cooperatives.[2] Building on the resilience of peasants, federated cooperatives

---

[1] Moyo et al., "The Classical Agrarian Question", p. 105.

[2] https://icaafrica.coop/en/alliance-africa-agricultural-cooperative-organisation-aaaco (accessed 20 January 2023). Cooperatives are expected to contribute to "Social Solidarity Economy" in Africa. See the research conducted in Cameroon, Morocco, Senegal, South Africa, and Tunisia. International Labour Organization (ILO), *Social and Solidarity Economy: Social Innovation Catalyst in Africa?* (Geneva: ILO, 2022).

will have to meet both long-term and short-term challenges, which go beyond the immediate needs of agricultural family enterprises.

Long-term challenges include how to respond strategically to demographic transformation as well as to the increased engagement of traditional and emerging donors, which sometimes compete fiercely with each other in Africa. Short-term challenges include how to organise effective responses of rural populations to sudden, critical, and pervasive threats such as COVID-19. Although the 2021 report of the United Nations Secretary-General highlighted the role of cooperatives in "building back better" from the pandemic, social distancing and other restrictive measures appear to have negatively affected the resilience of agricultural cooperatives. It was extremely difficult for rural leaders to reach out to their members.[1] However, as long as peasant families harbour the motivation and expectation to organise themselves, agricultural cooperatives will rise up time and again from below.

---

[1] *Cooperatives in Social Development,* Report of the United Nations Secretary-General, A/76/209, 22 July 2021; Nicola Francesconi, Fleur Wouterse, and Dorothy Birungi Namuyiga, "Agricultural Cooperatives and COVID-19 in Southeast Africa: The Role of Managerial Capital for Rural Resilience", *Sustainability* 13, no. 3 (2021), 1046. Surveys about COVID-19 were conducted in Madagascar, Malawi, Rwanda, and Uganda.

变局下的非洲能源转型与路径创新

罗 楠[*]

摘 要：世界正在经历百年未有之大变局，而非洲能源转型的内涵也在这种变局中愈加复杂。2020年以来，以气候变化、新冠疫情、俄乌冲突、地区发展等要素为内容的全球形势，塑造着非洲能源的多重挑战，从现代化、清洁化、可及性、能源安全等多个维度对非洲能源转型提出要求。当发达国家在世界变局中自顾不暇时，非洲各国采取积极行动探索能源转型的创新之道。从应对之策可以看出，非洲国家越来越重视激发内生的可持续发展动力，而非仅仅依赖国际社会的外部援助。非洲着力发展新能源，因为传统开发和应用路径不足以应对多重能源挑战，亟待自主探索更多创新开发之路。本文基于世界变局下非洲能源转型的多重目标，围绕离网型太阳能这一分布式新能源方式探讨非洲的能源创新实践，试图探索非洲能源发展的未来新路径。

关键词：非洲 能源 离网型太阳能 能动性 可持续发展

引 言

作为现代经济增长和繁荣的关键，能源的持续有效供给影响着人类的可持续生产、生活与安全。在联合国可持续发展目标中，第七项就是确保人人获得负担得起、可靠和可持续的现代能源。如果将可持续发展整体目标视作一个金字塔，那么能源目标就是位于塔底作为实现人最基本发展需求的要素而存在。放眼全球，拉丁美洲和加勒比地区、东亚和东南亚等多个地区的电力供应在近年都取得长足进展。相比之下，全

---

* 罗楠，中山大学马克思主义学院助理教授。

球超过 80% 无法接入电力的人口生活在撒哈拉以南非洲。[①] 自 2020 年以来，新冠疫情大暴发、全球能源结构转型和国际格局动荡等复杂的国际政治经济因素使得非洲能源发展更加举步维艰。2021 年撒哈拉以南非洲地区无法获得电力和清洁能源的人数，较 2019 年增加了 4%，实际上抵消了之前五年取得的所有进展。[②] 在严重的能源赤字面前，非洲能否实现可持续发展的能源目标充满变数。[③]

主流的国际发展话语认为，非洲的能源发展需要依靠外部力量的扶持，才能获得能源发展所需的工业基础和能源治理能力。[④] 这是一种基于传统能源发展模式的思路，即依靠政府能源部门自上而下的规模化开发和国家电网的集中传输分配。由于非洲大部分国家工业化水平较低，自身不具备有力的政策制度支持、成熟的技术和完善的基础设施等条件，想要使得能源规模化开发的条件全部到位，需要借助大量外部的技术和资金投入以推动能源设施建设的第一步。可现实是，国际社会对非洲能源转型的投入与支持长期不到位。例如，美国的"通电非洲"（Power Africa）项目计划到 2030 年为非洲提供超过 3 万兆瓦的新增发电

---

① 国际能源署：《全球能源回顾 2021》，2022 年 2 月，https://www.iea.org/reports/global-energy-review-2021?language=zh，2022-3-18。

② IEA, *Africa Energy Outlook* 2022, June 2022, https://www.iea.org/reports/africa-energy-outlook-2022, 2022-11-25. p 35.

③ United Nations Economic Commission for Africa, *Economic Report on Africa* 2021: *Addressing Poverty And Vulnerability In Africa During The Covid*-19 *Pandemic*, 2022, https://repository.uneca.org/bitstream/handle/10855/47592/ERA%202021%20En%20%28b12002963%29.pdf?sequence=10&isAllowed=y, 2022-11-25.

④ 如 Ann Johnston and Albert Sasson eds., *New technologies and development: Science and technology as factors of change: Impact of recent and foreseeable scientific and technological progress on the evolution of societies, especially in the developing countries (Notebooks on world problems)*. Paris: UNESCO, 1986; Rebecca Clay, "A continent in Chaos," *Environment Health Perspective*, Vol.102, No. 12, 1997, 1018-1023; Ashley Eva Millar and Malan Rietveld, "Natural Resources: A Blessing or a Curse?" in Ewout Frankema et al. *The African History of Development: An Online Textbook for a New Generation of African Students and Teachers*, African Economic History Network (AEHN), 2022, Chapter 16; Ramez Abubakr Badeeb et al., "The evolution of the natural resource curse thesis: A critical literature survey," *Resources Policy*, Vol. 51, 2017, pp.123-134. 从这些文献可以一窥学界和政界对于非洲能源治理的保守态度。他们的主要思路还是延续着传统能源发展逻辑，即非洲自身缺乏能源治理能力，其能源发展需要以大量外部投资和援助支撑的国家电力系统为基础。

量，但截至 2019 年该项目的新增发电量仅为不到 4 千兆瓦。[①] 近年来，传统发达国家在国际变局冲击下自顾不暇，导致有限的外部支持进一步被压缩。"外来论"视角的局限性在于，它不仅在实践中无法很好地解决非洲国家现代化和人口增长迫在眉睫的能源需求痛点，并且在认识论上忽视了非洲本土探索能源发展的努力。在内部需求迫切和外部支持薄弱的双向压力下，非洲如何探索能源发展的自主新路径，是一个重要课题。正是因为非洲国家所面临的能源发展挑战之复杂性和紧迫性，非洲行为体探索能源应用新途径的各类尝试和努力更应该被研究者和政策界关注到。只有将非洲的本土知识与实践纳入政策和学术的观察范围中，才能因地制宜地建设现代能源体系。[②]

本文结合非洲所处的世界变局分析该地区能源转型的任务，认为传统能源的开发模式不足以应对现代化、清洁化、安全化、可获取性等复杂的能源发展需求，并在此基础上探析能源路径创新的可能。文章以肯尼亚的离网型太阳能市场为例，展示非洲发展可再生能源尤其是太阳能的重要性，以及新能源应该以何种适当的方式生产和供应。文章对非洲能源发展这一议题给予了除了技术和制度层面以外的更多关于本土推动力的观察和理解，并从能源推及其他领域，思考这是否体现了非洲国家整体发展进路的迥异之处。

一、世界变局下非洲能源转型的多重挑战

能源是奠定国家经济发展的重要基础和动力，也是维护国家政治与社会稳定的资源保障，因此非洲各国需要有利的国内国际政治环境来支持能源相关的支柱性产业。20 世纪末、21 世纪初，非洲国家克服了经济结构调整和国内政治安全动荡的阵痛后进入新一轮和平发展期，各国竞先施展自主发展的雄心并制订中长期工业化与现代化战略规划，确定

---

① 马汉智：《美国"电力非洲倡议"新进展》，澎湃政务，2020 年 7 月，https://m.thepaper.cn/baijiahao_8493293。

② 张永宏、王达：《撒哈拉以南非洲应对环境与气候变化的本土选择》，《西亚非洲》2022 年第 1 期，第 31—50 页。

清晰的能源转型目标，即通过开发和使用清洁能源实现电力普及，实现能源的现代化，促使非洲整体进入电气化时代。能源不仅关系到非洲国家能否实现长期自主发展的远景，更直接影响非洲的社会发展与民生福利。目前非洲通电率仅约40%，有超过6.4亿非洲人生活在无电地区。非洲能源的现代化任务首先需要兼顾经济适用性与可获取性，让人民尽快切实获得电力。[①]

1. 全球气候变化趋势下的能源清洁化

随着气候变暖问题逐渐取得国际社会共识，致力于控制温室气体减排的能源转型成为国际趋势，全球能源格局正在世界范围内发生深刻的变化。一方面，以美国、丹麦、德国等国为首的发达行为体已逐步为本国搭建起以可再生能源为基础的能源供应系统，成为应对气候变化的有力倡导者和全球领先的参与者。另一方面，国际资本在传统能源投资趋势下降成为全球趋势。作为最大的燃煤电厂境外融资方，2021年中国承诺不再新建境外煤电项目，这势必对非洲获取电力投资产生影响。中国气候变化事务特使解振华表示："在绿色低碳发展的国际大趋势下，全球资金正在大规模转向绿色产业，非洲可乘此东风，加速相关产业布局，在打造产业发展新赛道的同时，提升自身应对气候变化的能力。"[②]

能源清洁化不仅仅是全球能源格局转变的外部要求，更是来自非洲发展过程中绕不开的内部需求。非洲是遭受全球气候变化和生态环境退化影响最严重的地区之一，且气候变化加剧了尚未解决的饥荒问题，甚至导致安全问题——许多证据揭示了环境恶化阻碍和平与发展。[③]此外，传统能源的不当获取和使用方式（如伐木、燃烧粪便或使用煤油），也对人们的生活环境造成显见的破坏，严重影响生存条件与生活质量。全球由于空气污染而导致肺部疾病死亡的人数中，有超过一半是因为使用

---

① 王珊:《助力非洲新能源发展，中非共同打造绿色发展新模式》，中国环境网，2022年11月18日，http://cenews.com.cn/news.html?aid=1018953, 2022-11-25.

② 同上。

③ 例如尼日利亚北部生态环境退化与博科圣地扩张之间的相关性，以及肯尼亚北部生态破坏与索马里恐怖主义入侵的关系。

煤炭或者木材做燃料烹饪和空气不流通及室内空气污染所导致的；^①在非洲，普遍存在焚烧农作物秸秆、产生大量烟尘现象，加之室内煤油或柴油不完全燃烧释放的有毒物质，都使得空气污染正在成为同艾滋病和疟疾一样威胁非洲人口健康的头号杀手之一。^②

最易受气候变化影响的非洲（排放量仅占世界总量的 4%，是世界上人均排放量最低的地区），同时由于缺乏资金与技术又是适应气候变化能力最脆弱的地区。关于非洲能否通过全球投资实现能源转型，目前存在不同的观点，有的研究认为国际金融机构撤出传统能源项目的趋势将促使非洲主要发展新能源；^③也有研究发现，当全球在致力于实现能源绿色转型的时候，外国金融机构仍在非洲不断投资化石能源，这进一步将非洲锁困在了一个高碳排放、极度脆弱性之间的不断恶性循环中。^④总之，非洲大陆摆脱化石能源依赖、向低碳清洁能源的转型异常艰难。非洲内部对此也存在争议，特别是财政严重依赖原油出口的国家和其他国家之间的主张明显不同。

在俄乌冲突带来欧洲能源短缺、各国纷纷加大与非洲合作开发天然气，特别是欧洲国家急于寻找替代俄罗斯能源供应的背景之下，《联合国气候变化框架公约》第二十七次缔约方大会（COP27）在埃及沙姆沙伊赫举行，非洲能源发展何去何从似乎又站在一个新的十字路口上。大会上，非洲各国政府提出三大诉求：认识到非洲的特殊情况、气候融资及清洁能源转型。"非洲的特殊情况"，是指其温室气体排放量与所遭受的气候变化负面影响之间的不对等性。包括南非、肯尼亚在内的一些非洲气候活动家认为，COP27 更加关注非洲天然气的开发，而天然气作为

---

① WHO, *9 out of 10 people worldwide breathe polluted air, but more countries are taking action*, May 2, 2018, https://www.who.int/news/item/02-05-2018-9-out-of-10-people-worldwide-breathe-polluted-air-but-more-countries-are-taking-action, 2022-11-25.

② Samantha Fisher et al. "Air pollution and development in Africa: impacts on health, the economy, and human capital," *Lancet Planet Health*, 2021 (5), p. 683.

③ 非洲咨研：《气候变化与非洲发展概述》，发展论坛·气候变化，第一期，2020 年 8 月，https://mp.weixin.qq.com/s/a5JV2nEzYYh1DdYcA4FqQw，2021-8-20。

④ 350 Africa et al., "Locked Out of A Just Transition: Fossil Fuel Financing in Africa," March 3, 2022, https://www.banktrack.org/download/locked out of a just transition fossil fuel financing in africa/07 md banktrack fossil fuels africa rpt hr 1.pdf, 2022-3-30.

化石燃料不仅不能缓解气候变化的问题，也无法支撑非洲经济长久发展。但非洲各国领导人回应称，西方国家在使用更具污染性的其他化石燃料（煤炭和石油），因此也不应阻止非洲开发相对清洁的天然气以提高非洲大陆的生活水平。[①] 也就是说，外部和内部呼声都推动着非洲国家的能源清洁化转型，但同时如何使之与急切的工业化发展要求相适应和平衡也是题中应有之义；即使停止使用化石燃料、将每个发电站都转向可再生能源，非洲国家往往仍需被迫开发其油田，从而为这一过渡转型筹集资金。如坦桑尼亚提出了 2050 年实现 100% 清洁能源供电的目标，但该国目前规划的大型电站仍全部为燃油电厂、燃气电厂。[②] 总之，非洲国家需要在实施本国工业化等发展目标的同时，追求开发侧与用能侧加速清洁能源对化石能源的替代、减少能源系统的碳排放、提高清洁能源在整个能源结构中的占比。总的来说，实现能源结构的低碳化，任重而道远。

2. 新冠疫情冲击下的能源贫困

能源贫困通常是指发展中国家的人们无法获得充足且稳定的现代能源，往往包括现代能源的可获取性和可负担性两个问题。2020 年初以来的全球新冠疫情大流行从这两个方面都对非洲追求能源可持续的努力造成了冲击。在可获取性方面，新冠疫情加剧了许多非洲能源公司尤其是电力公司本已岌岌可危的财务状况，削弱了能源部门提供公共服务的能力，导致整个大陆的发电能力受到影响。应对疫情冲击而采取的紧急救济计划虽然减轻了因疫情而贫困的终端用户电费支付负担，但同时往往严重限制了能源部门的运营成本和偿债能力。[③] 在 2020 年初因新冠疫情导致的封锁期间，近 60% 的非洲公用企业运营成本收益，没有恢复到新冠疫情大流行前的水平，其中进口燃料用于发电的国有企业受到的打击

---

① CNN, "Activists hoped Egypt's COP27 would bring a focus on Africa. They were disappointed," November 17, 2022, http://edition.cnn.com/2022/11/17/africa/cop27-egypt-africa-climate-intl-cmd/index.html, 2022-11-25.

② 张锐：《非洲能源转型的内涵、进展与挑战》，《西亚非洲》2022 年第 1 期，第 56 页。

③ IEA, *Africa Energy Outlook 2022*, June 2022, https://www.iea.org/reports/africa-energy-outlook-2022, 2022-11-25. p. 40.

最大。非洲的输配电网建设进程本来推进缓慢，而且许多既有能源供应基础设施亟须扩建和维修，新冠疫情开始后的财政困境基本上使得基础设施新建和维修工作都停滞不前。

就可负担性而言，疫情阴霾下全球经济复苏极不平衡，供应链和投资周期的中断，导致各类能源价格上涨，与能源相关的设备价格也上涨，这对非洲大多数家庭的生活产生了严重影响。在肯尼亚，不断上涨的液化石油气价格，导致液化石油气在贫困家庭月收入中的占比从7.5%增加到10%以上；在尼日利亚，该比例甚至翻了一番，从3.3%上升到7%。[1] 新冠疫情导致项目延误和家庭收入的下降，使得人们负担首次能源供应或维持最近获得能源的能力下降，从而导致现代能源供应受阻，抑制了非洲扩大清洁烹饪燃料使用的努力。液化石油气价格的上涨，导致非洲许多家庭重新使用木柴等污染性烹饪燃料，对人类健康和森林砍伐造成严重的后果。由于新冠疫情大流行，部分原本使用清洁燃料和技术的人迫于成本压力，放弃使用清洁燃料和清洁技术，2021年超过9.7亿非洲人（几乎占总人口的四分之三）无法使用清洁燃料和烹饪设施。[2] 由此可见，新冠疫情对能源供应影响严重，打断了非洲实现能源获取目标的努力，甚至在非洲多处出现能源返贫的现象。

大封锁等社会限制措施造成供应链中断，经济活动减少也致使家庭、公用事业和设备供应商财务困难，电网连接进度更是放缓。国际能源署因此提出，新冠疫情影响下，非洲已经偏离了实现可持续发展目标七的轨道。[3] 尽管目前新冠疫情在全球范围内整体趋向平稳，非洲地区也因其及时有效的举措而大大减缓了疫情的冲击，但是生产、贸易、医疗等各方面活动受限依然暴露了非洲能源供给的脆弱性。

疫情导致的国家财政困难、公共服务减少以及政府对军队的掌控力削弱等原因，也增加了非洲地区的安全风险和不确定性。在过去两年中，西非多国发生政变事件，如马里、几内亚和布基纳法索，也有几内

---

① IEA, *Africa Energy Outlook* 2022, June 2022, https://www.iea.org/reports/africa-energy-outlook-2022, 2022-11-25. p. 40.

② 同上。

③ 同上注，第35页。

亚比绍、圣多美和普林西比、冈比亚发生了未遂政变。此外，撒哈拉以南非洲其他地区也呈现多点不稳定状态，埃塞俄比亚政府与"提格雷人民解放阵线"的武装冲突持续了将近两年；刚果（金）和卢旺达的争端冲突不断升级对发电设备和电网的打击破坏、政权不稳定导致的能源部门服务能力削弱，都使得非洲能源供给更加雪上加霜，充分凸显发展和安全的互动关联性，也证明长远解决问题的艰难程度。

3. 俄乌冲突影响下非洲的能源安全

俄乌冲突为全球变局增添了更多不确定因素，其中最直接的影响是国际能源价格剧烈波动，从而冲击了全球能源供应链的稳定性。由于俄罗斯供应的石油产品已不能再采购，尽管欧盟转向清洁能源的长远决心并未动摇，但在巨大的能源需求压力下，一些欧洲国家不得不暂缓能源低碳化转型并重新加大对化石能源的使用。[1] 同时，作为非洲油品进口的主要来源，欧洲供应商大大减少了对非供应，转而留在欧洲市场以满足本土需求。这暴露了非洲能源安全的致命缺陷——尽管非洲原油产量充足，但炼油能力不足意味着该地区几乎所有的化学燃料都依赖进口。非洲大陆最大的原油生产国尼日利亚仅有少数几家炼油厂，且炼油量远未达到官方产能。安哥拉作为撒哈拉以南仅次于尼日利亚的非洲第二大产油国，也仅拥有一家运营中的炼油厂，该国五分之四的燃料需求依赖进口。[2] 因此，尽管俄乌冲突以来，国际市场对非洲原油的需求非常强劲，非洲的十几个产油国能够从国际石油价格上涨中受益，但是原油出口收入几乎无法覆盖巨额的油品进口支出——大多数非洲国家将不得不承受能源价格上涨所带来的额外经济支出。俄乌冲突爆发以来，包括南非、尼日利亚（非洲第一大石油生产国、原油出口国但必须进口汽油）、埃及、埃塞俄比亚、摩洛哥、肯尼亚等主要经济体在内的大部分非洲国家都经历了燃油供应紧张和价格飞涨，这也成为制约非洲经济复苏的重

---

① 杨永明：《地缘影响下欧洲能源政策及发展形势分析》，2022 年 6 月 6 日，https://baijiahao.baidu.com/s?id=1734876627972354193&wfr=spider&for=pc，2022-11-25。

② 新浪财经：《俄乌冲突暴露能源安全脆弱性，一场燃料短缺危机正席卷非洲》，2022 年 6 月 6 日，https://baijiahao.baidu.com/s?id=1734876627972354193&wfr=spider&for=pc，2022-11-25。

要因素。

俄乌冲突所暴露的非洲能源安全脆弱性不仅限于能源供给，还外溢到国家经济和民生问题上。燃料价格上涨促使非洲各国采取更强硬的货币政策，并通过贬值、加息等方式以支撑不断减少的外汇储备和遏制不断攀升的通胀。在国际油价上涨的背景下，政府燃油价格补贴的暂停、减少和延迟发放，都不可避免地造成非洲本地能源涨价与抢购，进而影响到其他工农业领域的生产。因为化肥、农业所需燃料和粮食运输等方面，能源不足也连带着影响非洲的农业——柴油价格上涨已经导致种植成本上升，迫使农民减少犁地次数和缩减种植面积，进而影响粮食产量，并导致食品价格上涨，加剧了粮食危机。

二、非洲能源发展的创新路径

世界变局对非洲能源转型提出的多重挑战，加之非洲国家在能源领域面临的其他诸多挑战——包括意愿与能力的矛盾、资金短缺的困境、同外部合作方的利益协调等问题——反映了传统能源开发和供电模式不足以应付国家战略层面的能源转型和底层人口用电需求不足的双重能源需求。对于每个非洲国家而言，要开发既具有融入现有系统的便利性，又高度匹配民众现实需求的新型能源系统，就必须超越单一的能源发展路径，在多个方面尽可能地探索本土创新的方法。正如一位肯尼亚官员曾说："当你没有稳定的电力供应时，你必须尝试任何事情来确保电力供应。"①

1. 新能源种类

非洲大陆拥有巨大潜力发展可再生能源，不但能减缓全球气候变暖带来的冲击，还将为非洲大陆的经济发展提供动力，帮助数百万人摆脱贫困。在过去10年，可再生能源中，在岸风能发电、离岸风能发电、聚光太阳能发电的装机成本都有一定程度下浮，但是降幅最大的仍属太阳能光伏

---

① Adekoke Oke, Nathanial Boso and John Serbe Marfo, "Out of Africa," *Supply Chain Management Review*, January 5, 2022, https://www.scmr.com/article/out_of_africa, 2022-3-21.

发电。由于技术进步及以中国为代表的上游生产商大规模生产和价格下降，2010 年至 2018 年，太阳能光伏发电的每兆瓦装机成本已从 4621 美元下降至 1210 美元，年平均变化幅度为 –15.4%。目前，部分太阳能光伏发电投用项目的平均能源成本已低于火力发电。[①] 随着可再生能源市场的发展，投资新能源将逐渐在包括非洲在内的世界各地区成为常态，为非洲国家将可再生能源作为主要能源的发展方向提供了巨大的机会。

在非洲，除了全球层面的能源结构转型与区域内部发展极大的电力需求推动之外，良好的资源禀赋和新能源发电成本下降为非洲国家的新能源技术发展提供可行性。从资源分布来看，风力资源集中在埃塞俄比亚、肯尼亚、塞内加尔、南非等国，地热能集中在肯尼亚，天然气资源则集中在莫桑比克、坦桑尼亚、埃及、塞内加尔、毛里塔尼亚以及南非，太阳能更是覆盖 2/3 的非洲大陆。从能源类型上看，水电已经是商业领域较为成熟和可行的项目，在许多非洲国家，大规模水电站已成为主要的电力来源。

然而新能源产业在非洲的发展并不充分。作为资源丰富的大陆，非洲的可再生能源规模发电水平仍然很低，总装机容量仅占世界总量的 1.9%，并主要集中在水力发电，新能源开发尚未获得显著发展。[②] 作为太阳能资源最丰富的大洲，截至 2019 年，非洲仅建设了 5 吉瓦太阳能光伏，不到全球装机容量的 1%。[③] 成规模的能源市场只出现在南非和部分北非国家。[④] 制约非洲可再生能源规模发电的瓶颈主要是基础设施、发电量和电网。为应对翻倍的用电需求，非洲需要建设可靠的供电系统，包括更稳定的发电设备、覆盖面更广的电力传输与容量更大的电力储蓄。但是相对较小的市场份额和贷款不可偿付的高风险使得在非洲发展

---

① 平均能源成本衡量的是一个发电项目未来折现总成本除以未来折现总发电量的每千瓦时成本，即理想情况下一个发电项目可以平衡盈亏的最低电价。非洲咨研：《非洲新能源行业概况与市场特征》，行业观察·新能源，第 1 期，2020 年 9 月，https://mp.weixin.qq.com/s/_lQv6U9eg3M61JI7rcN-6A，2021-8-20。

② 由于水力发电开发程度已经比较成熟，因此水力只是可再生能源而不是新能源。

③ 非洲咨研：《非洲新能源行业概况与市场特征》，行业观察·新能源，第 1 期，2020 年 9 月，https://mp.weixin.qq.com/s/_lQv6U9eg3M61JI7rcN-6A，2021-8-20。

④ 国际能源署：《全球能源回顾 2021》，2022 年 2 月，https://www.iea.org/reports/global-energy-review-2021?language=zh，2022-3-18。

新能源基础设施充满挑战。规模化发电基础问题并非能一蹴而就地解决。虽然在近年，不少非洲国家对制度框架做出了修改与调整，但基础设施和法规仍然处于无法吸纳大量投资、大规模生产和调配可再生能源的窘境。

2. 新开发方式

如前所述，以集中供电来开发清洁能源在非洲面临较大困难。可再生资源丰富的地带大多距离电力负荷中心较远，清洁能源在集中式开发后需要通过电网外送，因此大多数清洁能源基地都需配套建设较长距离的输电线。[①] 然而，电网薄弱是制约非洲电力开发的主要瓶颈，各国电网普遍存在覆盖范围小、输送能力弱、电能损耗率高、供电可靠性低的问题。非洲当地由于供应链的体系未臻完善，因此项目开发多半需仰赖海外业者完成。关于非洲电力发展的未来，一种较为流行的观点认为可以通过引进先进技术跳过中间阶段，一步到位地建设适应清洁能源发电特性的电网系统，从而在能源领域实现"蛙跳式"发展。然而问题在于，当今世界先进的清洁能源技术大多数被欧美发达国家所垄断，非洲国家要想获得先进的清洁能源电网系统，容易再次陷入资源或市场换取技术的新剥削陷阱。

放眼全球，那些致力于可再生能源发展的欧美国家进行能源系统转型的共同经验是，在高度动态和国际化的复杂背景下将以化石燃料为基础的集中供电方式转变为基于可再生能源发电的分散式系统。由此可见，能源转型不仅发生在能源类型上，对能源供应方式也提出了新的思路。同样在非洲，当政府自上而下铺就新能源规划面临基础设施、制度、资金、治理能力等各方面掣肘的同时，围绕太阳能等新能源的草根式离网应用已在悄然展开。利用分布式清洁能源破解无电困局，是多数非洲国家的优先行动重点。分布式清洁能源从技术层面突破了传统电网成本高、投资回收期长、运维难度大的困境，广大乡村居民能够通过分布式光伏和风电、小水电、小型生物质发电系统实现能源的就地开发和自给自足，还能将成本控制在较小规模。对于非洲不少决策者而言，当

---

① 张锐：《非洲能源转型的内涵、进展与挑战》，《西亚非洲》2022年第1期，第58页。

前的能源转型就等同于通过分布式利用可再生能源快速实现乡村电气化，而离网型太阳能就是可再生能源与分布式发电结合的代表性应用。

离网型太阳能是利用光伏面板或组件将太阳能转化为电能的独立发电系统，多应用在远离电网的地区。无源特性使离网型太阳能系统区别于分布式光伏的微网系统，较低的功率范围也使得离网型太阳能产品主要集中在家用功能。根据世界银行的分类，目前离网型太阳能家用产品有三类：微型太阳能产品（Pico，峰值功率在 3 瓦以内）、家用太阳能系统（SHS，峰值功率在 11 瓦及以上）和直流电驱动的节能太阳能电器（包括家用电器和生产用设备）。[1] 对于大多数农村低收入家庭来说，微型太阳能产品的购买门槛最低，也是离网太阳能市场的主要产品。自 2010 年以来，Pico 始终占据市场销售量的八成以上。SHS 可提供的能源功能更加多样，如为电器供电，但价格相对较高。近年来 SHS 销量同步稳定增长，意味着超过一半以上的离网太阳能用户已经接入了一级（Tier 1）乃至更高级别的清洁、可靠的现代太阳能电力。[2] 此外，离网太阳能市场已经从为家庭和微型企业提供照明和消耗性能源的服务迅速拓展至可以提供一系列的应用于生产的离网型太阳能电器。尤其在农村地区，农业生产过程中许多环节都能使用离网太阳能系统，如太阳能水培、太阳能灌溉（滴灌和抽水）、太阳能或沼气驱动的冷藏和烘干机、谷物碾磨等等。

离网型太阳能在非洲的应用具备良好的自然条件。非洲的地理位置使其拥有丰富的太阳能资源，除刚果雨林和几内亚湾，几乎整个非洲大陆都有充足的日照时长。目前，非洲已发展为全球离网太阳能最大的市场地区之一，仅东非就占据了全球离网型太阳能系统过半的投资。肯尼

---

[1] 世界银行：《2020 年离网太阳能市场趋势报告》，2020 年 3 月，第 1 页，https://www.lightingglobal.org/wpcontent/uploads/2020/04/14005VIV_OFF%20GRID%20SOLAR%20REPORT%20Exec%20Sum%20V14-CHINESE.pdf，2021-8-13。

[2] 能源部门管理援助计划（ESMAP）开发了多级能源框架（the Multi-Tier framework, MTF），对能源用户的接入程度进行 0—5 级的划分。其中，0 级是完全无法接电，1 级是每天接电时长达 4 小时，这也是国际标准中判别电力接入的最低标准。Mikul Bhatia and Nicolina Angelou, Beyond Connections: Energy Access Redefined, Technical Report 008/15 (Washington, DC: ESMAP, July 2015), https:// www. esmap.org/node/56715.

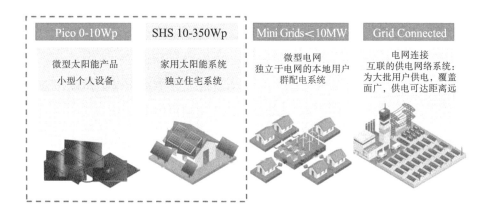

图1　太阳能细分市场与离网型太阳能的范围
图片来源：世界银行《2020年离网太阳能市场趋势报告》，2020年3月，第iv页

亚和坦桑尼亚培育了多个非洲主要的离网型太阳能企业（例如M-Kopa，Azuri等），并继续为希望涉足该行业的公司提供最理想的落地机会。稳定的政治和经济条件、相对较高的业务便利性、政府对该行业的支持，使得这些东非国家成为离网太阳能市场主要领导者。近年来，随着东非市场的成熟和外溢，离网型太阳能在非洲的市场重心开始逐渐转移至中非、西非等无法接入电力或电网供电不稳定而人口集中的地区。在西非，几内亚和尼日利亚大部分已接入电网的家庭表示，家里"一半时间"没有电。[1]这些情况都为离网型太阳能进入当地市场提供了空间。实际上，笔者在广州调研时向一些供应商了解到，近年来华采购离网型太阳能产品的非洲商人主体已从东非国家转变为以尼日利亚为主的西非国家群体，也从侧面佐证了这一市场变化的趋势。

3. 新商业模式

随着互联网的发展，新的金融技术越来越多地应用在分布式可再生能源的开发上，形成新商业模式助力新能源、新应用的三角创新。使用移动货币来支付和获取离网型太阳能商品和服务贷款就是一个例子。太阳能

---

[1]　非洲晴雨表：第七轮数据，https://afrobarometer.org/publication-round/round-7，2021-7-31。

产品的传统交易都是在商店柜台以一次性付清现金的方式进行。自 2010 年前后随着非洲手机革命兴起，基于移动支付的"即付即用"模式（Pay As You Go, PAYG）开始出现，帮助更多金字塔底端的消费者获取到各类电力产品，同时实现资本积累和融资。事实上，"即付即用"这一模式对于很多人来说并不陌生。在买房、买车的时候，消费者常常采用由租赁到产权（lease-to-own）的付款模式，以缓解短期巨额资金的压力。[①] 当这种方式与移动手机结合应用在离网型太阳能领域时，用户只需支付少量预付款即可获得设备，然后通过手机按月或按周支付余款。[②] 在家用离网电力支付系统中，这种灵活的付款模式对于整体收入较低或收入不固定的非洲城郊和农村家庭来说，恰好贴合其需求。而对于资金匮乏的供应链运营商而言，这种金融科技解决方案也能够为其经营活动融资。

随着"即付即用"模式成熟，大量投资流入非洲的离网型发电企业，支持基于这一模式的太阳能发电技术。多家公司推出灵活搭配的产品套餐，促进"家电下乡"，包括太阳能电视机、太阳能剃须刀、智能手机等等。还有的企业通过"2G"网络就可以获得太阳能设备使用后的性能数据，让运维团队能在设备即将报废或出现故障时主动与用户联系。[③] 创新的商业模式加速了离网型太阳能市场的发展。根据世界银行的统计，非洲已有过半国家出现"即付即用"模式并取得很好的经济效益，而且该模式的销量占全球离网太阳能市场收入的 62%，其中大部分来自非洲地区。[④] 除了经济效益，"即付即用"的新商业模式还具有深远的社会意义。它使清洁能源产品在非洲逐渐告别"人道主义产品"的标签，缺电的居民们可以不再倚赖政府或国际社会的援助，而是通过市场化手段、发扬自食其力的精神去获得清洁电力，并在这种创新型实践中拓展生产生活的更多可能。[⑤] 从这个角度来看，"即付即用"的商业模式有可能像

---

① The Intelligent Unit, *Power Up: Delivering Renewable Energy in Africa*, The Economics, 2016.

② 张锐：《非洲能源转型的内涵、进展与挑战》，《西亚非洲》2022 年第 1 期，第 62 页。

③ 同上注，第 63 页。

④ 世界银行：《2020 年离网太阳能市场趋势报告》，2020 年 3 月，第 5 页，https://www.lightingglobal.org/wpcontent/uploads/2020/04/14005VIV_OFF%20GRID%20SOLAR%20REPORT%20Exec%20Sum%20V14-CHINESE.pdf, 2021-8-13。

⑤ 张锐：《非洲能源转型的内涵、进展与挑战》，《西亚非洲》2022 年第 1 期，第 63 页。

手机冲击座机那样对传统能源应用模式产生深刻挑战。

但是这一创新的商业模式在非洲本土也遇到不少困难。尽管大多数"即付即用"产品符合市场标准，但许多非洲消费者更看重价格低廉而非产品质量。实际上，在非洲流通的大多数离网型太阳能产品并未经过国际标准认证，反而在街上经营的商店拥有大量设备，其中许多设备不合格。此外，自然灾害、政治动荡或经济低迷会使得"即付即用"模式失去金字塔底端的客户群，具有不稳定性。但如果非洲的太阳能企业能够克服重重困难和残酷竞争，那么"即付即用"模式具有扩大规模的潜力。一项关注中东非地区推出太阳能家庭系统时遇到的"最后一英里"挑战的研究指出，在增加穷人获得可负担得起的清洁能源方面，"即付即用"的模式提供了潜在的突破性积极影响，然而，技术和商业模式都比目前的替代能源更复杂，因此需要一个更发达的市场战略。与零散地销售能源产品相比，实现技术和产品广泛传播的成本更高，也要求采用更加快速灵活的策略。①

三、案例分析：肯尼亚的离网型太阳能市场

在撒哈拉以南非洲，肯尼亚的能源应用表现不凡。虽然并非传统上的化石能源大国，肯尼亚却能成为东非电气化率最高的国家。它不仅是少有的以可再生能源实现电力供应，还拥有世界最活跃的离网型太阳能市场。无论是开发类型还是应用路径，肯尼亚都是非洲探索能源发展新路径的最佳案例，也为其他非洲国家提供了样本。

1. 肯尼亚的能源现状

从整体来看，肯尼亚的能源结构呈现传统能源和新能源"花开两朵，各表一枝"的态势。一方面，传统生物质能（包括木柴、木炭等木质燃料和农业废弃物等）和化石能源作为燃料分别主导着农村地区和城

---

① Jack Barrie and Heather J. Cruickshank, "Shedding light on the last mile: A study on the diffusion of Pay As You Go Solar Home Systems in Central East Africa," *Energy Policy*, Vol. 107, 2017, pp.425-436.

市工业地区。肯尼亚对木质燃料的依赖程度很高，目前全国三分之二的能源来自生物能源，尤其是木质燃料。据估计，肯尼亚人现在每年消耗240万吨木炭。[①] 考虑到传统燃料的环境不可持续性和它在国民生活中的占比之重，肯尼亚能源转型现代化任务十分紧迫，通过开发和使用清洁能源实现电力普及，实现用能的现代化，促使肯尼亚全国进入"电气化时代"。由于肯尼亚地热资源和石油的使用增加，预计到2040年，传统木质燃料的份额将从三分之二缩减至15%。[②] 与此同时，化石能源的使用约占肯尼亚总能源的20%。随着500万辆汽车的投入使用，石油在公路运输中的使用量增加了两倍。[③] 此外，液化天然气依然是城镇地区烹饪燃料的主要来源。虽然肯尼亚并非传统的化石能源生产国，但出于国家发展的考虑，政府采取了一系列措施开发其相对有限的资源。2012年，肯尼亚北部图尔卡纳（Turkana）发现石油，此后又在拉穆（Lamu）等地区进行了广泛的石油勘探。在肯尼亚的姆温吉（Mwingi）中东部和姆提图（Mutitu）地区均发现了可进行商业开采的煤矿床。[④] 如果要如期实现到2030年跨入中等收入国家行列的现代化目标，肯尼亚仍有较高的经济增长任务，这支撑了化石燃料需求的强劲增长。

另一方面，肯尼亚的电力部门由可再生能源主导。水力曾经是肯尼亚高度依赖的发电来源。然而在过去的10年中，由于全球变暖的影响，江河流量、湖泊水位、水库蓄水大幅减少，多个大型水电站都出现水量危机，进而造成全国性的电力短缺。2018年9月，肯尼亚由于干旱气候不得不关闭多个水电站，松杜（Sondu Miriu）水力发电站的发电量只能达到设计容量的1/8。[⑤] 为解决缺电问题，肯尼亚将地热、风电、太阳

[①] 能源界：《肯尼亚能源概况：生物质能》，2018年9月14日，http://www.nengyuanjie.net/article/18447.html，2022-2-23。

[②] International Energy Agency (IEA), *Africa Energy Outlook 2019: Overview Kenya*, November 2019, p. 24, www.iea.org/reports/africa-energy-outlook-2019, 2022-3-21.

[③] 同上。

[④] David Obura, "The Environmental Impact of a Coal Plant On Kenya's Coast Is Being Underplayed," The Conversation Africa (Johannesburg), *AllAfrica*, September 19, 2017, https://allafrica.com/stories/201709220670.html.

[⑤] 同上注，第56页。

能等绿色能源作为未来优先发展目标。奥尔卡里亚地热发电厂（Olkaria Geothermal Power Station）2019 年 10 月完成新一轮的扩建，实现了非洲同类型项目的最大发电能力。预计到 2040 年，它将占肯尼亚发电量的近 50%。[1] 肯尼亚的图尔卡纳湖风电项目（Lake Turkana Wind Power Station）2019 年 8 月投运，是肯尼亚最大的风电项目，总规模达 310MW，已于 2019 年中旬全数完工并网，连带使得风电的装机量增加，跃升为仅次于水电及地热第三高的再生能源项目。[2] 加里萨太阳能电站是肯尼亚太阳能标志性项目，该项目由中国进出口银行提供融资、中国江西国际技术合作有限公司负责实施。[3] 2020 年肯尼亚 92.3% 的电力来自可再生能源，预计在 2030 年实现 100% 再生能源发电量占比的目标。[4]

尽管肯尼亚已是撒哈拉以南非洲电气化率增长最快的国家之一，并在可再生能源开发方面取得了一些进展，但是依然存在许多电力开发和应用上的问题。第一，现代清洁能源和传统能源之间存在巨大张力。虽然在过去 10 年间，肯尼亚的石油发电量在该国总发电量的占比迅速下降，而清洁能源则占了绝对主导地位，[5] 但考虑到肯尼亚的现代化发展任务，这是否仅仅是因为能源系统短期的结构变化仍需要继续观察。肯尼亚政府在拉穆岛建造燃煤电厂的计划恰是一例——尽管该计划最终因为环境问题和社会抗议而终止。此外，在日常生活层面，对传统能源使用的路径依赖使得现代能源的需求受限。例如，2020 年曾有媒体指出，肯尼亚石油和矿业部与能源部在推广清洁能源的工作方向上产生了巨大矛盾。石油部的目标是通过突出环保和健康优势来尽可能地提升液化石油

---

[1]　David Obura, "The Environmental Impact of a Coal Plant On Kenya's Coast Is Being Underplayed," The Conversation Africa (Johannesburg), *AllAfrica*, September 19, 2017, https://allafrica.com/stories/201709220670.html. p. 18.

[2]　《全球光伏新兴市场需求解析—非洲地区：肯尼亚》，北极星太阳能光伏网，https://guangfu.bjx.com.cn/news/20210104/1126919.shtml, 2022-3-1。

[3]　《加里萨太阳能电站有望今年 7 月开工建设》，中国商务部网站，http://ke.mofcom.gov.cn/article/jmxw/201604/20160401288673.shtml, 2022-3-1。

[4]　IEA, *Africa Energy Outlook 2019: Overview Kenya*, November 2019, p. 36, www.iea.org/reports/africa-energy-outlook-2019, 2022-3-21。

[5]　张锐：《非洲能源转型的内涵、进展与挑战》，《西亚非洲》2022 年第 1 期，第 58 页。

气在全国的使用率；而能源部则通过建立区域能源中心，培训当地工匠制造改进的木材和木炭炉灶。两部门不仅各行其是，而且重点发展的能源方向也与清洁能源议程的本质背道而驰，人们对使用化石燃料和传统能源的路径依赖在国家政策制定层面可见一斑（甚至有报道称，2019 年的一次液化石油气公开招标活动让公众得以一窥总统的厨房，却发现他的家中也仍将木炭作为燃料）。[①] 第二，清洁能源规模化开发面临输送问题。与许多非洲国家一样，肯尼亚政府十分注重对电力进行自上而下的管理，始终认为拓展电网是实现电力覆盖成本最低的解决方案。因为肯尼亚预计有 63% 的人口生活在配电线路服务的区域，93% 的人口生活在电网可到达区域。[②] 在与法国开发署合作的"最后一英里电力连接"的项目中，其解决思路主要还是延伸电网。[③] 但是如前文所述，清洁能源在集中式开发后需要通过电网外送，而电网薄弱是制约非洲电力开发的主要瓶颈。因此，肯尼亚在解决电网建设以及人口无法连接电网的问题上进展缓慢。第三，能源需求量的估计偏差。非洲各地有很多大型水电的开发计划，但长期无法得到推进，其原因是非洲整体工业化水平较低，高载能产业较少，大型水电项目面临缺乏电力消纳市场的窘境。有研究称，肯尼亚能源需求的年增长率在 6%—8% 之间，这与政府估计的 15% 相差甚远。[④] 对能源需求的过度估计会导致对能源生产的投资未得到充分利用，而且高昂的开发成本最终将转嫁到消费者身上。

肯尼亚的能源结构中存在着非洲能源转型普遍面临的多重挑战，即清洁化、现代化、多元化和可及性。肯尼亚的能源现状折射出非洲电力

---

① Edwin Okoth, "Kenya: Puzzle of Two Energy Dockets Pushing Conflicting Agenda," *AllAfrica*, May 12, 2020, https://allafrica.com/stories/202005120310.html.

② 配电线路（distribution lines）服务区域是指电力通过电线从变电站传输到用电单位所经过的区域；电网（grid）可达区域指的是以配电线路为基础形成的电力网络可覆盖的范围。处于电网覆盖范围的居民，即便没有居住在配电线路沿线，也可以享受电力服务。Lighting Africa, "Policy Paper Note: Kenya," https://dev-lgla-merge.pantheonsite.io/wp-content/uploads/2012/01/24_Kenya-policy-report-note.pdf 2021-8-10.

③ Brian Sergi, et al., "Institutional influence on power sector investments: A case study of on- and off-grid energy in Kenya and Tanzania," *Energy Research & Social Science*, 2018 (40), p. 70.

④ Amos Wemanya, "Kenya: Renewable Energy Is the Key to Cheaper Electricity in Kenya," *AllAfrica*, August 25, 2020, https://allafrica.com/stories/202008250875.html.

开发始终存在的一个困局：有迫切的用能需求，但需求的有限规模无法支撑项目的落地及可持续运营。面对这种情况，肯尼亚国内的电力应该以何种方式生产和供应？是否有足够大的需求量去承接并且持续刺激新的电力供应？生产的电力能否有效分配抵达电力用户需求端？肯尼亚政府一直在研究寻找低成本的能源供应模式，以满足其国家发展和国民生活生计的能源需求，同时提高能源的可及性——这或许能够在离网型太阳能中找到答案。

2. 肯尼亚的离网型太阳能产业

肯尼亚是世界上最发达的离网型太阳能市场之一，这一事实鲜为人知。与撒哈拉以南非洲的其他国家相比，肯尼亚的离网型太阳能行业在市场活跃度、质量标准门槛和商业模式创新方面都表现得更为成熟。尽管离网型太阳能是一个较为新兴的市场，但是如果以动态的历史眼光去看，会发现孕育该市场的条件早已有之。肯尼亚最早的离网型太阳能应用可以追溯到 20 世纪 70 年代，经历了 70 年代末至 80 年代初的国际援助阶段、20 世纪 80 年代中期至 90 年代中期"援助 - 市场"并行的本土企业起步阶段、20 世纪 90 年代后期到世纪之交本土市场壮大阶段，以及 21 世纪第一个十年中期至今的离网型太阳能与互联网革命结合阶段。肯尼亚离网型太阳能的蓬勃势头正在向全球能源转型展现一种可能的本土实践，而这种示范成果离不开长期以来的本土化探索。肯尼亚之所以能够产生比邻国更高水平的离网型太阳能扩散市场，得益于许多因素，包括国家政策的有力支持、政府各部门的通力合作、不断增长壮大的中产阶级消费群体以及他们的购买力、与国际发展机构往来的有利地理条件、本地零部件供应商提供技术人才、当地活跃的离网型太阳能领军企业以及创新的商业模式等等。[1]

在宏观上有政策支撑——肯尼亚于 2018 年 12 月启动了国家电气化战略（Kenya National Electrification Strategy, KNES），原本计划于 2020 年实现全面通电，受疫情的影响，后将目标推迟两年至 2022 年。[2]肯政

---

① Ulrich Elmer Hansen, Mathilde Brix Pedersen & Ivan Nygaard, "Review of solar PV policies, interventions and diffusion in East Africa," *Renewable and Sustainable Energy Reviews*, 2015(46), pp. 236-248.

② 同上注，第 41 页。

府意识到，要想实现全面通电的目标，关键在于打通电网未架设地区的通电，而离网型太阳能就发挥了极为重要的作用。如今，肯尼亚已将离网解决方案纳入其国家电气化战略，致力于解决偏远地区供电不足的问题，以实现普遍电气化。[①] 2017 年 7 月，在世界银行的支持下，肯尼亚离网太阳能接入项目（Kenya Off-Grid Solar Access Project, KOSAP）开始实施。该项目旨在提高能源服务的覆盖范围，利用微网和离网型太阳能产品为 14 个偏远县的 130 万人口增加电力接入。[②] 该项目所覆盖的东北和北部地区人口高度分散，密度远远低于全国平均水平，而且存在基础设施不足的问题。KOSAP 利用离网型太阳能向偏远、低密度和传统上能源服务不足的地区提供电力服务，从而缩小国家电力供应缺口、减少贫困并推动实现国家平等供应能源的目标。因此，该项目既是肯尼亚国家电气化战略明确将离网型太阳能作为电力化途径纳入国家能源发展框架的重要举措，也是肯尼亚长期发展计划 2030 年愿景的关键部分。

在中观上有协作机制——作为国家级的能源旗舰项目，肯尼亚多个政府部门和产业界参与到 KOSAP 的工作当中，可见国家对离网型太阳能的鼓励力度。能源部作为决策部门统筹该项目，负责电力、石油、煤炭燃料和可再生能源政策以及整体行业发展，尤其还涉及偏远机构的太阳能和风能系统管理。由于 KOSAP 是实现农村电力化的重要内容之一，因此由肯尼亚电力和照明公司（KPLC）、农村电力化管理局（REA）共同管理。KOSAP 的工作内容之一是确定项目所在县可以获得符合质量标准的离网型太阳能产品，因此标准的设定是关键因素。在这个方面，世界银行是肯尼亚政府的重要合作伙伴，通过点亮非洲项目为政府提供有关标准的政策咨询。与此同时，肯尼亚可再生能源协会（KEREA）及以其成员为代表的地方社会团体也通过游说政府部门——例如负责监督法规与质量的肯尼亚标准局（KEBS）——或者参与国家能源政策草

---

① World Bank, *Kenya Launches Ambitious Plan to Provide Electricity to All Citizens by 2022*, news release, December 6, 2018, https://www.worldbank.org/en/news/press-release/2018/12/06/Kenya-launches-ambitious-plan-to-provide-electricity-to-all-citizens-by-2022, 2021-12-14.

② KPLC, "Kenya Off-Grid Solar Access Project," https://kplc.co.ke/content/item/1943/kenya-off-grid-solar-access-project-kosap.

案审议，以游说加快政府制定产业标准进程，从而更好地将分布式可再生能源技术（包括离网型太阳能）纳入国家能源政策。此外，质量保证

直是肯尼业离网型太阳能利益攸关方高度重视的问题。消费者意识计划、为高质量产品供应商提供的业务发展支持以及装运前验证过程都使优质产品在总销量中占有很大份额。在这个过程中，KEBS 专门负责确保符合国际质量标准的政府机构采用了与照明全球质量保证框架一致的国际电工委员会（IEC）标准。

在微观上有模式创新——从宏观和中观的层面看，肯尼亚政府重视私营企业在离网型太阳能方案中发挥的重要作用，鼓励公共部门和私人投资者进入发电行业，为能源企业营造良好的营商环境。在微观层面上，木土创新的商业模式加速了市场的发展——离网型太阳能产业在肯尼亚获得成功的关键，是其创新的终端支付模式。得益于移动钱包在非洲的飞速发展，用户可以使用各类移动支付系统，利用"即付即用"模式，为其家用太阳能设备支付少量预付款，再按月或按周支付余款。以肯尼亚著名的离网型太阳能品牌 M-Kopa 的一套家用发电套装为例，若单次购买其整套产品，需要约合 240 美元。如果使用"即付即用"模式，则只需先付 35 美元获得设备、通上电力，再按 0.5 美元 / 天的租金持续缴费一年，便可获得整套设备。这样分摊之后的用电成本，甚至比传统煤油灯还便宜。此外，在肯尼亚有许多公司在竞争和探索新市场和产品，包括通过提高效率和融资使人们负担得起越来越多的家电产品。他们通常提供灵活的付款条件和不同的租赁期限，一方面减少用户的付款压力，另一方面也有助于降低费用偿还风险。这些公司不仅向城郊和农村地区的低收入家庭提供产品，也向小型企业经营者提供服务。他们的目标通常不仅仅是提供产品，而是与客户建立长期关系，强化产品的服务性能。

3. 疫情期间肯尼亚离网型太阳能产业的作用

能源服务对预防疾病和抗击流行病尤为重要。在新冠疫情期间，能源服务从为医疗设施供电、为基本卫生提供清洁水，到实现通信服务，使得人们在保持社交距离的同时依然能够获得卫生和交流的保障。在过去三年，肯尼亚全国仍有四分之一的居民缺乏电力供应，偏远农村地区

这样的情况更是屡见不鲜。新冠病毒大流行导致大量人失业，许多人无法支付电费或燃料。2020年肯尼亚还遭遇了罕见的暴雨天气，导致农村电网严重受损。疫情期间的能源服务在肯尼亚这个较为发达的东非国家也面临严峻挑战。汤森路透基金会报告称："由于极端天气和新冠肺炎的经济影响，许多肯尼亚人陷入了黑暗，替代能源变得越来越重要，即使对接入电网的家庭也是如此。""随着新型冠状病毒在肯尼亚的病例不断攀升，缺乏可靠的电力可能是一个生死攸关的问题。"[①]

疫情期间，离网型太阳能产品在肯尼亚的医疗救援和通信照明等领域发挥重要作用。最具代表性的场景是将离网型太阳能的技术应用于疫苗的储藏和运输。肯尼亚女工程师诺拉·玛格罗（Norah Magero）设计的可移动太阳能冰柜Vaccibox能将新冠疫苗运送到电网无法覆盖的地区。[②]这一产品起初源于为当地奶农储藏运输牛奶，后来得以创新性地拓展到医疗领域，是由于该产品巧妙地将离网新能源技术和互联网模式结合起来，形成一个整体性的解决方案。线上监控功能使得人们可以随时查询到冰柜的位置，并监测疫苗的规定和实际储存温度，从而确保这些疫苗的活性。在肯尼亚这种热带地区国家，随时随地监测疫苗储存的温度、确保人们获得有效药物是十分必要的。除了疫苗和药物的储藏运输，离网型太阳能所提供的通信功能也极大地帮助了当地医疗救援服务。根据肯尼亚社区卫生志愿者的反映，许多家庭面临着在紧急情况之下手机没电而无法及时联系医疗机构的困难。因此拥有一个可以昼夜供电的太阳能电池组件，对于挽救生命而言至关重要。[③]此外，离网型太阳能还在照明这一最为常见的领域支持着肯尼亚的各类医疗机构和家庭用户。汤森路透基金会的报告，就以肯尼亚女性工人使用微型光伏系统的故事作为开头。文中表示，离网型太阳能帮助她度过疫情封锁失去收

---

① Kagondu Njagi, "Solar keeps lights, phones on for rural Kenyans during pandemic blackouts," Thomson Reuters Foundation, 23 July 2020, https://news.trust.org/item/20200723131328-2e2fg.

② Africanews , "Solar-powered fridges help transport COVID-19 vaccines in Kenya," 27 Jan 2022, https://www.africanews.com/2022/01/27/solar-powered-fridges-help-transport-covid-19-vaccines-in-kenya/.

③ Kagondu Njagi, "Solar keeps lights, phones on for rural Kenyans during pandemic blackouts," Thomson Reuters Foundation, 23 July 2020, https://news.trust.org/item/20200723131328-2e2fg.

入的困难时刻，不仅让她不需要购买煤油照明，还可以以较低的价格将光伏产品租借给邻居使用。

结　论

非洲能源转型受到当下变化莫测的全球局势影响。在全球气候变化、新冠疫情、俄乌冲突等不稳定因素交织叠加的影响下，非洲国家不得不在追求能源现代化的同时还要努力实现清洁化、解决能源贫困和能源安全等多重目标。全球变局对非洲能源发展提出的这些复杂挑战，促使非洲国家在能源发展领域不能再简单复制西方国家的模式，而是要从能源种类、开发路径、能源供应方式等诸方面皆取得一定的创新。近年来特别是在过去的 3 年里，非洲不乏追求能源可持续发展的创新举动，如大力开发可再生能源尤其是新能源以拓宽能源种类，从集中式发电到分布式发电来尝试解决能源获取和基础设施薄弱的问题，在商业模式上与时俱进以使得电力资源的分配更加民主化。从本质来看，非洲能源发展的挑战是西方既有的现代化发展逻辑与自身情况的不适配。非洲能源基础的薄弱和发展转型需求的紧迫，不允许它们像西方国家那样通过长时间、重资本的积累来实现能源设施和管理能力完全成熟到位。至少，这种以国家力量来主导能源发展的自上而下的路径不足以解决非洲的能源困境——在非洲，能源的生产和分配问题，同等重要也同等严峻。因此，非洲国家需要探索传统路径以外的其他道路来进行补充，从而形成多途径齐头并进的态势。本文所展现的能源创新举动都展示了应对多重挑战的方案最终要落脚到非洲本土的实际情况当中，发现更多自下而上的力量。

文章以肯尼亚为例，展示了非洲发展可再生能源尤其是太阳能的必要性和可行性，以及新能源以何种适当的方式生产和供应。建设电网并输送集中生产的电力的传统方式在非洲不足以应对能源转型多重困境的现实，突出了发展离网型太阳能的必要性与可行性。以肯尼亚为代表的非洲国家正在探索一条非洲能源可持续发展的创新之路。这一创新路径基于现代新能源技术，分布式利用可再生能源，是对政府主导、基建先行的传统能源开发模式的补充。离网型太阳能在肯尼亚的出现，回应了非洲底层电力需求巨大与自上而下电力供给能力薄弱之间的张力，展示了一种能源民主化的可能性。[①]与大型基础设施建设不可忽视的存在感和可见性相比，离网型太阳能在非洲社会的发展如草根式的"星星之火"，但在各利益攸关方的推动作用下，"星星之火"正在呈现"燎原之势"。因此，以离网型太阳能为切入点，理解非洲的能源可持续发展和现代新能源技术在非洲社会的传播是值得研究的课题。

本文旨在展现在中央集权的电气化因缺乏成熟到位的设备而进程缓慢时，非洲有别于传统国家发展路径的社会自主发展道路——与其等待未可期的电网拓展，不如主动探索自主供电的方案——尤其是在世界变局带来诸多不稳定因素的当下。离网型太阳能正是为这种能源自治提供了途径。通过离网型太阳能的技术，人们得以实现能源自主的愿景和由此产生的社会实践。因此，分布式的离网型太阳能在非洲应用的意义不能仅仅被简化为技术性或是金融性的问题，而是要讨论这些新能源技术如何可以与推动社会自主能源实践以及提升国家电力服务质量相结合，也就是思考能源与社会的互动关系，这才能有助于塑造能源可持续发展的远景。

---

① Raphael Obonyo, "Push for renewables: How Africa is building a different energy pathway," 6 January 2021, https://www.un.org/africarenewal/magazine/january-2021/push-renewables-how-africa-building-different-energy-pathway, 2021-12-13.

当下困境中的非洲经济一体化新进展

郑　宇　朱北思　周心培[*]

摘　要：促进非洲贸易是非洲发展战略的重要目标。作为经济一体化的里程碑，非洲大陆自贸区为规划统一的非洲大市场创造了契机。然而，非洲经济一体化仍面临执行意志不足、关税与非关税壁垒高筑、基础设施薄弱、区域组织碎片化、外部依赖等障碍。非洲大陆自贸区的启动在中短期面临着疫情蔓延、经济停滞和贸易阻隔的多重困境，但从长期看有望推动域内市场整合和资本流动，进而释放非洲大陆的发展潜力。在大国竞争白热化、全球化向区域化转向的背景下，中非发展合作既为非洲全方位、多层次的经济一体化提供重要机遇，也有利于中国团结非洲国家，实现共同发展，并加强在全球南方的经济外交。

关键词：非洲大陆自贸区　经济一体化　区域主义　中非合作

引　言

2021年1月，非洲大陆自由贸易区（以下简称"非洲自贸区"）的启动标志经济一体化从若干次区域的尝试迈入整个非洲大陆统合的新阶段。非洲自贸区并不是非洲首次尝试经济一体化战略。事实上，非洲经济一体化是一个延绵百余年的愿景。尽管表达、实现方式与时更新，但推动经济一体化始终是通向"非洲梦"的主要途径。在过去数十年中，经济一体化的进展参差不齐，而挑战则层出不穷。挑战体现在执行意志、关税与非关税壁垒、交通与能源基础设施、区域组织碎片化、贸易

---

　　* 郑宇，复旦大学国际关系与公共事务学院教授；朱北思（Smith Njumbe），复旦大学国际关系与公共事务学院博士生；周心培，复旦大学国际关系与公共事务学院研究生。本文系国家社会科学基金重点项目"大国竞合态势下的中非发展合作研究"（批准号：22AGJ005）的阶段性成果。

外部依赖性等多方面。正确认识这些挑战，有助于非洲管理期望、吸取教训、采取措施，确保非洲自贸区逐步实现可持续、包容性发展。[①]

非洲自贸区的成立之时正值新冠疫情肆虐全球之际。非洲经济结构单一，工业生产能力孱弱，严重依赖国际援助和贸易，医疗用品和药物的自给率仅为8%。[②] 疫情造成的全球供应链中断使非洲大陆陷入了多重危机中，包括公共卫生危机、粮食危机、贸易危机、债务危机。这些危机相互关联，对非洲的发展构成了空前挑战。

然而，非洲自贸区的启动，有望成为历史性转折，激活非洲经济一体化的发展潜力。在非洲自贸区启动一年后，非盟成员已就超过80%的非洲原产地商品的关税问题达成共识，并已启动争端解决机制。覆盖全非洲的泛非支付结算系统也已投入域内贸易使用，旨在减少非洲国家间跨境交易的货币兑换成本。非洲自贸区有望助力宏观规划、提高域内贸易占比、刺激投资流入、推动价值链深化、促进贫困治理，并发挥非洲能动性。不过，在新冠疫情、乌克兰危机的背景下，非洲自贸区要想真正推动经济一体化，既需要加强域内协同，也需要与国际社会良性互动。

自非洲自贸区实施以来，非洲经济一体化面临哪些机遇和挑战？本文首先回顾非洲经济一体化的五阶段进程，并聚焦非洲自贸区为经济一体化注入的崭新活力；接着，从贸易和投资两方面评估非洲的总体表现，列举阻碍经济一体化的种种挑战，探讨非洲自贸区将被激活的发展潜力；最后，研判全球化趋势与美欧对非政策调整，分析中国在非利益，呈现经济一体化带来的全球机遇。

一、经济一体化的非洲路径

非洲推动一体化的雄心由来已久，最初表现为在泛非主义思潮引

[①] Olabisi Akinkugbe, "Chapter 7: A Critical Appraisal of the African Continental Free Trade Area Agreement," in K. Kugler and F. Sucker, eds., in *International Economic Law*: (*Southern*) *African Perspectives and Priorities*, South Africa: Juta Law, 2021.

[②] International Trade Centre, *Medical Industries in Africa*: *A Regional Response to Supply Shortages*, July 2020. https://intracen.org/media/file/2476.

领下的次区域、小规模尝试。非洲的一体化运动始于前而民族国家成于后，[①] 兴起于 20 世纪初的泛非主义主张"非洲一体性"，追求非洲人民大团结，推翻殖民主义统治，取得非洲独立，最终统一非洲大陆，建立"非洲合众国"。[②] 20 世纪 60 年代以来，非洲开国领袖均积极倡导经济一体化，目的是建立覆盖非洲大陆的共同市场。1963 年，非洲联盟（以下简称"非盟"）前身非洲统一组织（以下简称"非统组织"）的成立使大陆一级的一体化成为可能。不过，在早期探索中，一体化运动由政治而非经济因素驱动，以政治宣言为主，而非具备约束力的法律文件。[③]

自 1979 年《蒙罗维亚宣言》和 1980 年《拉各斯行动计划》起，经济一体化进入第二阶段。《蒙罗维亚宣言》强调非洲国家将共同努力，为建立非洲共同市场铺平道路；《拉各斯行动计划》则承诺在 2000 年之前建立非洲经济共同体，并为此设置两个"十年规划"，预期先加强次区域与各行业一体化，再逐步建立非洲共同市场与非洲经济共同体。[④] 此外，在思想层面，该轮一体化强调非洲经济应自力更生、自主发展。然而，在实践层面，由于受到国际金融机构主导的结构调整方案的压力，经济危机加剧，非洲在 20 世纪 80 年代陷入"失去的十年"，《拉各斯行动计划》未能真正落地。

经济一体化的第三阶段始于 1991 年《阿布贾条约》。《阿布贾条约》宣告非洲经济共同体正式成立，并详细规划为期 34 年、分为 6 个阶段的一体化实施路线图。[⑤] 该条约有两大特征：一是法律性高于政治性，试图囊括强有力的体制机制，以确保一体化承诺得到遵守和有效履行；二是以区域经济共同体为支柱，并认为稳步推进次区域一级的经济一体化

---

① 刘鸿武、杨惠：《非洲一体化历史进程之百年审视及其理论辨析》，《西亚非洲》2015 年第 2 期，第 73—94 页。

② 舒运国：《泛非主义与非洲一体化》，《世界历史》2014 年第 2 期，第 27 页。

③ Luke, David, and Jamie MacLeod, eds., *Inclusive Trade in Africa: The African Continental Free Trade Area in Comparative Perspective*, Routledge, 2019.

④ Organization of African Unity (OAU), *Lagos Plan of Action*, 1980. https://www.nepad.org/publication/lagos-plan-of-action.

⑤ OAU, *Treaty Establishing the African Economic Community*, 1991. https://au.int/en/treaties/treaty-establishing-african-economic-community.

是实现非洲一体化的先决条件。在非洲自贸区实施之前，非洲大陆已有30个次区域自由贸易协定，[①] 而且54个国家共有132个区域经济组织的成员身份，平均每个非洲国家是2.5个区域组织的成员。[②] 区域经济共同体的井喷式发展也带来组织成员国身份重叠问题（见图1），形成"意大利面碗"效应（Spagetti bowl effect），[③] 在履约难度、管辖权冲突、协调负担等方面，阻碍非洲经济一体化。

自1994年生效以来，《阿布贾条约》一直是经济一体化的指导依据。1999年，非统组织第四届特别首脑会议通过《锡尔特宣言》，决定成立非盟。2002年，非盟取代非统组织，并将区域经济共同体作为建立非洲经济共同体的战略性支柱。非盟承认如下8个区域经济共同体：西非国家经济共同体（ECOWAS）、中部非洲国家经济共同体（ECCAS）、南部非洲发展共同体（SADC）、东部和南部非洲共同市场（COMESA）、东非共同体（EAC）、东非政府间发展组织（IGAD）、萨赫勒－撒哈拉国家共同体（CEN-SAD）和阿拉伯马格里布联盟（AMU）。[④]

在非盟的领导下，经济一体化步入第四阶段。《非盟宪章》明确指出，要加快《阿布贾条约》落实进度，以促进非洲经济社会发展，更有效地应对全球化挑战；然而，非洲区域经济共同体叠床架屋的现象愈演愈烈，各区域市场整合与制度建设程度参差不齐，对《阿布贾条约》的执行情况也大相径庭。[⑤] 有鉴于此，非盟意识到不能放任"自下而上"的小规模尝试，而需以"自上而下"的顶层规划统筹之。

2012年，非盟通过《促进非洲内部贸易的决定》，试图以顶层规划方式将现有区域经济共同体合并为分别覆盖非洲大陆东半部和西半部的

---

① 郑宇：《后疫情时代非洲发展前景展望》，《中国投资》2021年第1、2期，第39页。

② 朱伟东、王婷：《非洲区域经济组织成员身份重叠现象与消解路径》，《西亚非洲》2020年第2期，第99页。

③ "意大利面碗"效应一词源于美国经济学家巴格沃蒂1995年出版的《美国贸易政策》一书，指在许多自由贸易协定和区域贸易协定下，同一区域的不同优惠待遇和原产地规则像意大利面条那样，一根根绞在一起，剪不断，理还乱。

④ OAU, *Constitutive Act of the African Union*, 1991.

⑤ 朴英姬：《非洲大陆自由贸易区：进展、效应与推进路径》，《西亚非洲》2020年第3期，第95页。

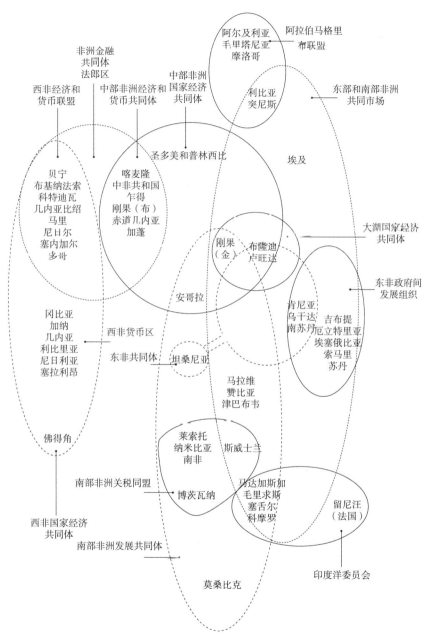

图1 非洲区域经济共同体成员身份重叠图

资料来源：朱伟东、王婷：《非洲区域经济组织成员身份重叠现象与消解路径》,《西亚非洲》2020年第2期，第101页，根据非盟官方网站的信息和非洲开发银行《2019年非洲经济报告》整理而成

两个"超级区域经济共同体"（super REC），进而将这两大超级区域经济共同体合并为"大陆自由贸易区"（CFTA）。纵向看，超级区域经济共同体注重区域经济共同体机制、层级协调与合理化；横向看，超级区域经济共同体替代原先小规模的次区域经济共同体，成为经济一体化的过渡机制。[1] 东部和南部非洲共同市场、东非共同体和南部非洲发展共同体也于2011年开启"三方自由贸易区"（TFTA）谈判，并于2015年发表《沙姆沙伊赫宣言》，下决心组建超级区域经济共同体。[2] 总之，非盟已付出种种努力推动超级区域经济共同体建设，但是收效未能尽如人意。

2018年，非盟大会通过了《非洲大陆自由贸易区协定》，2019年协定生效，并于2021年1月正式启动大陆自贸区，标志着经济一体化进入又一新阶段。该协定致力于促进非洲内部贸易、投资、工业化以及大陆一级的市场整合。[3] 非洲自贸区是迄今为止世界上成员最多的区域贸易集团，覆盖除厄立特里亚外的全部54个非洲国家、13亿人口和3.4万亿美元经济总额。根据该协定，非洲国家应在5到10年内，逐步对90%的区域内贸易商品削减97%的关税，非关税壁垒也会大幅减少。[4] 非洲自贸区虽然建立在现有的经济一体化（"大陆自由贸易区"）框架上（见图2），但超越了整合区域自贸区或超级区域共同体（如"三方自由贸易区"）关税同盟的线性逻辑，直接尝试在非洲大陆建立单一自贸区，而非等待次区域共同体成熟后再着手合并，故被称为经济一体化的最后阶段。非洲自贸区还纳入促进可持续绿色工业化和包容性社会经济进步目标，而不同于以往国民生产总值至上的发展主义考虑。[5]

---

[1]　AU, *Decisions and Declarations on Boosting Intra-African Trade* (*BIAT*) *and the Establishment of a Continental Free Trade Area* (*CFTA*), 2012. https://au.int/en/documents/20120731/decisions-and-declarations-boosting-intra-african-trade-biat-and-establishment.

[2]　Southern African Development Community, *Tripartite Declaration for the establishment of the COMESA-EAC-SADC Free Trade Area* (*FTA*), 2011. https://www.tralac.org/resources/by-region/comesa-eac-sadc-tripartite-fta.html.

[3]　AU, *Agreement Establishing the African Continental Free Trade Area*, 2021. https://au.int/en/treaties/agreement-establishing-african-continental-free-trade-area.

[4]　郑宇：《后疫情时代非洲发展前景展望》，《中国投资》2021年第1、2期，第39页。

[5]　David Luke and Jamie MacLeod, eds., *Inclusive Trade in Africa*: *The African Continental Free Trade Area in Comparative Perspective*, Routledge, 2019.

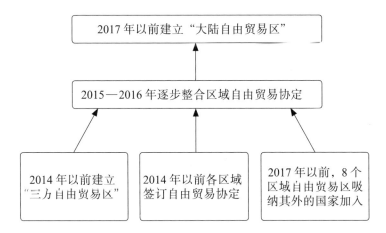

图2 "大陆自由贸易区"实现步骤设想

资料来源：David Luke et al. eds., *Inclusive Trade in Africa: The African Continental Free Trade Area in Comparative Perspective*, London: Routledge, 2019

此外，作为非盟《2063年议程》旗舰项目，非洲自贸区是非洲大陆实现包容性和可持续发展蓝图的核心组成部分，即将非洲大陆转变为一个未来的全球增长动力。[1]非洲自贸区目标是建立统一的自由市场、促进资本和人员流动，推动工业化、提升经济竞争力等。[2]非盟为非洲自贸区设计了三阶段方案：第一阶段是商品和服务贸易的关税减让；第二阶段涉及知识产权保护、投资自由化和竞争政策；第三阶段重点在数字经济的开放。目前正在推进的第一阶段预计需花费10年时间来消除非洲国家间97%的商品和服务贸易关税。这一目标能否顺利实现，取决于五个核心政策工具能否到位：一是原产地规则（Rules of Origin），二是关税减让，三是非关税壁垒的监督、报告和消除机制，四是泛非支付结算系统（PAPSS），五是非洲贸易观察站。[3]

① African Union Commission (AUC), *Agenda 2063: The Africa We Want*, Addis Ababa, 2015.

② AU, *Legal Text of the AfCFTA*, May 2018, Art.3 (f) and (g).

③ 郑宇：《非洲一体化是中国的机遇吗》，《文化纵横》2022年第5期，第153页。

二、经济一体化的曲折发展

自 20 世纪 80 年代开始，随着经济全球化的推进，非洲大陆融入国际贸易体系的程度不断加深。1990—2017 年，非洲贸易总额占 GDP 比值从约 53% 增至 67%，并在 2011 年前后，随大宗商品价格飙升而达到顶峰（见图 3）。在此期间，非洲服务贸易额显著增长，进口总额从 1990 年的约 270 亿美元增至 2017 年的约 900 亿美元，出口总额从 1990 年的 200 亿美元增至 2017 年的约 890 亿美元。[①]

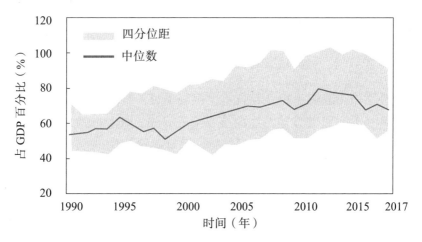

图 3　非洲贸易开放度变迁（1990—2017 年）

资料来源：国际货币基金组织（2019），根据世界银行"世界发展指标数据库"数据作图

同时，非洲贸易伙伴关系也趋多样化和自主化。以欧盟为代表的传统伙伴占比下降，以中国为代表的新兴市场占比上升，非洲域内贸易也大幅增加。域内贸易占非洲贸易总额的比重从 1990 年的约 5% 增至 2019 年的约 17%。[②] 此外，非洲非正规跨境贸易（即未纳入官方统计的小规

---

① IMF, *Regional Economic Outlook: Sub-Saharan Africa Recovery Amid Elevated Uncertainty*, Washington, DC, April 2019.

② Brookings, "Figures of the Week: Increasing Intra-regional Trade in Africa," 2019, https://www.brookings.edu/blog/africa-in-focus/2019/02/22/figures-of-the-weekincreasing-intra-regional-trade-in-africa, 查询时间：2023 年 1 月 13 日。

模边境贸易）举足轻重。在 21 世纪初，乌干达对东非地区非正规出口达正规贸易的三分之一；在南部非洲发展共同体，以农产品为主的非正规贸易达官方贸易的 30%—40%。[1]

但从贸易结构来看，非洲处于全球价值链的底端，主要以出口能源资源等初级产品为主，尚未形成区域和产业内的制造业生产链。不同非洲国家间和次区域间也存在巨大差异。科特迪瓦、肯尼亚、塞内加尔和南非是区域贸易枢纽。南非占非洲域内进口的 35%，占域内制造业进口的 40%。相比之下，同为域内大国的尼日利亚、阿尔及利亚和埃及共占非洲 GDP 总量一半，却仅占贸易份额的 11%。不同区域间的贸易份额则更低。这很大程度上是因为区域间关税较高，平均为 12%—15%。[2]

1. 多种融合障碍

根据非洲区域一体化指数（ARII）2019 年数据，经济一体化虽取得一定进展，却未达预期目标。[3] 经济一体化表现不佳是执行意志薄弱、关税与非关税壁垒高筑、基础设施欠完备、区域组织碎片化以及国际贸易中的外部依赖性等多重因素共同作用的结果。

执行意志

非洲次区域组织曾出台多份一体化纲领和文件，但执行意志不足，难以按期履约，致使目标实现往往滞后。马格里布联盟计划 1995 年前建立优惠贸易区和关税同盟，2000 年建立共同市场，最终却不了了之。西共体以埃科替代非洲法郎的想法由来已久，但至今也未实现。[4] 三方自贸区原计划于 2014 年组建，到 2015 至 2016 年再与其他自贸区整合成非洲自贸区，但延至 2019 年才初步实现。[5] 非洲国家推动经济一体化的政

---

① African Development Bank (AfDB), "Informal Cross Border Trade in Africa: Implications and Policy Recommendations," *Africa Economic Brief* 3, November 2012.

② AfDB, "Informal Cross Border Trade in Africa: Implications and Policy Recommendations," *Africa Economic Brief* 3, November 2012.

③ AUC, AfDB, and UNECA, *Africa Regional Integration Index Report* 2019, Addis Ababa, 2020. ARII 根据贸易、生产能力、宏观经济、基础设施和移民等指标，评估非洲区域融合情况。

④ 周心培：《西共体单一货币：埃科能否落地？》，《中国投资》2022 年第 19、20 期，第 96—99 页。

⑤ 姚桂梅：《非洲自贸区带来新希望，但需要耐心》，《世界知识》2019 年第 13 期，第 55 页。

治表态虽然坚定，但实际行动往往迟滞甚至与美好愿景背道而驰。

非洲自贸区能否顺利推进，很大程度上将取决于南非、尼日利亚、埃及等区域大国的决心和协调能力。经济一体化与国家产业政策往往存在张力。当经济一体化与国家产业政策目标发生冲突时，非洲国家常常走向保护主义，比如利用关税与非关税壁垒来促进和保护国内产业，免受来自非洲其他国家竞争。尼日利亚对邻国贝宁的封锁政策就是一例。2019 年 8 月，尼日利亚毫无预兆地关闭与贝宁的贸易边界，并声称旨在打击走私犯罪。这种保护主义做法违反了其对西共体做出的承诺。事实上，受益于贸易保护的政治和商业精英会更有动力和能力，游说政府维持贸易保护的举措，保护这些群体的既得利益，如此形成恶性循环。

关税与非关税壁垒

由于国内税基狭窄，关税是大多数非洲国家财政收入的重要来源。在有效补偿机制缺失的情况下，许多非洲国家不愿削减关税、开放国内市场。除了南部非洲关税同盟和东共体内部成员国之间实现零关税外，非洲其他区域经济共同体成员之间均保留不同程度的关税壁垒，而对非成员国的关税则更高。

另外，很多时候，关税削减也未能提高次区域贸易流量。比如，已成立 20 多年的中部非洲经济和货币共同体（CEMAC），6 个成员国之间的贸易量仍然很低。这表明关税以外的因素限制了贸易增长，包括非关税壁垒高筑以及产品类型单一。

非关税壁垒主要包括海关及物流体系低效、政府机构懒政怠政和权力滥用，以及法律、制度、技术规则和标准不统一等等。尤其是在微观一级，体制内腐败亟待彻查，以真正实现劳动力、资本跨国流动。

基础设施

基础设施落后导致非洲大陆物流成本高昂。绝大多数非洲国家财政紧张，无力为本国本区域的基础设施建设注入足够资金，被迫大规模依赖外部金融机构贷款。这给非洲国家带来债务攀升、依赖性强等问题。

新冠疫情加剧非洲国家财政危机，许多国家无力偿还基建贷款，融资可持续性堪忧。按照非盟《2063 年议程》规划，非洲大陆每年基建资金有 1300 亿美元到 1700 亿美元的缺口，[①] 其提出的以高铁网、高速公路网和区域航空网连接首都和商业中心的设想，可能因缺乏资金和技术支持迟迟不能落地。

此外，电力和能源基础设施短缺构成非洲大陆自贸区建设的另一大瓶颈。目前，非洲通电率仅约 40%，有超过 6.4 亿非洲人生活在无电地区，而电力短缺也成为非洲工业化发展的瓶颈。贸易政策无法代替产业政策，许多非洲国家尚缺乏工业生产能力，因而存在产品同质化强、互补性弱的问题。因此，即便在去除关税与非关税壁垒等方面取得进展，非洲经济一体化依然缺乏内生动力。非洲自贸区要获得生命力，必须解决非洲企业生产能力弱、市场主体参与不足的问题，而这还需从改善增加电能基础设施入手。[②]

成员国身份重叠

前文提到的"意大利面碗"效应极大地推高了非洲域内贸易成本。许多非洲国家同时隶属于不同的区域经济共同体，因而可适用不同的贸易规则（如决定出口商品能否享受优惠关税待遇的原产地规则）。

这种成员国身份重叠现象在非洲屡见不鲜，造成如下三方面困扰：一是区域经济共同体的运行成本可能加重成员国财务和行政负担；二是因相同贸易问题领域的管辖权，或因司法机构宽泛的管辖权而导致非贸易领域的管辖权冲突；三是不同区域组织之间或某区域经济组织与成员国国内法之间，在法律适用上产生冲突。[③]

欧盟一直试图同非洲大陆签订整体性贸易协定，但因非洲国家之间集体行动难以协调，只好退而求其次，分别与不同非洲国家或次区域组织签订经贸伙伴协议（Economic Partnership Agreement, EPA）。

国际贸易中的外部依赖

在国际贸易中，非洲经济体普遍呈现严重的外部依赖特征，尤其是

---

① AUC, *Agenda 2063: The Africa We Want*, Addis Ababa, 2015. https://au.int/en/agenda2063/overview.

② AUC, AfDB, and United Nations Economic Commission for Africa (UNECA), *Africa Regional Integration Index Report* 2019, Addis Ababa, 2020.

③ 朱伟东、王婷：《非洲区域经济组织成员身份重叠现象与消解路径》，《西亚非洲》2020年第 2 期，第 106 页。

尼日利亚、安哥拉等资源型国家深受国际大宗商品市场价格波动困扰。①
国际贸易的外部依赖性与殖民遗留的单一产业结构息息相关。非洲许多
国家的生产结构集中于一种或者几种农矿初级原料，在殖民时期，供宗
主国作为工业原料和生活消费品使用；而在独立后，这些生产品与国内
消费市场缺乏联系，因而仍以直接输往世界市场为主。

同时，非洲的经济发展长期失衡，粮食生产、制造业等其他经济部
门得不到应有发展，粮食和工业制成品依赖外部进口。在新冠肺炎疫情
期间，由于全球供应链被切断，非洲国家在粮食、化肥与医疗用品方面
受到巨大负面影响，更是凸显这种外部依赖性的弊端。②

政治与安全

非洲国家彼此之间虽然几乎没有战争，但一国内部的冲突和军事政
变接连不断，严重阻碍非洲经济一体化进程。首先，近年来，非洲萨赫
勒地区政变浪潮明显抬头，2022 年 2 月第 35 届非盟峰会专门讨论了中
西部非洲 18 个月内发生的 6 场政变或未遂政变的问题。同时，恐怖主义
威胁也在加剧，索马里青年党、伊斯兰国和"博科圣地"等极端主义暴
恐势力威胁非洲民众安全和经济生产秩序，严重打击经济合作信心。

此外，非传统安全威胁也逐渐凸显。新冠肺炎疫情导致非洲经济 25
年以来首次衰退，助长各国保护主义情绪，非盟也因此推迟《非洲大陆
自由贸易区协定》的实施日期。气候变化危及非洲经济和民生，旱灾、
洪灾、沙漠化、土地退化频发大大增加经济下行压力，并破坏民生和政
治稳定。以东部非洲地区为例，2018—2019 年，该地区遭受旱灾，2020
年又经历蝗灾和洪灾，伴随新冠疫情，造成粮食安全危机。民众的正常
生产生活都无法保障，更遑论推动非洲自贸区建设和经济一体化发展。

2. 一体化的发展潜力

在后疫情时代，非洲自贸区被各方寄予厚望，希望其逆势推动非洲
国家以统一大市场的面貌参与到全球经济活动中。具体而言，非洲自贸

---

① 刘海方:《被忽视的自强大陆——多重危机中的非洲能动性》,《文化纵横》2022 年第 4
期, 第 43—53 页。

② 刘海方:《变动世界秩序中的非洲》,《世界知识》2023 年第 1 期, 第 14 页。

区有望改善成员国身份重叠问题，提高域内贸易占比，刺激投资流入，促进价值链深化，推动贫困治理。

宏观规划

非洲自贸区为打破"意大利面碗"效应创造良机，它继承了《阿布贾条约》的经济一体化梦想，并改良了其不切实际的路径设计。《阿布贾条约》要求区域经济共同体在合并至大陆一级前先逐步发展为关税同盟，但对于很多区域而言，在区域一级建立关税同盟难比登天、遥遥无期。有鉴于此，非洲自贸区并没有无限期等待区域关税同盟合并，而是采取"自上而下"的方式，直接在整个非洲大陆建立自由贸易区。这将有助于非洲经济一体化的宏观规划与协调。

域内贸易

20 世纪 90 年代初，非洲域内贸易额占非洲贸易总额的比重仅为 4% 到 5%，该数据在 2017 年提升至 17%。非洲自贸区有望进一步提升非洲域内贸易比重，降低经济对外贸易依赖度。据联合国非洲经济委员会估算，到 2040 年，非洲域内贸易可增加 500 亿美元至 700 亿美元，比 2020 年增长 5% 至 15%，域内贸易占比达 50% 以上；其中，工业产品贸易额增加 360 亿美元至 440 亿美元，比 2020 年增长 25% 至 30%；农产品和食品贸易额增加 95 亿美元至 170 亿美元，比 2020 年增长 20% 至 30%；能源和矿产品贸易额增加 45 亿美元至 90 亿美元，比 2020 年增长 5% 至 11%。[①] 据世界银行和非洲自贸区秘书处估算，到 2035 年，非洲自贸区有望推动非洲域内出口增长超 109%，域外出口增长约 18%。[②]

直接投资

非洲自贸区逐步消除关税与非关税壁垒，建构覆盖 13 亿人口、GDP 总和达 3.4 万亿美元的单一大市场。由此产生规模经济效应，既能刺激非洲国家间相互投资，也能加速域外资本流入非洲大陆。更重要的是，

[①] UNECA, *An Empirical Assessment of the African Continental Free Trade Area Modalities on Goods*, November 2018, p. 3. https://archive.uneca.org/sites/default/files/PublicationFiles/afcfta_modalities_key_messages_eng.pdf.

[②] World Bank and AfCFTA Secretariat, *Making Most of the African Continental Free Trade Area: Leveraging Trade and Foreign Direct Investment to Boost Growth and Reduce Poverty*, 2022, p. 65.

非洲的外国直接投资流入将超越自然资源领域而走向多样化，从而降低对原材料出口驱动式的繁荣和面对全球性经济危机的脆弱性。非洲将吸引更多出口导向、追求效率的外国直接投资，发展商品和服务贸易等新部门，并助力非洲的工业化发展和经济多元化进程。政府招商引资政策在可信度和灵活性之间的权衡调整既可能增强投资信心，也可能削弱投资能力。[1] 就非洲现状而言，政府提高政策的可信度，有助于增强投资信心。

区域价值链

随着非洲域内贸易成本降低，以及投资的信心、质量、数量上升，区域价值链也将逐步深化。目前，非洲大陆从初级产品转化为工业制成品的区域价值链的发展潜力尚未得到充分发挥。例如，喀麦隆、科特迪瓦、加纳等西非地区可可生产国将绝大多数的可可原料出口到全球其他地区，而南非、埃及等区内主要巧克力生产国则主要从非洲大陆以外地区进口可可原料。非洲自贸区通过建立涵盖全非洲的统一大市场，扭转次区域经济共同体之间未能有效建立贸易联系的局面，进而构建起更复杂、高效而具有竞争力的区域价值链，增强非洲的全球竞争力。[2]

贫困治理

根据贫困治理的渐进平衡模式，检验一国减贫机制是否有效，可以重点考察该国发展制造业、减少不平等和治理多维贫困的表现。[3] 非洲自贸区是非洲消除贫困的重要催化剂。如果非洲自贸区成功实施，非洲制造业的规模有可能从 2015 年的 5000 亿美元增加到 2025 年的 1 万亿美元，创造 1400 万个稳定的就业岗位；到 2035 年，非洲自贸区有望促进非洲制造业出口增长 134%，在各产业中增速最快。在 29 个国家中，18 个国家非熟练女劳工工资增速高于平均水平，有助于削弱性别不平等。到 2035 年，非洲约 3000 万人将摆脱极端贫困，6790 万人将摆脱中度贫

---

[1] Yu Zheng, "Credibility and Flexibility: Political Institutions, Governance, and Foreign Direct Investment," *International Interactions*, Vol. 37, No. 3, 2011, pp. 293-319.

[2] 朴英姬：《非洲大陆自由贸易区：进展、效应与推进路径》，《西亚非洲》2020 年第 3 期，第 110 页。

[3] 郑宇：《贫困治理的渐进平衡模式：基于中国经验的理论建构与检验》，《中国社会科学》2022 年第 2 期，第 141—161 页。

困。① 同时，伴随交通道路、自来水等基础服务设施不断完善，非洲民众能从中获得的福祉和幸福感也会上升。从这些意义上看，非洲自贸区有望真正提高多维贫困治理水平。

非洲能动性

随着非洲自贸区正式启动，非洲国家将以统一大市场的崭新面貌，参与到全球经济活动中。这有望极大地提升非洲能动性（African agency）。一方面，非洲自贸区加速区域内贸易的整合和增长，促进形成统一大市场。当整个非洲大陆真正实现在经贸方面"用一个声音说话"，那么它在国际经贸谈判中的话语权也将显著提升，在与域外大国周旋时也将更有底气。

另一方面，非洲国家之间增强横向的合作协同，有助于逐步平衡在国际贸易中的外部依赖性。随着与原宗主国或某一西方大国的垂直型关系模式发生松动，非洲国家所谓的"外向性"大为改观，而这种强调通过横向合作，实现集体发展的趋势被称为"新泛非主义"。它在路径上区别于强调民族自觉与解放的传统泛非主义，致力于探索集体治理的新路径。②

三、非洲经济一体化的全球机遇

21世纪以来，非洲成为大国竞争的重要战场。中美欧竞相鼓动起"追求非洲"的热浪，加强同非洲的经贸合作。2000年是大国开启新非洲战略元年。这一年，美国通过《非洲增长与机遇法案》（African Growth and Opportunity Act, AGOA），允许对非洲国家出口到美国的部分商品免征关税；欧盟同非盟举行第一次首脑会谈，通过《科托努协定》，确立对非总体经贸战略；中国启动中非合作论坛，提出对非洲国家援助、贸易和投资等一系列合作计划。

美国和欧盟对非战略以改造非洲政治生态为条件，并未取得预期效

---

① World Bank and AfCFTA Secretariat, *Making Most of the African Continental Free Trade Area: Leveraging Trade and Foreign Direct Investment to Boost Growth and Reduce Poverty*, 2022, pp. 7, 65, 92.

② 刘海方:《被忽视的自强大陆——多重危机中的非洲能动性》,《文化纵横》2022年第4期, 第43—53页。

果，正进行重大调整转型。中国则以中非合作论坛和"一带一路"倡议为载体，开展全方位的对非经贸合作，后来居上，成为非洲最重要的贸易伙伴。在大国竞争加剧、全球化倒退的阴影下，非洲自贸区推动经济一体化取得实质进展，有助于中非伙伴关系，从而帮助中国对冲地缘政治风险，并为引领经济全球化重启发掘新的增长点。

1. 大国角逐非洲

美国对非经贸战略

普惠制，亦称特惠关税制度（Generalized System of Preferences，GSP），是发达国家对发展中国家部分出口商品给予非互惠关税减免的制度安排。AGOA 基于 1971 年的普惠制建立，将免税商品清单从普惠制的 4000 多种扩大到 6400 多种，但肉类、奶制品、烟草等非洲国家具有出口竞争力的产品未纳入清单。[1]AGOA 对非洲贸易整体促进不明显，仅南非、尼日利亚、安哥拉等大国从中获益较多。在 AGOA 实施的早期，非洲对美出口增长较快，从 2000 年的不足 200 亿美元增长到 2008 年的 820 亿美元。[2]但全球金融危机后，随着国际大宗商品价格下降，非洲经济增长放缓，美对非贸易和投资也显著下降。2020 年，美非贸易额不足美国全球贸易额的 1.5%，美对非投资不足其对外投资总额的 1%。

AGOA 的政治目标也未能实现。以埃塞俄比亚为例：作为从 AGOA 中获益最多的国家之一，该国对美出口总额在 20 年中增长了 10 倍，2020 年达近 3 亿美元，却未能实现美国所期望的政治民主化和改善人权的目标，甚至因内战导致国内局势不稳，而被取消 AGOA 的优惠待遇。因此，美国对 AGOA 政策的实施效果并不满意。

在 2014 年第一次美非峰会上，奥巴马政府承诺将 AGOA 延至 2025 年，但该决定在美国国内广受质疑。特朗普政府改变单方面给予非洲国家贸易优惠条件的做法，同肯尼亚谈判双边自由贸易协定。这是美国为同其他非洲国家谈判自由贸易协定的试点。拜登政府上台后，继续释放

---

① AGOA FAQs. https://agoa.info/about-agoa/products.html，查询时间：2022 年 12 月 15 日。

② Souleymane Coulibaly, Woubet Kassa, and Albert Zeufack, *Africa in the New Trade Environment Market Access in Troubled Times*, World Bank Publications, 2022, p. 87.

愿同非洲国家签订自由贸易协定的信号，并在 2021 年七国集团（G7）峰会上提出"重建更好世界"（B3W）的倡议，表示只要非洲国家认同西方价值体系，美国就会帮助其缩小基础设施建设赤字，将中国视为战略竞争对手之心昭然若揭。2022 年拜登政府借助国务卿访非之机，发布对非新战略，其中经贸、反恐和援助三大优先事项，都服务于遏制中国影响力这一目标。[①]

欧洲对非经贸战略

欧盟在 2000 年与非洲、加勒比海和太平洋地区的 77 个国家（简称"非加太集团"）签订《科托努协定》，旨在通过援助和扩大经贸合作帮助发展中国家实现可持续发展和民主转型。《科托努协定》的三根支柱是经济合作、贸易、政治对话。就贸易而言，欧盟对两类非洲国家给予不同的优惠待遇：一类是给予欠发达国家除武器外所有商品单项关税单方面免除（Everything but arms, EBA）；另一类是同经济发展水平相对较高的非洲国家签订的非对等互惠的经贸伙伴协议（Economic Partnership Agreement, EPA）。此外，欧盟还同北非国家签订联合协议（Association Agreement, AA），开展更广泛的政治经济合作。由此，非洲出口到欧盟的 90% 的商品都享受免征关税待遇，欧盟则得以保持对非影响力。

2015 年难民危机爆发后，移民问题成为欧非关系的讨论焦点，政策话语也从"移民—发展"向"移民—安全"关联转变。作为处理移民问题的核心政策工具，"欧非紧急信托基金"预算中，55% 用于移民管理，25% 用于遣返移民政策改革，13% 用于移民国籍甄别，仅 3% 用于安全和常规移民线路保障。[②] 可见，"阻遏性"在移民政策中渐占主导地位，而"遣返"和"再接收"变为关键词。同时，欧盟也致力于推动非洲和平发展，从根源上缓解移民和难民压力，进而维护自身安全。

2020 年，《科托努协定》到期之后，欧盟又同非加太集团国家续签《后科托努协定》，纳入欧盟关切的气候变化、人权、移民等问题，试图让对非战略更全面。欧非关系是法国 2022 年任欧盟轮值主席的优先事

---

① 张宏明:《拜登政府的非洲政策：优先事项与本质内涵》,《西亚非洲》2022 年第 4 期，第 70 页。

② 金玲:《欧盟的非洲政策调整：话语、行为与身份重塑》,《西亚非洲》2019 年第 2 期，第 50 页。

项，目标是"与非洲建立雄心勃勃又有前瞻性的联盟，创造团结、安全、可持续繁荣和稳定的环境"。与美国类似，欧盟全球门户投资计划也致力于加强对非基础设施投资，首期投入 1500 亿欧元，并与非洲发展平等的长期伙伴关系，加强绿色转型、数字化、移民和人口安全合作。

中非发展合作

2000 年以来，作为规范化的高层对话机制，三年一次的中非合作论坛有效推动中非经贸合作。自 2005 年开始，中国对 33 个非洲欠发达国家 97% 的输华产品提供零关税待遇，其政策效果与美国的 AGOA 和欧盟的 EBA 类似。2013 年"一带一路"倡议提出以后，中非经贸合作渠道拓宽，投融资、工程承包、工业园区建设都在迅猛增加。这深刻影响美欧对非战略变革，促使它们也开始加强对非投融资和基础设施建设。不过，中国对非贸易合作的制度化程度不高。直到 2021 年，中国才同毛里求斯签署第一个与非洲国家的自由贸易协定（FTA）。

从政策效果看，中非经贸增速远超美欧。2000—2020 年，中非贸易额增加 14 倍，从 120 亿美元增至 1760 亿美元；美非贸易额仅增加一倍，从 210 亿美元增长到 450 亿美元。2001 年，非洲出口商品中，超过一半的目的地是欧盟，输往美国的占 17%，中国份额仅为 3%。到 2020 年，欧盟仍是非洲最大出口地，但份额已降至 27%；美国份额降至 5%；中国份额则升至 14%，远超美国，也在缩小同欧盟的差距（见图 4）。

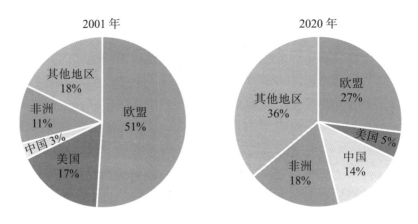

图 4　非洲对主要贸易伙伴的出口份额变化（2001—2020 年）

资料来源：Eurostat

总之，尽管美欧对非贸易都有所增加，但相对于中非经贸关系的迅猛发展态势，美欧对非经贸战略收效有限，因此急于调整对非战略，遏制中国不断扩大的影响力。对于非洲国家而言，大国竞争加剧虽然会带来不确定性，但也可能增加同域外大国谈判的筹码，前提是非洲国家需要团结一心，落实非洲自贸区建设，把握合作机遇。

2. 非洲一体化促进中非关系

非洲经济一体化进程将对后疫情时代的全球经贸格局产生重要影响。非洲大陆既是大国的必争之地，也是中国海外投融资的重要市场。因此，中非发展合作的双重目标在于保持良好稳定的外交关系以及平等互利的经贸关系。

全球趋势

全球贸易面临从全球化倒退到区域化的重大挑战。从发展增量看，金融危机以来，全球贸易增速显著放缓。新冠疫情前，全球贸易和GDP增速已大体相当，贸易不再是增长的"火车头"。尽管2021年全球贸易创28.5万亿美元的纪录，比2020年高25%，但这是疫情后报复式消费，恐难持续。从治理机构看，世界贸易组织（WTO）争端解决机制因美国阻挠上诉机构法官任命而停摆。拜登政府上台后，表面重申多边承诺，实则沿袭特朗普孤立政策，致力于与盟友"搞小圈子"。

与全球贸易陷入僵局相反，区域贸易蓬勃发展。WTO前身关贸总协定（GATT）运行46年间完成8轮多边贸易谈判，仅产生25个区域贸易协定。WTO成立27年来，未完成一轮多边贸易谈判，曾被寄予厚望的多哈回合谈判几经波折，最终搁浅，而同期却新增330个区域贸易协定。新冠疫情重创全球贸易，各国签署区域自贸协定的积极性反而更高。2021年，全球新增44个自贸协定，为历史最高纪录。[1]中国要适应全球化新态势，就要加强与在全球贸易体系中处于边缘地位的非洲国家的合作。

---

[1] WTO Regional Trade Agreements Database, https://rtais.wto.org/UI/PublicMaintainRTAHome.aspx，查询时间：2022年11月23日。

政治平等互信的伙伴

深度参与非洲经济一体化将有助于中国对冲地缘政治风险，进一步深化同发展中国家的团结合作，争取这支"天然同盟军"。就经济规模来看，非洲国家GDP仅占全球经济总量的2.9%，不足《区域全面经济伙伴关系协定》（RCEP）涵盖国家GDP的10%。但非洲自贸区是成员国最多的区域贸易集团，战略意义重大。

自2013年以来，中国与"一带一路"沿线国家的贸易投资额迅速增长，超过同其他地区的贸易和投资额的增速。自2013至2021年，中国与沿线国家贸易总值从占中国外贸总值比重的25%升至29.7%，[①]沿线投资占中国对外投资总额的比重更是从7%升至18%。[②]但目前来看，对外投资增量主要流向新加坡、印度尼西亚、马来西亚、越南等少数东南亚国家。同时，尽管中非经贸关系发展迅速，但中国对非投资额变化不大，占比甚至有所下降：2008年对非投资曾达中国对外投资总额的9.8%，而2020年这一数字仅为2.8%。在全球化退潮、大国竞争加剧的情况下，支持非洲经济一体化建设，对于巩固中非关系，营造可持续的投资环境格外重要。

经济互惠

非洲经济一体化建设有望带给中国巨大的潜在经济利益。这包括两方面：一是助力中国基建标准的推广。中国已成为非洲基础设施建设中最重要的域外参与者。根据德勤公司的统计，2013年，中国在非洲基础设施建设中的份额还远低于美欧，美欧提供了15%的非洲基础设施融资，建设了37%的项目，而中国仅提供了10%的融资，并建设了12%的项目；到了2019年，中国的融资和建设份额均为最高，分别为20.4%

---

① 《海关总署：我国与"一带一路"沿线国家进出口总值占比升至29.7%》，中国经济网，2022年5月20日，http://www.ce.cn/cysc/newmain/yc/jsxw/202205/20/t20220520_37602571.shtml，查询时间：2022年11月23日。

② 《2021年我对"一带一路"沿线国家投资合作情况》，中华人民共和国商务部官网，2022年1月24日，http://fec.mofcom.gov.cn/article/fwydyl/tjsj/202201/20220103239004.shtml，查询时间：2022年11月23日。

和 31.0%，而美国降至 1.3% 和 2.9%，欧盟国家降至 4.2% 和 12.2%。[①]

尽管新冠疫情以来，中国在非洲的基础设施融资和项目建设中的份额有所下降，但仍是最重要的参与者。对于交通和能源等基建项目，互联互通是降低运行成本、扩大规模效应的关键。"一带一路"倡议带来的双边互联互通对中国参与非洲基建非常关键，但如果没有非洲国家之间的互联互通，这些基础设施的长期运行将难以保障。因此，非洲自贸区建设对于维系中国的基建优势同样重要。

二是促使中国产能转出和非洲工业化进一步融合。21 世纪以来，非洲经济增长显著加快，但仍难摆脱资源依赖型经济结构，工业化异常艰难。2020 年，制造业在非洲 GDP 中仅占 12%，基本同 20 年前没有变化。非洲同域外国家贸易中，初级产品和能源占非洲的出口份额高达 75% 以上。不过，非洲对华出口中工业产品占比远高于对美欧出口，而非洲从中国进口的中间产品也更多地用于本地制造业生产。换言之，非洲同美欧的贸易结构体现传统商品贸易特征，同中国则体现全球价值链贸易特征，呈现出更强的互补关系。中国产业升级带来的商品和资本输出，提升了非洲国家工业生产能力，帮助其进一步融入全球价值链。[②]非洲自贸区的建设将扩大非洲的工业化产能和市场规模，推动中国和非洲建立更紧密的价值链生产合作。

谈判经验

中国政府明确表态支持非洲自贸区建立，但如何在制度和规则层面同非洲经济一体化对接，仍存在许多现实障碍。非盟和非洲自贸区可以各自通过非盟委员会和秘书处同中国建立经济合作专家组谈判，但整体性自贸协定的谈判仍需获得各国授权，包括未建交国的问题。尽管非盟呼吁非洲集体与域外大国谈判，但由于担心失去单向关税减免待遇，一些中等收入国家（如肯尼亚、毛里求斯）更倾向同域外大国签订双边贸易协定，而这又会提高谈判多边贸易协定协调成本。

中国同 26 个国家和地区签署 19 个自由贸易协定，其中半数在过去

---

① Deloitte, *Africa Construction Report Trends* 2019: *Capital projects in a digital age*, 2019, p. 8.
② 郑宇:《全球化、工业化和经济追赶》,《世界经济与政治》2019 年第 11 期, 第 105—128 页。

10 年中签署。在与东盟谈判的过程中，中国获得不少多边贸易谈判经验：先签订整体性和框架性的文件，再按货物贸易、服务贸易和投资协定的顺序逐步协商。与东盟类似，非盟内部千差万别，中国应以开放包容的心态、灵活务实的态度，全方位、宽领域、多层次推进合作，利用好当前的窗口期，在继续推进与单个非洲国家合作的同时，做好同非洲自贸区整体谈判的准备。当然，非洲经济一体化进程可能非常漫长，签署中非自由贸易协定的经济效应也难以立竿见影，但对后疫情时代的全球发展布局至关重要。①

结　语

为纪念 2019 年 7 月 7 日《非洲大陆自贸区协定》生效，非盟将每年的 7 月 7 日设为"非洲一体化日"，足见非洲自贸区成立之于非洲经济一体化的里程碑意义。作为泛非主义旗帜之下，先谋独立、再谋统一的"非洲梦"的重要组成部分，经济一体化是一代代非洲人锲而不舍、孜孜以求的目标：1963 年非统组织成立，奠定经济一体化的组织基础；1991 年《阿布贾条约》生效，为经济一体化提供指导依据；而 2019 年非洲自贸区协定生效，则预示着非洲单一大市场的曙光。非洲自贸区如果能顺利落地，那么它将成为 WTO 成立以来，覆盖国家最多、面积最大的自贸区。

然而，非洲经济一体化的落地却一波三折、举步维艰，毕竟要整合 54 个国家、14 亿人口谈何容易？事实上，早在非统组织成立之初，非洲一体化就有急渐之辩。经历 60 年逐步推进后，非洲经济一体化的基础渐臻成熟，但仍存在执行意志不足、关税与非关税壁垒高筑、基础设施薄弱、区域组织碎片化、外部依赖等重重障碍。非洲自贸区有望自上而下打破僵局，释放非洲大陆发展潜力。这一举措预计将带来五项实质性进展，包括改善成员国身份重叠问题、促进域内贸易、刺激投资流入、

---

① 本部分内容来源于郑宇：《非洲一体化是中国的机遇吗》，《文化纵横》2022 年第 5 期，第 146—155 页。

促进价值链深化和推动贫困治理。当然，落实情况仍待观察。

放眼世界，非洲经济一体化将带来经贸合作的机遇与竞争。21世纪以来，中美欧都愈发重视同非洲的合作。其中，美欧对非经贸战略未能达到政治和经济目标，正向基础设施建设投资、移民问题安全化等方向转型，以遏制中国不断扩大的影响力，维护自身利益。中国则以中非合作论坛和"一带一路"倡议为载体，灵活而全方位地开展对非经贸合作，取得良好成效。大国竞争白热化、全球化转向区域化之际，如果非洲自贸区能推动非洲一体化取得实质进展，那么中非伙伴关系也有望得到加强，一方面继续团结广大发展中国家，另一方面在经贸合作上进一步实现双赢。

总之，非洲自贸区意味着非洲一体化的"关键一跃"，机遇与挑战并存，合作与竞争同在。非洲国家如果能团结一心，将非洲自贸区落到实处，就有可能实现用"一个声音说话"，增加同域外大国谈判的筹码。对于中国而言，除经济利益外，非洲自贸区也为在后疫情时代平衡全球发展布局、对冲地缘政治风险提供机遇。

中非合作：老话题、新探索

多重危机下在非中国企业
人力资本投资新探索

王进杰　彭高杲　吴锦美　朱明明[*]

摘　要：自"一带一路"倡议提出以来，中国对非洲投资快速增长，成为非洲最重要的合作伙伴之一。然而，新冠疫情和俄乌冲突等因素造成了非洲大陆国际贸易萎缩、供应链断裂、通货膨胀、安全风险等多重危机。近年来新冠疫情等因素使得中国企业外派员工难度增大，加之本地员工技能有待提升，这暴露出长期以来中国在非企业难以本土化的困境，因此，中国亟待通过积极参与非洲本地人力资本发展来补齐短板。本文以案例研究法调查了四家典型的中国在非企业，通过深度访谈和资料分析，探讨了不同人力资本投资策略对于提升企业本地化经营能力的作用，同时结合非洲当地人力资本的特点和成长环境，分析了中方有效推动本地化人才建设应该采取何种策略的问题。本研究发现，中国企业突破了传统的"教育投资"的限制，新增了四个人力资本投资要素，分别为"制度投资""信任投资""文化投资"与"社区投资"。该五维度人力资本投资形式适应了非洲本地劳动力发展的需求，将当前局势与本地化人才培养相结合，以人才发展为核心来对抗不确定性，为当今复杂环境下中国企业在非洲进行本地化经营探索出值得广泛参考和借鉴的新道路。中国企业在非洲投资人力资本，不仅可以通过劳动力培养来促进企业的生产和管理，更带来了技术溢出和知识转移，从而创造就业并提升民生福祉，为当地可持续发展和提升经济竞争力贡献着力量。

---

*　王进杰，北京大学国家发展研究院、北京大学南南合作与研究院助理研究员，北京大学非洲研究中心副秘书长；彭高杲，中国传媒大学媒体融合与传播国家重点实验室舆情与社会治理专业硕士研究生；吴锦美，美国福坦莫大学金融管理专业博士生；朱明明，美国福坦莫大学金融管理专业博士，美国罗格斯大学访问学者。

关键词：人力资本　投资　劳动力　本地化　中国企业　非洲

引　言

自 2013 年"一带一路"倡议提出以来，中国企业对非洲的投资快速增长，成为非洲的重要合作伙伴之一。然而，新冠疫情、俄乌冲突等不确定因素的冲击，使得非洲大陆出现了国际贸易萎缩、供应链断裂、通货膨胀、安全风险等问题，这也为中国在非企业的经营带来了阻力。尤其是疫情蔓延全球，许多国家和地区对人员出入境采取了相关措施，造成国内人员外派难度增大，加之当地人才往往短缺，中国企业面临用工困难。促进本地人力资本水平提升、实现企业人力资源本土化变得迫在眉睫。

现有研究多基于传统的人力资本理论，关注常态环境下对员工的教育投资；后疫情时代如何开启，企业和政策决策层亟待了解在当前特殊变局下非洲经营时空环境以及所需人才的跟踪研究。尽管近年来学界和业界开始关注企业跨文化经营问题，但目前仍未将跨文化、本地化和人力资本投资结合起来。本文从人力资本投资的角度展开研究，探讨中国企业在当今多重危机下如何通过投资人力资本来提升企业在非洲进行本地化经营的能力，并实现技术转移、员工培养、当地发展等多个维度的企业社会责任。本研究以四家在非洲经营的中国企业为案例，基于深度访谈法和资料分析法展开研究，通过剖析中国企业所采用的不同人力资本投资策略，梳理中国企业应对多重危机，提升本地化经营能力并推进当地人力资本发展的新探索。

一、中国企业在"一带一路"国家的投资情况

自 2013 年"一带一路"倡议开启以来，中国与有关国家基于现有的多双边工商合作机制，建立了更为广泛、有效的区域合作平台，积极参与经济全球化、区域合作和文化多样性的建设。截至 2022 年 12 月，中国已与 150 个国家和 32 个国际组织签署 200 余份共建"一带一路"合作

文件，投资规模近 1 万亿美元。 如图 1 所示，自 2002 年以来，中国对外直接投资呈现稳步上升趋势。尽管近些年受到疫情暴发和俄乌冲突等多种不利因素的影响，中国对外投资仍在逆势增长，2021 年总投资流量为 1788.2 亿美元，比上年增长 16.3%。[2]

（亿美元）

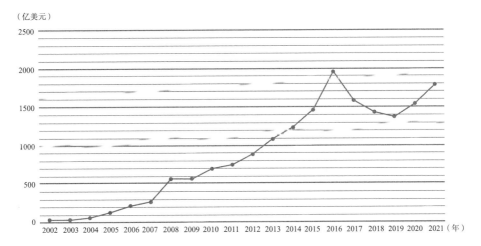

图 1 2002—2021 年中国对外直接投资流量情况

资料来源：历年《中国对外直接投资统计公报》

非洲是"一带一路"倡议的重要组成部分，拥有丰富的资源、巨大的人口红利和快速发展的城市化进程。中国则拥有资金、技术和发展经验的优势。这使得中非合作优势互补，提高了资源配置效率，在互利共赢的基础上，推动了双方经济的发展。然而，比较各地区之间的投资（见图 2），2021 年中国对非洲的直接投资存量仅占其全球对外投资的 1.6%，主要分布在南非、刚果（金）、赞比亚、埃塞俄比亚、安哥拉、尼日利亚、肯尼亚、阿尔及利亚、津巴布韦、坦桑尼亚、尼日尔、埃及、

---

① 国家发展改革委，中国政府与巴勒斯坦政府签署共建"一带一路"谅解备忘录，https://www.yidaiyilu.gov.cn/info/iList.jsp?cat_id=10002&info_id=295194&tm_id=126。

② 中华人民共和国商务部、国家统计局、国家外汇管理局：《2021 年度中国对外直接投资统计公报》2021 年版，https://www.xdyanbao.com/doc/v8oea59uzu?bd_vid=12202869823366793967。

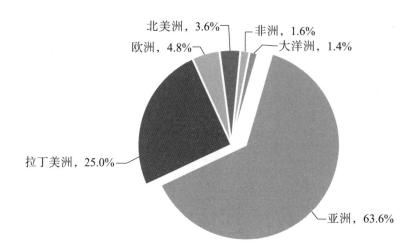

图2　2021年中国对外直接投资存量地区分布情况
资料来源：中华人民共和国商务部、国家统计局和国家外汇管理局

莫桑比克、苏丹、加纳等国家。[①]

　　虽然总体投资存量金额不高，但是中国对非洲的投资流量增速迅猛，2021年中国流向非洲的投资金额为49.9亿美元，比上年增长18%，约为2003年的66倍，在投资流量增速上比在亚洲、美洲、欧洲等地都要快。中国企业扎根非洲的同时，直接或者间接开展技术转让，传递生产经验，带动当地工厂提高劳动生产率，同时还创造了大量的就业机会，降低失业率，也间接降低了当地的犯罪率。[②]商务部数据显示，境外企业雇用外方员工占比逐年提高，2017年为50.4%，2018年为52.2%，2019年为60.5%，其中88%的中企在海外有用人需求，且未来人才需求更大（见图3）。[③]在人才需要的类型上，海外企业急需技术类和管理类人才，对语言人才、研发人才、政府和公关类人才、法律人才也有一定

　　① 中华人民共和国商务部、国家统计局、国家外汇管理局：《2021年度中国对外直接投资统计公报》2021年版，第23页，https://www.xdyanbao.com/doc/v8oea59uzu?bd_vid=12202869823366793967。

　　② 卡洛斯·奥亚、弗洛林·薛弗、齐昊：《中国企业对非洲就业发展的贡献——基于一项大规模调查的比较性分析》，《政治经济学评论》2020年11卷06期，第184—224页。

　　③ 中国贸易报社、中贸国际智库平台、领英中国：《中国企业海外人才发展白皮书》，2021年版。

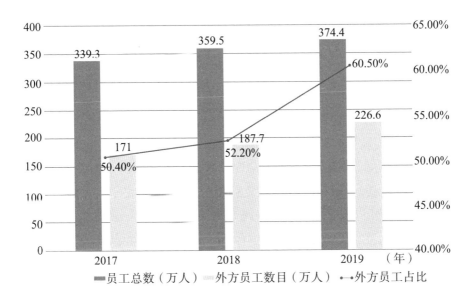

图3　2017—2019年中国企业海外用工情况

资料来源：领英中国《中国企业海外人才发展白皮书》

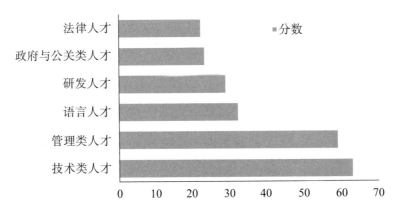

图4　中企海外人才急需类型

资料来源：领英中国《中国企业海外人才发展白皮书》

需求（见图4）。①

　　非洲富有挑战与充满前景的市场机会、中国国内的竞争压力和企业

———————

　　①　中国贸易报社、中贸国际智库平台、领英中国：《中国企业海外人才发展白皮书》，2021年版。

家精神带动着中国企业来到非洲开展投资，中国在非企业数量和投资规模都显著增加。[①] 然而随着疫情和俄乌冲突的爆发，中国在非企业面临着更多危机与挑战：第一，各国的防疫政策对企业正常生产经营造成影响，不定期停工停产导致了企业绩效严重下滑；第二，国际交通和物流与供应链的不通畅使得企业的生产、销售成本与外派用工成本升高，原有的经营计划被打破；[②] 第三，伴随经济下行，货币贬值风险激增，造成资金短缺，企业投资意愿降低；第四，恶性治安事件与恐怖袭击等发生频率增加，政府更替带来的不稳定性使得营商环境进一步恶化；第五，大国竞争激烈，暗流涌动，某些西方言论扭曲宣传中国政策和对外形象，这对中非企业员工的跨文化融合产生负面影响。[③]

2023 年 1 月 8 日，中国将新冠病毒感染由"乙类甲管"调整为"乙类乙管"，出入境管理放松，不再进行核酸检测与集中隔离，全球也逐渐进入防疫常态化阶段。这对国际贸易和国际合作来说无疑是一个利好的信号，在疫情动荡与封锁中开始恢复的国际投资市场或将迎来新的爆发。然而，在如今错综复杂的世界格局中，后疫情时代的不确定性仍然存在，良好营商环境的恢复需要缓冲时间，各国经济发展与贸易往来仍然受到影响，前景喜忧参半。

二、非洲国家的人力资本现状

"人力资本"是劳动力所拥有的技能总和，包括教育、培训和健康。[④] 进入 21 世纪，此概念在企业管理领域也得到了广泛应用。在企业中，"人力资本"是指员工为雇主提供的无形资源，它代表了员工带到

---

① Jing Gu, "China's private enterprises in Africa and the implications for African development," *The European Journal of Development Research* 21, no. 4, 2009, pp. 570-587.

② 全球化智库（CCG）：《中非对话：疫情下的挑战与合作机遇》，http://www.ccg.org.cn/archives/58561。

③ 邓斌、刘海风、袁帅：《新冠疫情背景下中资企业在非洲矿业投资面临的问题和对策研究》，《矿业研究与开发》2020 年第 9 期。

④ Frederick H. Harbison, "Human Resources Development Planning in Modernising Economies," *International Labour Review* 85, 1962, pp. 435-458.

工作中的内在能力、行为、智力敏捷性和个人精力。[1] 传统的人力资本投资主要分为两部分，一部分是教育，另一部分是健康，两者对提升人力资本具有不可替代的影响。[2] 许多学者的研究都证明了投资人力资本对企业发展是至关重要的。[3]

非洲的人口基数大，且增长速度快，具有充足且年轻的劳动力以及广阔的消费市场。然而，和世界其他国家相比，无论教育水平还是健康状况都存在差距，人口红利有待释放。[4] 如图 5 所示，在世界经济学（World Economics）统计的世界各国平均教育年限排名中，后 30 名中就有 23 个国家来自非洲，例如布基纳法索（2 年）、埃塞俄比亚（3 年）、卢旺达（4 年）、安哥拉（5 年）等，大多数非洲国家的平均教育年限都远远低于世界平均水平（8.7 年）。[5]

非洲人力资本的核心问题不仅仅是教育水平低，更源自就业市场中的技能错配（skill mismatch）。[6] 虽然有部分非洲国家在教育方面并不差，例如埃及的平均教育年限为 7 年，这表明其基础教育水平不低，但在世界价值观调查（World Value Survey）[7] 中有超过 60% 的埃及人认为，该国

---

[1] Hai-Ming Chen, and Ku-Jan Lin, "The measurement of human capital and its effects on the analysis of financial statements," *International Journal of management* 20, no. 4, 2003, pp. 470-478.

[2] Kolawole Ogundari and Titus Awokuse, "Human capital contribution to economic growth in Sub-Saharan Africa: does health status matter more than education?" *Economic Analysis and Policy* 58, 2018, pp. 131-140.

[3] Ioana Julieta Josan, "Human capital and organizational effectiveness," *Manager* 17, 2013, p. 39. Linda Brazen, "The ROI of human capital: measuring the economic value of employee performance," *AORN Journal* 80, no. 6, 2004, pp. 1146-1147. Onyebuchi Obiekwe, "Human capital development and organizational survival: A theoretical review," *International Journal of Management and Sustainability* 7, no. 4, 2018, pp. 194-203. Jens M. Unger, Andreas Rauch, Michael Frese, and Nina Rosenbusch, "Human capital and entrepreneurial success: A meta-analytical review," *Journal of business venturing* 26, no. 3, 2011, pp. 341-358.

[4] 王进杰：《新一轮中国资本与非洲人口红利——基于中非工业园区的调查分析》，载《中国非洲研究评论：一带一路与一洲：中国与非洲新合作调研专辑》，社会科学文献出版社，2022 年，第 129—155 页。

[5] World Economics, https://worldeconomics.com/Indicator-Data/ESG/Social/Mean-Years-of-Schooling, 2022.

[6] Alexandra Doyle, Amos C. Peters, and Asha Sundaram, *Skills mismatch and informal sector participation among educated immigrants: Evidence from South Africa*, 2014.

[7] World Value Survey, Accessed from https://www.worldvaluessurvey.org/wvs.jsp, 2022.

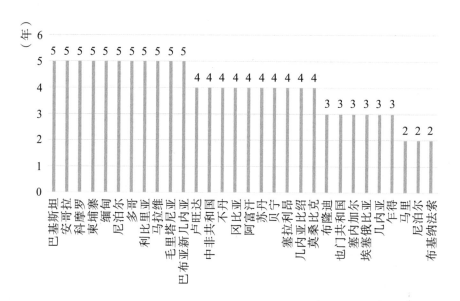

图 5　按国家划分的平均上学年限

资料来源：作者根据 World Economics 数据自制表

　　的教育系统不足以提供就业市场所需的技能和培训。由于非洲各地劳动力人口普遍缺乏适应工业化发展的技术和技能，"所学非所用"现象普遍，所以无法及时承接外资企业所带来的技术转移。[1]

　　技能错配是一个用来描述现有技能与经济所需技能之间差距的术语，可以从微观和宏观两个层面观察到。[2]在宏观方面，总技能需求和供给的匹配程度是影响经济增长、竞争力和生产率的主要因素。[3]在微观层面，技能错配与劳动力市场结果有关，如工作流动性、基于工资的工人福利和工作满意度。[4]技术错配包含不同类别，如教育不足（under-education）、教育过度（over-education）、技能不足（under-skilling）、技能

---

　　① 王进杰：《中非合作工业园区助力非洲工业化》，《世界知识》2022 年第 17 期，第 23—26 页。

　　② Seamus McGuinness, Konstantinos Pouliakas, and Paul Redmond, "How useful is the concept of skills mismatch?" 2017.

　　③ ILO, *Global Employment Trends for Youth 2013: A generation at risk*, Geneva: International Labour Office, 2013.

　　④ Jim Allen, and Rolf Van der Velden, "Educational mismatches versus skill mismatches: effects on wages, job satisfaction, and on-the-job search," *Oxford economic papers* 53, no. 3, 2001, pp. 434-452.

鸿沟（skill gaps）四个方面。[①] 同时，职业技能错配也是企业所面临的问题，这是由工作所需技能与个人技能之间的差异造成的。[②] 国际劳工组织也强调，对熟练劳动力需求与供给之间的不匹配将导致非洲经济不平等加剧。[③]

因此，企业为了降低生产成本和提高运营效率，投资和提高人力资本成为了重要举措。研究发现，人力资本对企业绩效有直接影响，包括生产力、市场份额、盈利能力、客户满意度、创新、工作流程改进和技能发展。[④] 另外，人力资本也是公司的重要资源，与公司实现目标的能力密切相关。[⑤] 这些研究证明了人力资本对企业绩效的重要性，它直接关系到员工能力的发展，影响着企业凝聚力，决定着企业业绩和增长潜力。

三、多重危机下中国在非企业所面临的劳动力挑战

尽管疫情对世界的影响已经减弱，但是多重经济和政治危机正威胁着非洲劳动力市场的复苏，如新冠疫情和俄乌冲突引发国际需求下降，石油和大宗商品价格下跌，预计造成高达2700亿美元的非洲进出口贸易损失；另外，虽然停航和航班限制已经全面恢复，但是疫情期间

[①]　Seamus McGuinness, Konstantinos Pouliakas, and Paul Redmond, "How useful is the concept of skills mismatch?" 2017.

[②]　ILO, *Measuring informality: A statistical manual on the informal sector and informal employment*, Geneva: International Labour Office, 2013.

[③]　Robert Palmer, "Jobs and skills mismatch in the informal economy," *ILO*. https://www. ilo. org/ wcmsp5/groups/public/---ed_emp/---ifp_skills/documents/publication/wcms_629018. pdf, 2017.

[④]　Lawrence Arokiasamy, and Maimunah Ismail, "The background and challenges faced by the small medium enterprises. A human resource development perspective," *International Journal of business and Management* 4, no. 10, 2009, p. 95. Hasliza Abdul Halim, Noor Hazlina Ahmad, T. Ramayah, and Haniruzila Hanifah, "The growth of innovative performance among SMEs: Leveraging on organisational culture and innovative human capital," *Journal of Small Business and Entrepreneurship Development* 2, no. 1, 2014, pp. 107-125.

[⑤]　I-Chieh Hsu, Carol Yeh-Yun Lin, John J. Lawler, and Se-Hwa Wu, "Toward a model of organizational human capital development: Preliminary evidence from Taiwan," *Asia Pacific Business Review* 13, no. 2, 2007, pp. 251-275.

造成的非洲航空业、旅游业和餐饮服务业低迷仍需时间来重振。[①] 这些挑战为中非在设施联通、贸易往来、投资合作、民间交流等多方面带来冲击。例如，非洲是中国第二大海外工程承包市场，疫情期间一些非洲国家由于融资能力有限，应对疫情冲击的财力不足，使得很多中非合作工程项目出现停建、缓建、放慢提款和拖欠工程承包商应收账款等现象。[②]

自 2020 年疫情暴发以来，虽然中国对外投资流量保持稳定，但是企业一直承受着多重压力，不得不抗衡来自各方面的挑战，如能源和各种投资要素价格的上涨增加了企业成本，高利率不但限制了企业的投资，还增加了债务风险，加上汇率不稳定所带来的货币贬值风险，多重危机造成了投资环境的高度不确定性，进一步抑制了投资意愿，从而影响了就业机会的创造。随着世界范围内对疫情管制的解除，虽然就业率有稳步回升的趋势，但是许多企业仍然面临劳动力短缺的困境。近些年随着中国国内劳动力价格的提升，外派成本也大幅度增加，中国企业也更加认识到培养和发展当地人才的迫切性。领英中国对中国海外企业的调查结果显示，企业出海的阶段已经从"走出去"迈向"走进去"，正加速在东道国的本地化进程，但还没有做到全面本地化运营的程度，特别是在本地员工占比上，虽然近些年有所提升，但是占比仍然很低，本地员工拥有率 10% 以下的企业高达 44%，仅有 24% 的中国企业的本地员工拥有率超过 50%。[③]

在中非合作的过程中，中国企业在直接和间接培养当地员工技能方面卓有成效，[④] 但是也有学者对中国企业是否可以助力非洲人力资本发展提出了质疑，如企业管理者忽略了与当地人在文化认同和人际关系方面的融入，缺乏对彼此的信任，这造成了中国外派人员无法和社区及当地

---

① 姚桂梅：《新冠肺炎疫情对中非经贸合作的影响及应对》，《中国非洲学刊》2020 年第 2 期，第 85—99 页。

② 同上。

③ 中国贸易报社、中贸国际智库平台、领英中国：《中国企业海外人才发展白皮书》，2021 年版。

④ Michael Mitchell Omoruyi Ehizuelen, "Education and skills development in China-Africa cooperation," *Frontiers of Education in China* 13, no. 4, 2018, pp. 553-600.

人产生深入交流，此外，这也大大降低了当地员工的晋升前景和担任高级职位的可能。[①]另外，也有学者发现中国企业在培训当地员工、与当地社区和其他企业互动，以及从当地环境中学习等方面仍有很大改进空间。[②]这些研究说明了中国企业在非洲本地化经营之路仍很漫长，尤其在培养当地劳动力方面的投入远远不够。提升人力资本，培养高水平的劳动力，是对企业抵抗不确定风险的有效手段，这需要企业不能仅局限在培养员工技能上，更应该在文化融入、社区建设、公司制度等方面进行系统和全方位的人力投资。

尽管中国企业在非洲的生产经营情况备受关注，但是对于如何进行人力资本投资的系统性研究仍很缺乏，亟须对本地化经营成功的案例进行深入分析，总结出发展人力资本的规律，为在出海过程中摸索的中国企业提供参考和借鉴。

四、中国在非企业投资人力资本的案例研究

本文采用案例研究的方法，对四家在非洲经营的中国企业进行了研究。在数据收集时，文本数据从公司网站、社交媒体和新闻中进行收集。同时，使用半结构式访谈法，对四家企业的创始人和负责人力资源管理的高层管理人员进行采访，探讨后疫情时代中国在非企业的人力资本投资状况。所选案例企业重视通过提升人力资本来增强企业核心竞争力，并且关注跨文化差异，在疫情冲击下利用各种策略提升员工劳动技能，以此带动本地化运营，助力当地建设。

四个案例的选取是基于三点原因：首先，四家企业人力资本投资的侧重点和改善企业的劳动力水平的着力点均不相同；其次，这些公司进驻非洲的时间不同，其中有过去五年刚刚进入非洲的新兴企业，也有在非洲发展近 40 年的成熟企业，研究可以为处于不同发展阶段的海外

---

① Terence Jackson and Frank M. Horwitz, "Expatriation in Chinese MNEs in Africa: An agenda for research," *The International Journal of Human Resource Management* 29, no. 11, 2018, pp. 1856-1878.

② Terence Jackson, "Employment in Chinese MNEs: Appraising the dragon's gift to sub-Saharan Africa," *Human Resource Management* 53, no. 6, 2014, pp. 897-919.

企业提供参考；最后，这些案例的行业覆盖具有代表性，分别为矿产开采、基础设施建设、通信技术和农业领域，每一家企业在该东道国中已经占据翘楚地位，为当地创造了大量就业岗位，是相对具有代表性的中国企业（案例企业概况见表 1）。

表 1　案例概况表

序号	案例企业	所在行业	代表性	人力资本的新探索
1	JCX	矿山开采	曾承接中国在海外的第一个大型有色金属项目，并获得过"中国矿山采掘行业最佳自主创新企业"的荣誉称号	制度投资：通过标准化操作流程对员工的工业化思维和工作行为进行培养
2	ZT	工程承包	是中国最早进入国际工程承包市场的企业之一，曾组织并实施了中国最大的援非基础设施项目	信任投资：信任当地员工，给予他们担任重要职位的机会
3	TS	智能终端	2021 年在非洲的手机出货量排名第一，荣登"2022年度最受非洲消费者喜爱的品牌"百强榜	文化投资：致力于跨文化建设，建立与推动员工文化交流政策
4	CG	生物科技	拥有 20 多项国家专利技术，辣椒红色素产销量世界第一	社区投资：具有高度的社会责任感，投资非洲当地社区的基础设施和儿童教育，体现了中国企业的责任担当

在这些案例中，JCX 是行业内备受赞誉的矿山开采企业之一，曾承接中国在海外的第一个大型有色金属项目，并获得过"中国矿山采掘行业最佳自主创新企业"的荣誉称号。ZT 公司是中国最早进入国际工程承包市场的企业之一，曾组织并实施了中国最大的援非基础设施项目。

TS 2021 年在非洲的手机出货量排名第一，荣登"2022 年度最受非洲消费者喜爱的品牌"百强榜。CG 拥有 20 多项国家专利技术，其中辣椒红色素产销量世界第一。这四家企业均重视本地化经营，虽然都对人才发展重视，但是各有所长。其中 JCX 重视通过标准化操作流程对员工的思维和行为进行培养，ZT 信任当地员工，给予他们担任重要职位的机会，TS 致力于文化投资，建立与推动员工交流政策，CG 具有高度的社会责任感，投资非洲当地社区的基础设施和儿童教育，体现了中国企业的责任担当。

1. JCX 矿业公司

JCX 是一家专业从事有色金属矿山、黑色金属矿山和化工矿山工程建设、运营管理、设计和技术研发业务的管理服务企业。自 2003 年启动铜矿项目以来，JCX 在非洲逐步获得声誉，并在赞比亚、刚果（金）等国家开展了矿产服务业务。他们在非洲的员工规模约为 1 万人，员工大多受过小学和中学教育。JCX 在员工管理规范上进行了大量的投入，根据非洲当地人力资本基础和工人工作习惯等实际情况，建立了适合当地员工作业情况的标准操作流程和配套的激励系统。严谨和规范的制度在疫情肆虐的特殊时期保障了企业的正常运转，避免了大量员工流失。JCX"有条不紊，有章可依"地来管理员工，这成为企业稳步推进本地化的基础。

JCX 的人力资源经理任总认为，非洲当地员工主要来自农村地区，对于工业社会的工作模式及其背后的职业规范和规则比较陌生。相对而言，当地人会更关注工资和工作时间，觉得在工作时间内完成一定量任务就可以了，对工作质量并不重视。因此，他们在工作中常常存在一部分敷衍了事的情况，造成工程进度较慢、项目质量不过关等问题。新冠疫情期间，员工离职率增加，流动性增强。新员工对工程、工作中的操作方法等并不熟悉，企业对员工的培训成本随之提升。为解决此问题，JCX 高度重视制度对员工工业化思维的训练，制定了一种便于员工理解和遵循的标准化操作流程，它主要规定了每个特定人员在生产和作业等工作活动中的职责和权限。英美企业已于多年前就开始尝试实施这种管理方法，为中国企业在非洲制定相应操作流程奠定了良好的基础。在日常的工作管理中，JCX对员工进行标准化流程培训，而后要求他们按照流程进行工作。同时，企业会根据员工遵守流程规范程度与最终工作成果等，给予他们奖金、岗位晋升等奖励，这已经成为该企业员工努力进步的动力源泉。新冠疫情期间，JCX以此方法有效提升了培训效率，保证了员工工作质量，避免了无效人员流动，降低了公司损失。

JCX还采用了导师制来加强"传帮带"效果。任总认为建立这种固定关系对师徒双方都产生了长期而深远的影响，有利于拉近企业内部员工之间的距离，增强企业凝聚力，有效减少人才流失。虽然在疫情期间，由于防疫政策使得人员聚集受限，影响了导师制的展开，但是在做好安全防护措施的前提下，公司采用了灵活工作制度，有序且分时段地进行错峰工作，避免大规模人员聚集。这个制度既不影响正常工作，又极大保护了员工的健康和安全。

任总对公司的人力资本投资与本地化的阶段性成果感到满意，他总结道：

> 近几年公司经营虽然遭遇了疫情影响，但是我们公司仍然积累了一支数百人的管理团队。赞比亚员工在管理模式和对中国的看法上发生了巨大变化，他们开始认识与了解中国文化，并感到有趣、尝试学习。在一开始的时候，他们做错事时不会觉得有什么问题，也不会认为错误与他们有关。通过制度约束，他们变得更加有责任心了。现在，他们会跟我们一样积极管理下属，倡导并谈论企业的理想。[①]

JCX从企业制度层面出发，完善制度规范，不生搬硬套中国经验，而是结合本地人的工作特色，有针对性地建立起一套规范流程。JCX对制度的投资完善了从培训、考核、奖励到惩戒的闭环管理系统，不但规范了员工行为，还保障了员工利益并提高了他们的工作积极性。当其他同行因为疫情冲击带来人员离职，造成停工停产或者减工减产的时候，

---

① 来自JCX人力资源经理任总的在线视频访谈记录，2021年12月22日。

JCX 的考核和奖惩机制不但留住了员工，还使得企业绩效事半功倍。

2. ZT 建筑公司

ZT 成立于 1979 年，是中国最早进入国际工程承包市场的四家企业之一，曾负责中国援外项目坦赞铁路的组织、设计及建造，雇用了约 30 万名员工。该企业经过 40 年的发展，秉承"全球经营，非洲为主"的经营理念，市场占有率不断提高。截至 2019 年，在非洲 54 个国家中，ZT 开拓的国别市场已有 40 个。该公司采用了独特的人力资本投资策略来推动企业的本地化，即信任当地员工，对他们委以重任。在疫情期间，非洲安全形势也随之恶化，ZT 给予当地员工的信任提升了他们对公司的忠诚度和执行力。从制度规训到给予员工信任的人性化管理方法，这是中国企业本地化迈出的一大步。

与其他高层人员几乎全是外派员工的公司不同，ZT 倾向于雇用非洲本地员工担任重要的管理职位，他们愿意给予当地人充分发挥能力、人脉、天赋的机会，以此建立信任关系。ZT 资深的驻埃塞俄比亚总部经理郑先生讲述了他们的岗位分布："当地员工除了应聘普通工人之外，也可以来做我们的技术人员和工程师。他们完全可以参与我们的投标、财务管理等，甚至是我们在当地的人事管理。"[①]

在语言交流方面，让非洲当地员工担任经理职务比中国员工更有优势。他们可以跟当地员工、当地人、合作企业以及当地政府等更好地沟通。在企业面临问题时，他们拥有当地的人脉基础，往往能更快解决问题。其次，选择非洲当地员工做经理会减少他们及其他当地员工的工作流动，从情感的层面考虑，这些员工会更愿意留在公司，降低跳槽的可能。郑先生解释道：

> 非洲地区的员工普遍存在流动性强的问题。普通员工第一天来，第二天不来都是很常见的，疫情和社会安全问题使得这个问题更为明显。一些地方大学的毕业生跳槽的频率甚至更高。因此，让当地员工拥有权利和晋升机会是留住他们的一种方式。这样可以鼓

---

① 来自 ZT 驻埃塞俄比亚区域经理郑先生的在线语音访谈记录，2022 年 2 月 11 日。

励他们长期在企业工作，带动其他员工的工作积极性。然后，他们会逐渐融入我们的团队，了解工作项目，接受我们企业文化甚至是中国文化，最终提高公司的业绩。①

与此同时，ZT 希望让员工拥有归属感和集体荣誉感，让他们相信在 ZT 工作是一件值得骄傲的事情。每年，他们都会在固定时间召开表彰会，隆重表彰一批"海外先进工匠"和"海外先进员工"，颁发荣誉奖章和奖金，鼓励他们继续发挥模范作用。这些沉甸甸的信任和荣誉不断地加深当地员工对 ZT 的感情，带动公司更加团结、和谐地运行。虽然信任是有风险的，但是 ZT 员工心往一处想，力往一处使，对公司渡过难关尤为重要。郑先生深有感触地表示：

> 这些非洲当地员工愿意与公司同心协力，在关键时刻支持我们，帮助我们一起解决了很多意想不到的困难。如果只有中国员工，遇到这种事情，他们可能不熟悉当地情况，又不具备过得去的语言交流能力，处理起来就很棘手。这个时候真的要感激当地人帮助我们，保护了我们的员工，保护了企业项目和财产的安全。②

ZT 在非洲大地扎根 40 年有余，已经与海外员工建立了代际信任与忠诚。他们充分重视员工的管理，重视信任投资，愿意相信当地人的才干和能力，对他们委以重任。ZT 充分给予当地员工工作晋升机会，把他们当作中国员工一样对待，所以自然也赢得了当地人的信任。当地人愿意和中方员工一起工作，在安全和生产等大小事上支持公司，长期与企业共成长。尤其是近几年来，由于疫情和当地武装冲突频发，在面临重大灾难，如撤侨、绑架、偷盗和营地遇袭时，ZT 的当地员工因为认可公司的价值与文化，总是会挺身而出帮助公司解决问题和化解矛盾。ZT在信任投资上的举措大大带动了本地员工的工作积极性，即使在近几年

---

① 来自 ZT 驻埃塞俄比亚区域经理郑先生的在线语音访谈记录，2022 年 2 月 11 日。
② 同上。

营商环境不理想的情况下，公司本地化运营仍然稳中有增。

3. TS 通信公司

TS 主要从事以手机为核心的智能终端设计、研发、生产、销售和品牌运营。该公司已于上海证券交易所科创板上市，曾荣获"中国企业 500 强"等称号，同时，在非洲智能手机的市占率超过 40%，排名第一，被誉为"非洲手机市场之王"。该公司在非洲的 40 多个国家开展业务，在尼日利亚、埃塞俄比亚等地建立了部门和工厂，员工总数超过 1 万人。TS 在非洲的员工以当地人为主，占比 90% 以上，主要从事营销、销售和生产、售后服务等工作。中国员工占比约 10%，主要从事技术开发、新产品维护、培训和管理等。

虽然 TS 在雇用员工数量上本地化程度很高，但是克服中非双方员工的文化隔阂一直是该公司提升本土化经营努力的方向。除了定期的培训和学习，公司一直关注缓减中国和非洲员工之间的跨文化差异。虽然在疫情管控期间，中非员工的线下交流受到限制，但是 TS 进行线上文化投资的措施卓有成效。TS 联合创始人兼总经理秦总解释道：

> 疫情前，我们定期或不定期安排非洲员工来中国的研发中心交流，学习前沿技能和技术，提高他们的日常工作能力和产品开发能力。同时，我们还将中国研发中心的员工派往非洲出差，让他们深入了解当地市场，增强对市场需求的理解。更重要的是，经过交流，他们有机会生活在彼此的环境中，进一步接触不同的文化。员工会更理解来自其他国家的同事，因为他们亲身体验过了当地的氛围和文化。因此，员工内部会更加团结，对公司也更加忠诚。虽然疫情限制了双方员工的线下交流，但是线上的交流互动和学习机会一直在持续，这是增进双方员工彼此理解的重要途径。[①]

面对文化冲突，TS 很早就明确规定，企业对所有员工，无论白人、黑人或黄种人的说法，都一视同仁。秦总表示："我们不应该也绝对不会

---

① 来自 TS 的联合创始人秦总的在线视频访谈记录，2022 年 1 月 23 日。

因为员工的肤色而区别对待或区别称呼，因为大家在听到后肯定会不舒服，这会产生隔阂的。"[1] 为此，公司还成立了独立于人力资源部门的培训学校，鼓励拥有五年以上工作经验的员工在培训学校的线上平台上自主开发培训课程，分享和交流经验。在疫情期间，这个线上平台为员工之间沟通和理解架起了一座文化交流和互相学习的桥梁。

TS 的领导层始终相信，当地员工和中国员工都有各自擅长的事情，如果将两者的优势结合起来，工作将更高效地完成，公司将更高效地运转。例如非洲员工往往更了解当地市场，他们在与当地人对接、销售产品和制定产品战略等方面的工作更切合当地实际情况。因此，TS 的经理往往是由非洲本地员工和中国外派员工共同担任。每当企业决定前往非洲新的地区扩大业务时，他们会派遣两名总经理，一名是中国人，另一名是当地人，让两人互相学习、互相监督，一起进行区域管理和合作。

总之，TS 在文化交流和文化融合上有独到且成功的经验，疫情期间，遵循技术和才干至上、人人平等的原则，充分利用互联网的优势，借助自主开发的在线学习平台，坚持开展员工交流活动。该企业在文化投资方面为中国企业树立了标杆，大大减少甚至避免文化冲突带来的不良后果，促进了企业在非洲顺利经营和对本地员工的跨文化培养。在经济下行、社会环境紧张的局面下，这样的人力投资方式更加难得，体现了中国企业的人文关怀温度。

4. CG 农业生物公司

天然植物色素行业的 CG 于 2018 年进入非洲，在赞比亚投资并不断扩大生产规模。作为全球植物提取行业的龙头企业，CG 曾两次荣获国家科技进步二等奖。他们的辣椒红、辣椒精、叶黄素三个产品的销量达世界第一，并让我国自主生产的辣椒红色素在国际市场的占有率由不足 2% 增加到 80% 以上。现今，他们在非洲拥有大约 1 万名员工。其中 300 名是由当地大学生和有农场管理经验的当地人组成的正式队伍，负责领导整个团队的运行。另外约 8000 名当地工人在田里作业，进行浇水和采摘。CG 对人力资本的投资不仅体现在对员工的培养上，还辐射到周边地区，为当地的社区建设做贡献。尤其是疫情期间，他们修桥建路，投资当地医疗设施，为当地疫情救治做出了贡献。从企业内部人力投资到外部社区投资，这是 CG 在非洲摸索出的一条共赢发展之路。

CG 来到非洲两年后就遇到疫情暴发，这对于新兴投资非洲的企业来说无疑是巨大的挑战。由于疫情期间跨境人员流动受限，国内外派人员无法及时到岗，CG 就因地制宜，积极融入当地社区，依靠当地民众发展生产，先后在赞比亚开发了辛纳宗纬农场和齐邦博农场。随后，企业从赞比亚首都卢萨卡的贫民窟吸纳了数千名失业人员，给他们提供食宿，传授农业技术，提供工作机会。这些举措赢得了当地人的认可，也提升了 CG 本地化运营的成果。

CG 董事长卢总介绍道："CG 的核心文化理念是'人与企业共同发展'，'人'并非仅指代企业员工，还包括了企业所在的当地社区。"[1]CG 在赞比亚经营的 5 年时间里，一直致力于促进当地经济的发展，帮助当地人民过上富裕幸福的生活。CG 对社区的贡献主要体现在以下五个方面。

第一，CG 提升了当地人的温饱水平。赞比亚普通人的生活条件艰苦，他们以玉米粉为主食，且没有存钱的习惯，经常没钱购买食物。针对这一问题，公司规定如果员工每月工时达到标准，会免费为他们提供足够一家人食用半个月的玉米粉。这个举措既提高了员工的工作积极性，又解决了他们的粮食问题。这成为了在 CG 工作的员工及其家庭的重要生活保障，哪怕是在物价上涨的新冠疫情期间，他们的生活质量依然得到提升。

第二，CG 帮助员工解决了住房问题。当地家庭条件较好的人会烧砖建房，但大多数人仍然住在用茅草搭建的房子里，甚至有些人没有房子，无家可归。在 CG 开始管理农场后，他们就着手改善员工的住宿条件。在辛纳宗纬农场，CG 建设了几十栋楼房，符合公司要求的员工分批次拥有了免费的宿舍。同时，房间内的水、电都是免费的。齐邦博农

---

[1]　来自 CG 创始人兼董事长卢总的在线语音访谈记录，2022 年 10 月 3 日。

场也正在为当地人建造住房和生活区。此后，CG 还计划建造数千栋房屋，并向员工分发生活必需品。

第三，CG 为当地社区的基础建设提供支持。赞比亚农村的道路和其他基础设施非常简陋，为了方便当地人出行，CG 使用公司的平地机和铲车等施工机械，帮助附近村庄修路，指导他们如何挖掘排水沟、疏导道路积水。他们在辛纳宗纬农场附近修建了 20 多公里的道路和五六座桥梁，还在农场门口安装了路灯，照亮从村庄通往农场的道路，使员工和当地人更安全地在夜间出行。齐邦博农场附近同样也已经修建了 15 公里的公路和 40 公里的电线，CG 计划以此为基础，进一步改善周边村庄的电力供应情况。

第四，CG 积极助力提高当地的医疗水平，投资员工健康。新冠疫情期间，企业向当地社区捐赠了一系列包含口罩、医疗包在内的医疗物品，并向农场周围的诊所捐赠了资金和物资，以提高诊所的医疗条件。非洲当地人因为不了解新冠疫苗而抗拒接种。CG 直接以现金为奖励，鼓励当地人接种。无论是企业的经理、司机或维修技术人员、村庄里的人，只要他们愿意接种疫苗，直接获得现金奖励。

最后，CG 关注当地儿童与老人等弱势群体。CG 在农场地区建立了小学，企业员工或当地居民的子女都可以享受免费教育，以及获得免费书籍和文具。CG 还定期组织孤寡老人关爱活动，每月将玉米面、油等生活必需品送给农场附近的孤寡老人。2022 年 9 月，辛纳宗纬农场与当地教会联合举办了孤寡老人关怀会，慰问了 10 余名当地老人。疫情阴霾逐步散去，人员流动放开，CG 还将计划为当地建造教堂和超市，向当地社区提供进一步帮助。

虽然在来到非洲两年后就遇到疫情的冲击，但是 CG 一直秉持以人为本的经营理念，将公司利益和当地社区利益视为一体，与非洲民众患难与共，用实际行动赢得了当地员工和社区的认可。

五、案例研究总结

中国在非企业一直以来面临着提升本地员工技术技能[①]、管理人才缺失[②]、化解跨文化冲突[③]等挑战，但是近些年疫情和俄乌冲突等因素激化了这些原本就存在的常态化问题，使得中国企业更加意识到依靠非洲当地人和社区共渡难关的重要性，从关注公司盈利向制度完善、企业文化构建、员工提升、社区融入等方面过渡，这些策略的转变大大增加了企业对当地员工和社区的投入。

尽管近年来学者们越来越关注跨文化经营问题，为企业管理、培训当地员工及解决跨文化差异等提出了一些有意义的观点，但学界仍然缺乏企业投资人力资本的综合策略。本文选取了四个应对多重压力并取得一定成果的中国在非企业，梳理出"制度投资""信任投资""文化投资"与"社区投资"四个新路径，成为助力企业在常态化工作中提升抗压和抗风险能力的新举措。

"制度投资"是企业本地化的起点，强化内部制度规范是应对外部不确定环境的核心。JCX 在投资的初期，根据非洲国家的实际情况（如人力资本基础、员工工作习惯、企业用工要求等），建立员工作业时完整、严谨和规范的标准化操作流程。由于用制度来规定每个特定人员在生产和作业等工作活动中的职责和权限，所以在制度的基础上建立配套的培训、考核、奖励和惩戒系统，使得企业经营事半功倍。因为这种方法不仅量化体现了员工的工作价值，提高了员工的积极性，还确保了每个成员拥有合理的工作强度，并提高了工作质量。在特殊时期，标准化操作流程让员工能够尽快熟悉工作流程和公司政策，以最快速度上手工作，激励员工提高能力和效率，带动企业的顺利运营。

---

① 袁立、李其谚、王进杰：《助力非洲工业化——中非合作工业园探索》，中国商务出版社，2020 年。

② 中国贸易报社、中贸国际智库平台、领英中国：《中国企业海外人才发展白皮书》，2021 年版。

③ Anedo Onukwube, "China-Africa culture differences in business relations," *African Journal of Political Science and International Relations* 6, no. 4, 2012, pp. 92-96.

　　"信任投资"是企业本地化的重要推动力。ZT 给予当地员工信任，放权于当地人，给予他们担任重要岗位的机会，这是留住员工的理想方式。舍得在管理风险上投入成本，真诚地信任员工，鼓励员工长期为企业工作，带动了员工的工作积极性。即便当地员工的基础人力资本较外派员工偏弱，但他们同样具有外派员工不具备的优势，即拥有当地的人脉、资源，熟悉当地社会运作规律与语言沟通便利等，尤其在对抗外部环境压力的艰难时候，员工和企业之间的信任变得更为重要。信任并不意味着业绩损失，反而可能获得预料之外的收获，尤其是在疫情期间，信任规避了大面积离职和消极怠工。患难与共的团队合作机制，最终会提高公司业绩，加强组织凝聚力。

　　"文化投资"对于企业在异国他乡的本地化经营至关重要。TS 公司为了规避文化差异造成的工作氛围僵化和工作效率下降，平等地对待双方员工，通过交流、互动等方式进行文化投资，带来相互的理解和认同。此外，TS 还努力搭建多国员工线上和线下的开放沟通平台，加速员工之间互相熟悉的过程。依据当地的节日、习俗等组织团建活动，进行文化建设，形成了团结和谐的企业文化。以彼此尊重、重视跨文化差异为基础的经营理念使得不同文化转化成一种积极的、互补的资源，为企业带来创造力和新活力。①

　　"社区投资"是企业在人力资本投资与本地化过程中为非洲国家做出的最重要贡献，具有深远价值与长久影响。CG 不但重视提升企业内部的人力资本，更将人力资本发展辐射到更大范围的周边社区，助力社区基础设施建设，改造当地居民的生活环境，疫情期间为儿童、老人等社会弱势群体提供相应的教育与医疗健康帮助。在外部大环境不理想的状态下，团结、依靠并助力当地民众，有利于企业和社区的互利共赢，体现人文情怀与责任担当，为可持续发展的中非合作打下坚实基础。

　　综上所述，本文总结出中国企业在多重危机下以人力资本投资为核心的本地化经营路径图，理清了应对多重危机的人才发展方案，拓展了

---

　　①　Günter K. Stahl and Rosalie L. Tung, "Towards a more balanced treatment of culture in international business studies: The need for positive cross-cultural scholarship," *Journal of International Business Studies* 46, no. 4, 2015, pp. 391-414.

传统人力资本投资的定义，将其与企业面临的实际管理问题及复杂多变的时代背景相结合，总结出五维度的人力资本投资策略，从"教育投资"这个基础出发，逐步发展为对制度、信任、文化和社区的层层深入和递进的投资理念，最后再回归到对教育的继续投资，从而形成完整的投资闭环。如图6所示，进行人力资本投资不仅对企业发展有着积极影响（如提升劳动力技能和劳动生产率、降低离职率、促进技术溢出和知识转移、提高企业绩效等），更会为非洲当地发展带来益处（如提升人力资本、为当地创造就业、促进区域减贫、加速工业化进程等），是实现中非合作可持续发展的重要基石。

当然，这个五维度框架是在理想状态下综合全面的投资策略，企业在实践运营中需要结合各自需求，从中甄别出适合当下企业需要的投资组合模式。值得注意的是，不同的企业类型首选的人力资本投资形式可能会略有偏重。如劳动密集型产业对于员工的技能要求相对初级，但是对于规范员工行为、提升生产率有更高要求，所以需要在完善和健全"制度投资"上多下功夫；对于高新技术类产业，需要持续提升员工的技术技能，所以进行"教育投资"和搭建和谐的"企业文化"留住人才是首要任务；而对于从事基础设施类公司，需要团结当地民众并得到他们的信任和支持，才有可能在"人家的土地上"顺利地开土动工；而对于农业类投资企业，往往会在相对贫瘠的非城镇区域建厂，所以加大社区发展的投入变得尤为迫切。

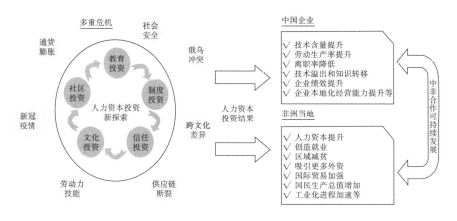

图6　多重危机下中国企业投资非洲人力资本的新探索框架图

结　语

四家典型的中国企业采用了不同的人力资本投资策略，有效推动了企业的本地化进程，在疫情时期努力带动了员工发展与企业业绩的提升，为中国企业在海外扎根奠定了坚实的基础。他们善待员工，重视企业形象，积极承担社会责任，参与非洲当地发展。本研究从教育、制度、信任、文化和社区五个维度，总结归纳了人力资本投资的五要素框架，不同企业可以结合自身需求，从该模型中选取人力资本投资组合策略，有助于化解企业跨文化差异，以人才发展为核心应对外部多重危机带来的不确定性。文章总结了中国企业海外经营的独特方法，拓展了传统人力资本理论的边界，为当前以教育和培训为主的非洲人力资本研究填补了一定的学术空白。

在当今充满不确定性的世界大格局下，非洲作为基础相对薄弱的地区，经济建设与国际市场开发将面临更大挑战。不过，危险与机遇并存，这也同样意味着越来越多的中国企业可以利用自身优势，谋求海外发展的新机会。中国企业应看准时机，把握当今世界格局与非洲的实际状况，充分认知本地化人才培养的重要性，探索中国企业在非洲本地化经营的全新之路。中国企业在非洲投资人力资本，不仅仅可以提升企业的核心竞争力，更可以实现知识转移，为非洲当地创造就业，提升民生福祉。中国企业在中非合作中发挥着重要作用，后疫情时代将继续推动中非经贸和人文交流的深度合作，并为非洲当地经济和社会发展贡献力量。

非洲工业化与华人工厂

许　亮[*]

摘　要： 本文选取三处华人工厂为案例，即尼日利亚卡杜纳的纺织业、南非新堡的制衣业与埃塞俄比亚亚的斯亚贝巴的皮鞋业，对非洲的华人工厂历史做了简要回顾和分析。本文强调，华人工厂自非洲独立之初就深度参与了非洲国家工业化的探索，在20世纪60至70年代、20世纪80至90年代和21世纪这三个不同阶段对于非洲国家引进生产技术、创造就业和融入全球产业链等方面做出了重要贡献。这些华人工厂来自中国大陆和香港、台湾地区，其生产规模大小不一，经营策略也有差异，在非洲产生了不同的社会经济影响。华人工厂在非洲能否长期成功既受其本身的经营模式的影响，也取决于当地政府的工业政策、劳工状况以及全球产业环境的变动。

关键词： 非洲工业化　华人工厂　卡杜纳　新堡　亚的斯亚贝巴

引　言

过去三年，全球新冠疫情和俄乌冲突对经济全球化进程产生了深远影响，给始于20世纪90年代的"超级全球化"[①] 来了一次急刹车，也对国际金融市场、能源、粮食和供应链造成重大冲击。早在新冠疫情暴发前，由于世界经济增长乏力以及中美之间的贸易战，全球化进程放缓已初现端倪；2019年初英国《经济学人》杂志曾专门就《慢全球化》予

---

[*] 许亮，北京大学国际关系学院助理教授。本文为国家社会科学基金一般项目"中国新移民与非洲工业化研究"（项目编号：20BGJ078）的阶段性研究成果。

[①] 有关"超级全球化"的论述，可参见 Dani Rodrik, "Globalization Dilemmas & the Way Out," *The Indian Journal of Industrial Relations* 47, no. 3, 2012, pp. 393-404; Dani Rodrik, "Globalization's Wrong Turn: And How It Hurt America," *Foreign Affairs* 98, no. 4, 2019, pp. 26-33。

以讨论。[1] 这些变化给非洲在内的发展中国家的经济前景带来了挑战和不确定性，也给过去十年被热议的"非洲崛起"的乐观期待蒙上一层阴影。[2] 不过，"慢全球化"迫使各国政府将注意力从外部转向内部，也将促进区域内深层经济联系。因此，后疫情时代或将成为非洲发展的机遇期。非洲近期最重要的发展进程是 2021 年 1 月 1 日正式启动的《非洲大陆自贸区协定》。纵观历史，非洲经济长期依赖外向型融入，但非洲对外贸易只有 20% 是域内贸易（即非洲国家间贸易），这一比例远低于亚洲国家（61%）和欧洲国家（70%）。[3] 非洲自贸区不仅将促进非洲经济的内向型融入，更重要的是，它将给非洲工业化带来发展契机。20 世纪 60、70 年代，非洲国家曾实施了进口替代工业化，但都以失败告终，其中一个重要经验教训是单一非洲国家的狭小市场不足以支撑过剩的工业产能和昂贵的生产设施与成本。[4] 非洲共同市场的建立使得非洲一国的产能可以辐射整个非洲，为非洲重新思考工业化道路提供了可能性。

在非洲新一轮工业化进程中，中国制造业投资和工厂将发挥重要作用。在中国自身经济结构转型过程中，由于中国国内产能相对过剩，国内消费出现瓶颈，企业对资源、原材料以及海外市场增长的需要，大批中国投资者选择在非洲拓展业务。截至 2020 年，中国在非洲对外直接投资的存量已超 430 亿美元，是非洲国家最大投资来源国之一。[5] 中国国有企业在非业务大多集中在能源、矿产与基建产业，而数量众多的私营企业更倾向于从事制造、贸易和服务业。2017 年一份调查报告显示，在非洲的中国企业数量已经超过 1 万家，其中 90% 为私营企业，约 30% 为

---

① "Slowbalisation: The Steam has Gone Out of Globalization," *The Economist*, January 24, 2019, https://www. economist. com/ leaders/2019/01/24/ the-steam-has-gone-out-of-globalisation, 查询时间：2022 年 11 月 15 日。

② "Africa Rising," *The Economist*, December 3, 2011.

③ 数据来源：UNCTAD, https://unctad.org/press-material/facts-figures-0, 查询时间：2021 年 11 月 20 日。

④ Emmanuel Akyeampong, "Early Independent Africa's Abortive Attempt at Industrialization: The Case of Ghana under Kwame Nkrumah," lecture at STIAS Public Seminar, Stellenbosch University, May 12, 2021.

⑤ 中国对非投资存量数据来自中国国务院新闻办：《新时代的中非合作》（白皮书），2021 年 11 月 26 日，http://www.gov.cn/zhengce/2021-11-26/content_5653540.htm, 查询时间：2022 年 11 月 15 日。

制造业企业，员工中近 90% 为当地非洲雇员。[①] 因此，随着中国工业资本和制造业企业大规模进入非洲并在当地投资兴业、创造就业，有分析认为非洲或将开启工业化新阶段，并有潜力成为"下一个世界工厂"。[②]

针对中国制造企业在非洲日益增长的经济活动，学界现有研究可以分为三种类型。第一类研究是从全球产业链的宏观视角研究中国企业在非洲的机遇，同时也强调非洲的资源优势、人力成本以及相关国际贸易政策给非洲工业化带来的契机。[③] 第二类研究侧重分析非洲中国工厂内部的劳资关系，特别是中国管理人员如何管理当地员工以及中国企业薪资待遇等问题，强调中国与非洲所处的不同发展阶段和文化差异给企业内部劳资关系带来的挑战。[④] 第三类研究则聚焦中国企业在非洲的人力资源培训、技术转移以及如何促进当地上下游产业的增长与变化。[⑤] 总体而言，现有研究主要关注最近 10 多年中国企业在非洲的发展趋势和面临的挑战。同时，虽然有部分学者做了一些国际比较（例如对比在非洲的中国企业和其他外国企业），但大多数研究的分析视角仍是以中国

① Irene Sun, Kartik Jayaram, and Omid Kassiri, *Dance of the Lions and Dragons*: *How are Africa and China Engaging, and How Will the Partnership Evolve*? McKinsey & Company, 2017.

② Irene Sun, *The Next Factory of the World*: *How Chinese Investment Is Reshaping Africa*, Boston: Harvard Business Review Press, 2017.

③ 林毅夫:《中国的崛起和非洲的机遇》，载《中国非洲研究评论（2013）》，社会科学文献出版社，2014 年，第 28—29 页；Justin Yifu Lin and Yan Wang, "China–Africa Cooperation in Structural Transformation: Ideas, Opportunities, and Finances," in *Oxford Handbook of Africa and Economics Volume* 2: *Policies and Practices*, eds. Célestin Monga and Justin Yifu Lin, New York: Oxford University Press, 2015, pp. 792-812；唐晓阳:《中非经济外交及其对全球产业链的启示》，世界知识出版社，2014 年。

④ Carlos Oya and Florian Schaefer, *Chinese Firms and Employment Dynamics in Africa*: *A Comparative Analysis*, IDCEA Research Synthesis Report, SOAS, University of London, 2019; Xiaoyang Tang and Janet Eom, "Time Perception and Industrialization: Divergence and Convergence of Work Ethics in Chinese Enterprises in Africa," *The China Quarterly* 238, 2019, pp. 461-481；袁立、李其谚、王进杰:《助力非洲工业化——中非合作工业园探索》，中国商务出版社，2019 年，第 146—169 页；Liang Xu, "Engendering China–Africa Encounters: Chinese Family Firms, Black Women Workers and the Gendered Politics of Production in South Africa," *The China Quarterly* 250, 2022, pp. 356-375。

⑤ Deborah Brautigam, Toni Weis, and Xiaoyang Tang, "Latent Advantage, Complex Challenges: Industrial Policy and Chinese Linkages in Ethiopia's Leather Sector," *China Economic Review* 48, 2018, pp. 158-169; Oya and Schaefer, *Chinese Firms*；袁立、李其谚、王进杰:《助力非洲工业化——中非合作工业园探索》，中国商务出版社，2019 年。

大陆企业或工厂为中心。

本文试图从历史视角来考察非洲的华人工厂，希望能对既有研究做一些有益补充。具体而言，本文借助一手的民族志资料与相关二手研究，选取了三处华人工厂为案例，即尼日利亚卡杜纳的纺织业、南非新堡的制衣业与埃塞俄比亚亚的斯亚贝巴的皮鞋业。一方面，本文通过回顾这三个案例强调非洲华人工厂不仅是最近 20 年的新现象，事实上在20 世纪 60 年代非洲国家独立初期，20 世纪 80、90 年代非洲经济转型期和 21 世纪非洲快速发展时期这三个阶段，非洲国家都曾主动邀请华人工厂深度参与非洲工业化进程。这种视角既可凸显非洲国家在吸引中国企业过程的主动性，避免中非关系叙事中以中国为中心的分析倾向，[①]也反映出华人工厂在非洲国家工业化探索历程中的积极贡献，进而超越中国向非洲转移血汗工厂的狭隘叙事。另一方面，研究中非关系的学者们对来自中国不同性质的资本做了区分，如国有资本、大型私营资本以及中小规模的民营资本，进而可以更为立体地呈现"全球中国"（Global China）或"中国走出去"这一概念和进程内部的多样性和复杂性。[②]借由这一分析框架，本文也反对对来自中国的经济行为体做单一化的简单定义。本文选取的三个案例涵盖了来自中国大陆、香港与台湾地区的企业，同时在分析过程中也注意区分国有企业、大型跨国集团以及小型家庭工厂等不同类型的华人企业。

一、卡杜纳：尼日利亚棉纺业的兴衰与转型

卡杜纳是尼日利亚北部城市，建立于英国殖民统治时期，在尼日利

① 刘海方近期呼吁从非洲本身视角出发讨论非洲经济转型和中非合作，参见刘海方：《导论："一带一路与一洲"新在哪里？》，载《中国非洲研究评论（第九辑）》，社会科学文献出版社，2021 年，第 1—22 页。

② Ching Kwan Lee, *The Specter of Global China: Politics, Labor, and Foreign Investment in Africa*, Chicago: Chicago University Press, 2017; Ching Kwan Lee, "Global China at 20: Why, How and So What?" *The China Quarterly* 250, 2022, pp. 313-331; Chengxin Pan, "What Is Chinese about Chinese Businesses? Locating the 'Rise of China' in Global Production Networks," *Journal of Contemporary China* 18, no. 58, 2009, pp. 7-25.

亚 1960 年独立以前曾是北方保护领的首府。自 20 世纪 50 年代起，卡杜纳逐渐发展为当地重要的工业核心区域，也因其繁荣的棉纺织业收获"尼日利亚的兰开夏"之誉。[①] 与其他独立后的非洲国家类似，尼日利亚政府在独立后选择以轻纺业为切入口，大力推行进口替代的工业发展战略。[②] 为了减少对英国纺织品的依赖，卡杜纳政府积极利用当地工业基础，在尼日利亚北部地区发展集团（Northern Nigerian Regional Development Corporation）的支持下，在卡杜纳扶持建立了 4 家大型纺织厂。[③]

1964 年，来自香港的查氏纺织集团创立了尼日利亚联合纺织有限公司（United Nigerian Textile Ltd），后者迅速成为尼日利亚北部地区最大的纯棉与印花布生产厂家。查氏集团随即在尼日利亚扩大经营，并向整个西非地区销售成衣。得益于在尼日利亚的成功，查氏从此发展为大型跨国集团，建立起涵盖亚洲、西非、欧洲与美国的全球生产销售网络。查氏集团的查济民也因此成为享誉世界的"纺织大王"，但鲜有人知道其第一桶金中很大一部分来自西非市场。

值得一提的是，在查氏集团投资卡杜纳的同一时期，中国政府也在开展对非洲社会主义国家发展工业化的援助。中方资料显示，从 1961 年到 20 世纪 80 年代，中国以财政、技术支持等形式援助了非洲各国共计九家大型棉纺工厂，这一政策称作"纺织援非"。[④] 然而，除达累斯萨拉姆的中坦友谊纺织厂外，其余所有中方援助纺织厂都于 20 世纪 90 年代末关停。这些工厂关停的原因有很多，既有非洲国家经济结构调整改革的影响，也有因基础设施水平有限导致的生产效率低下，还包括 20 世纪 90 年代以来廉价进口商品的冲击。目前，中坦友谊纺织厂成了"纺织

---

① 兰开夏，即 Lancashire，是英国 19 世纪和 20 世纪初最重要的棉纺工业城市。

② 有关非洲国家独立后实施进口替代工业化的分析，参见舒运国、刘伟才：《20 世纪非洲经济史》，浙江人民出版社，2013 年，第 105—107 页；李智彪：《非洲工业化战略与中非工业化合作战略思考》，《西亚非洲》2016 年第 5 期，第 125—126 页。

③ Salihu Maiwada and Elisha Renne, "The Kaduna Textile Industry and the Decline of Textile Manufacturing in Northern Nigeria, 1955-2010," *Textile History* 44, no.1, 2013, pp. 171-196; Elisha Renne, *Death and the Textile Industry in Nigeria*, New York: Routledge, 2020.

④ 杜英、陈金龙：《中国纺织援非的历史作用论析》，《当代中国史研究》2018 年第 5 期。

援非"时期兴建的仅存的一座工厂。虽然中坦友谊纺织厂于1995年进行过一次重大的所有权改革，试图重整旗鼓，但此后还是经历了大幅裁员，盈利之路极为坎坷。[①]

在过去50年里，查氏集团在卡杜纳创办的联合纺织公司走过了相似的发展与衰落路程。尼日利亚纺织产业在20世纪70年代的石油繁荣时期显示出迅速增长的态势。据相关研究，联合纺织公司的员工一度超过5000人，主要是男性员工。[②]然而，好景不长，1986至2006年，国际货币基金组织在尼日利亚推行了经济结构调整改革。这一改革对尼日利亚的纺织产业是一次巨大打击。由于货币贬值，进口外国织机和设备极其昂贵，几乎成了奢望。而尼日利亚政府在基础设施与棉花生产方面也几乎毫无投资。21世纪初以来，廉价的中国纺织品的进口量持续增长，其在尼日利亚的市场份额大幅提升，对当地纺织品造成了冲击，进一步加深了尼日利亚国内纺织企业困境。[③]截至2007年，建于20世纪60年代的卡杜纳四大纺织厂都已停产。

不过，联合纺织公司在最近10多年里获得了一次转型契机。2010年，在尼日利亚棉纺服装发展基金会（Cotton, Textile and Garment Development Fund）的帮助下，查氏集团重启了联合纺织公司的工厂。然而，重启后的新工厂仅保留了此前员工数量的四分之一，布匹产量也显著减少。虽然工厂店生产规模今非昔比，但查氏集团开始在尼日利亚转变发展思路，试图与来自中国的纺织品形成差异化竞争。查氏集团凭借对西非当地纺织品市场的了解，积极利用其国际一线设计师的人脉，开始聚焦生产高品质纺织品，并设立自有高端品牌"达维瓦"（Da Viva）。[④]这些中高端纺织品以现代蜡染技术打入西非当地市场，由尼日利亚与加纳的多家工厂同时生产，在西非地区成功建立了品牌形象，并在消费者群体中拥有不错口碑。

---

① 陈晓晨：《一家中坦合资样板企业的45年荣衰》，《中国中小企业》2013年第5期。

② Elisha Renne, "United Nigerian Textiles Limited and Chinese-Nigerian Textile-Manufacturing Collaboration in Kaduna," *Africa* 89, no. 4, 2019, p. 707.

③ Shaonan Liu, "China Town in Lagos: Chinese Migration and the Nigerian State Since the 1990s," *Journal of Asian and African Studies* 54, no. 6, 2019, pp. 783-799.

④ Renne, "United Nigerian Textiles Limited," pp. 696-717.

回顾查氏集团在尼日利亚的经营历程，它虽然没能在独立后初期帮助尼日利亚完全实现工业化，但其近期的转型或许代表着中非服装产业合作的一种潜在模式。中国学者刘少楠通过对联合纺织公司老员工进行访谈指出，查氏集团在尼日利亚经营的几十年中，通过企业内部职业培训和引入现代设备等方式在当地真心实意地推进技术转让，许多工人表示非常怀念联合纺织公司内部良好的劳资关系以及比同行业更高的工资和遣散费。[1]美国学者勒内在总结查氏集团在尼日利亚投资的主要特征时强调，"（联合纺织公司）高效生产与营销，迅速应对变化的经济形势，尊重尼日利亚政府项目与工人的需求"，而在集团面对亏损时，它"牢牢守住了底线"，没有彻底放弃西非当地市场，而是努力通过科技与营销创新将生意扩展到高端纺织品牌。[2]

二、新堡：血汗工厂还是包容二元？

新堡是位于南非夸祖鲁－纳塔尔省的一个工业城镇。[3]南非种族隔离时期曾对南非的黑人民族进行强制的迁移和定居，新堡正好位于当时的"白南非"和祖鲁人聚居的"夸祖鲁"的交界地带，属于"白南非"一侧，但是会吸纳周围的黑人前来就业。[4]20世纪60、70年代，新堡拥有比较现代化的基础设施和一定规模的煤炭、钢铁产业，曾一度被认为是一座种族隔离的"模范城镇"。[5]

自20世纪80年代起，新堡逐渐吸引了台湾与香港的企业家（以台湾企业家为主），并成功地转型成南非重要的服装生产基地。新堡在台湾和香港的招商引资策略在一定程度上是当时南非国家政策所决定的，当时

---

[1] Shaonan Liu, *The History of Chinese Presence in Nigeria* (1950s-2010s): *Factories, Commodities, and Entrepreneurs*, London: Routledge, 2022, see discussion in Chapter 4.

[2] Renne, "United Nigerian Textiles Limited," p. 712.

[3] 新堡的英文名称为 Newcastle，由于当地华人称其为"新堡"，故本文也沿用此中文名。

[4] 有关南非黑人家园政策，参见杨立华:《列国志：南非》，社会科学文献出版社，2010年，第95页。

[5] Alison Todes, "Newcastle: The Development of a Model Apartheid Town and Beyond," *South African Geographical Journal* 83, no. 1, 2001, pp. 69-77.

的南非种族隔离政府正遭受越来越严苛的国际制裁，很难从主要西方国家吸引投资。南非政府期望绕开国际社会制裁，来到台湾和香港吸引外资，前往指定的黑人聚居区附近设立工厂，进而吸收黑人劳工，使得黑人和黑人聚居区在经济上能够维系下去。促成台湾和香港企业来到新堡有多重原因。南非当时处于种族隔离制度之下，黑人权益受打压，黑人的工会组织程度不高，薪资水平低，对于港台企业家具有较大的吸引力。当时的南非不仅在"外交"上与台湾省政府保持友好关系，还给前来投资设厂的外商提供了极为慷慨的优待政策，包括高额的工人工资补贴、外商安家费、优惠的美元汇率和申请南非永居权和国籍的便捷通道。①

需要强调的是，虽然南非吸引港台企业有其种族隔离制度的特殊原因，但 20 世纪 80、90 年代有大批港台企业家来到南部和东部非洲国家投资兴业，在南非、毛里求斯、莱索托、斯威士兰和马拉维等国都能见到他们的身影。例如，被人津津乐道的"睡衣岛国"毛里求斯在 20 世纪 70 年代中后期，从原先的进口替代工业战略转向包含出口导向的混合型战略，成为非洲工业化相对成功的范例。②一方面，香港和台湾在 20 世纪 60、70 年代经历了高速增长期之后，很多中低端产业特别是劳动密集型制造业，出现了劳动力成本快速上升，行业内部过度竞争以及市场饱和的局面。在这一转型过程中，香港和台湾地区在 20 世纪 80 年代开始重点鼓励发展电子、半导体等新兴产业，以服装、制鞋为代表的劳动密集型的"夕阳产业"逐渐开始外移。为了寻找更低的制造成本，一部分劳动密集型产业迁往了东南亚国家，一部分迁往中国大陆；而与此同时，得益于非洲国家的招商引资政策，也有一

---

① John Pickles and Jeff Woods, "Taiwanese Investment in South Africa," *African Affairs* 88, no. 353, 1989, pp. 507-528; Song-Huann Lin, "The Relations between the Republic of China and the Republic of South Africa, 1948-1998", PhD diss., University of Pretoria, 2001; Gillian Hart, *Disabling Globalization*: *Places of Power in Post-Apartheid South Africa*, Berkeley: University of California Press, 2002.

② Gilles Joomun, "The Textile and Clothing Industry in Mauritius," in *The Future of the Textile and Clothing Industry in Sub-Saharan Africa*, eds. Herbert Jauch and Rudolf Traub-Merz, Bonn: Friedrich-Ebert-Stiftung, 2006, pp. 193-211.

部分产业开始迁往非洲。另一方面，港台地区以服装、制鞋为代表的一些产品在进入欧美市场时也开始不断受到配额和高关税的限制，相关制造企业迫切需要寻求新的生产基地来规避欧美市场对于产品来源国的限制，进而选择来到非洲国家设厂。

根据笔者的研究，1983 年第一家来自香港的华人服装工厂入驻新堡，1996 年新堡拥有的华人工厂增至 48 家。这些企业主要来自台湾，香港企业只有 3 家。截至 2020 年，新堡大约设有 120 家华人开办的制衣厂，雇用当地祖鲁女工约 20000 人，享有"南非的服装圣地"之誉。目前，新堡几乎所有华人服装公司都是以家庭为单位的小型工厂。每家工厂的雇工规模为 50 至 400 人不等，其生产主要是面向南非国内消费者生产基础服饰、校服以及快销时装。需要指出的是，在 20 世纪 80、90 年代有 3 家大型香港企业与多家台湾企业曾在新堡从事出口服装的生产业务，但此类大型出口企业都已于 2005 年前后关停。其背后的原因也是多重的。一方面是南非当地人工成本增加和工会的涨薪罢工活动频繁；[1]另一方面，美国政府 2001 年出台的《非洲增长与机遇法案》(African Growth and Opportunity Act)给予了非洲国家产品优惠的关税，但是对南非这样的中等收入国家则在原材料来源地和生产过程有严格规定，相比于莱索托、斯威士兰、埃塞俄比亚等落后国家，南非的生产和贸易优势被削弱。[2]因此，现存于新堡的华人工厂大都经历过规模缩减与业务调整。2005 年前后，港台大型出口型企业纷纷退场之际，起先担任这些工厂的大陆管理人员抓住机会，通过或租或买的方式取得了廉价厂房与二手设备，就此成为新一拨的工厂经营者。因此，目前新堡的华人服装厂中大陆人经营的比例占多数，约 80 家，剩下 40 家为台湾人工厂。虽然也受到廉价的中国出口产品打击，但新堡的华人工厂比上文提及的尼日利亚纺织企业更加顽强，凭借南非国内大型超市、连锁店以及一些企业和机构的小额、短期订单成功守住了自己的市场份额。当地的华人工厂

---

[1]　Nicoli Nattrass and Jeremy Seekings, *Job Destruction in the South African Clothing Industry*, Johannesburg: Center for Development and Enterprise, 2013.

[2]　Jeffrey Herbst and Greg Mills, *How South Africa Works and Must Do Better*, Johannesburg: Pan Macmillan, 2015, pp. 102-103.

主们表示，他们生产灵活、交付周期快，成本控制合理，因此能够一直持续经营至今。

过去 20 年间，新堡华人服装工厂始终位于南非国内关于创造就业与产业政策争论的风口浪尖。1994 年，南非种族隔离终结后，由于非洲人国民大会（African National Congress）、南非工会大会（Congress of South African Trade Unions）、南非共产党（South African Communist Party）结成"三方联盟"在南非长期执政，南非的工会组织迅速发展壮大，拥有很大的政治话语权和政策影响力。2003 年成立的"全国服装产业议价委员会"（National Bargaining Council for the Clothing Manufacturing Industry，简称 NBC）就是一个例证。该议价委员会旨在提高全国服装生产部门的最低工资标准，进而削减地区间报酬差距，并要求企业主强制执行。为了回应上浮的工资以及工会的罢工活动，新堡的华人工厂也组织了好几次"资方罢工"以示抗议，即集体关门停业。由于工资是当地工人的唯一生机来源，因此"资方罢工"后，工会往往会与华人工厂达成妥协，要求恢复生产。

在新堡的华人工厂看来，"全国服装产业议价委员会"里面的资方代表大多是来自富裕的西开普地区的大企业，它们主要生产利润丰厚的奢侈时尚类服饰。而新堡经济发展和生活水平处于相对欠发达地区，工人的技能和生产效率也较低，并且新堡华人工厂主要生产薄利多销的中低端服装产品，供应当地超市和连锁店销售。因此，华人工厂认为"全国服装产业议价委员会"确定的最低工资水平非常"不公平"，决定诉诸法律行动。2013 年，位于彼得马里茨堡（Pietermaritzburg）的高等法院宣告谈判委员会和南非劳工部的行为非法，理由是谈判委员会里面中小企业代表性不足，新堡的华人工厂可以不执行上述机构提出的最低工资标准。鉴于南非失业率高达 30%，劳资双方"罢工"同时出现的奇特现象揭示出后种族隔离时期南非的高失业率与强大工会之间的深刻悖论。就像工人们常说的，"半块面包总比没有好"[①]。因此，部分南非学者

[①]　Jon Herskovitz, "The Cost of No Sweatshops: South Africa Struggles Not to Be Bangladesh," *Reuters*, May 16, 2013, https://www.reuters.com/article/us-safrica-labour-idUSBRE94F08Q20130516.

呼吁出台一种"包容二元"的工业政策，即在提高工人生产效率和薪资待遇、促进"体面工作"（decent work）的同时，也给低薪、低技术、劳动密集的企业留下生存空间。[①]

性别在新堡华人服装产业的劳工关系中也尤为突出。纵观全球工业发展史，我们常常将服装产业与"工厂女孩"或"厂妹"（factory girls）联系起来。她们十七八岁或二十出头，尚未结婚，通常在工厂里劳作几年后回到自己的家乡结婚生子，开启人生下一个阶段。但笔者的访谈资料显示，新堡的祖鲁女工80%以上是年龄在20到50岁不等的未婚母亲。[②] 当地的祖鲁人将这些工人称为"mama mabhodini"，意为"工厂母亲"或"厂妈"。研究南非社会经济变迁的学者曾指出，20世纪70年代中期以来，随着南非经济下行，很多矿业企业和白人农场开始大规模裁员，并通过机械化转型减少薪资支出，随之南非社会特别是黑人成年男性大规模失业，进而造成南非黑人家庭的分崩离析。[③] 由于失去了原先可以在矿区和农场的工作机会，南非黑人男性也失去了组建家庭的经济基础，新堡的"工厂母亲"们便在家庭内部依赖不同代际女性成员之间的相互扶持，组建"以女性联结的家庭"（the female-linked family）。因此，虽然华人服装厂并非导致上述女性互助家庭产生的原因，但祖鲁女性这种家庭结构是劳动密集型的低薪制衣产业能在新堡等地发展存续的重要的社会基础之一。在新堡，家庭中通常有一位女性进厂工作挣取一份工资，另一位女性留守家中，进而实现照顾孩子和处理家务的责任以及完成她们劳动与情感再生产。[④]

① Nicoli Nattrass and Jeremy Seekings, *Inclusive Dualism*: *Labour-intensive Development, Decent Work, and Surplus Labour in Southern Africa*, Oxford: Oxford University Press, 2019.

② Liang Xu, "Factory, Family, and Industrial Frontier: A Socioeconomic Study of Chinese Clothing Firms in Newcastle, South Africa," *Economic History of Developing Regions* 34, no. 3, 2019, pp. 300-319.

③ Shireen Hassim and Jo Metelerkamp, "Restructuring the Family? The Relevance of the Proposed National Family Program to the Politics of Family in the Natal Region", Unpublished paper, presented at Workshop on Regionalism and Restructuring in Natal, University of Natal, Durban, January 28-31, 1988; Mark Hunter, *Love in the Time of AIDS*: *Inequality, Gender, and Rights in South Africa*, Indianapolis: Indiana University Press, 2010.

④ Liang Xu, "Factory, Family, and Industrial Frontier."

三、亚的斯亚贝巴："埃塞俄比亚制造"（Made in Ethiopia）的可能性

过去几十年中，埃塞俄比亚始终位于世界上最贫困国家之列。但在总理梅莱斯·泽纳维（Meles Zenawi）执政时期，埃塞俄比亚通过积极制定工业政策，在过去15年中经济始终保持着两位数增长。自2002年起，埃塞俄比亚各类全国工业政策文件都将创造就业与出口创收视作生产领域的重点。其中，皮革产业则因为涉及埃塞俄比亚国家工业的未来而得到格外关注。直至近期，埃塞俄比亚虽然拥有非洲最多的牲畜总量以及悠久的制革历史，但该国的皮革产业仍旧工业水平低下、增长缓慢。[①] 埃塞俄比亚政府很清楚，其皮革产业要想腾飞，需要一个"头雁"公司打入国际市场。[②]

21世纪初，梅莱斯·泽纳维开始接触意大利及德国几家公司，但尝试无果，他随即将目光投向东方，并收到成效。[③]2011年，中国最大的女鞋生产品牌、来自广东的华坚集团来到亚的斯亚贝巴城外中资运营的东方工业区（Eastern Industrial Zone），建立了第一家海外工厂。促使华坚迈出这一步的原因很多，既有中国政府的"走出去"战略，也有埃塞俄比亚诱人的鼓励政策、廉价的劳动力和皮革原材料。此外，还有一个关键原因是不受限制的广大海外市场。由于华坚主要面向欧美消费者，为卡尔文·克莱恩（Calvin Klein）、马克·费舍尔（Marc Fisher）、寇驰（Coach）和盖斯（Guess）等欧美品牌代工，从埃塞俄比亚生产出口可以不受配额限制并享受相关的关税优惠。因此，与早期尼日利亚的查氏集团以及现在新堡的华人服装厂不一样，华坚主要依托的是埃塞俄比亚出口导向发展政策。华坚在埃塞俄比亚投资获得成功后，随即于2015年兴建第二厂房，位于亚的斯亚贝巴近郊的集团自建的工业园内。如今，两家工厂合计雇用埃塞俄比亚劳工近8000人，

---

① Arkebe Oqubay, *Made in Africa: Industrial Policy in Ethiopia*, Oxford: Oxford University Press, 2015.

② Brautigam, Weis and Tang, "Latent Advantage."

③ 同上。

年产 500 万双皮鞋，占埃塞俄比亚皮鞋出口的 65%，每年创造外汇收入 3100 万美元。①

恰如在非洲的许多中国企业，华坚面临的最大挑战是埃塞俄比亚员工缺乏现代工业职业规范和相对较低的技能水平。华坚集团运用了多种方法提升车间工作的准点率与生产效率，比如开设班车线路助力工人按时到岗、管理人员按迟到扣除奖金、在生产小组之间开展生产竞赛以及采取类似军训的方式管理培训新员工等。② 华坚集团还会将工人干部送到中国南方的东莞总部培训，回国后他们则在工厂里担任中层管理岗位。关于劳动状况与薪酬水平，近期一项基于纵向数据比对的研究表明，埃塞俄比亚的中国制造企业与当地其他外资龙头企业相差无几。③ 但这并不代表工人没有怨言。有研究表明，由于埃塞俄比亚政府惯于以比较威权的手段来调控经济，工人运动和工会组织的发展受到一定程度的打压和限制。这使得工人缺少集体发声机制，只能以个人行动表达不满。④ 其直接后果就是，在埃塞俄比亚皮革与纺织部门员工出现较高的离职率。作为应对，企业通常需要提供工资以外的一些福利来安抚并留住员工，增强待遇吸引力，比如免费伙食、补贴、奖金及医疗服务。⑤

从性别角度看，在埃塞俄比亚的皮革与纺织产业雇用的劳工当中，女性员工至少占全体工人一半左右，人数可观。以阿瓦萨工业园为例，近 2 万名当地女工在园区内工作，她们大多来自农村，居住在园区附近的小镇上。⑥ 研究显示，在埃塞俄比亚工厂中的女性员工比男性的离职率低，经验丰富且绩效表现优异的男性员工最容易离职。⑦ 毫无疑问，

---

① Wencheng Gao,"Chinese Factory in Ethiopia ignites African dreams," *Xinhua News*, March 31, 2018, http://www.xinhuanet.com/english/2018-03/31/c_137079548.htm.

② Tang and Eom, "Time Perception and Industrialization."

③ Oya and Schaefer, *Chinese Firms*.

④ Vincent Hardy and Jostein Hauge, "Labor Challenges in Ethiopia's Textile and Leather Industries: No Voice, No Loyalty, No Exit?" *African Affairs* 118, no. 473, 2019, pp. 712-736.

⑤ 同上。

⑥ 袁立、李其谚、王进杰:《助力非洲工业化——中非合作工业园探索》，中国商务出版社，2019 年，第 23 页。

⑦ R. Renjith Kumar, "Turnover Issues in the Textile Industry in Ethiopia: A Case of Arba Minch Textile Company," *African Journal of Marketing Management* 3, no. 2, 2011, pp. 32-44.

工业园区提供的就业机会有助于提升当地女性的社会经济地位，但这并不意味着当地女性满足于工厂里的流水线工作。牛津大学长期研究埃塞俄比亚中资企业的学者戴梦涵（Miriam Driessen）指出，随着中国企业近年来在埃塞俄比亚投资的增长，前往海湾国家打工的埃塞俄比亚妇女数量也在增长。这说明很多埃塞俄比亚女性将华人工厂的工作视作积累资金的跳板，她们当中的一部分人通过挣取工厂工资，攒足旅费，然后选择前往海湾国家从事家政服务，以谋取远高于流水线工人的薪酬待遇。[1]

如今"埃塞俄比亚制造"的鞋履已得到全世界的青睐。华坚在埃塞俄比亚经营的成功也鼓舞了其他企业。好几家大型皮革产品公司随后都在亚的斯亚贝巴的工业园区建厂，其中包括一家台湾制鞋厂和一家中资手套厂。过去的 10 多年里，埃塞俄比亚工业发展战略很大程度上效仿了东亚发展型国家模式，即吸引轻型制造业投资，鼓励出口导向的工业，促进经济的转型升级。有学者警告称，在皮革与制衣产业当中，国际价值链已经开始挤压供应端，国际竞争也愈加激烈，这意味着供应商入行门槛提升，产量要求增加，容错空间更小以及产品单价更低。[2]这种挑战同样适用于眼下其他试图实施出口导向发展战略的国家，因为自 20 世纪 90 年代以来越来越多的国家采取出口导向工业化政策，导致在技术门槛相对较低的中低端制造业出现了空前竞争，客观上也增强了跨国公司的议价能力。[3]因此，对于像埃塞俄比亚这些渴望复制东亚奇迹的低收入国家，此等变化将会造成新的挑战。与此同时，埃塞俄比亚近两年的内战也干扰了包括华坚在内的当地企业生产和政府工业政策的安排。故此，埃塞俄比亚工业化的中期前景还不明朗，有待进一步追踪与观察。

---

[1] 英国广播公司新闻（中文版）：《中资涌入涟漪效应 非洲妇女走出国门》，2018 年 2 月 24 日，https://www.bbc.com/zhongwen/simp/world-43146420，查询时间：2022 年 11 月 15 日。目前，这方面还未有已发表的学术研究，不过在新闻报道中是戴梦涵博士受访提及这一观察，具有一定权威性和参考价值。

[2] Lindsay Whitfield, Cornelia Staritz, and Mike Morris, "Global Value Chains, Industrial Policy and Economic Upgrading in Ethiopia's Apparel Sector," *Development and Change* 51, no. 4, 2020, pp. 1018-1043.

[3] 李智彪：《非洲工业化战略与中非工业化合作战略思考》，《西亚非洲》2016 年第 5 期，第 127 页。

结　论

本文回顾了三个具有代表性的非洲华人工厂案例，强调华人工厂自非洲国家独立至今一直是非洲国家工业化探索的重要参与者。尽管中国国有企业涉足非洲轻工业较早，可以追溯至20世纪60年代，但中国私营企业在非洲大陆轻工业发展中更为活跃，国际化程度也不断提升。本文介绍的华人工厂分别涉及纺织、服装和皮鞋行业，都属于轻工业生产部门，它们均为私营企业，来自中国大陆和香港、台湾地区，其规模大小不一，经营策略迥异，塑造了多样的劳资关系，也产生了不同的社会经济影响。可以说，华人企业在20世纪60至70年代、20世纪80至90年代和21世纪这三个不同阶段，对于非洲国家引进生产技术、创造就业和融入全球产业链等方面做出了重要贡献。

虽然卡杜纳、新堡和亚的斯亚贝巴的华人工厂源自不同的时代，但通过比较分析可以发现这三处华人工厂的两个相同点和一个重要差异。首先，这三处华人工厂都是受到所在国邀请参与当地工业化发展。例如，查氏集团于20世纪60年代在卡杜纳设立纺织厂，参与尼日利亚的进口替代工业化，并在此后半个多世纪里经历了兴盛、衰落和品牌升级转型。20世纪80、90年代大批台湾企业家前来新堡兴办工厂，是南非种族隔离政府为规避西方国家制裁，在黑人聚居区创造就业以限制黑人流动的重要举措。同样，埃塞俄比亚政府大力扶持的出口导向型工业园吸引了中资企业前来打造新的皮鞋生产基地，助力"埃塞俄比亚制造"的腾飞。其次，这三处华人工厂都雇用了大量非洲本地工人，成为当地经济的重要支柱之一。查氏集团的联合纺织公司、新堡华人服装厂和华坚在当地创造的就业岗位分别高达5000个、20000个和8000个，产生了积极而广泛的社会经济影响。再次，这三处华人工厂经营策略存在明显差别。联合纺织公司在成立之初着眼于尼日利亚国内棉纺织品进口替代，但在近10年转型过程中则是依靠增加品牌价值和西非内部的区域性市场。新堡华人工厂最初也是着眼欧美市场，但近20多年逐渐演变为以南非国内市场为主的生产模式。虽然南非国内市场容量相较于其他非洲国家要更大一些，但新堡华人工厂面临的工人涨薪和产品升级压力与日俱增。华坚采用的是典型的出口导向模式，较好地结合华人资本和技术、埃塞俄比亚当地劳动力和皮革资源以及欧美市场三方面要素，但也面临国内政局影响和全球产业链挤压的竞争压力。这三个案例表明，进口替代工业化在非洲也具有重要潜力，非洲国家可因地制宜，加强内部市场整合，在发展中同时重视进口替代和出口导向战略。

上述分析为我们审视非洲华人工厂和非洲工业化提供了三个重要视角。首先，政府的作用很关键。政府的作用既体现在中非政府之间的国际合作，也包括所在国政府制定的工业政策，它们都会促进、塑造在非的华人制造业。历史表明，一套能够充分挖掘本国的潜在资源优势、推动跻身全球价值链的工业政策对当地华人工厂的繁荣壮大都至关重要。其次，中资企业的性质也很关键。本文涵盖了多种中资生产企业，从香港的跨国集团到台湾的家族企业，再到大型出口商以及小型华人家庭生产者。以大型出口商为例，其全球关系网络与大规模商业活动是一把双刃剑，因为这些优势也令他们对人工成本上涨、汇率波动与国际竞争更为敏感。相反，新堡的小型华人家庭生产者虽然并不属于利润丰厚的生产者，但表现出极强的经营韧性，在劳资的谈判中也不太容易妥协。最后，当地劳工状况也是影响生产经营的关键要素。非洲的华人工厂已经成为全球产业链重要组成部分。新堡和亚的斯亚贝巴的案例表明，当地工会运动和劳工性别深刻影响华人工厂的生产实践，并在全球价值链中体现出来。它们在非洲雇用了大量的非洲女性员工，进一步分析劳工性别问题也将有助于揭示全球产业链更深远的社会经济影响。因此，华人工厂在非洲能否长期成功既受其本身的经营模式的影响，也取决于当地政府的工业政策、劳工状况以及全球产业链大环境。

疫情前后中国与非洲合作的环境视角

拉瓦尔·马路华著　姚　航译*

摘　要: 蓬勃发展的中非关系持续引发争论,有人提出这样的问题:中非合作关系也对非洲环境产生了负面影响,甚至在某些方面导致了环境退化。值得注意的是,随着中国成为非洲繁荣发展的重要伙伴以及中国不断在全球舞台上寻求资源和合作伙伴,这些关于中非关系的负面评论就已经开始,而且在过去的20多年间不断甚嚣尘上。尽管中国最初被视为非洲援助的提供者,但这种关系很快转变为寻找自然资源和制成品市场——中国也随之成为许多非洲国家的主要贸易伙伴,同时仍然是援助提供者。随着中国经济的蓬勃发展,中国与非洲的关系不断提升,创建了中非合作论坛(FOCAC)以加强与非洲的多方面接触。中国由此向非洲提供进一步的援助,成为了非洲多国包括建设铁路、公路、水坝、体育场等基础设施在内的主要融资来源。除此之外,中国还持续从非洲采购矿产资源、石油以及农产品。这些发展令将非洲视为自己的传统合作伙伴的西方国家感到懊恼。即使在疫情期间,中国与非洲的合作也在不断迭代翻新、迅速发展,基础设施建设、贸易活动和公共卫生合作项目都在持续增长,在非洲大陆留下了实实在在的足迹。西方国家的传统叙事,缺乏对于中非关系带来的大量真实可触的发展的观照,而是更多讨论这些包括基础设施建设项目在内的中非合作对非洲大陆的负面影响。

关键词: 非洲　中国　环境　基础设施　疫情　可持续发展

---

　*　拉瓦尔·马路华(Lawal Marafa),香港中文大学地理和资源管理系、饭店和旅游管理学院(Department of Geography and Resource Management and the School of Hotel and Tourism Management at The Chinese University of Hong Kong)教授,来自尼日利亚;姚航,北京大学国际关系学院博士生,2022年伦敦政治经济学院硕士毕业。
　〔注〕本文由刘海方、王进杰进行中文翻译校对。

引　言

中非如今的交往故事可以追溯到近 2 个世纪以前。[①]然而，当前对资源和外交优势的争夺已经将西方国家和中国（非洲目前的主要投资者和贸易伙伴）置于讨论的对立面。[②]长期以来，西方一直是非洲的主要贸易伙伴；[③] 2009 年中国成为非洲的第一大贸易伙伴和主要投资者，格局发生了彻底改变。虽然中国是一个单一的经济合作对象，但非洲大陆各国的人口和经济发展水平千差万别。从这个角度来说，研究作为单一国家的中国与拥有 54 个国家的整个非洲大陆的联系具有一定挑战性。现有研究成果为中非关系蓬勃发展的原因提供了不同解释，其中包括：历史背景、地缘政治问题、资源导向的贸易和商业活动，[④]也有的解释关注援助和金融的可及性等视角。[⑤]尽管包括中国在内的许多国家都在向非洲寻求资源，但需要研究的是这些活动是在怎样的背景下进行的。[⑥]

这个讨论需要回答如下几个问题：随着中非关系的发展，中非近期

① Emma Mawdsley, "China and Africa: Emerging Challenges to the Geographies of Power," *Geography compass* 1, no. 3, 2007, pp. 405-421; Chris Alden and Christopher R. Hughes, "Harmony and Discord in China's Africa Strategy: Some Implications for Foreign Policy," *The China quarterly* (*London*) 199, no. 199, 2009, pp. 563-584; Howard W. French, *China's Second Continent*: *How a Million Migrants Are Building a New Empire in Africa*, First edition. New York: Alfred A. Knopf, 2014.

② Bernt Berger, "China outwits the EU in Africa," *Asia Times Online I*, 13, 2007, A1.

③ Denis M. Tull, "China's Engagement in Africa: Scope, Significance and Consequences," *The Journal of modern African studies* 44, no. 3, 2006, pp. 459-479; Alex Vines, "The Scramble for Resources: African Case Studies," *The South African journal of international affairs* 13, no. 1, 2006, pp. 63-75; Chris Alden, *Emerging powers and Africa*: *From development to geopolitics*, Istituto Affari Internazionali (IAI), 2019.

④ Chris Alden, *Emerging powers and Africa*: *From development to geopolitics*, Istituto Affari Internazionali (IAI), 2019; Deborah Brautigam, *The Dragon's Gift*: *the Real Story of China in Africa*, Oxford: Oxford University Press, 2009; Kieran E. Uchehara, "China-Africa Relations in the 21st Century: Engagement, Compromise and Controversy," *Uluslararasi Iliskiler / International Relations* 6, no. 23, 2009, pp. 95-111.

⑤ Machiko Nissanke, and Marie Söderberg, "The Changing Landscape in Aid Relationships in Africa: Can China's engagement make a difference to African development?" *UI Papers* 2011/2 (2011).

⑥ Kent H. Butts and Brent Bankus, "China's Pursuit of Africa's Natural Resources," *CSL Issue Paper*, Volume 1, 09, June Collins Center Study, 2009.

的贸易、援助和全面合作伙伴关系的增长态势是否会持续？中国与非洲的接触和投资非洲大陆的发展有何影响，特别是在疫情之后？有些学者和评论家对中国与非洲的交往提出了批评，认为中国开展的勘探、采矿、基础设施建设和运营等项目与当地自然环境不相适应，从而对环境产生了负面影响。[①] 这样的种种批评，基于这样的事实，即非洲大陆面临着对自然资源的需求、环境退化和掠夺性贷款等众多问题，但随着与"一带一路"最新发展战略的不断推广和实施，中非关系中的积极成果也在整个非洲大陆得到了真实而清晰的记录。因此，证实这些基础设施能为当地带来双方期待的社会整体可持续发展。有鉴于此，必须承认，在中国实现战略目标的过程中，非洲一直被视为重要的合作伙伴。

一、非洲的丰富资源与中国的参与

毫无疑问，非洲拥有丰富的自然资源和原材料，包括石油、黄金、钻石、铁矿石等。其中一些矿物储量丰富，分布在各个国家，这将在后文进行讨论。这些资源长期引起发达国家的巨大兴趣，并吸引着贸易和投资。令人感到奇怪的是，既然资源富足，完全可以用于经济增长、工业化和社会发展，为什么发展却迟迟不能光顾非洲大陆呢？[②] 相反，随着更多国家试图从非洲获取这些资源，种种危机却更加频发，不安全、战争、自然灾难和最近的全球新冠疫情不一而足。

正是在这重重危机中，非洲国家和中国等伙伴国家开始尝试不断加强国家之间更加有意义的合作，以便更好利用资源、促进发展。中国因其在自身发展、基础设施建设和消除贫困上的历史成就，可以向非洲

① Axel Berger, Deborah Bräutigam and Philipp Baumgartner, "Why are we so critical about China's engagement in Africa," *The Current Column* 15, 2011; David Dollar, "China's Engagement with Africa – From Natural Resources to Human Resources," *John L. Thornton China Center Monograph Series*, Number 7. The Brookings Institution, 2016.

② Bei Jin, "The relationship between resource and environmental regulation and industrial competitiveness," *China Economist*, July-August, Focus, 2009, pp. 37-45.

分享宝贵的经验，解决其迫切的发展问题。[1] 1989 年至今，甚至在全球疫情期间，中国凭借年均 9% 的增长率，一直是世界上发展最快的经济体。[2] 同样的，据世界银行统计，非洲也有许多在过去十年中经济发展迅速的国家，例如卢旺达、塞舌尔、博茨瓦纳、肯尼亚等等。

一般而言，讨论非洲与中国的交往，必须参照非洲最早以及当前的西方伙伴关系，包括那些非洲国家的前宗主国和美国的影响。尽管很难把非洲与传统合作伙伴的交往作为分析背景，但以组合投资为代表的中国对非合作，以自然资源为主，而且具有战略性投资的性质。[3] 比如说，虽然对非贸易之间只是中国对外贸易总额的约 4%，但中国参与投资了其他领域，包括制造业（3%）、服务业（25%）、贸易（22%）、基础设施（15%）。中国在双边活动中采取了一种双赢的策略，如表 1 所示，在贸易和投资领域，中国已经领先于其最接近的竞争对手美国。

表 1 中美在非洲的贸易和投资

	中国	美国
与非洲的贸易（2019）	2087 亿美元	568 亿美元
FDI 存量（截至 2019）	500 亿美元	490 亿美元
优先国家	南非、刚果民主共和国、赞比亚、尼日利亚、埃塞俄比亚	尼日利亚、毛里求斯、南非、加纳

---

[1] World Bank and the Development Research Center of the State Council, "the People's Republic of China. Four Decades of Poverty Reduction in China: Drivers, Insights for the World and the Way Ahead," Washington, DC: World Bank. License: Creative Commons Attribution CC BY 3.0 IGO., 2022, doi:10.1596/978-1-4648-1877-6.

[2] Obert Hodzi, "China and Africa: Economic Growth and a Non-Transformative Political Elite," *Journal of contemporary African studies* 36, no. 2, 2018, pp. 191-206; Isaac Abekah-Koomson, and Nwaba Eugene Chinweokwu, "China-Africa Investments and Economic Growth in Africa," *Regional Development in Africa* 27, 2020.

[3] Chris Alden and Christopher R. Hughes, "Harmony and discord in China's Africa strategy: some implications for foreign policy," *The China Quarterly* 199, 2009, pp. 563-584.

续表

	中国	美国
优先部门	采矿业、建筑业、制造业（占中国在非投资总量的65%）	采矿业（占美国在非投资总量的60%）

资料来源：收集多位学者的研究编制

　　大量的投资和非洲国家对这一趋势似乎非常合作和接受的态度，引起了非洲传统伙伴的大量关注，如前所述，突出的问题之一是自然资源和环境问题。中国与非洲的交往很大一部分集中在自然资源和基础设施建设上，对此事实，那些不愿意看到中国投资增长的人不以为然，争议这些基础设施项目为何大多数由中国公司和专家建设。[①] 西方国家和他们的小群体认为，大型基础设施项目和自然资源开采会对环境造成影响。显然这类观点不利于非洲对现实发展的渴望，而是反映了非洲传统合作伙伴的担忧。中国在大型项目上的经验，已经经历时间的检验。正如金碏指出，获取资源是社会发展和工业化的基础，这也证明了非洲对经济发展的需求具有合理性。[②]

　　随着国家的持续发展，中国对资源的需求是无可否认的，而非洲也必须将其资源用于发展。经济发展、人口的增长、可支配收入增加都会使对资源的需求激增。例如，众多分析师认为，到2030年，中国预计成为世界上最大的石油消费国，每天约消费1500万桶，占全球需求增长的近80%。[③]

　　除其他消费需求，包括中国在内的大多数国家都必须关注资源安全

① Jamie Farrell, "How do Chinese contractors perform in Africa? Evidence from World Bank projects," *China Africa Research Initiative Working Paper* No. 3, Johns Hopkins University, School of Advanced International Studies, 2016; Xiao Han and Michael Webber, "From Chinese Dam Building in Africa to the Belt and Road Initiative: Assembling Infrastructure Projects and Their Linkages," *Political geography* 77, 2020, p. 102.

② Bei Jin, "The relationship between resource and environmental regulation and industrial competitiveness," *China Economist*, July-August, Focus, 2009, pp. 37-45.

③ Bojie Wen, Yuchuan Chen, Gaoshang Wang and Tao Dai, "China's demand for energy and mineral resources by 2035," *Strategic Study of Chinese Academy of Engineering* 21.1, 2019, pp. 68-73.

等诸多方面。尽管所有大国都对非洲资源感兴趣，但中国在获取和采购这些资源上已经成为无可争议的佼佼者。①

始于2000年的中非合作论坛系列活动，在将中非关系提升到更高水平的同时，也引发了各界人士的大量评价和反响。②一方面，这些会议将各国政府和政策制定者聚集在一起开展讨论，加强了贸易和商业联系以及战略伙伴关系；而另一方面，它也给了中国怀疑论者更多的机会来评价和分析非洲和中国之间日益紧密的关系。③

如今的现实是，世界经济正在被中国所塑造。中国是通过诚诚恳恳地在兑现投资、新技术、服务、商业和贸易关系以及消除贫穷战略方面的承诺来实现发展的；认真学习和采取这些策略，大部分都可以使非洲获益。Bikales等人认为，在消除贫困方面，中国提前实现了联合国千年发展目标（MDGs）和可持续发展目标（SDGs），并取得了重大成就。④国际知识发展中心同样认为，中国是实现千年发展目标的领先国家，也将领先实现可持续发展目标。⑤

当西方把非洲贬为一个持续需要帮助、贫穷和不稳定的地方时，非洲在中国的形象反而是被重视被倡导的伙伴关系，中国语境中非洲人的文化、多样性和活力以及这个大陆所拥有的潜力都是被关注的。因此，在贸易、制造业、农业、资源、能源、基础设施和人员交流上的外交关系，是非洲和中国领导人会晤时最被关注的。

---

① Kent Hughes Butts and Brent Bankus, "China's pursuit of Africa's natural resources," *Collins Center Study* 1.9, 2009, pp. 1-14.

② Garth Shelton, "The FOCAC process and Sino-African strategic partnership," *China Quarterly of International Strategic Studies* 2.02, 2016, pp. 259-276.

③ Denis M. Tull, "China in Africa: European perceptions and responses to the Chinese challenge," Washington, DC: The Johns Hopkins University, 2008.

④ Bill Bikales, "Reflections on poverty reduction in China," Swiss Agency for Development and Cooperation, 2021.

⑤ Center for International Knowledge on Development, "Poverty reduction in China: 40 years of experience and insights for the world," forthcoming, 2022.

二、合作中的互补性

鉴于这些合作正在发生、扩大和几何性地增长，不同的非洲国家有不同的反应。总体而言，中国在非洲的活动在不同程度上得到了自上而下的承认。中国所有领导人都长期强调"平等互信的政治关系"，强调"对非经济合作共赢"，强调"人力资源开发升级"，强调"扩大人文合作和人文交流"。在众多双方领导人交流的场合，中国国家主席习近平都以各种形式强调了以上内容。

在与中国交往的过程中，技术官僚往往能够将这些声明转化为行动，私营部门也同样将它们转化为进一步合作的机会。特别是对非洲人来说，中国在农业、教育、体育、旅游等诸多领域都带来了机遇，在国际事务中，相互合作、相互支持、追求共同发展的前景广阔。此外，非洲领导人在各种场合表示，正是中国通过本国大大小小的企业家参与非洲的基础设施发展和进行外国直接投资（FDI），促进了许多非洲国家的经济增长。[1]

尽管新冠疫情在全球蔓延，非洲仍然持续吸引着投资者，2021 年外国直接投资流量达到了历史最高点，《2022 年世界投资报告》统计结果显示了这一增长现实（见图 1）。然而，即使出现了这样的发展，非洲吸引的投资流量仅占全球外国直接投资总量的 5.2%。这直接表明，共同发展图景的实现还有很多工作要做，正如中国领导人不断强调的推动合作共赢战略所言。

---

[1] Mohamed Abdouli and Anis Omri, "Exploring the nexus among FDI inflows, environmental quality, human capital, and economic growth in the Mediterranean region," *Journal of the Knowledge Economy*, 2020, https://doi.org/10.1007/s13132-020-00641-5; Stephen Morgan, Jarrad Farris and Michael E. Johnson, "Foreign Direct Investment in Africa: Recent Trends Leading up to the African Continental Free Trade Area (AfCFTA)," *A report summary from the Economic Research Service. Economic Research Service. U. S. Department of Agriculture*, 2022; Michale Ehizuelen Mitchell Omoruyi, "The impact of China's economic activities in Africa on economic growth of African countries," *The Bangladesh Development Studies* 38.4, 2015, pp. 47-90.

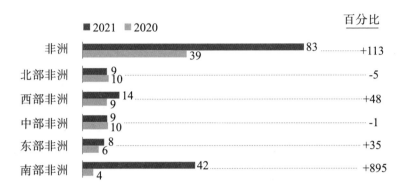

图1　2020—2021年流入非洲大陆和次区域的外国直接投资（10亿美元）

资料来源：联合国贸易和发展会议组织（United Nations Conference on Trade and Development, UNCTAD），2022年

三、非洲的发展与环境

中非交往所产生的贸易、投资和其他活动必然会对环境产生积极的影响，但在某些情况下，也带来消极的影响。对环境的影响因国家而异，在某些情况下因区域而异。例如，反映生活标准的能源等资源消耗在不同国家和地区并不相同。[①]如表2所示，大多数非洲国家拥有丰富的自然资源和矿产资源。

表2　部分非洲国家的主要矿产和产量

国家	主要矿产	年产量（百万美元）
津巴布韦	铂、铬、黄金、煤、钻石	9.967
加蓬	锰、铁矿、铀、黄金	10.920
刚果民主共和国	黄金、钻石、钴、铜	13.688

---

① Adel Ben Youssef, Laurence Lannes, Christophe Rault and Agnès Soucat, "Energy consumption and health outcomes in Africa," Discussion Paper No. 10325SSRN *Electronic Journal*, 2016, pp. 175-200.

国家	主要矿产	年产量（百万美元）
加纳	黄金、铁矿、铌钽石、长石、石英、盐、钛铁矿、磁铁矿、金红石	14.970
埃及	黄金、铜、银、锌、铂	23.225
利比亚	黏土、水泥、盐、铌钽石、钾碱、磁铁矿、磷酸盐岩、硫	27.027
安哥拉	钻石、黄金、石油	32.042
阿尔及利亚	非烃化合物、制氢	38.699
尼日利亚	石油、黄金、铌铁矿、钨锰铁矿、钽铁矿、沥青、铁矿、铀	52.678
南非	金矿、煤、钻石、铁矿、铬、锰、铂族金属	124.963

资料来源：根据多位学者成果编写

　　虽然观察者们倾向于讨论自然资源开发与工业发展之间的矛盾，但政府和投资者有责任为了人民的利益干预和规范这一过程。在开采矿产资源的地区，必须采用使收益、利润和利益归于人民且有助于国家整体发展的方式。工业化需要利用技术来开采和使用自然资源，以便限制在开采资源的地区产生对环境的不利影响。因此，为了国家整体经济增长，发现、采购和开发资源是必要的，这是中国过去几十年里在实现双赢方面发挥的领导作用。

　　谈及中国与非洲，总有人倾向于认为这是一种由资源开发、贸易不平衡、债务、援助主导的关系，[①]进而总是贬抑双方合作的精髓和发展潜力。

　　正是因为中非合作论坛建立前后的合作，以及"一带一路"倡议的

---

　　① Pádraig Carmody and Ian Taylor, "Flexigemony and force in China's resource diplomacy in Africa: Sudan and Zambia compared," *Geopolitics* 15.3, 2010, pp. 496-515.

发起，中国成为非洲基础设施建设融资的最大来源国。观察家们明显增加了对中国不断寻求某种更宽松环境监管的指责，也即所谓"污染的天堂"假说。在这方面，许多环境条例不太严格的非洲国家更能吸引到外国直接投资。约翰·霍普金斯大学中非研究院指出，由于宽松的环境法规，中国公司在非洲的工程和建筑项目的年总收入约为 40 亿美元（几乎占这些公司全球收入的 27%）。^①虽然这是中国的重大投资行业之一，但它为那些急需此类基础设施的非洲国家带来了双赢的局面。随着"一带一路"倡议在全球范围内获得成功，基础设施建设是实现这一倡议、促进国家间的高水平融合目标的关键。

随着与非洲交往政策的蓬勃发展，中国政府强调在气候变化、清洁和可再生能源产业以及其他环境保护和关注方面合作的重要性，这是 2006 年中非合作论坛的一个重要特征。因为非洲继续欢迎中国参与基础设施融资、贸易和其他领域的伙伴关系，有必要强调指出，经济增长和发展对解决非洲的贫困、疾病、人类安全、粮食安全等问题至关重要。不管是双边还是多边渠道，这些都是在非洲与中国交往过程中得到确认的。

本部分意在集中讨论中国和非洲交往的环境维度，重要的是首先要明确，中国在非洲国家的各种经贸活动和投资，尤其是基础设施建设，往往就是环境敏感地区。其所在社区从这些建设活动中受益是显而易见的，但对此持续关注的现有研究和当前很多政治化的叙事，导致了包括采矿、林业和农业项目在内的很多中方投资都受到批评。

实际上，随着中国力图在其国内和海外投资活动中推动可持续发展、减少对环境的影响，中国进出口银行等金融机构都敦促其贷款人在其活动地区实施严格的环境政策。作为对庄严写入中非合作论坛文件的该项自上而下政策的承诺，进出口银行制定了一个框架标准，鼓励中国企业遵守东道国在可持续发展和环境保护方面的政策。这个框架文件声明，中国将高度重视非洲对环境保护和可持续发展的关切，致力于帮助

---

① CARI, "Data: Chinese Investment in Africa (2003-2020)," http://www.sais-cari.org/chinese-investment-in-africa.

非洲国家将能源资源优势转化为发展优势。在对非洲有利益和愿意进行投资的所有发展伙伴中间,这是在非洲环境问题上做出的第一份承诺。

四、疫情前后中国与非洲的合作

从历史上看,非洲人民很看好中非关系,也很认可中国对非洲经济发展产生的积极贡献。正如肯尼亚一家报纸在一篇文章中所指出,非洲目前仍然深陷不发展窘境,"中国是打破这一贫困陷阱的值得合作的伙伴",中国迄今为止显然已经对非洲的发展做出了贡献,并在整个非洲大陆留下了发展印记。[①] 中国在基础设施领域的发展印记,包括但不限于铁路、公路、学校、体育场、政府办公室、机场、港口、信息通信技术等。另外也包括培训、技能培养、农业发展和现代化。随着中国的进入,非洲在增长、发展和减贫领域的进步已经赫然在案,而且这种合作仍将长期持续,尽管全球疫情已经带来了经济动荡和诸多不利影响。[②]

最近一段时间,尽管中国在非洲的组合投资逐渐不再以自然资源为主,在非洲的经济和投资关系主要是共建"一带一路"基础设施项目。[③] 原来主要由采掘和自然资源驱动的贸易关系,已逐渐转向其他部门,如建筑业、制造业、通信技术行业以及越来越明显的民间合作。这恰恰可以澄清那些所谓日益发展的中非关系产生了负面环境影响的叙事。非洲所处的地理环境及其与中国的合作交往,恰恰凸显了非洲大陆及其人民

---

① Peter Bosshard, "China's environmental footprint in Africa," *SAIS Working Papers on African Studies. The Johns Hopkins University*, 2008, retrieved from https://www.sais- jhu.edu/sites/default/files/China's-Environmental-Footprint-in-Africa.pdf; Vincent Konadu Tawiah, Abdulrasheed Zakari and Irfan Khan, "The environmental footprint of China-Africa engagement: an analysis of the effect of China–Africa partnership on carbon emissions," *Science of the Total Environment* 756, 2021, pp. 143-603.

② John C. Anyanwu and Adeleke O. Salami, "The impact of COVID-19 on African economies: An introduction," *African Development Review* 33, Suppl 1, 2021, S1-S16.

③ Julia Breuer, "Two Belts, One Road? -The role of Africa in China's Belt & Road initiative," *Blickwechsel*, 2017, pp. 1-8; Xiao Han and Michael Webber, "From Chinese dam building in Africa to the Belt and Road Initiative: Assembling infrastructure projects and their linkages," *Political Geography* 77, 2020, p. 102.

面临的核心挑战。[①]地理条件恰恰是欠发达和解决贫困问题的根本挑战，决策者和投资者需要获得机会、绕开困难以取得进步。以非洲大陆已经拓展的广阔可耕地而言，迄今成功保障粮食生产和粮食安全之计仍然付诸阙如。这是因为，非洲的发展及其相关的交通和商业领域长期以来持续受到地理因素的限制，包括高原、不可通航的河流等。

同样，中国的陆地面积和地形也为其带来了诸多挑战。黄土高原就是一个典型案例，那里的生态过程并不有利于实际发展，但政府的承诺和人民的创新被证明是成功的。由于非洲大陆的很多问题都具有全球相关性，中国获得的成功也可以在其他地区复制。在这方面，气候变化问题为中国与非洲合作提供了一个平台。2021年中非合作论坛上中国国家领导人提出支持绿色项目，指出了进一步投资与合作的方向，中国领导人确认的绿色投资，可以为中非双方进一步在气候变化和可持续发展领域的创新合作奠定基础。[②]

五、中国对非合作新动力：超越疫情

根据美国企业研究所（AEI）对中国全球投资活动的跟踪调查数据，自2005年以来，中国在非洲的投资和建设总额接近2万亿美元。中国最近启动了10亿美元的"一带一路"非洲基础设施基金，并提供了600亿美元的非洲一揽子援助计划，旨在支持多项倡议。中国已经成为发展融资的主要捐赠国和提供者，挑战了西方在过去的几十年里作为非洲捐赠国的垄断地位。[③]

---

① Chris Alden and Daniel Large, "China's exceptionalism and the challenges of delivering difference in Africa," *Journal of Contemporary China* 20.68, 2011, pp. 21-38.

② Akoyoko Astrid, "Africa, China, and the 'Green' Factor," *Consultancy Africa Intelligence*, 2012, http://www.consultancyafrica.com/index; Motolani Agbebi and Petri Virtanen, "Dependency theory–a conceptual lens to understand China's presence in Africa?" *Forum for Development Studies*, Vol. 44. No. 3, 2017, pp. 429-451.

③ Raphael Kaplinsky and Mike Morris, "Chinese FDI in Sub-Saharan Africa: engaging with large dragons," *The European Journal of Development Research* 24.1, 2009, pp. 1-23; Jon Lomøy, "Chinese aid–a blessing for Africa and a challenge to western donors," CMI - Chr. Michelsen Institute, 2021, pp. 1-6.

非洲国家正遭受粮食和医疗用品等关键产品全球供应链中断的困扰。疫情导致了全球贸易急剧收缩，对撒哈拉以南非洲的经济增长、贫困和粮食不安全带来了严重的连锁反应。[①] 对于每个非洲国家而言，贸易关系的变化情况在一定程度上取决于疫情前的贸易模式。[②] 例如，非洲大陆的三个最大经济体（尼日利亚、南非和安哥拉），疫情后的经济衰退可能相当严重，因为它们依赖的大宗商品出口价格大幅下降；同样，佛得角和毛里求斯等小岛屿国家也受损严重，因为边境关闭和随之而来的国际旅游业下降，这占据这些国家收入的很大比例。

全球疫情预计将对非洲国家和世界其他地区之间的经济相互依赖产生长期影响。然而，由于中国在疫情爆发时反应迅速，向非洲提供了最早的援助，非洲和中国之间的关系实现了加速发展。全球贸易模式的变化，加上世界面临的地缘政治挑战，以及随之而来的全球外交关系变化，必然对非洲国家和世界产生重大的地缘政治影响。Catherine Wong 在《南华早报》上发文称，"中国在疫情下也不会缩减在非洲的投资"[③]。中非关系十分密切，中国近年来也成为非洲最大的债权人之一，为非洲的大部分基础设施建设提供资金。在所有与中国签署了跨大陆基础设施战略"一带一路"倡议（BRI）的国家中，有三分之一来自非洲。尽管非洲在疫情期间经历了相对严重的经济衰退，但中国仍然对非洲保持信心，加强合作，共克时艰。

这一持续合作的信心可见于很多事实，比如 2013 年至 2018 年，中国对外援助中 45% 用于非洲（根据中国外交部公布的数据统计）。据《2022 年世界投资报告》计算，中国是非洲最大的双边贸易伙伴，2021 年达到 2540 亿美元，比美非洲贸易额高出 4 倍。

中国致力于维持中非关系，捐赠了 10 亿支新型冠状病毒疫苗，并

① Moustapha Mbow, et al., "COVID-19 in Africa: Dampening the storm?" *Science* 369.6504, 2020, pp. 624-626, https://doi.org/10.1126/science.abd3902.

② John C. Anyanwu and Adeleke O. Salami, "The impact of COVID-19 on African economies: An introduction," *African Development Review* 33, Suppl 1, 2021, S1-S16.

③ Catherine Wong, "China still committed to Africa despite Covid-19 disruption, minister says," *South China Morning Post*, Nov 26, 2021, https://www.scmp.com/news/china/diplomacy/article/3157549/china-still-committed-africa-despite-covid-19-disruption.

进而为非洲贸易和基础设施建设提供了数十亿美元，用于非洲疫情期间和之后的缓冲和恢复。中国政府还免除了对非洲国家的无息贷款，以帮助非洲大陆从疫情中恢复。这些公告是习近平主席在塞内加尔达喀尔的中非合作论坛上发表讲话时作出的。习主席还表示，中国将鼓励扩大非洲农产品进口规模，扩大免税商品范围，力争未来 3 年中国从非洲进口总额达到 3000 亿美元。

分析人士认为，非洲经济的各个领域在未来很长一段时期有着巨大的吸引国际投资的潜力，尤其是在绿色经济和海洋经济以及基础设施建设上。[①] 总之，中国在非洲活动的指数级扩张，一直是许多研究和报告讨论的重要主题——既有研究虽然充分地展示合作全面增长的趋势，但鲜有全面视角来公正地讨论环境视角，有也往往是讨论其负面影响。本文致力于从环境视角全面反思中非合作中的贸易、基础设施，特别是政策，也希望能够带来进一步的讨论，并有机会根据情况进行深入的客观调查。

结 论

纵观历史的发展规律，任何国家的基础设施落后和交通匮乏（甚至难以进入社区），都构成农业和农村发展以及整体经济增长的主要阻碍。基础设施（公路、铁路、能源等）是促进这些地区开放、使其参与经济活动的钥匙，尽管建设这些项目难免也经常威胁到所在地区环境的可持续性。中国的参与可以说为非洲大陆提供了获取自然资源的途径，也同时打开了进入那些洪荒之地或具有生态重要性地区的大门。

从中非合作论坛到中国领导人最近在金砖国家峰会上的声明可见，在与非洲交往过程中，中国已经准备好纳入气候变化、可再生能源投资和促进绿色经济等问题。不难看出，对替代能源、生态基础设施、可持续农业和绿色经济的投资，必将促进经济增长、创造就业机会、减少贫

---

① Akoyoko Astrid, "Africa, China, and the 'Green' Factor," Consultancy Africa Intelligence (2012), http://www.consultancyafrica.com/index.

困，同时应对环境和气候挑战。

迄今为止，中国与非洲的交往和接触已经促进了非洲的经济增长，创造了就业机会，减少了贫困，同时也在应对环境和气候变化挑战。据统计，近几十年来，中国企业和投资者通过提供技术和培训，为非洲大陆创造了数以百万计的就业机会，也确保了非洲的可持续发展趋势。

中国秉持合作与伙伴关系原则，发布了"非洲政策文件"，文件表明，中国将确保在与非洲大陆的合作中，"高度重视非洲对环境保护和可持续发展的关切，帮助非洲国家将能源和资源优势转化为发展优势"。因为以这些声明和承诺为基础，双方未来的合作项目和投资将满足中非都可以接受的环境可持续发展目标。

总之，中非关系仍然在锐意进取，研究的方法也有必要设计得更加深入，特别是从全面的视角来看待中非关系中的环境维度，这也将助力于这一双方都获益的合作关系能最大限度地维持双赢的局面。

附：本篇英文

Environmental Context of China-African Engagement in Pre and Post Pandemic

Lawal Marafa [*]

Abstract: The bourgeoning context of China Africa relationship has continued to generate comments and observations leading to issues raised from observers that the relationship of this engagement has also been generating negative impacts on the African environment and in some aspects leading to degradation. It is important to note from the onset that these comments on the relationship that has been brought to the fore escalated over two decades ago when China became a formidable partner in Africa's thrive for development and Chinas quest for resources and partnerships in the global arena.

Although in the beginning, China was initially seen as an aid provider to Africa, the engagement quickly transformed into China seeking natural resources and market for their manufactured goods. Consequently, China became a leading trading partner with many African countries as well as an aid provider. As China's economy blossomed, it upgraded its relationship with Africa and created the FOCAC, a platform that enhanced engagement with Africa on many fronts. Accordingly, China provided further aid and became a major source of Africa's infrastructure financing with rail roads, highways, dams, stadia, etc., constructed in many countries. In addition to these, China continue to source mineral resources, oil, as well as agricultural products from Africa. These developments were to the chagrin of many western observers who saw Africa as their traditional partners. The trend of engagement with Africa soared and blossomed even at the time of the pandemic. It is the footprint of the tangible development devoid of the traditional rhetoric of western countries that are being represented as negative to the African continent.

---

 * Lawal Marafa, Professor of the Chinese University of Hong Kong.

Keywords: Africa; China; Environment; Infrastructure; Pandemic; Sustainable development

1. Introduction

The recent and current story of China and Africa engagement is centred on a relationship that goes back almost two Centuries.[①] However, the scramble for resources and diplomatic advantage has put the West, for a long-term, African traditional partners, and China, the current leading investor and trading partner with Africa at opposite sides of the discussion.[②] Historically, the west has been the leading trading partners.[③] This changed since 2009 when China became the number one trading partner and leading investor in Africa. While China stand alone as an economic partner, countries on the African continent are at different levels of demographic and economic development. In this regard, it is challenging to study the engagement of China as a country with a whole continent of 54 countries. Many scholars have enumerated several reasons for the booming China-Africa relations that include historical antecedents, geo-political issues, trade and business to the quest for resources.[④] Others include aid, access to finance etc..[⑤] It is true that many countries including China seek

---

① E. Mawdsley, "China and Africa: Emerging Challenges to the Geographies of Power", *Geographic Compass* Vol. 1, (2007). p. 1-17; C. Alden and C. R. Hughes, "Harmony and Discord in China's Africa Strategy: Some Implications for Foreign Policy", Ource. *The China Quarterly*, No. 199,(2009). pp. 563-584; H. W. French, "China's Second Continent: How a Million Migrants Are Building a New Empire in Africa," Knopf Doubleday Publishing Group (2014).

② B. Berger, "China Outwits the EU in Africa", *Asia Times Online*, (13 December 2007). p. A1.

③ D. Tull, "China's engagement in Africa: Scope, significance and consequences", *Journal of Modern African Studies*, (2006). 44(3), 459-479; A. Vines, "The Scramble for Resources: African Case Studies", *South African Journal of International Affairs*, Vol. 13, (No 1, Summer/Autumn, 2006), p. 71; C. Alden, "Emerging Powers and Africa: From Development to Geopolitics", Istituto Affari Internazionali (IAI) Papers 19/23, (November. 2019).

④ C. Alden, "Emerging Powers and Africa: From Development to Geopolitics", Istituto Affari Internazionali (IAI) Papers 19/23, (November. 2019); D. Brautigam, "China in Africa: The Real Story", Oxford University Press (2009); K. E. Uchehara, "China-Africa Relations in the 21st Century: Engagement, Compromise and Controversy", *Uluslararası İlişkiler*, Volume 6, (2009). No 23 (Fall).

⑤ M. Nissanke and M. Söderberg, "The Changing Landscape in Aid Relationships in Africa: Can China's Engagement Make a Difference to African Development?" *UI Papers*, (2011).

resources from Africa.[①] The context in which the search for resources operates is subject to scrutiny.

Some of the questions that will need to be answered include whether or not the growing engagement and the recent acceleration of trade, aid, and overall partnership of engagement will continue as the relationship between China and Africa move forward. There is also the need to understand how China's engagement and investment in Africa influence the continent's growth and development, particularly in the aftermath of the pandemic. Some scholars and commentators have also criticized China's engagement with Africa alluding that the projects undertaken including exploration, mining and infrastructure construction and operations are not in conformity with the natural environment and consequently generates negative environments.[②] It is such allegations and the fact that Africa's abundant resources have remained irrelevant in the development process for over one century of its relationship and partnership with others. Consequently however, the strategic analysis of the evolution of China Africa relationships and engagement have been well documented.[③]

2. Africa's abundant resources and China's engagement

There is no doubt that Africa has abundant natural resources and raw materials including oil, gold, diamond, iron ore, etc. Some of these minerals have substantial deposits and are located in various countries as will be shown in the ensuing discussion. These resources continue to generate huge interest from developed countries and attract trade and investment. With the amount of resources that Africa has, it is a wonder as to why

---

① K. H. Butts and B. Bankus, "China's Pursuit of Africa's Natural Resources", *CSL Issue Paper*, Volume 1, 09, June Collins Center Study, (2009).

② A. Berger, D. Brautigam and P. Baumgartner, "Why are we so critical about China's engagement in Africa?" *The Current Column* of 15 August 2011; D. Dollar, "China's Engagement with Africa – From Natural Resources to Human Resources", John L. Thornton China Center Monograph Series, Number 7. The Brookings Institution, (2016).

③ D. J. Muekalia, "Africa and China's Strategic Partnership", *African Security Studies*, Vol.13, No. 1, (2004). pp. 5-12; P. Konings, "China and Africa: Building a strategic partnership", *Journal of Developing Societies*, (2007). 23(3), pp. 341-367.

development has eluded the continent for so long, given that the availability and use of resources is fundamental to economic growth, industrialization and development of societies.[①] As many countries seek to source these resources from Africa, various crises become imminent that include insecurity, wars, natural disasters and very recently the global COVID-19 pandemic.

It is in the middle of all these Africa and its partners especially China continue to push for meaningful engagement in order to use the resources to enhance development. Given China's own history in development, infrastructure and poverty eradication, it therefore has experience that can be valuable in dealing with Africa's needs.[②] In the past few years, China became the fastest growing economy in the world averaging 9% from 1989 until recently, even despite the pandemic.[③] Africa also has some of the countries with fast growing economies in the past decade including but not limited to Rwanda, Seychelles, Botswana, Kenya to name a few, according to a World Bank data.

Generally, if African and Chinese engagements are discussed, there must be some references on the initial and current partnerships with Western countries including those that colonised Africa and the role of the United States of America. While it is difficult to contextualize the engagement with African traditional partners, the Chinese engagement represented by the investment portfolio is not only dominated by natural resources, but is strategic in nature (Alden and Hughes, 2009). For example, while trade with Africa is about 4%, other estimates of engagement and investment include manufacturing (3%), services (25%) trade (22%) infrastructure (15%). With the trend of activities between the two sides, China has adopted a strategy for a win-win situation. In

① B. Jin, "The relationship between resource and environmental regulation and industrial competitiveness", *China Economist*, July-August. Focus. (2009). pp. 37-45.

② World Bank and the Development Research Center of the State Council, the People's Republic of China, "Four Decades of Poverty Reduction in China: Drivers, Insights for the World, and the Way Ahead", Washington, DC: World Bank (2022). doi:10.1596/978-1-4648-1877-6. License: Creative Commons Attribution CC BY 3.0 IGO.

③ O. Hodzi, "China and Africa: Economic growth and a non-transformative political elite", *Journal of Contemporary African Studies*, (2018). 36(2), pp. 191-206; J. C. Anyanwu and A. O. Salami, "The impact of COVID-19 on African economies: An introduction", *African Development Review*, Apr, (2021), 33(Suppl 1): S1-S16.

trade and investment for example, China has forged ahead of its closest rival, the United States of America as seen in Table 1.

Table 1 Chinese and U. S. Trade and Investment in Africa

	China	United States
Trade with Africa (in 2019)	$208.7 billion	$56.8 billion
FDI Stock (by the end of 2019)	$50 billion	$49 billion
Priority Countries	South Africa, Democratic Republic of Congo, Zambia, Nigeria, and Ethiopia	Nigeria, Mauritius, South Africa, and Ghana
Priority Sectors	Mining, Construction, and Manufacturing (accounting for 65% of total Chinese investment in Africa)	Mining (accounting for 60% of total U. S. investment in Africa)

Source: Compiled from multiple authors

The enormous amount of investment and seeming acceptance of this trend has caused a lot of concern to Africa's traditional partners. As indicated previously, one of the issues highlighted is that of natural resource and environment. The fact that a large percentage of China's engagement with Africa is on natural resources and infrastructure construction, those opposed to the growing Chinese investment see this as a controversy including also that the infrastructure that is being built by majority Chinese companies and experts.[①] The western countries and their coteries argue that big infrastructure projects and the extraction of natural resources result in environmental impacts. It is clear that such arguments do not favour Africa's yearn for tangible development,

---

① J. Farrell, "How do Chinese contractors perform in Africa? Evidence from World Bank projects", *China Africa Research Initiative Working Paper* No. 3, Johns Hopkins University, School of Advanced International Studies, (2016); X. Han and M. Webber, "From Chinese dam building in Africa to the Belt and Road Initiative: Assembling infrastructure projects and their linkages", *Political Geography* 77, (2020), p.102.

rather it reflects uneasiness on the part of Africa's previous leading partners. But China has experience in large projects that have passed the test of time. Indeed, Jin had indicated that the availability of resources is fundamental to the development and industrialization of societies, a thesis that vindicates Africa's need for economic growth and development.[①]

As China continue to develop, the need for resources is undeniable. The need for Africa to use its resources for development is also incumbent. The economic growth, the development and the demography including the rise of disposable income makes the demand of resources soar. According to many analysts for example, China will certainly be the world's largest oil consumer by 2030 with about 15 million barrels per day representing almost 80 % of global demand growth.[②]

In addition to other demands for consumption, most countries, and China is one, must be concerned with various aspects of resource security. While all major powers have been interested in African resources, China has since become the undisputed leader, sourcing and purchasing of these resources in this context.[③]

The series of the Forum on China-Africa Cooperation (FOCAC), started in 2000, has taken China-Africa relationship to a higher level and at the same time it has generated several comments and reactions from all groups of people.[④] On one hand, the meetings have brought governments and policymakers together for discussions and enhanced trade and businesses, strategic partnerships, while on the other hand, it has given China-sceptics further opportunities to comment and

---

① B. Jin, "The relationship between resource and environmental regulation and industrial competitiveness", *China Economist*, July-August. Focus. (2009), pp. 37-45.

② B. Wen, Y. Chen, G. Wang, T. Dai, "China's demand for energy and mineral resources by 2035", *Chinese J Eng Sci.* (2019), 21(1):68. https://doi.org/10.15302/j-sscae-2019.01.010.

③ K. H. Butts and B. Bankus, "China's Pursuit of Africa's Natural Resources", *CSL Issue Paper*, Volume 1, 09, June Collins Center Study, (2009).

④ G. Shelton, "The FOCAC Process and Sino-African Strategic Partnership", World Century Publishing Corporation and Shanghai Institutes for International Studies. *China Quarterly of International Strategic Studies*, Vol. 2, No. 2, (2016). pp. 259-276.

analyze the growing relationship between Africa and China.[1]

The reality these days is that the world economy is being shaped by China. This is done in earnest by commitment in investment, new technologies, services, business and trading relations and poverty eradication strategies, most of which, if carefully studied and adopted, can benefit Africa. In poverty eradication, China has made significant achievements even before the advent of the Millennium Development Goals (MDGs) and the Sustainable Development Goals (SDGs) as also observed by others like Bikales.[2] It is indeed the leading country in the achievement of the MDGs at that time and is set to lead in the pursuit of the SDGs as well.[3]

While the West have since relegated Africa to a place continuously needing help, poor and unstable, in comparison the images of Africa in Beijing is that of a relationship where Africa is celebrated. What is noted in this context is the culture, diversity, and resilience of the African people and the potential that the continent has. In this regard, forging relationships are on trade, manufacturing, agriculture, resources, energy, infrastructure, and people to people exchanges, that are mostly emphasized where the leadership of Africa and China meet.

3. Complementarity in the engagement

Given that these engagements are happening, expanding and growing exponentially, different countries have different responses. In general, however, there is clear acknowledgement of China's activities in Africa which has variously been acknowledged top down. Historically, all leaders emphasized "*political relations of equality and mutual trust*", broadening of

---

① D. M. Tull, "China in Africa: European Perceptions and responses to the Chinese Challenge", SAIS, *Working Paper in African Studies*. John Hopkins University, (2008).

② B. Bikales, "Reflections on Poverty Reduction in China", Swiss Agency for Development and Cooperation, (2021).

③ Center for International Knowledge on Development, "Poverty reduction in China: 40 years of experience and insights for the world", forthcoming, (2022).

"win-win economic cooperation with Africa", *"upgrading of human resource development"*, *"expansion of cultural cooperation and people-to-people exchanges"*. Most of these statements have been variously emphasized by President Xi Jinping on numerous occasions where the leadership of the two sides are discussing.

In dealing with China, these are statements that technocrats tend to turn into action and private sector have similarly turned them into opportunities for further engagements. For Africans in particular, China provides opportunities in so many fields with examples in agriculture, education, sports and tourism and many other sectors including the prospects of cooperation and mutual support in international affairs as well as in the pursuit of common development. Also, at various occasions, African leaders have indicated that it is China's involvement in African infrastructure development, in foreign direct investment (FDI) through its own entrepreneurs both large and small that has helped economic growth in many African countries.[1]

As the pandemic became ubiquitous, Africa continued to attract investors with FDI flows reaching a record high in 2021. This growth was recorded by the World Investment Report 2022, despite the pandemic (Figure 1). Despite this growth, investment flows to Africa accounted for only 5.2% of the global FDI. This certainly indicates that there is much to do in attracting a win-win scenario and in the pursuit of common development strategy as has been promoted by the Chinese leadership.

---

[1] M. Abdouli and A. Omri, "Exploring the nexus among FDI inflows, environmental quality, human capital, and economic growth in the Mediterranean region", *Journal of Knowledge Economics*, (2020). https://doi.org/10.1007/s13132-020-00641-5; M. Mbow, et al, "COVID-19 in Africa: Dampening the Storm?" in: *Science*, 369, 6504, 624-626, https://doi.org/10.1126/science.abd3902 (28 September 2020); M. E. M. Omoruyi, "The Impact of China's Economic Activities in Africa on Economic Growth of African Countries", *Bangladesh Development Studies*, Vol. 38, No. 4. (2015), pp. 47-90.

Figure 1 FDI inflows to the African continent and subregions, 2020–2021 (Billions of USD)

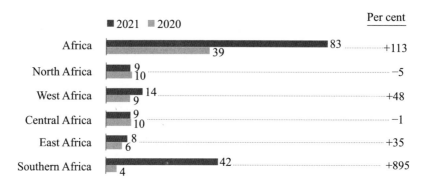

4. African development and the environment

Trade, investment, and other activities resulting from the engagements between China and Africa certainly influences the environment both positively and, in some instances, negatively. The effects on the environment differ by country and in some cases by region. For example, consumption of energy and other resources that reflect standard of leaving is not the same across countries and regions.[①] This is despite the fact that most African countries are endowed with natural resources and huge mineral deposits as indicated in Table 2.

Table 2 Selected African countries showing predominant minerals and production

Country	Predominant minerals	Annual Production (USD millions)
Zimbabwe	Platinum, chrome, gold, coal, diamond	9.967
Gabon	Manganese, iron ore, uranium, gold	10,920
DRC (Congo)	Gold, diamonds, cobalt, copper	13,688
Ghana	Gold, Iron ore, limestone, columbite – tantalite, feldspar, quartz, salt, ilmenite, magnetite, rutile	14,970

① A. B. Youssef, L. Lannes, C. Rault and A. Soucat, "Energy Consumption and Health Outcomes in Africa", Discussion Paper No. 10325SSRN *Electronic Journal.* 10.2139/ssrn.2864825, (2016).

continued

Country	Predominant minerals	Annual Production (USD millions)
Egypt	Gold, copper, silver, zinc, platinum	23,225
Libya	Clay, cement, salt, limestone, potash, magnetite, phosphate rock, sulphur	27,027
Angola	Diamond, gold, oil	32,042
Algeria	Non-hydrocarbons, hydrogen production	38,699
Nigeria	Oil, gold, columbite wolframite, tantalite, bitumen, iron ore, uranium	52,678
South Africa	Gold mines, coal, diamonds, iron ore, chromium, manganese, platinum group metals	124,963

Source: Compiled from multiple documents

Although observers tend to explore the contradiction of natural resource exploitation and industrial growth, it is the government and investor's responsibility to intervene and regulate this process for the benefit of the people. Where mineral resources are extracted and mined, it has to be in such a way that the proceeds, profits and benefits go to the people and help in the overall development of the country. There is the need for the use of technology in industrialization to develop and utilize natural resources so that there will be limited negative environmental impact where such resources are mined. It is therefore necessary for these resources to be located, sourced and developed for the overall economic growth of the country. In the last few decades, this is the role that China plays leading to a win-win situation.

Whenever China and Africa are discussed, it has always been seen as a relationship dominated by exploitation of resources, unbalanced trade, debt, aid and so on.[1] The essence of the engagement and the potential for development on the two sides is always relegated.

---

① P. Carmody and I. Taylor, "Flexigemony and force in China's resource diplomacy in Africa: Sudan and Zambia compared", *Geopolitics*, 15(3), (2010), pp. 496-515. doi:10.1080/14650040903501047.

As a result of previous engagement pre and post FOCAC, and with the launch of the Belt and Road Initiative (BRI), China became the largest source of construction financing for infrastructure. As this became apparent, observers, accused China for seeking some sort of looser environmental regulations often referred to as the pollution haven hypothesis. In this regard, many countries in Africa with less stringent environmental regulations attracted FDI. As a result of the lax in environmental regulations, the China Africa Research Institute at the John Hopkins University indicated that the gross annual revenues of Chinese company's engineering and construction projects in Africa total about $4 billion (almost 27% of global revenues for the companies). While this is a substantial sectoral investment by China, it created a win-win situation for those African countries that critically need such infrastructures. As the BRI becomes successful globally, it focuses on promoting high level integration between countries and the development of infrastructure is key to this.

As policies of engagement with Africa flourishes, the Chinese government emphasized the importance of cooperation on climate change, clean and renewable energy industries among other aspects of environmental protection and concern. This was identified as a key feature in FOCAC 2006. As Africa continuously welcomes China's engagement on infrastructure financing, trade and other types of partnerships, it is necessary to highlight the need for economic growth and development that will address issues such as poverty, diseases, human security, food security, etc. The relationship with China thus identified these in both bilateral and multilateral engagements with the continent.

As we focus this discussion on an environmental context of engagement between China and Africa, it is important to understand that China's activities and investments in African countries particularly in construction of infrastructure can often be located in environmentally sensitive areas. While such developments are necessary for the benefit of the communities where they are carried out, the literature and current political narratives continue to express concerns leading to criticisms of such investments including in mining, forestry and agricultural projects.

As China attempts to promote sustainable development, mitigation and environmental impacts in their activities, both at home and in overseas investments, financial institutions like the Exim Bank of China urges beneficiaries to embark on better environmental policies where ever they are active. As a commitment to the top down policy enshrined in the FOCAC document, the bank developed a framework that encouraged Chinese companies to comply with host country policies regarding sustainable development and environmental protection.

In this regard, the documents indicated that China will give high priority to African concerns of environmental protection and sustainable development, and help African countries turn their advantages (in energy and resources) into development strengths. This commitment was the earliest undertaking on African environment by any of the development partners with interest and investment in Africa.

5. Africa China-Cooperation before and after COVID pandemic

Historically, Africans have appreciated the relationship with China and the impacts that China brought on African economic growth and development. In a Kenyan newspaper recently, an article indicated that "China is a worthy partner in Africa's effort to break the poverty trap" due to its current underdevelopment status. It is clear that China has contributed to African development thus far, and has left development footprint across the continent.[①] There are development footprints facilitated by China in infrastructure that include but not limited to railway lines, highways, Schools, stadia, government offices, airports, ports, ICT, to mention a few. Others include training, skills development, agricultural development and modernization. With the advent of China in Africa, improvement in growth, development and poverty alleviation has been recorded

---

① P. Bosshard, "China's Environmental Footprint in Africa", *SAIS Working Papers on African Studies*. The Johns Hopkins University, (2008), Retrieved from https://www.sais- jhu.edu/sites/default/files/China's-Environmental-Footprint-in-Africa.pdf; V. K. Tawiah, A. Zakari and I. Khan, "The environmental footprint of China-Africa engagement: An analysis of the effect of China – Africa partnership on carbon emissions", *Science of the Total Environment* 756. 143603, (2021).

and is set to continue despite the ensuing economic instability and the impact brought by the covid pandemic.[1]

In the most recent times, China's economic and investment relationship in Africa are directed towards supporting the BRI infrastructure projects.[2] Increasingly though, the Chinese investment portfolio in Africa is no longer dominated by natural resources. There has been a gradual shift from a predominantly extractive, natural resource-driven trading relationship to other sectors that include construction, manufacturing, ICT and increasingly, people to people, etc. This is a vindication from those that highlight environmental consequences as a result of this growing relationship. The geography of the African environment and its relation to China's engagement highlights the essence of the challenges that the continent and its people faces.[3] While the geography poses challenges to addressing underdevelopment and impoverishment, there are windows that will allow decision makers and investors to circumnavigate and make progress. For example, despite the large expanse of arable land on the African continent, satisfactory food production and food security has not been recorded. In addition, its development and associated aspects of transportation and commerce have historically been constrained by physiography that include high plateaux, unnavigable rivers, river basins, etc.

Similarly, China's landmass and physiography posed challenges. One particular example is on the loess plateau where the ecological process does not favour tangible development. But the government and people had commitment and innovation that proved successful. As some of these issues on the African continent have global relevance, the successes that China recorded can be replicated elsewhere. In this regard, the issue of climate change provided a

---

① J. C. Anyanwu and A. O. Salami, "The impact of COVID-19 on African economies: An introduction", *African Development Review*, Apr. (2021), 33(Suppl 1): S1-S16.

② J. Breuer, "Two Belts, One Road? The role of Africa in China's Belt & Road initiative", *Blickwechsel*, (2017), pp.1-8; Han, X. and Webber, M., From Chinese dam building in Africa to the Belt and Road Initiative: Assembling infrastructure projects and their linkages. *Political Geography*, (2020), 77, 102102.

③ C. Alden and D. Large, "China's exceptionalism and the challenges of delivering difference in Africa", *Journal of Contemporary China*, (2011), 20(68), 21-38.

platform on which China can work with Africa. At the FOCAC meeting in 2021, President Xi Jinping indicated that China would support green development projects in Africa, signalling new opportunities for cooperation and investment. This aspect of green investment identified by the Chinese leadership can set the stage for further innovation and cooperation particularly in the aspects of climate change and sustainable development.[①]

6. The China's initiatives in Africa and beyond the pandemic

The total value of Chinese investments and construction in Africa is almost $2 trillion since 2005, according to the American Enterprise Institute (AEI) China Global Investment Tracker. China recently launched a $1 billion Belt and Road infrastructure fund for Africa, and recently delivered a $60 billion African aid package, designed to support numerous initiatives. Over the last few decades, China has emerged as a substantial donor and provider of development finance challenging the monopoly western donors have held, particularly over the last few decades.[②]

African countries were being affected by disruptions of global supply chains of critical goods, such as food and medical supplies. The pandemic resulted in a sharp contraction of trade worldwide, with severe knock-on effects in sub-Saharan Africa on economic growth, poverty and food insecurity.[③] For individual African countries, the degree of change in trade relations depends to some extent on trade patterns before covid-19.[④] For example, economic downturns following the pandemic are likely to be sizeable in the continent's

---

① A. B. Akoyoko, "Africa, China, and the 'Green' Factor, Consultancy Africa Intelligence", 2012, http://www.consultancyafrica.com/index; M. Agbebi and P. Virtanen, "Dependency theory – A conceptual lens to understand China's presence in Africa?" *Forum for Development Studies*, (2017), 44(3), pp. 429-451.

② R. Kaplinskyand M. Morris, "Chinese FDI in Sub-Saharan Africa: Engaging with large dragons", *European Journal of Developing Research*, (2009). 24(1), pp. 1-23; J. Lomøy, "Chinese aid – a blessing for Africa and a challenge to western donors", CMI - Chr. Michelsen Institute, (2021), pp. 1-6.

③ Moustapha Mbow, et. al, "COVID-19 in Africa: Dampening the Storm?" in: *Science*, 369, 6504, pp. 624-626, https://doi.org/10.1126/science.abd3902 (28 September 2020).

④ J. C. Anyanwu and A. O. Salami, "The impact of COVID-19 on African economies: An introduction", *African Development Review*, Apr.(2021); 33(Suppl 1): S1-S16.

three largest economies (Angola, Nigeria and South Africa) because they rely on commodity exports that have strongly declined in price. Small island states such as Cabo Verde and Mauritius have been affected by border closures and the subsequent decline of international tourism that reflects a substantial part of the income of those countries.

The covid pandemic is projected to have long-lasting effects on economic interdependence between African countries and the rest of the world. However, there has been an acceleration of ties between Africa and China due to the rapid response with which China provided the initial aid to Africa at the onset of the pandemic. The shifts in global trade patterns combined with geopolitical challenges that the world suffers and the ensuing global diplomacy changes certainly have significant geopolitical implications for African countries and the world. Writing in the South China Morning Post, Catherine Wong observed that despite the advent of the covid 19, China will not scale back its investment in Africa.

The relationship of China and Africa is such that Beijing has become one of Africa's largest creditors in recent years financing the bulk of their infrastructure. Africa is also home to a third of the countries that have signed up to China's transcontinental infrastructure strategy, the Belt and Road Initiative (BRI). Although Africa has experienced some kind of severe economic recession within the period of the pandemic, China still maintains a confidence level on Africa that ensures the strengthening of cooperation that will go beyond the pandemic.

This commitment stems from the fact that between 2013 and 2018, 45 per cent of China's foreign aid went to Africa (according to statistics released by the Chinese Foreign Ministry). China is Africa's largest two-way trading partner, hitting $254 billion in 2021, exceeding by a factor of four U. S. A-Africa trade according to the World Investment Report, 2022.

To buttress the fact of this relationship, China donated a billion coronavirus vaccines and further advanced billions of dollars for African trade and infrastructure as a palliative within and further after the covid pandemic. The Chinese government also wrote off interest-free loans to African countries to help the continent heal from the coronavirus pandemic. These announcements were made by President Xi Jinping while addressing the Forum on China-Africa Cooperation, in Dakar, Senegal. President Xi also said China would encourage more imports of African agricultural products, and increase the range of zero-tariff goods, aiming for US$300 billion of total imports from Africa in the next three years.

According to analysts, for the long-term prospects, Africa will continue to have great potential to attract international investment in all aspects of the economy particularly in both green and blue economies as well as in infrastructure development.[1] Generally, China's exponential expansion of activities in Africa has been a major subject of discussion by many scholars and reports. While these trends are well documented, the extent of the environmental footprint is fragmented with some presenting a negative perspective. This article tends to reflect on the environmental context in which both trade, infrastructure and indeed policy are involved in the context of China Africa engagement. It is hoped that this will generate further discussion and the opportunity to conduct in depth objective investigation as the case may be.

Conclusion

Historically, poor infrastructure and lack of access even to communities hold back growth indices even in agriculture and rural development and in the overall trend of economic growth. While infrastructure (roads, rails, energy, etc.) can open up such areas and expose them to economic activities, they also tend to threaten the environmental sustainability of locations where they are located. With China's activities, it arguably provides access to the continents natural resources which also facilitate access to places that are either pristine or ecologically important.

Following from FOCAC and recent pronouncements by Chinese leaders at the BRICS summits, China has shown preparedness to integrate concerns of climate change, investment in renewable energy and promote green economy

① A. B. Akoyoko, "Africa, China, and the 'Green' Factor", Consultancy Africa Intelligence, http://www.consultancyafrica.com/index, 2012.

in dealing with Africa. It is indicated that investing in alternative sources of energy, ecological infrastructure, sustainable agriculture and green economy will certainly stimulate economic growth, create jobs and employment, reduce poverty while addressing environmental and climate challenges.

The relationship and engagement of China with Africa has thus far stimulated economic growth creating jobs and employment and reducing poverty while addressing environmental and climate change challenges. *Statistics have indicated that some million African jobs had* been created by China on the African continent in the last decades with many of the companies and investors providing skills, training, while ensuring the trend of the continent's sustainable development.

In adherence to the principles of cooperation and partnership, China released an African Policy Paper in which it indicated that the government will ensure that its relationship with the continent "will give high priority to African concerns of environmental protection and sustainable development, and help African countries turn their advantages in energy and resources into development strengths". With these statements and commitments, the stage was set for the future cooperation in which the projects and investments will leave behind footprints that are environmentally acceptable to Africa and China.

In conclusion, and as this relationship continue to grow, it is necessary to device ways and framework for further research in this context so as to maximize the win-win situation of the benefits that continues to come out of this partnership to the both sides.

附录 北京大学非洲研究中心 2022 年度学术成果汇总

交流活动

2 月 1 日，非洲晴雨表与北大非洲研究中心工作会议召开，刘海方和何则锐、陶蒴、Sena 同学与会，晴雨表的 Dulani 主任、Carolyn Logan 研究员、Nkomo 研究员和 Josephine 研究员参会。

2 月 25 日，程莹主持并评议 CAAC（Chinese in Africa/Africans in China Research Network）的第十次线上讨论会，主题为"冷战与第三世界之间：跨越民族国家的中非文学档案"。讨论会由康奈尔大学比较文学系博士候选人黄琨和拜罗伊特大学非洲研究院博士候选人袁明清先后就相关主题发表演讲，挖掘 20 世纪 60 年代的中非文学交往（包括文本的翻译、个体作家的旅行等等）的历史材料，讨论冷战政治与第三世界思想如何影响了非洲文学文本的世界流通。

3 月 11 日，非洲研究中心师生 20 余人与公共外交学会副会长胡正跃大使、苟皓东公使一起访问位于顺义国际文化中心的谢燕申先生的非洲艺术博物馆，受到谢先生热情接待和讲解，老师和同学们受益良多。程莹、刘海方老师带队，来自非洲的 4 位同学和北大出版社"理解非洲"丛书赵聪编辑、深圳市文化广电旅游体育研究中心傅瑞强特约研究员也参与了活动。

4 月 13—14 日，中心主任刘海方应邀线上参加睿纳新国际咨询与非盟驻华代表处共同主办的"协调非盟非洲基础设施发展计划（PIDA）下的区域基础设施项目建设"特别对话活动。

4 月 16 日，北京大学区域与国别研究院举办了第二届"博望天下"区域与国别研究博士生论坛，本届论坛主题为"青年和区域与国别研究：新视角、新理论、新方法"。非洲分论坛有来自北京大学、北京外国语大学、浙江师范大学、外交学院、澳门城市大学等多所高校博士生参加。博士生何则锐、邹雨君分别作题为《困境中的摩洛哥青年及其能动性研究》《推动需求：中国在非企业参与中非教育和培训合作》的报告。论坛邀请北京外国语大学非洲学院院长李洪峰教授及北京大学区域与国别研究院谭萌博士后担任评议老师。

7月4日，北京大学非洲研究中心和国际组织与公共政策专业、大数据分析实验室的师生们，应邀来到位于朝阳区望京的国际竹藤组织总部参观交流，副总干事陆文明先生、原驻埃塞俄比亚办公室代表傅金和博士及项目官李婷女士热情接待了北大团队。刘海方、刘莲莲、董盼等老师与10余位同学参访。

7月27日，刘海方赴呼和浩特市参加北京大学暑期学堂活动，为来自内蒙古各地的中学生宣讲北京大学人文社会科学的教学和研究，特别穿插讲授了国际关系学院和北京大学的非洲研究教学与社会参与。

7月28日，刘海方应 CGTN-Radio 邀请，就刚刚举办的中非智库论坛、女性在中非关系中的作用接受著名主持人 Bridget 女士（津巴布韦人）的采访，与来自阿尔及利亚的女学者 Lina Benabdallah 一起对话。对话实况请参考链接：Happy African Women's Day!!! today we look at The role of women in bridging relations between China and Africa!

8月5日，王进杰老师接受 CGTN-Radio 专访，以"China—Africa cooperation in science and technology"为题进行报道。

中心人才培养

7月15日，由中心组织的"2022年北京大学保平非洲研究优秀论文奖"颁奖典礼线上公开隆重举办，本次活动为非洲研究基金重要子项目之一。颁奖活动分别邀请了北京大学非洲研究基金募捐人徐勤霞老师及基金首批捐赠人董艳红女士出席。来自社会学系、新闻与传播学院、国际关系学院、国家发展研究院、政府管理学院、燕京学堂的10名获奖学生各自陈述论文的要义，中心学术委员会评审老师许亮老师、王进杰老师、程莹老师进行精彩点评。同时线上颁奖活动也得到李安山教授、苟皓东参赞的线上鼓励和支持。本次活动由中心主任刘海方老师主持。

出版物

2月，李安山教授的《非洲现代史》（上、下卷）入选2021年度国家社科基金中华学术外译项目。国家社科基金 2010 年设立中华学术外译项目，主要立足于学术层面，资助中国现当代哲学社会科学优秀成果、近现代以来的名家经典以及国家社科基金项目优秀成果的翻译出版。北京大学社会科学部对这一消息进行了报道和宣传（https://news.pku.edu.cn/xwzh/00e0398e954f43888f8d414c4dc07be5.htm）。该著作也被列入 "十四五" 时期国家重点出版物出版专项规划中，详情见 2021 年 12 月 31 日《出版商务周报》的专题报道《〈出版业 "十四五" 时期发展规划〉发布，首批 1929 个项目有哪些？》，《出版业 "十四五" 时期发展规划》八. 社会科学与人文科学出版规划 6. 历史类，相关链接为：https://www.163.com/dy/article/GSGNNBB00512DFEN.html。

11 月，李安山教授的《我的非洲情缘——中非关系的话语、政策与现实》由中国社会科学出版社出版。

公开发表

1 月 13 日，中心成员刘少楠博士的文章《非洲历史研究的中国视角——评〈非洲现代史〉》，发表在《中国社会科学报》。

1 月 14 日，李安山教授的文章《论非洲教育的起源与现代模式的引进和改革》，发表在北京外国语大学非洲学院的院刊《非洲语言文化研究》（第一辑）。

2 月，李安山教授的文章《南非发展进程中史学学派纷争与主题演变》，发表在《非洲发展研究（2019）》，江苏人民出版社，2022 年 2 月。

2 月 16 日，许亮博士受邀参加英国《时尚理论》（*Fashion Theory*）杂志 "全球中国专刊" 的发布研讨会，其英文文章 "Chinese Investment and the Rise of 'Made in Africa' Fashion Production in Africa" 发表在该刊物（*Fashion Theory*, Vol. 25, No. 7, pp. 975-982）。

李安山教授的英文文章《全球化背景下的中国非洲研究（1950—2020）》，发表在《巴西非洲研究杂志》，6:12（2021），第 107—169 页。"African Studies in China in Global Context (1950-2020)," *Brazilian Journal of African Studies*, Porto Alegre, v. 6, n. 12, Jul., Dez. 2021, pp. 107-169.

李安山教授的英文著作 *China and Africa in Global Context: Encounters, Policy, Cooperation and Migration*（《全球化背景下的中国与非洲：相遇、政策、合作与移民》，共 546 页），作为 "中国观点"（China Perspectives）系列之一在

英国 Routledge 出版社出版。相关链接为：https://www.routledge.com/China-and-Africa-in-the-Global-Context-Encounter-Policy-Cooperation-and/Anshan/p/book/9781032114996。

3月3日、5日，微信公众号"非洲研究小组"和"印度洋岛国研究中心"分别发表了李安山教授的英文著作 *China and Africa in Global Context: Encounters, Policy, Cooperation and Migration*（《全球化语境下的中国与非洲：交汇、政策、合作与迁移》）的推介文章。

3月7日，《经济观察报》发表了李安山教授的访谈文章《李安山：重新发现现代非洲》。

3月17日，李安山教授的文章《解析西方文明的三个悖论》，刊登在中国社会科学网、《中国社会科学报》上。

4月19日，李安山教授的文章《论非洲教育的起源与现代模式的引进和改革（上）》，通过北外非洲研究中心微信公众号发布。

4月20日，李安山教授的文章《中国的非洲研究——回顾与展望》，通过中国非洲学刊微信公众号发布。

4月23日，标题为《南非的人与环境——包茂红导读〈环境、权力与不公〉》一文，发布在澎湃私家历史上，北京大学世界环境史研究中心微信公众号全文转发。

6月，李安山教授发表在《国家安全论坛》2022年第1期的《中国国际移民安全问题刍议》一文，分别在暨南大学"海外发展与利益维护"微信公众号、温州大学"温州侨乡研究"微信公众号、北大新闻网转载发布。

7月1日，李安山教授的文章《如何加强对中国国际移民的安全保护？》，发布在北京大学中外人文交流基地微信公众号。

7月18日，李安山教授的文章 "China-Africa in the Context of BRI-B3W"（《"一带一路倡议"与"建设更好世界"背景下的中国与非洲》），发表在《巴西非洲研究杂志》v. 7 n. 13(2022)。阅读链接：v. 7 n. 13 (2022): *Revista Brasileira de Estudos Africanos* (ufrgs.br)。

林丰民教授的论文《〈一千零一夜〉的中国形象与文化误读》，被《中国文学研究文摘》创刊号收录，该论文原载《国外文学》2020年第4期。

刘海方的论文《被忽视的自强大陆——多重危机中的非洲能动性》，发表在

《文化纵横》2022 年 8 月号。

8 月 9 日，李安山教授为旅非华侨于宝盛先生的新书《白鹭，双飞（Nature's Fortune）》所作的序言，在"非洲研究小组"微信公众号以新书荐评方式发表。

8 月 22 日，李安山教授的文章《中非合作，后劲可嘉——推介两部有关中非关系的新作》，发表在东非之角微信公众号（上海）。

李安山教授的英文文章"African Students in China: Research, Reality and Reflections"（《非洲学生在中国：研究、现实与反思》），被收在以下论文集：Xinfeng Li & Chunying An, eds., *Changing World and Africa*（《变化的世界与非洲》），Palgrave, 2022, pp. 459-512。

中心成员王渊助理教授发表英文文章"Island Narrative and Bridge-Building: Postapocalyptic Isle of Love in Agualusa's Os Vivos e os Outros"（《岛屿叙事与桥梁建构：阿瓜卢萨〈生者与余众〉中的末日爱之岛》），*Journal of Lusophone Studies*, vol. 7, no. 1, 2022, pp. 55-75. 阅读链接：https://jls.apsa.us/index.php/jls/article/view/473/460。

10 月 22 日，原中心成员、毕业于北京大学国际关系学院的博士生，现刚果（金）知名学者龙刚的文章《中国共产党第二十次全国代表大会国际影响深远》，发表在中国驻刚果民主共和国大使馆微信公众号上。在校学习期间，李安山教授任龙刚的博士生导师。详情见链接：https://mp.weixin.qq.com/s/fV5x_Z9F03BT2_gfsVGnGA。

11 月 23 日，李安山教授的文章《论非洲共享价值观的源流、内涵及其实践》，发布在"西亚非洲"微信公众号的非盟 20 年栏目。详情见链接：https://mp.weixin.qq.com/s/lidw61nWVwFs2WsPkRMPCg。

2022 年，李安山教授的英文文章"Emerging Themes in African Studies in China"和潘华琼博士的英文文章"Cultural Heritage's Value in African Sustainable Development"，发表在由 Augustin F. C. Holl 主编的 *Studying Africa and Africans Today*。

许亮博士的书评文章《从"未闻之地"到"泪之地"》，发表在《解放日报》2022 年 12 月 17 日版。

许亮博士的论文《试析非洲酋长制的复兴》，发表在《中央民族大学学报》2022 年第 6 期。

讲座

3月7日，北京大学人文社会科学研究院微信公众号发表了《"另一种现代的尺度——〈非洲现代史〉研读会"嘉宾发言纪要》，详情见链接：https://mp.weixin.qq.com/s/-Nw1emUJdc7rBEqnal1FFg。

3月7日，刘海方应邀为中国人民警察大学维和警察培训中心的教官们作题为《看非洲：全球化时代有关非洲的知识是如何生产的》的讲座，何银教授主持讲座。

4月18日，李安山教授通过飞书线上直播方式作题为《尼罗河流域文明巡礼》的讲座。本次讲座由大学生文化素质教育中心主办，电子科技大学西非研究中心承办。

5月13日，北京大学外国语学院魏丽明教授为北京师范大学珠海园区的同学们带来了精彩讲座——《东方文学史可能吗》。本场讲座由北京师范大学文理学院中文系主办，由姚建彬教授主持。讲座采用线上线下结合的方式进行，在线观看直播的师生人数超过600人次。魏教授回顾亚非系在非洲文学学科建设与发展的历程，从东方文学回归亚非文学、世界文学视野中的东方文学以及"学科要公平"之理解等视野，介绍了亚非系非洲语言文学学科建设的历程和展望。

5月20日，北京大学外国语学院西葡意语系《米亚·科托与莫桑比克木通贝拉剧团》讲座于线上顺利举办。本讲座受北京大学国际合作部"海外学者讲学计划"支持，邀请美国威斯康星大学麦迪逊分校非洲文化研究系路易斯·马杜雷拉教授担任主讲人，由西葡意语系王渊助理教授主持、亚非系程莹助理教授评议。

5月22日，由中国侨乡（福建）研究中心、福州大学人文社会科学学院主办的旗峰侨学论坛第二期，邀请李安山教授作题为《世界历史进程中的非洲与中非关系》的线上讲座。中国侨乡福建研究中心主任林胜教授主持讲座，福州大学嘉锡学者甘满堂教授为点评人。

5月26日，李安山教授应邀作题为《世界历史进程中的非洲与中非关系》的线上讲座，该讲座得到国际学术重大平台专项支持，由武汉大学外国语言文学学院等主办。

5 月 27 日，李安山教授应邀在"风云大外交"线上直播间作题为《中国的非洲研究：历史、现状与展望》的讲座。中央财经大学政府管理学院国际政治系主任白云真博士主持讲座，大外交智库创始人、研究员王盖盖为本场讲座对话提问嘉宾。

6 月 10 日，中共湖北工业大学委员会党校 2022 年第 2 讲暨湖北工业大学中非工业创新合作中心《走进非洲》国际讲坛第 1 期邀请李安山教授作题为《世界历史进程中的非洲与中非关系》的线上讲座，湖北工业大学党委书记刘德富教授主持讲座。

6 月 19 日，五邑大学通识教育高端讲座第 44 讲邀请李安山教授线上讲授《中非关系与中国对非战略》。

10 月 21 日，刘海方应北京大学国关学院学生会邀请，做客"外交面对面"，为同学们作题为《全球非洲，中非炙热》的讲座，并与来自各年级同学进行了热烈的互动。

10 月 31 日，李安山教授受洛阳信息工程大学邀请，作题为《中非关系与中国对非政策》的线上讲座。

12 月 8 日，中国公共外交协会会员、社科院中国非洲研究院特聘研究员、全球化智库 CCG 高级研究员苟皓东先生与中国国家图书馆副研究馆员、多年从事文化外交工作、在非洲多国出任文化参赞的严向东先生，联袂做客刘海方老师课程，与来自全球多国的学子进行专题对话《中非合作中的人文交流》，受到热烈赞扬。

12 月 9 日，由广西侨乡文化研究中心主办的"华人华侨学系列讲座"邀请李安山教授线上讲授《华侨华人研究：学科整合与当前议题》，该讲座由广西民族大学郑一省教授主持。

12 月，由北京大学外国语学院亚非系非洲语言文化教研室、国别和区域研究专业、北大非洲研究中心共同主办"北京大学非洲文化研究系列讲座"。12 月 8 日，浙江大学传媒与国际文化学院百人计划研究员张勇博士讲授《中非影视交流史的"发生学"》，中心成员程莹主持讲座，刘海方老师和沙宗平老师参与评议。12 月 22 日，德国埃尔朗根－纽伦堡大学人文社科学院讲师、拜罗伊特大学非洲研究博士袁明清老师受邀进行《跨越非洲 * 中国：非洲文学在中国的翻译和流转》（Crossing Africa*China: Translations and Travels of African Literary Texts

in China）英文讲座，讲座由英国非洲研究协会主席 Dr Carli Coetzee 评议，中心成员程莹主持。

12月20—21日，由山东省委外事办公室非洲处、济南大学社科处、济南大学外国语学院共同主办，济南大学非洲研究中心承办，主题为"人类命运共同体——新时代中非交流新趋势国际研讨会"线上召开。李安山教授应邀出席开幕式并发言，并在研讨会学术讲座模块作题为《尼罗河流域文明巡礼》的学术讲座，讲座由济南大学外国语学院院长李常磊教授主持。

研讨会

1月6日，刘海方应邀参加临界咨询和丝路社会科学研究院联合举办的"投资非洲：机遇、挑战及风险管理"研讨会并以《中美竞争视角下中非合作前景展望》为题作演讲。国内诸多企业界、商会、智库和高校代表130多人参会。会议相关报道请参见链接：https://mp.weixin.qq.com/s/DahtPaiddHPREFRsBZXc-w。

2月3日、9日，刘海方两次参加"中国在非洲／非洲在中国"执委会会议，讨论目前这个跨国学术共同体的组织法规章改革、主要活动以及即将召集的线上研讨会等事宜。会议分别由密歇根州立大学非洲研究中心主任 Jamie Monson 和乔治城大学非洲研究中心非-中项目主任 Yoon Park 主持。

2月11日，北大非洲中心与南非金山大学合作举办中国-南非合作研究课题组内部线上研讨会，邀请来自林波波大学 Metji 教授、金山大学 Pooe 教授、西开普亚洲商会的 Benjamin 先生、Brand South Africa 中国主任 Malele 先生、约堡大学 Sandile 先生等演讲，天佑主持会议，杨燕博士、王进杰、刘海方、陶蒴参会交流。

3月23日，中心主任刘海方接受媒体"长江新闻号"视频连线就"阿尔及利亚、坦桑尼亚、赞比亚非洲三国外长访华并举行会谈"进行时事评论。访谈详情见微信视频号内容《刘海方：平等互利是中非友好合作的基础》。

4月1日，北京大学国际关系学院举办"俄乌冲突对国际关系的影响"研讨会。刘海方作关于《俄乌冲突对非洲影响以及非洲态度》的报告。

4月9日，李安山教授应邀参加由中国社会科学院主办，中国非洲研究院、非洲联盟驻华代表处承办的首届中非文明对话大会主题为"文明交流互鉴推动构建新时代中非命运共同体"学术研讨会，并作题为《文明：悖论、相似性与互鉴》的主旨演讲。

4 月 19 日，许亮博士受邀在法国高等社会科学院的研究生课程"中国与海外华人"上作题为"Black Women Workers and Chinese Factories in Africa: A Preliminary Analysis of Race, Gender, and Class"的发言。该课程由法国国家科学研究院（CNRS）的社会学研究员王思萌主持。

4 月 23 日，北京大学国际关系学院举行"北京大学国家安全学学科建设研讨会暨北京大学国际关系学院国家安全学系成立大会"。刘海方在分论坛中作关于《如何认识非洲当前安全形势及其相关学理思考》的报告。

5 月 13 日，中心副秘书长王进杰老师受邀参加由中非（重庆）职业教育联盟主办的"中非（重庆）职业教育联盟 2021 年年会暨职业教育服务中非能力建设交流会"，并作题为《职业教育服务中非合作能力建设》的主题演讲。

5 月 27 日，中心主任刘海方老师与许亮博士受邀参加由欧亚系统科学研究会、《文化纵横》杂志社主办的"乌克兰危机与新型国际体系视野下的非洲问题"研讨会。刘海方同时担任分论坛的评议人参与讨论。

5 月 28 日，莫桑比克诗人若泽·克拉韦里尼亚中译版诗选发布会在澳门葡文书局举办，王渊作为该书校译者线上参与，并作题为《莫桑比克文学中译史》的报告。

6 月 1 日，刘海方应邀参加中国石油经济技术研究院主办的题为"乌克兰危机及新地缘政治下非洲地区局势及我在非能源投资如何驾驭风险"研讨会，陆如泉副院长主持会议，来自中国石油的高级经理人、专家与几位非洲研究学者共同研讨了非洲地区当前的局势。

6 月 11 日，李安山教授应邀参加由华侨大学和华人华侨与区域国别研究院主办的"华人华侨与区域国别研究院（RIGCAS）揭牌仪式暨学术研讨会"。

6 月 18 日，李安山教授应邀参加由上海师范大学非洲研究中心主办的"新形势下中非共建'一带一路'的机遇与挑战"研讨会，作题为《"一带一路"倡议与"重建更好世界"倡议背景下的中非关系》的学术报告。

7 月 16 日，李安山教授应邀参加由江南大学外国语学院、华中师范大学外国语学院、中外语言文化比较学会世界族裔文学研究专业委员会联合主办的"文学的族裔性与族裔文学的普遍性：第八届族裔文学国际学术研讨会暨（中国）中外语言文化比较学会世界族裔文学专业委员会成立大会"，并用英文作

"Civilization: Paradox, Redefinition and Mutual Learning"（《文明：悖论、再定义与互相学习》）的主题报告。

7月20日，由中非合作论坛中方后续行动委员会秘书处主办，中国非洲研究院承办的中非智库论坛第十一届会议在北京开幕。李安山教授应邀线上参加开幕式全体会议，并用英文作 "Two Documents, Common Vision: Challenge and Action"（《两个文件共同愿景：挑战与行动》）的主题发言。

7月21日，王进杰老师受邀参加中非智库论坛第十一届会议北大分议题，并发表题为 "Educated Youth for Industrialization Development in Africa" 的主题演讲。

7月23日，李安山教授应邀参加由中国中东学会、内蒙古民族大学主办的"第四届埃及历史和埃及发展"高层学术论坛，并作题为《中国与非洲哲学史比较研究之体会：以古埃及与中国的"宇宙"概念为例》的主题报告。

7月23—24日，中心成员、哲学系副教授沙宗平应邀参加中国中东学会与内蒙古民族大学共同举办的"第四届埃及历史和埃及发展高层学术论坛"，提交《20世纪中埃文化交流与文明互鉴的重要学术成果——以马坚译阿拉伯语〈论语〉（1935）和汉语〈古兰经〉（1978）为例》（沙宗平、张秀兰）的会议论文，并在分组会议上发言。

7月25日，刘海方应邀参加凤凰卫视"龙行天下"栏目与福特基金会合作举办的以"从分享到合作：中国对外农业援助的实践、争议与可持续"为主题的线上研讨会，并就非洲案例发表评论。

7月26日，刘海方应邀参加国际NGO组织南方国家女性网络"新世纪妇女发展选择"（Development Alternatives with Women for a New Era，DAWN）举行的题为"中国全球的参与的性别影响"（Gender Impact of China's Global Engagement）的线上研讨会，并就非洲案例发表评论。

8月16日，刘海方应邀参加由香港中文大学前海国际事务研究院主办的"非洲之角局势与中国海外利益"研讨会，发表主题演讲并作最后会议的总结发言。

8月31日，刘海方应邀参加由中国驻南非使馆支持、南非国际问题研究所主办的题为"中非基础设施合作，一起向未来"（Future-Proofing Africa–China Infrastructure Cooperation）的国际会议，并就铁路领域的合作发表专题演讲。

11 月 18 日，刘海方应邀参加北京服装学院艺术设计学院举办的题为"以建筑为改变的媒介：探索作为未来实验室的非洲"线上研讨会，建筑和景观研究院许立言老师也应邀参会。

11 月 26 日，由西北大学外国语学院、西北大学中东研究所、西北大学非洲研究中心共同主办的第二届"长安非洲论坛"暨全国北非问题学术研讨会在线召开，李安山教授应邀在开幕式致辞。

12 月 3—4 日，李安山教授受邀线上出席由中国华侨历史学会、中国华侨华人研究所、福建社会科学院、福建社会科学院华侨华人研究所、平潭综合实验区共同主办的"海外侨胞与平潭国际旅游岛建设"学术研讨会，并以《如何设身处地关心侨胞的切身利益和自身发展》为题展开发言。详情见链接：http://www.fj.chinanews.com.cn/news/2022/2022-12-07/514510.html。

12 月 5 日，李安山教授在中国非洲史研究会换届大会暨学术会议开幕式上的致辞内容，发布在中国社会科学院世界历史研究所主办的"中国世界史研究网"网站上。详情见链接：http://iwh.cssn.cn/xhzx/xh_zx_zgfzsyjh/zgfzsyjh_dt/202212/t20221205_5568656.shtml。

12 月 5 日，由电子科技大学西非研究中心主办的"2022 年国别与区域研究工作座谈会暨第四届西非论坛"举行，李安山教授应邀参加并作题为《从文明概念到"中国方案"：有关区域研究的批判性思维》的主旨发言。

12 月 6 日，刘海方应邀参加加纳智库"非洲国际关系研究中心"（ASCIR）举办的研讨会"非洲的疫后重建与中国的作用"，获得主办方感谢。

12 月 7 日，北京大学非洲研究中心多位成员应《世界知识》邀请，以论坛形式回顾 2022 年的非洲形势。沙宗平教授、林丰民教授、王进杰博士、许亮博士、中山大学助理教授罗楠博士、何则锐、田泽浩、杨光（加纳）、姚航等同学参加并发言，刘海方和来自《世界知识》的赵萌编辑共同主持活动。

12 月 14 日，中心秘书长王进杰老师参加由教育部中外语言交流合作中心和浙江师范大学组织承办的"非洲中文教育研讨会"，并作主题演讲《中国对非投资与中非教育合作》。

12 月 16 日，许亮博士受邀参加清华大学国际与地区研究院举办的"南部理论研究论坛"，并在撒哈拉以南非洲研究分论坛作为发言人对论文进行评议。

12 月 17 日，李安山教授应邀参加由福建江夏学院非洲研究中心主办，福建江夏学院外国语学院承办的主题为"人类命运共同体理念下的非洲安全与发展"研讨会，李安山教授出席开幕式并致辞，并在研讨会第一单元作题为《中国国际移民的安全保护：机遇与挑战》的学术发言。北京大学国际关系学院博士候选人门杜（Joseph Olivier Mendo'o）和托马（Donglona Adawa Thomas）也一同参加本次研讨会，并在研讨会的第二单元分别作题为《非洲大陆的集体安全观与安全治理实践——以中部非洲经济共同体为例》《非洲能动性之韧性：多重危机背景下非洲维护和平与安全的努力》的学术报告。详情见链接：https://m.huanqiu.com/article/4Av8pUCI3uu。

咨政服务

6月23日，李安山教授的文章《必须制止伤害中国国际形象的短视频》被中国新闻社第30期（总160期）采用上报。

9月2日，刘海方应邀参加卫生部国际司举办的"新时代的中国医疗队专家座谈会"，与多位业内官员、专家和学者共同研讨商议新时代中国的卫生国际合作方式方法。

9月2日，林丰民老师代表北京大学非洲研究中心参加教育部国际司和留学基金委共同举办的有关评估和改进来华留学生工作的会议，北京大学国际合作部主管留学生工作的匡老师一同参加。

10月13日，李安山教授的文章《有关中国国际移民安全问题的建议》被中国新闻社内参部采用，发表在中新内参第44期（总第174期）。

10月26日，刘海方应邀参加教育部国际合作与交流司和教育部中外人文交流中心合作召开的中南人文交流专家工作会议，亚非处杨洲处长与会，夏娟副主任主持会议。

北京大学非洲研究中心简介

    北京大学非洲研究中心正式成立于 1998 年,是中国国内最早的高校非洲研究中心之一。北京大学的非洲研究的源起则可以回溯到 1958 年杨人楩先生的非洲历史研究和教学奠基工作。到了 60 年代初,季羡林先生领导的亚非所依托北京大学历史系的亚非拉教研室和东方语言文学系、西方语言文学系、政治学系、哲学宗教系、社会学系等学科的师资力量进一步推动了北京大学的非洲研究,发挥了重要的引领方向、输送人才的作用。1998 年,当时国内的非洲研究处于低潮时期,陆庭恩、何芳川、郑家馨等老一辈学者,倡导集中全校各学科的优势,对非洲开展多学科综合研究。目前,中心挂靠在北京大学国际关系学院,现有校内专家20 位,特邀研究员 10 位。

    目前,中心比较有影响力的教学和科研工作包含以下四个方面。

    第一,在教学方面,中心一直致力于整合全校的非洲教学资源,培养复合型的非洲研究人才。从 2017 年开始,中心与研究生院和国际关系学院合作启动了"北京大学非洲研究课程证书"项目,旨在向对非洲研究感兴趣的本科生和研究生提供优质的师资和课程,帮助学生系统地学习非洲和中非关系。中心试图通过这一课程证书项目进一步整合北大的非洲教学研究力量,推动非洲研究的学科建设,把非洲研究打造成北大国别区域研究的一个重要品牌。

    第二,在科研出版方面,中心每年通过出版《中国非洲研究评论》学术年刊,荟萃海内外研究非洲的众多名家作品。《中国非洲研究评论》在国内是第一本定位为综合性的、有关国际非洲研究动态的学术期刊,每期都邀请国际知名学者撰写原创性论文,赢得了学界的肯定和认可。同时,中心前主任李安山教授出版的《非洲华人华侨史》和《非洲华人社会经济史》(三卷本)是国内外有关非洲华人华侨研究的代表性著作,具有广泛的学术影响。

    第三,中心自主创办的电子周报《北大非洲电讯》是中心的一项重要学术品牌。自 2010 年创办以来,《北大非洲电讯》致力于免费为社会各界提供有关非洲和中非关系的最新资讯,并及时介绍国内外非洲研究进展的重要电子刊物。目前,通过邮件和微信订阅的用户达数千人。

    第四,中心自 2014 年起创办了"博雅非洲论坛"。该论坛是中心最重要的学术年度论坛,在岁末年初邀请中非各界人士相聚博雅塔下,共同讨论非洲和中非关系的重大议题。

    除了致力于非洲研究的学科发展和促进国内外的学术交流外,中心也承担了重要的智库功能,及时给国家相关部门提供涉非问题的政策咨询。

ABOUT THE PEKING UNIVERSITY CENTER FOR AFRICAN STUDIES

Peking University is one of China's foremost hubs of learning about Africa. Established in 1998, the Peking University Center for African Studies is the first university-based Africa research center in the country. African Studies at Peking University dates back to the 1950s when Professor Yang Renpian in the History Department started to teach and conduct research about Africa. In the following decade, the Peking University Institute of Asia and Africa, under the leadership of Professor Ji Xianlin, had become a renowned interdisciplinary body that brought together faculty members from linguistics, history, philosophy, politics, and other social sciences to broaden knowledge about Asia and Africa and nurture the next generation of scholars and experts. By the 1990s, African Studies had been relatively marginalized in academic research, receiving inadequate attention and support. During this time, Professors Lu Ting'en, He Fangchuan, and Zheng Jiaxin at Peking University decided to launch the Center to promote comprehensive African Studies and develop interdisciplinary programs and teaching that foster student and faculty engagement with the continent.

The Peking University Center for African Studies now has more than 20 faculty members and ten guest researchers. The Center prioritizes four areas of work. First, the Center collaborates with the Peking University Graduate School and the Peking University School of International Studies to offer graduate and undergraduate students the Peking University Certificate in African Studies — the first African Studies curriculum program in China. The program will promote African Studies as a core component of Area Studies at Peking University and help cultivate the next generation of Africanist scholars and experts, including future policymakers and applied practitioners. Second, the Center publishes the *Annual Review of African Studies in China*. The Review is an edited volume that promotes original and evidence-based research by both Chinese and international Africanist scholars. Third, the Center also has an obligation to present timely and accurate information about the African continent to the public. Toward that end, the Center publishes the *PKU African Tele-Info*, a weekly newsletter to disseminate positive news and commentaries on Africa to the general public. Finally, in collaboration with African Student Association, the Center organizes its annual Boya Africa Forum at the end of every year. The Forum invites scholars, policymakers, and business leaders worldwide and functions as a crucial intellectual bridge that connects the Center with the larger world.

While the Center's primary mission is to create new knowledge and train future talents, it also has the obligation to apply the knowledge toward solving problems that confront the Africa continent and jeopardize China-Africa relations. Therefore, to achieve this goal, the Center periodically conducts research projects commissioned by and provides consultation for government agencies, non-governmental organizations, and private enterprises.